Unless Recalled

New Methods for the Analysis of Change

New Methods for the Analysis of Change

Edited by Linda M. Collins and Aline G. Sayer

DECADE
of BEHAVIOR
2000-2010

AMERICAN PSYCHOLOGICAL ASSOCIATION
WASHINGTON, DC

First Printing April 2001
Second Printing January 2002

Published by
American Psychological Association
750 First Street, NE
Washington, DC 20002
www.apa.org

To order
APA Order Department
P.O. Box 92984
Washington, DC 20090-2984

Tel: (800) 374-2721, Direct: (202) 336-5510
Fax: (202) 336-5502, TDD/TTY: (202) 336-6123
Online: www.apa.org/books/
Email: order@apa.org

In the U.K., Europe, Africa, and the Middle East, copies may be ordered from
American Psychological Association
3 Henrietta Street
Covent Garden, London
WC2E 8LU England

Typeset in Berkeley Book by EPS Group Inc., Easton, MD
Printer: Sheridan Books, Ann Arbor, MI
Dust jacket designer: Berg Design, Albany, NY
Technical/Production Editor: Amy J. Clarke

The opinions and statements published are the responsibility of the authors, and such opinions and statements do not necessarily represent the policies of the American Psychological Association.

Library of Congress Cataloging-in-Publication Data
New methods for the analysis of change / edited by Linda M. Collins and Aline G. Sayer.—1st ed.
    p. cm. (Decade of Behavior)
Based on a conference held in 1998 at Pennsylvania State University.
Includes bibliographical references and index.
ISBN 1-55798-754-8 (cb : acid-free paper)
1. Change (Psychology). 2. Psychometrics. I. Collins, Linda M. II. Sayer, Aline. III. Series.
BF637.C4 N47 2001
155.2'4—dc21   00-052161

British Library Cataloguing-in-Publication Data
A CIP record is available from the British Library.

Printed in the United States of America

637/030

APA Science Volumes

Attribution and Social Interaction: The Legacy of Edward E. Jones

Best Methods for the Analysis of Change: Recent Advances, Unanswered Questions, Future Directions

Cardiovascular Reactivity to Psychological Stress and Disease

The Challenge in Mathematics and Science Education: Psychology's Response

Changing Employment Relations: Behavioral and Social Perspectives

Children Exposed to Marital Violence: Theory, Research, and Applied Issues

Cognition: Conceptual and Methodological Issues

Cognitive Bases of Musical Communication

Cognitive Dissonance: Progress on a Pivotal Theory in Social Psychology

Conceptualization and Measurement of Organism–Environment Interaction

Converging Operations in the Study of Visual Selective Attention

Creative Thought: An Investigation of Conceptual Structures and Processes

Developmental Psychoacoustics

Diversity in Work Teams: Research Paradigms for a Changing Workplace

Emotion and Culture: Empirical Studies of Mutual Influence

Emotion, Disclosure, and Health

Evolving Explanations of Development: Ecological Approaches to Organism–Environment Systems

Examining Lives in Context: Perspectives on the Ecology of Human Development

Global Prospects for Education: Development, Culture, and Schooling

Hostility, Coping, and Health

Measuring Patient Changes in Mood, Anxiety, and Personality Disorders: Toward a Core Battery

Occasion Setting: Associative Learning and Cognition in Animals

Organ Donation and Transplantation: Psychological and Behavioral Factors

Origins and Development of Schizophrenia: Advances in Experimental Psychopathology

The Perception of Structure

Perspectives on Socially Shared Cognition

Psychological Testing of Hispanics

Psychology of Women's Health: Progress and Challenges in Research and Application

Researching Community Psychology: Issues of Theory and Methods

The Rising Curve: Long-Term Gains in IQ and Related Measures

Sexism and Stereotypes in Modern Society: The Gender Science of Janet Taylor Spence

Sleep and Cognition

Sleep Onset: Normal and Abnormal Processes

Stereotype Accuracy: Toward Appreciating Group Differences

Stereotyped Movements: Brain and Behavior Relationships

Studying Lives Through Time: Personality and Development

The Suggestibility of Children's Recollections: Implications for Eyewitness Testimony

Taste, Experience, and Feeding: Development and Learning

Temperament: Individual Differences at the Interface of Biology and Behavior

Through the Looking Glass: Issues of Psychological Well-Being in Captive Nonhuman Primates

Uniting Psychology and Biology: Integrative Perspectives on Human Development

Viewing Psychology as a Whole: The Integrative Science of William N. Dember

APA Decade of Behavior Volumes

Computational Modeling of Behavior in Organizations: The Third Scientific Discipline

The Nature of Remembering: Essays in Honor of Robert G. Crowder

New Methods for the Analysis of Change

Personality Psychology in the Workplace

Psychosocial Interventions for Cancer

Unraveling the Complexities of Social Life: A Festschrift in Honor of Robert B. Zajonc

Contents

Contributors   xi

Foreword   xv

Preface   xvii

Acknowledgments   xix

Introduction: Organization of This Book   xxi

CHAPTER 1   Differential Structural Equation Modeling of   3
              Intraindividual Variability
              Steven M. Boker

              COMMENT: Dynamical Models and "Differential   29
              Structural Equation Modeling of
              Intraindividual Variability"
              Andrea M. Piccinin

CHAPTER 2   Toward a Coherent Framework for Comparing Trajectories   33
              of Individual Change
              Stephen W. Raudenbush

CHAPTER 3   A Structural Equations Modeling Approach to the General 65
              Linear Mixed Model
              Michael J. Rovine and Peter C. M. Molenaar

              COMMENT (on Chapters 2 and 3): Advances in the   97
              Application of Multilevel Models to the
              Analysis of Change
              D. Wayne Osgood

CHAPTER 4   The Best of Both Worlds: Combining Autoregressive and 105
              Latent Curve Models
              Patrick J. Curran and Kenneth A. Bollen

CHAPTER 5   Latent Difference Score Structural Models for Linear   137
              Dynamic Analyses With Incomplete Longitudinal Data
              John J. McArdle and Fumiaki Hamagami

CHAPTER 6   Second-Order Latent Growth Models   177
             Aline G. Sayer and Patricio E. Cumsille

CHAPTER 7   The Role of Factorial Invariance in Modeling Growth   201
                and Change
             William Meredith and John Horn

CHAPTER 8   Trait–State Models for Longitudinal Data   241
             David A. Kenny and Alex Zautra

             COMMENT: The Trait–State Distinction and Its Dialectic   265
                         Balance
                       Adam Davey

CHAPTER 9   Reliability for Static and Dynamic Categorical Latent   271
                Variables: Developing Measurement Instruments Based
                on a Model of the Growth Process
             Linda M. Collins

CHAPTER 10   Second-Generation Structural Equation Modeling With a   289
                Combination of Categorical and Continuous Latent
                Variables: New Opportunities for Latent Class–Latent
                Growth Modeling
             Bengt Muthén
             COMMENT (on Chapters 9 and 10): The Next Steps   323
                         in Latent Variable Models for Change
                         David Rindskopf

CHAPTER 11   Planned Missing-Data Designs in Analysis of Change   333
             John W. Graham, Bonnie J. Taylor, and
                Patricio E. Cumsille

CHAPTER 12   Multiple Imputation With PAN   355
             Joseph L. Schafer
             COMMENT (on Chapters 11 and 12): An Analysis of   379
                         Incomplete Data
                         Adam Davey

Additional Research (Abstracts)

APPENDIX A   Cluster Analysis of Developmental Profiles: Relations   385
Between Trajectories of Aggression and Popularity
Over Adolescence
Daniel J. Bauer and David B. Estell

APPENDIX B   Change in the Field of Study Among Science Majors: 388
A Multilevel Longitudinal Analysis
Dale J. Brickley, Joanne M. Cawley, and
Maria Pennock-Roman

APPENDIX C   A Latent Growth Modeling Approach to Mediation   390
Analysis
JeeWon Cheong, David MacKinnon, and Siek Toon Khoo

APPENDIX D   A Comparison of First- and Second-Order Latent Growth   393
Models of Alcohol Expectancies in Adolescence
Patricio E. Cumsille and Aline G. Sayer

APPENDIX E   A Latent Growth Curve Analysis of the Effects of Maternal   395
Well-Being and Cocaine Use on the Home Environment
and Infant Behavior From Birth to 24 Months
Evangeline R. Danseco and Paul R. Marques

APPENDIX F   Testing Mediational Effects of Competence on Drug Use   397
Propensity in Childhood With Structural Equation
Modeling
Zhihong Fan, Mary Ann Pentz, James Dwyer, and
Gencie Turner

APPENDIX G   Modeling Transitions in Two-Stage Sequences   399
Simultaneously
Brian P. Flaherty and Linda M. Collins

APPENDIX H   Stability and Change in Grip Strength During Adulthood: 400
An Examination of Genetic and Environmental
Influences
Julia D. Grant, Stig Berg, and Gerald E. McClearn

APPENDIX I   Tapestry Over Time: A Way to Visualize the Dynamics of   402
Multivariate Data
John C. Hanes, Jr.

APPENDIX J   Multivariate Survivorship Analysis Using Two   404
Cross-Sectional Samples
Mark E. Hill

APPENDIX K   Gun Availability and Adolescent Substance Use: 405
              Using Multiple Imputation to Get Standard Errors
              Stephanie L. Hyatt, Linda M. Collins, and
              Joseph L. Schafer

APPENDIX L   Unraveling Alcohol–Tobacco Cormorbidity Over Seven   407
              Years: A Latent Class Analysis
              Kristina M. Jackson, Kenneth J. Sher, and Phillip K. Wood

APPENDIX M   Longitudinal Analysis of Complex Survey Data: Math and 409
              Reading Achievement From the National Longitudinal
              Survey of Youth, 1986–1994
              Chi-Ming Kam and David A. Wagstaff

APPENDIX N   Latent Ordinal Markov Models of Attitude Change   411
              Jee-Seon Kim and Ulf Böckenholt

APPENDIX O   Estimating Cognitive Growth Curves From Environmental   414
              Risk Factors: Mediating the Role of Parenting and Child
              Factors
              Ambika Krishnakumar and Maureen Black

APPENDIX P   Modeling Prevention Program Effects on Growth in   416
              Substance Use
              Bonnie Taylor, John W. Graham, and
              Patricio E. Cumsille

APPENDIX Q   Linking Children's Poverty History to Change in Behavior 418
              Problems and Self-Concept: Latent Growth Curve Versus
              Piecewise Models
              Peter C. Tice and Steve Carlton-Ford

APPENDIX R   Understanding Caregiver Stress: Scalar and System Models 420
              Virginia Moore Tomlinson and Patrick Doreian

APPENDIX S   Measuring the Zone of Proximal Development: 422
              An Application of Individual Growth Analysis
              Zheng Yan

Author Index   425

Subject Index   433

About the Editors   441

Contributors

Daniel J. Bauer, University of North Carolina at Chapel Hill

Stig Berg, Institute of Gerontology, Jonkoping, Sweden

Maureen Black, University of Maryland School of Medicine, Baltimore

Ulf Böckenholt, University of Illinois at Urbana–Champaign

Steven M. Boker, University of Notre Dame, Notre Dame, IN

Kenneth A. Bollen, University of North Carolina at Chapel Hill

Dale J. Brickley, Pennsylvania State University, University Park

Steve Carlton-Ford, University of Cincinnati, Cincinnati, OH

Joanne M. Cawley, Pennsylvania State University, University Park

JeeWon Cheong, Arizona State University, Tempe

Linda M. Collins, Pennsylvania State University, University Park

Patricio E. Cumsille, Pennsylvania State University, University Park

Patrick J. Curran, University of North Carolina at Chapel Hill

Evangeline R. Danseco, Pacific Institute for Research and Evaluation, Landover, MD

Adam Davey, University of Georgia, Athens

Patrick Doreian, University of Pittsburgh, Pittsburgh, PA

James Dwyer, University of Southern California, Los Angeles

David B. Estell, University of North Carolina at Chapel Hill

Zhihong Fan, University of Southern California, Los Angeles

Brian P. Flaherty, Pennsylvania State University, University Park

John W. Graham, Pennsylvania State University, University Park

Julia D. Grant, Washington University School of Medicine, St. Louis, MO

Fumiaki Hamagami, University of Virginia, Charlottesville

John C. Hanes, Jr., University of North Carolina at Chapel Hill

Mark E. Hill, Pennsylvania State University, University Park

John Horn, University of Southern California, Los Angeles

Stephanie L. Hyatt, Pennsylvania State University, University Park

Kristina M. Jackson, University of Missouri–Columbia

Chi-Ming Kam, Pennsylvania State University, University Park

David A. Kenny, University of Connecticut at Storrs

Siek Toon Khoo, Arizona State University, Tempe

Jee-Seon Kim, University of Illinois at Urbana–Champaign

Ambika Krishnakumar, University of Maryland School of Medicine, Baltimore

David MacKinnon, Arizona State University, Tempe

Paul R. Marques, Pacific Institute for Research and Evaluation, Landover, MD

John J. McArdle, University of Virginia, Charlottesville

Gerald E. McClearn, Pennsylvania State University, University Park

William Meredith, University of California, Berkeley

Peter C. M. Molenaar, University of Amsterdam, Amsterdam, The Netherlands

Virginia Moore Tomlinson, Westminster College, New Wilmington, PA

Bengt Muthén, University of California, Los Angeles

D. Wayne Osgood, Pennsylvania State University, University Park

Maria Pennock-Roman, Pennsylvania State University, University Park

Mary Ann Pentz, University of Southern California, Los Angeles

Andrea M. Piccinin, Pennsylvania State University, University Park

Stephen W. Raudenbush, University of Michigan, Ann Arbor

David Rindskopf, City University of New York, New York

Michael J. Rovine, Pennsylvania State University, University Park

Aline G. Sayer, Harvard University, Cambridge, MA

Joseph L. Schafer, Pennsylvania State University, University Park

Kenneth J. Sher, University of Missouri–Columbia

Bonnie Taylor, Pennsylvania State University, University Park

Peter C. Tice, University of Cincinnati, Cincinnati, OH

Gencie Turner, University of Southern California, Los Angeles

David A. Wagstaff, Pennsylvania State University, University Park

Phillip K. Wood, University of Missouri–Columbia

Zheng Yan, Harvard University, Cambridge, MA

Alex Zautra, Arizona State University, Tempe

Foreword

In early 1988, the American Psychological Association (APA) Science Directorate began its sponsorship of what has become an exceptionally successful activity in support of psychological science—the APA Scientific Conference program. This program has showcased some of the most important topics in psychological science, and the conference participants have included many leading figures in the field.

As we enter a new century, it seems fitting that we begin with a new face on this book series—that of the Decade of Behavior (DoB). The DoB is a major interdisciplinary initiative designed to promote the contributions of the behavioral and social sciences to address some of our most important societal challenges and will occur from 2000 to 2010. Although a major effort of the initiative will be related to informing the public about the contributions of these fields, other activities will be put into place to reach fellow scientists. Hence, the series that was the "APA Science Series" will be continued as the "Decade of Behavior Series." This represents one element in APA's efforts to promote the DoB initiative as one of its partner organizations.

Please note the DoB logo on the inside jacket flap and the full title page. We expect this logo will become a familiar sight over the next few years. For additional information about DoB, please visit http://www.decadeofbehavior.org.

As part of the sponsorship agreement with APA, conference organizers commit themselves not only to the conference itself but also to editing a scholarly volume that results from the meeting. This book is such a volume. Over the course of the past 12 years, we have partnered with 44 universities to sponsor 60 conferences on a variety of topics of interest to psychological scientists. The APA Science Directorate looks forward to continuing this program and to sponsoring other conferences in the years ahead.

We are pleased that this important contribution to the literature was supported in part by the Scientific Conferences program. Congratulations to the editors and contributors on their sterling effort.

Richard McCarty, PhD
Executive Director for Science

Virginia E. Holt
Assistant Executive Director for Science

Preface

This book is a follow-up to *Best Methods for the Analysis of Change: Recent Advances, Unanswered Questions, Future Directions,* published by the American Psychological Association in 1991. Since that book was published, there have been tremendous advances in the field of measurement and analysis of change. We felt strongly the need for highlighting some of these.

In reviewing areas in which there has been much recent activity, we took stock of the field of the analysis of change and made some interesting observations. When *Best Methods for the Analysis of Change* was published, researchers were using primarily traditional procedures that emphasized interindividual variability. These procedures often effectively ignored change, which manifests itself in the form of intraindividual variability. In fact, an important theme of the first book was the exhortation to researchers to emphasize intraindividual variability. No such exhortation is needed today. Nearly all of the chapters of this book strongly emphasize intraindividual variability. Another important emergent theme is that of missing data. This topic was just beginning to be considered in 1991. John J. McArdle and Fumiaki Hamagami's chapter in the 1991 volume was the only one to address missing-data issues in any depth. Now missing data is recognized as an important subdiscipline within statistics, one of great interest to longitudinal researchers. We also noticed that the field is moving toward integration of methods that previously were thought to be separate — for example, growth curve and autoregressive models, factor analysis and latent class models. This is an indication of how much the field of analysis of change has matured since 1989.

This book is based in part on presentations given at the conference "New Methods for the Analysis of Change," held at the Pennsylvania State University (Penn State) in 1998. This conference was a follow-up to the Los Angeles conference "Best Methods for the Analysis of Change?" (the question mark is correct!), which resulted in the 1991 book. The second conference was the equal of the first event in terms of excitement, exchange of ideas, and lively discussion. However, there were some procedural differences between the Los Angeles conference and the Penn State conference. First, at the Los Angeles conference, we included a few presentations from substantive researchers in which they expressed their opinions about unsolved issues they would like to see methodological researchers address; we did not include this feature in the Penn State conference. There simply was not room on the program because there was so much methodological research we wanted to include. Second, when planning the Los Angeles conference, we struggled for a way to involve graduate student and postdoctoral participants and ultimately decided to hold a special poster session, which was a resounding success. The poster abstracts appear in the appendixes (at the end of the volume); we hope that readers will take the time to examine them. Readers will surely be seeing the names again in the analysis-of-change literature of the future.

Finally, we would like to say a word about the title of this book. The 1989 conference was titled "Best Methods for the Analysis of Change?" Note the question mark—John Horn and Linda Collins meant the title as a wry way of posing the question "Are these the best methods?" For various reasons, the question mark was removed some time before the book was published, inadvertently producing a rather grandiose title. One reviewer of the book even called it offensive. Thus, we chose not to name the current volume *Best Methods II* or something similar (some of our colleagues jokingly suggested *Even Better Methods*). Instead, we chose the title *New Methods for the Analysis of Change*. We hope that readers will find this book as stimulating as we have.

Acknowledgments

We gratefully acknowledge financial support from two major sources for the 1998 *New Methods for the Analysis of Change* conference and subsequent preparation of this volume. The first is the American Psychological Association Science Directorate, which funded about half of the expenses associated with the conference and the book. The second is the Program Innovation Fund of the Division of Continuing Education at Pennsylvania State University (Penn State). We particularly thank Sara Parks, who at the time was the Associate Dean for Outreach, Cooperative Extension, and International Programs in the College of Health and Human Development at Penn State, for valuable feedback on our proposal to the Program Innovation Fund.

Andrea Piccinin generously helped us organize the conference at a critical time when we badly needed such help (she also contributed a trenchant commentary on the Boker chapter). Tina Meyers provided her usual smooth, cheerful, and invaluable help with organizing the conference and preparing the manuscript.

It has been a privilege to work with the group of presenters and discussants who participated in the New Methods for the Analysis of Change conference. All were enthusiastic; came prepared; delivered their talks well; listened; and where appropriate, challenged and spoke out. They were also cooperative about chapter deadlines and revisions. We particularly wish to acknowledge the time that Patrick Curran and David Rindskopf spent preparing reviews of chapters for the book. Their efforts helped improve this volume. We also thank the graduate and postdoctoral students who contributed the excellent posters that made the poster session such an unqualified success.

While we were preparing this book, our families were most supportive. We thank John and Matthew and Gus and Gabriel, and we express our gratitude by dedicating this book to them.

Introduction: Organization of This Book

In *Best Methods for the Analysis of Change*, Linda Collins and John Horn argued that the chapters could not profitably be ordered in a single way. Several themes ran through the book, and depending on which theme was being emphasized, the ideal arrangement of the chapters would be quite different. So instead of presenting a single order, Collins and Horn listed these themes and indicated in a table which chapters were relevant to which themes. We do the same here, with a different set of themes appropriate to the present volume. The themes are outlined in Table I.1, along with an indication of the themes within which each chapter falls. Readers who wish to pursue a particular theme may then choose a suitable course of reading.

In the following sections, we discuss each category in greater detail. Also each chapter begins with an editors' introduction, which contains a brief dis-

TABLE I.1
Chapter Relevance to Themes Underlying This Volume

CHAPTER AUTHORS	INTRAINDIVIDUAL CHANGE	MEASUREMENT	DISENTANGLING STABILITY AND CHANGE	AIMING FOR A LARGER FRAMEWORK	MISSING DATA
Boker	X				
Collins	X	X	X		
Curran & Bollen	X		X		
Graham et al.					X
Kenny & Zautra			X	X	
McArdle & Hamagami	X		X		X
Meredith & Horn		X	X		
Muthén	X			X	
Raudenbush	X			X	
Rovine & Molenaar	X			X	
Sayer & Cumsille	X	X	X		
Schafer					X

cussion of the aspect of change that the chapter addresses and a note directing readers to other relevant chapters. Several chapters have interesting commentaries, an outgrowth of the conference setting from which this volume evolved. We hope that the identification of themes, the editors' introductions, and the commentaries help readers integrate the rich diversity of perspectives and depth of information about analysis of change contained in the 12 chapters in this book.

Models of Intraindividual Change

These chapters emphasize methods for estimating and evaluating models of growth and change over time at the level of the individual. Most of these chapters take a growth curve modeling approach. Patrick Curran and Kenneth Bollen (chapter 4) present a method for integrating intraindividual change with stability or autoregressive growth. John McArdle and Fumiaki Hamagami (chapter 5) discuss a very flexible approach based on latent difference scores. Bengt Muthén (chapter 10) offers a broad framework that allows the identification of subgroups of individuals exhibiting similar growth patterns. Stephen Raudenbush (chapter 2) discusses several types of intraindividual change and links these to appropriate mathematical models. Michael Rovine and Peter Molenaar (chapter 3) show how to address frequently posed research questions about intraindividual growth within the structural equations modeling framework. Aline Sayer and Patricio Cumsille (chapter 6) illustrate how to model intraindividual growth on the latent level. Two of the chapters deviate from the growth curve modeling perspective: Steven Boker (chapter 1) presents a radically different conceptualization of intraindividual change, based on engineering principles, and Linda Collins (chapter 9) presents an approach for categorical, stage-sequential change.

Measurement

The chapters in this category address issues of measurement that are important in analysis of change. Collins presents a method for developing instruments that are tailored to particular kinds of stage-sequential development. William Meredith and John Horn (chapter 7) discuss some thorny issues in factorial invariance and demonstrate results that may surprise many readers. Sayer and Cumsille (chapter 6) illustrate how to measure growth on the latent level and how to separate measurement error from deviations from the growth curve.

Disentangling Stability and Change

Several chapters emphasize methods for separating intraindividual growth from aspects of phenomena that are stable across time. Curran and Bollen (chapter 4) illustrate very clearly a method for separating systematic change over time from stability over time. David Kenny and Alex Zautra (chapter 8) discuss methods for identifying variance due to stable traits and variance due to transient states. McArdle and Hamagami (chapter 5) show how it is possible to assess change and stability simultaneously using their latent difference score approach. Meredith and Horn (chapter 7) discuss factorial invariance, which is a necessary underpinning of any attempt to assess stability and change. Sayer and Cumsille (chapter 6) illustrate an approach that permits identification of changing and stable true score variance. The latent transition analysis approach, discussed by Collins (chapter 9), estimates the proportion of individuals who remain stable and the proportion who change over time.

Aiming for a Larger Framework

The field of methodology for analysis of change has matured sufficiently so that now researchers have begun identifying larger frameworks in order to integrate knowledge. Several chapters in this volume are examples of this. Kenny and Zautra (chapter 8) discuss a larger framework within which they place several approaches to trait–state analyses. Muthén (chapter 10) presents an exciting and very general approach to analysis of change that integrates latent class and factor analysis methods. Raudenbush (chapter 2) reviews a wide variety of growth models and shows their interrelationships. Rovine and Molenaar (chapter 3) place several frequently used models of growth into the general linear mixed model and then place all of these into a structural equation modeling framework.

Missing Data

The increased attention that has been paid to missing data in longitudinal research since the 1989 Los Angeles "Best Methods for the Analysis of Change?" conference has been dramatic. Joseph Schafer (chapter 12) provides an accessible introduction to multiple imputation, a highly versatile and robust missing-data procedure, and discusses his new multiple-imputation method, designed for longitudinal research. Also taking a multiple-imputation approach are John Graham, Bonnie Taylor, and Patricio Cumsille (chapter 11), who discuss methods for imposing experimenter-controlled missing data on longitudinal research designs. McArdle and Hamagami (chapter 5) take an alternative perspective and illustrate how to deal with missing data in a structural equation modeling framework.

New Methods for the Analysis of Change

Editors' Introduction

This chapter presents a radically different conceptualization of intraindividual change. Most social scientists are accustomed to thinking in terms of the familiar parameters of growth models, such as intercept and slope. Steven Boker's approach is based on engineering principles, however, and it includes ideas about the form of change that are foreign to social scientists. For example, one model of change Boker advances is that of the dampened linear oscillator, which is like a pendulum with friction—swinging back and forth, gradually petering out. These kinds of severely nonmonotonic processes are impossible to deal with using standard growth modeling procedures. Boker's work has revealed a world of new models of change. Although in 2001 Boker's approach may seem like a methodology in search of a substantive application, we predict that social scientists will readily adopt this approach and that it will influence them to think in terms of new models of change. Andrea Piccinin's commentary nicely helps the reader place Boker's ideas in the context of more familiar ideas. Readers may wish to compare the Boker perspective on analysis of change with perspectives presented elsewhere in this volume by Muthén (chapter 10), Curran and Bollen (chapter 4), McArdle and Hamagami (chapter 5), Raudenbush (chapter 2), Rovine and Molenaar (chapter 3), and Sayer and Cumsille (chapter 6).

Differential Structural Equation Modeling of Intraindividual Variability

Steven M. Boker

The world in which we are immersed exhibits both invariant characteristics and continuous change. For an organism to successfully flourish in such an environment the predictable regularities of the environment must be recognized while simultaneously the ever-changing characteristics of new conditions must be perceived, and adaptations to these perceived changes must be made. If successful adaptation is to be attained, the organism must at some level be able to monitor changes in its internal state and the relation of that state to the environment. Such monitoring might be a high-level cognitive process or could alternatively be a part of a low-level, autonomic, self-regulatory system.

For the purposes of this discussion, the term *self-regulation* is used to describe a process by which an organism modifies its own behavior in a systematic way by using information about change. This information about change might be estimates of differences in internal states of the organism. In another case, information about change might be derived from an estimate of changes that have occurred in the environment. More complex, derived information about change might involve estimates of the relative change in the estimated differences in internal states as compared to the differences that have occurred in the environment during the same time period.

In this chapter I examine models that use change as a predictor, an outcome variable, or both. This form of model is appealing because it allows one to test theories of self-regulation or organism–environment coupling (Warren, 1990) as a mechanism for observed patterns of intraindividual variability. In particular,

I thank John Nesselroade, Jack McArdle, John Horn, Linda Collins, and Aline Sayer for their dynamic and systematic support of the analysis of variability and intraindividual change. I also sincerely thank Bennett Bertenthal for giving me permission to use the example data presented in this chapter and Jim Rose for the hard work of collecting postural data from 40 (potentially less than ideally cooperative) infants.

I focus on a method that models processes in which there is a covariance structure relating the value of a variable, its first derivative and its second derivative.

As a concrete example of first and second derivatives, consider taking an automobile trip from your house to a friend's house 10 miles away. Luckily, there are no stop signs or traffic that will interfere with your trip. Figure 1.1A plots the distance of your automobile from your house as a function of time. You start your car about 9 min. after this thought experiment begins, you accelerate toward your friend's house, reaching a peak velocity of about 55 miles per hour midway in the trip. Then you begin to decelerate, first gradually, and then braking decisively, finally arriving at your friend's house about 17 min. after you started your car. Figures 1.1B and 1.1C plot the velocity and acceleration of your automobile, respectively.

These three quantities—displacement and the first and second derivatives of the displacement—can each be thought of as ways of measuring change. Consider how they can be applied to psychological variables.

Self-Regulation and Dynamical Disease

It is convenient to think about a first derivative as the *slope* of a variable at a particular instant in time and the second derivative as the *curvature* of a variable at a particular instant in time. For instance, if the variable of interest were depression, one could devise an instrument that would, given repeated measurements, provide an estimate of the rate at which an individual was becoming more depressed and whether that rate of change was itself accelerating or decelerating. A normal individual might have a self-regulatory mechanism that would respond to increasing levels of depression by decelerating that increase. Eventually, the level of depression would begin to decrease, but the self-regulatory mechanism would need to slow that rate of decrease at just the right

FIGURE 1.1

(opposite page) Position and derivatives of automobile traveling between two locations 10 miles apart. Panel A: The abscissa plots time in minutes, and the ordinate plots the distance from the original location. Panel B: The ordinate plots the first derivative of the automobile's distance from the original location; the velocity of the automobile at each instant in time. Panel C: The ordinate plots the second derivative of the automobile's distance from the original location; the acceleration (or deceleration) of the automobile at each instant in time.

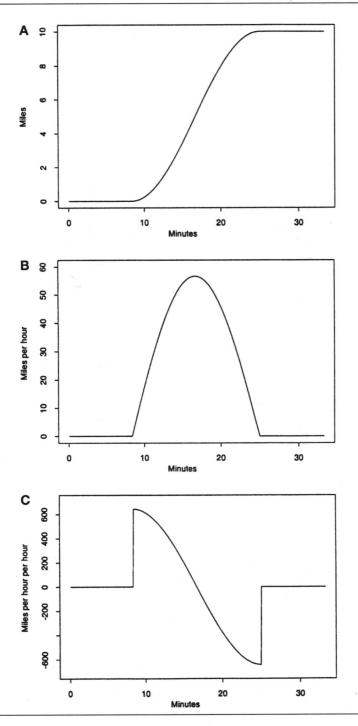

time if it were to reach a point of equilibrium at a mood balanced between depression and elation.

Pezard, Nandrino, Renault, and Massioui (1996) advanced the hypothesis that clinical depression might be a disease that affects the mechanism of self-regulation, a *dynamical disease* (Glass & Mackey, 1988). A different type of breakdown in such a self-regulatory mechanism might underlie rapid cycling bipolar disorder (RCBD) (Gottschalk, Bauer, & Whybrow, 1995). In normal individuals, one might characterize the likely day-to-day changes in mood scores as having a *point attractor*: an equilibrium point somewhere between elation and depression. Individual differences in these equilibrium points would be characterized by a distribution of more or less stable trait scores on this dimension. Thus, given some outside influence that perturbs a normal individual's mood away from equilibrium, one would expect that, over time, the mood would move back toward equilibrium. Conversely, in RCBD individuals, one might characterize the likely day-to-day changes as some sort of limit cycle attractor—that is, given an outside effect that perturbs an RCBD individual's mood, he or she might be expected to return to a characteristic pattern of cycling between elation and depression.

A dynamical model produces a prediction about the attractor that best fits the data. This is the basic difference between a dynamical model and a growth curve model, which produces a prediction about a best-fitting growth curve (what a dynamical modeler would call a single best-fitting *trajectory*).

One of the most exciting aspects of the use of dynamical models—and by this I mean models that include change as predictors and outcome variables—is that simply by varying the coefficients of the model one can produce expected attractors that have very different shape (Boker & Graham, 1998; Hubbard & West, 1991). Thus, for some dynamical models, the structure of the model does not need to change in order for the expected attractor to change from a point attractor to a limit cycle; only the coefficients need to change (see, e.g., Kaplan & Glass, 1995). This means that if, for instance, depression were to be a dynamical disease then a single structural equation model might account for normal, clinically depressed, and RCBD attractors with between-group differences in coefficients for the model.

Developmental Change in Attractors

One does not expect that mechanisms for self-regulation or environmental–organism coupling are limited to any particular time scale except those limits imposed by biology; that is, there is no apparent logical reason that the phenomena of self-regulation would be limited to, for instance, the time scale at which the endocrine system operates. Similarly, logic alone offers no reason that the mechanisms of self-regulation could not operate at the time scale of a life-time. Thus, one might reasonably expect to observe dynamical processes in human behavior operating at time scales measured in milliseconds to time scales measured in decades (Nesselroade & Boker, 1994).

Another possible way that one might observe change is through a developmental change in an existing behavioral attractor (Clark & Phillips, 1993; Thelen, 1995); that is, a behavioral attractor might change shape during the process of development. Thus, one pattern in short-term intraindividual variability might morph over time into another pattern in short-term intraindividual variability. Thus, one might not only plausibly study individual differences in change and changes in individual differences (Nesselroade, 1991a) but also may be able to model intraindividual change in intraindividual variability using dynamical models.

An example of the way that a behavioral attractor would exhibit developmental change might be observed as an infant becomes capable of self-supported sitting (Bertenthal & Bai, 1989). In this chapter, I use data from a study of postural control in infants to illustrate techniques that can test hypotheses about the structure of the covariances in short-term intraindividual variability as well as to test hypotheses about developmental change in attractors. Although this data set contains many observations per individual, these same techniques, given an assumption of homogeneity of attractor shape over individuals, can be applied to multiwave panel data with few observations per individual (Boker & Graham, 1998).

Example: Development of Postural Control

In this analysis I use an example data set that comes from a moving-room experiment performed on a group of infants (Bertenthal, Rose, & Bai, 1997). These infants were selected to have ages that straddled the average age of onset of self-supported sitting: 6.5 months (Bayley, 1969). The data from this experiment hold interest for examination using dynamical systems methods because developmental changes in the dynamics of the postural control mechanism can be studied simultaneously with the coupling between perception and action. By studying developmental changes in the coupling between visual perception and postural action I hope to better understand the nature of the postural control system.

Participants and Procedure

Forty infants participated in the study, 10 in each of four age groups: 5, 7, 9, and 13 months. The moving room consisted of a 1.2 m × 1.2 m × 2.1 m open-ended enclosure, the walls and ceiling of which were constructed of fiberboard covered in green and white vertically striped cloth that was mounted on small rubber wheels that rolled on tracks fixed to the floor. A small window in the middle of the front wall of the moving room provided a view to a small electronically activated toy dog that was used to fix the gaze of the infant at the beginning of each trial. A potentiometer was attached to one wall of the moving room such that the position of the room could be measured by the voltage drop through the potentiometer. The position of the room was sampled at 50 Hz and converted to a digital time series using an 8-bit A/D converter, thereby creating a time series $R = \{r_1, r_2, r_3, \ldots, r_N\}$, representing the room movement.

A forceplate was set in the middle of the floor of the moving room, and an infant's bicycle seat was mounted on the center of the forceplate facing parallel to the direction of room movement. The forceplate consisted of a rigid metal plate suspended from four pressure transducers that effectively sampled the center of pressure of the infant at 50 Hz synchronously with the measurements of room position.

An infant sat in the infant bicycle seat, and at the beginning of each trial the toy was activated to direct the infant's attention to the front of the room. The walls were then moved in one of six movement conditions for a period of approximately 12 s, during which time the infant's center of pressure (COP) was measured. Four of the movement conditions consisted of a 2 × 2 design in which the room oscillated at 0.3 or 0.6 Hz and the amplitude of the oscillation was either 9 or 18 cm. The remaining two movement conditions were a pseudorandom oscillation and a control condition in which the room did not oscillate. Each infant performed two trials in each movement condition. For the purposes of the present analysis, only the movement conditions in the 2 × 2 design are considered.

During each trial, the forceplate measured changes in the infant's COP along two axes: the anterior–posterior axis (X), aligned with the movement of the room, and the lateral axis (Y), orthogonal to the movement of the room. As the room began to move, the two axes of COP and the unidirectional position of the room were simultaneously sampled at 50 Hz (20-ms sampling interval) for 10.25 s. Thus, each trial generated three synchronized time series containing 512 samples: X, Y, and R.

Postural Control as a Dynamical System

Figure 1.2 shows the fore–aft movement of one infant and the corresponding movement of the room plotted against time for one trial in the 0.6-Hz–9-cm condition. By inspection, it appears that while the infant is accommodating to the room to some degree, the coupling between the room movement and the infant's COP is not strong. I will model and test how individual differences in this coupling may be related to the room movement conditions and to age-related change.

Note that in Figure 1.2 the room movement describes an oscillation similar to a sine wave. If the infant's COP were to exactly mimic a sine wave oscillation, then the resulting time series would be expected to exactly fit a linear oscillator. I use a dampened linear oscillator as a first approximation to the movement of the infant.

A dampened linear oscillator can be thought of as a pendulum with friction. When a pendulum with friction is given a single push, it will swing back and forth for awhile, until it comes to rest at its equilibrium point. If one models the infant's COP as a dampened linear oscillator, one is proposing the hypothesis that the postural-control system in the infant is attempting to return the COP to a point of equilibrium. Perceptual input that drives the infant's COP away from this point of equilibrium induces compensatory applications of muscular force that will eventually return the COP to the single point of equilibrium.

I now explore the consequences of the hypothesis of an undampened linear oscillator for postural control in sitting. An undampened linear oscillator suggests that the acceleration toward the equilibrium point is proportional to the distance from the equilibrium point. This mechanism has face validity in that

FIGURE 1.2

Time series plot of room movement (dotted line) and anterior–posterior center of pressure (solid line) for one trial for one 7-month-old infant.

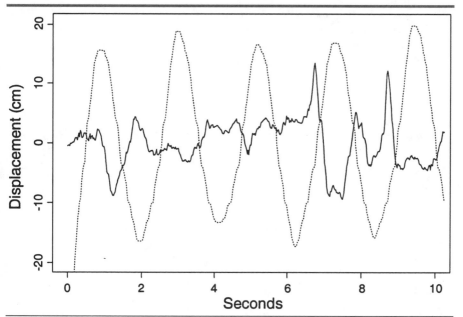

the farther one is from equilibrium—that is, the more off balance one is—the more force one would tend to exert in order to attempt to return to equilibrium.

Suppose that the infant's COP was at some distance anterior to the equilibrium point. Through some sensory mechanism the infant acquires the information required to produce a compensatory posterior movement toward the equilibrium point. As the infant applies muscular force, the COP will accelerate in a posterior direction toward the equilibrium point.

If the postural-control system were to use only information about how far the COP was from the point of equilibrium, then the COP would continue to accelerate toward the equilibrium point until it passed the equilibrium point. As long as the COP is anterior to the equilibrium point, the control system would apply muscular force to produce acceleration in the posterior direction. However, as soon as the COP passes the equilibrium point the control system would begin to exert force in the opposite direction; small amounts at first but, as the COP became farther from the equilibrium point, proportionally more force would be exerted. The COP would decelerate, eventually stop, and begin to accelerate in the anterior direction. This process would continue indefinitely, and the maximum velocity of the COP would always be attained exactly at the equilibrium point. The system would always overshoot the equilibrium point, and the resulting movement would be exactly that described by a frictionless pendulum, as shown in Figure 1.3A.

Consider the consequences of adding dampening to the linear oscillator model. As for the undampened oscillator model previously discussed, in response to a displacement from equilibrium the postural-control system produces a proportionate acceleration toward equilibrium. In addition, however, a dampening force is added: COP velocity produces a proportionate acceleration in the opposite direction. Thus, the faster the COP is traveling, the greater is the opposing muscular force applied to decelerate the postural movement. In

FIGURE 1.3

Time series plot of undampened (A) and dampened (B) linear oscillators.

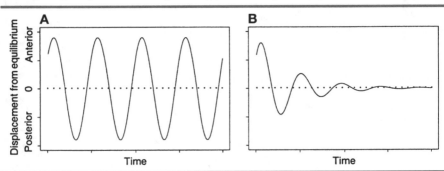

the undampened oscillator the greatest velocity occurred as the COP was passing over the point of equilibrium. Thus, this is the point at which the dampening force will be the greatest. At the extreme values of displacement, the velocity is zero, so the dampening force is zero at those points as well. Adding a dampening force to the linear oscillator produces a trajectory, as shown in Figure 1.3B, in which the COP eventually comes to rest at the equilibrium point.

Differential Equation Model of a Linear Oscillator

This dampened oscillator can be expressed as a multiple regression in which the acceleration of the system is predicted by the displacement from equilibrium and the velocity. If one uses the standard notation for instantaneous velocity and acceleration, this equation can be written as

$$\frac{d^2x(t)}{dt^2} = \zeta \frac{dx(t)}{dt} + \eta x(t) + e(t), \tag{1.1}$$

where $x(t)$ represents the displacement from equilibrium at time t, $dx(t)/dt$ represents the velocity at time t, and $d^2x(t)/dt^2$ represents the acceleration at time t. The parameter η is the square of the frequency of the resulting oscillation, ζ is the dampening (or friction), and $e(t)$ is the residual error (see, e.g., Thompson & Stewart, 1986).

Many may be unfamiliar with the use of *velocity* and *acceleration* in a psychological context. However, velocity is simply linear change, often referred to in growth curve models as *slope*. In the same context, acceleration would be referred to as *curvature*. It is important to realize that the techniques applied here to long-time series can also be applied to longitudinal data sets with as few as three time points (Boker & Nesselroade, in press). A minimum of six waves of measurement would be ideal because this would allow a wider range of models to be tested. However, the techniques applied here are not limited to data sets with hundreds of occasions of measurement.

Attractors

The three variables in the dampened linear oscillator—displacement, velocity, and acceleration—are related as a dynamical system; that is, the specific relations among these three variables specify a central tendency of a family of trajectories that any one individual might have. This is different than a growth curve type of model in that a growth curve model makes a prediction about a single trajectory of central tendency. The set of equilibria for this family of trajectories is called the system's *attractor*. In this case the attractor is a single point. A best-fitting family of trajectories for a dynamical systems model is called a *basin of attraction*, which can be visualized using a *vector field* plot.

One possible shape for the basin of attraction for a dampened linear oscillator is plotted in Figure 1.4, in which a grid of possible combinations of displacement [$x(t)$] and velocity [$dx(t)/dt$] is plotted. For each of these combinations an arrow is plotted, the direction and length of which are determined by the predicted value of the acceleration such that the end of the arrow points to where the expected values of position and velocity will be after a short interval of time.

By selecting a pair of initial values for velocity and displacement, one may follow the arrows and determine the trajectory that would evolve from that original set of starting values. Every trajectory, in this case, ends up at the equilibrium point of zero displacement and zero velocity. Just as there are infinitely many possible starting values for velocity and displacement, there are infinitely many expected trajectories that conform to the shape of a basin of attraction. The shape of the basin of attraction and the attractor itself are determined by the values of the parameters that are estimated from Equation 1.1. Individual differences in these parameters would indicate that individuals have basins of attraction with different shapes and may have attractors with different shapes. If these parameters change with development, then there would be a developmental change in the shape of the basin of attraction and possibly in

FIGURE 1.4

Vector field plot of the point attractor for a dampened linear oscillator with frequency and dampening parameters similar to a pendulum with friction.

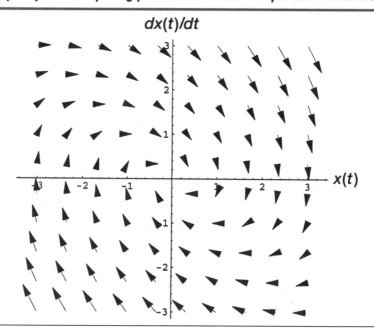

the attractor itself (Clark, 1997; Geert, 1997; Hopkins & Butterworth, 1997; Thelen, 1995).

Local Linear Approximation to Derivatives

To fit a differential equation model to data, at each available occasion of measurement an estimate for the first and second derivatives of the variable must be calculated. Many estimation methods may be used (e.g., Cleveland & Devlin, 1988; Gu, 1990), but local linear approximation is easy and works well in simulations (Boker & Nesselroade, in press).

Suppose the variable X is measured on three occasions, resulting in the measurements $x(1)$, $x(2)$, and $x(3)$. A local linear approximation for the derivative of X at the second occasion of measurement is given by the average of the two slopes between $x(1)$ and $x(2)$ and between $x(2)$ and $x(3)$ (see Figure 1.5),

$$\frac{dx(1 + \tau)}{dt} \approx \frac{x(1 + 2\tau) - x(1)}{2\tau\Delta t} \tag{1.2}$$

where in this case $\tau = 1$ because $x(1)$, $x(2)$, and $x(3)$ are successive occasions of measurement and Δt is the interval of time between measurements. Every

FIGURE 1.5

Local linear approximation of the derivative of X at the second occasion of measurement.

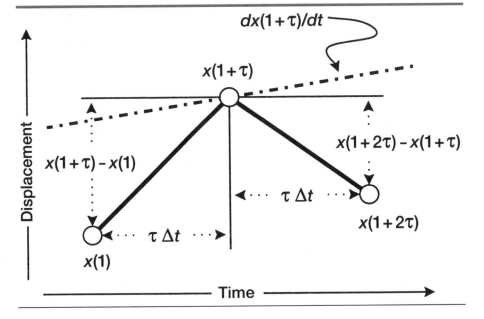

other measurement in a sequence (e.g., $x[1]$, $x[3]$, and $x[5]$) could be used if one substituted $\tau = 2$ into Equation 1.2.

Similarly, the local linear approximation for the second derivative of x at the second occasion of measurement can be calculated from the same triplet of scores $x(1)$, $x(2)$, and $x(3)$ as simply the change in the slopes,

$$\frac{d^2x(1 + \tau)}{dt^2} \approx \frac{x(1 + 2\tau) - 2x(1 + \tau) + x(1)}{\tau^2 \Delta t^2}. \tag{1.3}$$

Differential Structural Equation Models

The dampened linear oscillator defined in Equation 1.1 can be considered an ordinary multiple regression equation. If one supposes that variables outside the dampened linear oscillator might have an effect on it, a system of linear equations will result. Structural equation modeling provides a powerful tool for estimating parameters of systems of linear equations and can be effectively used here. This technique is called *differential structural equation modeling* (dSEM).

In the example data, a model can be fit to each individual trial in which the infant's anterior–posterior COP and room movement were recorded. Each trial consists of 512 data points, so if one assumes that the basin of attraction is not changing shape during the trial, one has more than 500 observations of the three values—displacement, velocity, and acceleration—with which to estimate the shape of the basin of attraction.

For each trial, five structural models were fit to the data generated by the room movement and infant anterior–posterior COP. The first model, shown in Figure 1.6, is one in which the movement of the room provides no prediction of the position, velocity, or acceleration of the infant. This model will be used as a null model for comparison with other models that make specific predictions about how the room affects the infant's posture.

The three variables R, dR, and d^2R at the top of Figure 1.6 represent the displacement, velocity, and acceleration of the room, respectively. The remaining three variables—X, dX, and d^2X—represent the displacement, velocity, and acceleration of the infant's anterior–posterior center of pressure (A–PCOP). The variables X, dX, and d^2X form the hypothesized dampened linear oscillator for the infant such that the coefficient η is the proportional effect of the A–PCOP displacement on the acceleration of the A–PCOP, and the coefficient ζ is the proportional effect of the velocity of the A–PCOP on the acceleration of the A–PCOP. The loops from a variable to itself represent the variance of that variable, according to the reticular action modeling path diagram form introduced by McArdle (McArdle & Boker, 1990; McArdle & McDonald, 1984) and used by the Mx structural equation modeling software (Neale, 1994).

Because the expected movement of the infant is a swaying motion with a frequency equal to the frequency of the moving room, the value of η was fixed

FIGURE 1.6

Model A: differential structural equation model in which the moving room does not predict infant's anterior–posterior center of pressure (A–PCOP). The variables in the model include R, which is room displacement; dR, which is room velocity; d²R, which is room acceleration; X, which is A–PCOP displacement; dX, which is A–PCOP velocity; and d²X, which is A–PCOP acceleration.

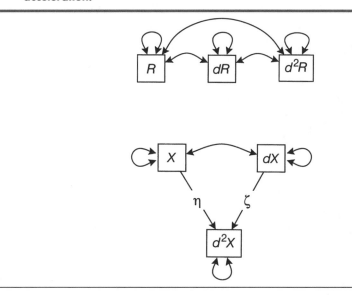

so that the frequency of the linear oscillator comprising the three variables X, dX, and d^2X would be forced to match the frequency of the moving-room condition. If the estimated value of ζ is negative, then one expects a dampened linear oscillator, but if the estimated value of ζ is positive then, rather than dampened oscillations over time, one expects to see amplified oscillations over time. If the estimated value of ζ is near zero then the oscillator is a "frictionless" system, one that does not dampen or amplify over time.

There are two sources of potential for misfit in Model A. First, because the value of η is fixed, then, to the degree to which the postural control system of the infant is not well described by a linear oscillator at a frequency equal to the frequency of the room, the model does not fit the data. The second source of misfit is the strong assumption of zero covariance between all of the room variables and all of the infant variables. The covariances between the room variables are completely saturated, so the structure of their covariances fits exactly and thus cannot contribute to model misfit.

The other four models that were fit to each trial are shown in Figure 1.7. Each of these models explores a different structure for the effect of the room's displacement, velocity, and acceleration on the A–PCOP of the infant.

FIGURE 1.7

Four differential structural models of the effect of the moving room on the infants' anterior–posterior center of pressure (A–PCOP). R represents room displacement; dR represents room velocity; d²R represents room acceleration; X represents A–PCOP displacement; dX represents A–PCOP velocity; d²X represents A–PCOP acceleration.

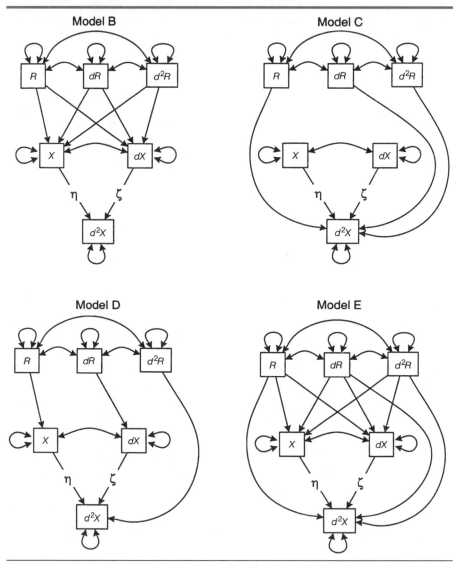

Model B and Model C provide two alternative ways in which the room variables could influence the acceleration of the infants' A–PCOP. In Model B the effect of the room on the A–PCOP acceleration is mediated through the displacement and velocity of the A–PCOP. On the other hand, in Model C the effect of the room variables is directly on the A–PCOP acceleration. These two models form an interesting dichotomy from a dynamical systems perspective.

In Model B, there is no possibility for the coefficients linking the room variables to the A–PCOP variable to affect the estimates of the parameters of the A–PCOP oscillator. Thus in Model B, the shape of the basin of attraction for the A–PCOP oscillator is independent of the moving room. If Model B were preferred, the theoretical conclusion would be that visual perception is an input to the postural control system but not an intrinsic part of it.

In Model C, however, changes in the coefficients linking the room variables directly to the A–PCOP acceleration could cause changes in the A–PCOP oscillator coefficients. In this case, the effect of the moving room includes a change in shape of the basin of attraction for the A–PCOP oscillator, and if Model C were to be preferred, the theoretical conclusion would be that the perception of the visual stimulus was incorporated as an intrinsic part of the postural control system. Model D tests the hypothesis that the room displacement affects only the A–PCOP displacement, the room velocity affects only the A–PCOP velocity, and the room acceleration affects only the A–PCOP acceleration.

Model E fully saturates the paths between the room and the A–PCOP oscillator and thus provides an anchor as the best the model could fit, given that the frequency of the A–PCOP oscillator has been fixed. Model E has 1 degree of freedom, and its misfit will give an indication of how well the fixed-frequency oscillator model fits the infants' responses to the moving room.

Results

Each of the five differential structural models were fit to each of the 320 individual trials. To remove artifacts possibly associated with the start of the trial and the end of the trial, the first 100 samples and final 200 samples of the trial were ignored, leaving 212 samples of room position and A–PCOP from the middle of each trial. The derivatives were calculated using linear interpolation with a time lag of $\tau = 24$. The value of τ was chosen as the value that would induce the least bias in the parameter estimation given the two moving-room frequencies (Boker & Nesselroade, in press). When the correlation between the displacement and its first derivative is minimized, the bias in η is minimized. A τ equal to the number of samples in one quarter the average period (1.92 s = 96 samples, 96/4 = 24) minimizes the correlation between displacement and its first derivative for a sine wave. After choosing $\tau = 24$, first and second derivatives were calculated for each trial using local linear approximation. The resulting number of samples of displacement, velocity, and acceleration for room and A–PCOP was $N = 165$ for each trial. Next, a covariance matrix was calculated for the room, and A–PCOP displacement, velocity, and acceleration (a 6×6 covariance matrix) was calculated for each trial. Finally, parameter estimates and fit statistics were obtained by fitting the previously described models individually to each trial's covariance matrix. Thus for each trial there were obtained individual parameter estimates for each model.

Table 1.1 presents the overall mean values of the estimated parameters and fit statistics for the five models tested as averaged across all conditions and all infants. On first inspection, none of the fit statistics appear promising, with root mean square error of approximation in the range of .42 to .97. From this one can conclude that, on average, a model of infant postural control based on a linear oscillator with a frequency fixed to the room frequency is not sufficient to account for the variance in the acceleration of the infant. Although the mean multiple R^2 values for A–PCOP acceleration are in the range of .40 to .46, these

TABLE 1.1

Mean Coefficients and Fit Statistics Over All Infants, All Conditions, and All Trials

COEFFICIENT	MODEL				
	A	B	C	D	E
η	−8.05	−8.05	−8.05	−8.05	−8.05
ζ	−.01	−.01	.00	−.04	.00
$R \rightarrow X$		−1.49		−1.07	−1.49
$dR/dt \rightarrow X$		0.14			0.14
$d^2R/dt^2 \rightarrow X$		−0.06			−0.06
$R \rightarrow dX/dt$		−2.80			−2.80
$dR/dt \rightarrow dX/dt$		−1.03		−0.98	−1.03
$d^2R/dt^2 \rightarrow dX/dt$		−0.02			−0.02
$R \rightarrow d^2X/dt^2$			9.86		9.86
$dR/dt \rightarrow d^2X/dt^2$			0.38		0.38
$d^2R/dt^2 \rightarrow d^2X/dt^2$			0.86	0.12	0.86
R^2 for d^2X/dt^2	0.40	0.40	0.46	0.42	0.46
N	165	165	165	165	165
df	10	4	7	7	1
χ^2	322	182	304	254	165
RMSEA	.42	.51	.49	.45	.97

Note. RMSEA = root mean square error of approximation.

are not sufficiently large to suggest that the linear oscillator model is doing an adequate job of accounting for the intrinsic dynamic of the infant.

Perhaps it is not so surprising that the movement of an infant would have a large degree of unpredictability, and one might consider that a poorly fitting model is to be expected. If one accepts the linear oscillator model as a first approximation, then the mean values of the parameters η and ζ can be examined. The mean value of $\eta = -8.05$ was predetermined: It is the average of the ηs for the two moving-room frequencies, which were fixed when the model was fit. The values of η for the 0.3-Hz (-3.21) and 0.6-Hz (-12.88) conditions were determined empirically by fitting an oscillator model to the moving-room data. It is interesting to note that the range of mean values for ζ across the five models is $-0.04-0.00$. These values are very close to zero, indicating that if the linear oscillator model is used as an approximation to the infants' A–PCOP, then the system is essentially "frictionless": It has neither dampening nor amplification over the course of a single trial.

Regardless of whether the linear oscillator portion of the model is rejected as a first approximation, there are still several interesting differences among these models. Recall that there are two sources of potential misfit in the model. Model A and Model B are nested, and their chi-square difference is 140 for 6 degrees of freedom (df). However, Model A and Model C are nested, and their chi-square difference is only 18 for 3 df. It seems evident that Model B is doing a better job of accounting for the covariance between the room and the infant than is Model A, whereas Model C does not do much better than Model A, the hypothesis of no influence of the room on the infants' A–PCOP.

Similarly, the chi-square difference between the nested models Model B and Model E is 17 for 3 df, whereas the chi-square difference between the nested models Model C and Model E is 139 for 6 df. Thus, Model B fits almost as well as the model that fully saturates the paths between the room and the infant variables, whereas Model C fits almost as poorly as the model that fixes to zero the effect of the room variables on the infant variables.

Model D, which posits that the room displacement affects infant A–PCOP displacement, room velocity affects infant A–PCOP velocity, and room acceleration affects infant A–PCOP acceleration, has a mean chi-square fit statistic that is approximately halfway between the null room effect model and the fully saturated room effect model.

Examining the mean parameters for Model B suggests that one may be able to create a model that fits almost as well as model B by fixing to zero the effects of the room velocity and acceleration on infant A–PCOP displacement as well as fixing to zero the effect of the room acceleration in infant A–PCOP velocity. The parameter values from Model B suggest that the displacement and velocity of the room were the primary visual cues used by these infants to control their sitting posture.

Age-Based Increase in Model Misfit

The infants in this study were in one of four age categories at the time of testing: 5, 7, 9, or 13 months. In Figure 1.8 the mean chi-square fit statistics for each model within each age category are plotted. There is an age-related increase in the chi-square for Model A and Model C that appears to reach an asymptote around 9 months of age. There is a much smaller increase in chi-square for Model B and Model E that follows the same general pattern. Again, the mean fit for Model D is approximately midway between the best- and worst-fitting models.

The difference between the misfit of Model A and Model E increases between the ages of 5 and 9 months. At each age, this difference in misfit is attributable to the degree to which an existing predictive effect of the room on the infants' A–PCOP is not captured by the null effect model, Model A. Thus, there appears to be a substantial age-related increase in the effect that the room variables have on the infants' A–PCOP. This may be interpreted as an age-related increase in the infants' response to the moving room, an increase that reaches an asymptote at around 9 months of age. This finding is in accordance with other correlational (Bertenthal et al., 1997) and nonlinear (Boker, 1996) analyses of these data.

FIGURE 1.8

Mean model fit (chi-square) as a function of age of infant for the five models: A, B, C, D, and E.

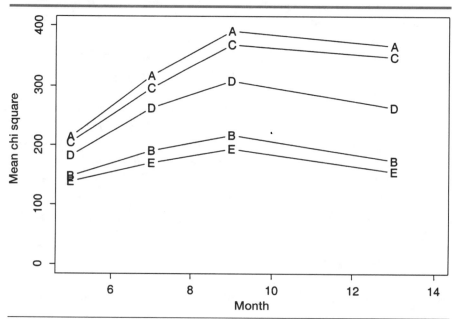

Predicting Coefficients and Fit of Trial Level Differential Structural Models

The coefficients from Model B that predict the infants' A–PCOP from the room variables are likely candidates for a second level of analysis. Because on each trial the room was moved with one of two different frequencies and one of two different amplitudes, it might be that the infant responded to one of these frequencies or amplitudes more than another. It might also be the case that there are age-based differences in these parameters.

As a first approximation to answering these questions, a series of multiple regressions was performed, predicting each of the six parameters linking the room variables to the infant variables in Model B from the age, frequency, and amplitude of each trial. The results of these analyses are presented in Table 1.2.

Scanning down the column of R^2 values in the table, it is interesting to note that the experimental manipulations and age of the infant predict between 11% and 20% of the variance in four of the coefficients for Model B but predict only less than 4% of the variance for the remaining two coefficients. These two coefficients, $d^2R/dt^2 \rightarrow X$ and $d^2R/dt^2 \rightarrow dX/dt$, also do not have an intercept

TABLE 1.2

Coefficients From Model B as Predicted by Unstandardized Multiple Regressions From Age, Frequency, and Amplitude Conditions Within Each Trial

COEFFICIENT	INTERCEPT	MONTHS	FREQUENCY	AMPLITUDE	R^2
$R \rightarrow X$	2.076	−0.344	−2.020	0.020	.116
$p()$	0.017	0.000	0.068	0.593	
$dR/dt \rightarrow X$	−0.900	0.040	1.530	0.001	.160
$p()$	0.000	0.000	0.000	0.900	
$d^2R/dt^2 \rightarrow X$	0.041	−0.025	0.101	0.005	.032
$p()$	0.747	0.003	0.538	0.383	
$R \rightarrow dX/dt$	11.037	−0.483	−23.605	0.066	.199
$p()$	0.000	0.001	0.000	0.495	
$dR/dt \rightarrow dX/dt$	1.082	−0.226	−0.640	0.007	.148
$p()$	0.024	0.000	0.293	0.715	
$d^2R/dt^2 \rightarrow dX/dt$	0.387	0.002	−0.994	0.002	.038
$p()$	0.080	0.873	0.000	0.860	
χ^2	145.943	8.781	−28.318	3.405	.064
$p()$	0.000	0.000	0.516	0.020	

Note. Probability values were derived using the simplifying assumption that individual trials are independent. Predictor variables were left in their raw metric: months of age, frequency in cycles per second, and amplitude in centimeters.

that is significantly different than zero. This again suggests that acceleration of the room may not play a part in the infants' postural sway responses.

However, 16% of the variance in the Model B coefficient $dR/dt \rightarrow X$ can be accounted for by the age of the infant and experimental conditions. Although the mean value for this coefficient over all conditions and all ages is near zero, the coefficient's value does appear to covary with the age of the infant and with the frequency condition ($p < .01$). This suggests that both room displacement and room velocity affect the infants' A–PCOP displacement and velocity.

It is interesting to note that the Model B coefficient $dR/dt \rightarrow X$ changes sign depending on the frequency condition. For the mean age of 8.5 months and the slow frequency of 0.3 Hz, this coefficient has a predicted value of $-.10$, whereas for the fast frequency of 0.6 Hz this coefficient has a predicted value of .36. Thus, the velocity of the room is predictive of A–PCOP displacement in the direction opposite of the room velocity in the slow-frequency condition but in the same direction in the fast-frequency condition.

The age of the infant is a significant predictor ($p < .01$) of the four Model B coefficients with $R^2 > .11$, suggesting that there is an age-related change in the effect of the room displacement and velocity on the infants' sway responses. The room frequency is a significant predictor for only two of the selected four Model B coefficients: (a) the effect of the room velocity on the A–PCOP displacement and (b) the effect of the room displacement on the A–PCOP velocity. This interesting symmetry may be an important clue to the functional form of a better model for perception–action coupling in visually guided postural control.

Finally as I noted previously, in the plot of the Model B chi-square as a function of age there is a significant ($p < .01$) age-related change in the fit of Model B. The linear oscillator model fits the younger infants' data better than it does the older infants' data.

Discussion

This chapter illustrated techniques that might be applied to a wide range of longitudinal data. For a dynamical systems theoretic approach to be appropriate, one must have a theory that suggests that changes in the individual, in the environment, or in the differences between the individual and the environment are predictive of future behavior of the individual. To apply dSEM, one needs at least several hundred triplets of measurements (a triplet consisting of displacement and the first and second derivatives of a variable). These triplets could be sampled from a single individual or across individuals.

For second-level analyses, one must have several groups of individuals or several experimental conditions such that in each group there are at least several hundred triplets of observations. This data limitation may seem daunting, but an attempt is being made to capture variability at short time scales while at the same time estimating longer term change or between-groups differences.

I recommend that if one is designing a study in hopes of being able to test theories that predict the attractor that best fits a covariance structure in intraindividual variability or changes in the shape of a basin of attraction, one should gather a burst measurement sample on each individual (Nesselroade, 1991b). A *burst measurement* is a group of repeated observations gathered with a short time interval between observations. The number of observations in the burst will be determined by whether an assumption of homogeneity of attractor shape can be supported or whether individual or group differences in attractor or basin-of-attraction shape are to be examined.

If homogeneity of attractor shape can be assumed, then I recommend no fewer than six observations per burst measurement on an individual. If group differences in attractor or basin-of-attraction shape are to be examined, then I recommend no fewer than six observations in a burst measurement for an individual and a few hundred bursts per group. If individual differences in attractor or basin-of-attraction shape are to be examined, then I recommend at least 200 measurements per burst measurement on each individual, and the number of individuals may be determined using a power calculation based on expected between-individual differences in the coefficients of the structural model.

I expect that there are many problems in developmental, clinical, and cognitive psychology—as well as in biology, sociology, and economics—for which differential structural models may prove to be useful. There seems at present to be a change in direction of psychological theory in order to take into account processes by which an individual's behavior may evolve. This, coupled with the growing number of tools available to examine the issues of change, makes for an especially exciting time to be involved in psychological research.

References

Bayley, N. (1969). *Manual for the Bayley Scales of Infant Development*. New York: Psychological Corporation.

Bertenthal, B., & Bai, D. (1989). Infants' sensitivity to optical flow for controlling posture. *Developmental Psychology, 25*, 936–945.

Bertenthal, B. I., Rose, J. L., & Bai, D. L. (1997). Perception–action coupling in the development of the visual control of posture. *Journal of Experimental Psychology: Human Perception and Performance, 23*, 1631–1643.

Boker, S. M. (1996). *Linear and nonlinear dynamical systems data analytic techniques and an application to developmental data.* Unpublished doctoral dissertation, University of Virginia, Charlottesville.

Boker, S. M., & Graham, J. (1998). A dynamical systems analysis of adolescent substance abuse. *Multivariate Behavioral Research, 33,* 479–507.

Boker, S. M., & Nesselroade, J. R. (in press). A method for modeling the intrinsic dynamics of intraindividual variability: Recovering the parameters of simulated oscillators in multiwave panel data. *Multivariate Behavioral Research.*

Clark, J. E. (1997). A dynamical systems perspective on the development of complex adaptive skill. In C. Dent-Read (Ed.), *Evolving explanations of development: Ecological approaches to organism–environment systems* (pp. 383–406). Washington, DC: American Psychological Association.

Clark, J. E., & Phillips, S. J. (1993). A longitudinal study of intralimb coordination in the first year of independent walking: A dynamical systems analysis. *Child Development, 64,* 1143–1157.

Cleveland, W. S., & Devlin, S. J. (1988). Locally weighted regression: An approach to regression analysis by local fitting. *Journal of the American Statistical Association, 83,* 596–610.

Geert, P. van (1997). Nonlinear dynamics and the explanation of mental and behavioral development. *Journal of Mind and Behavior, 18,* 269–290.

Glass, L., & Mackey, M. (1988). *From clocks to chaos.* Princeton, NJ: Princeton University Press.

Gottschalk, A., Bauer, M. S., & Whybrow, P. C. (1995). Evidence of chaotic mood variation in bipolar disorder. *Archives of General Psychiatry, 52,* 947–959.

Gu, C. (1990). Adaptive spline smoothing in non-gaussian regression models. *Journal of the American Statistical Association, 85,* 801–807.

Hopkins, B., & Butterworth, G. (1997). Dynamical systems approaches to the development of action. In G. Bremner, A. Slater, & G. Butterworth (Eds.), *Infant development: Recent advances* (pp. 75–100). Hove, England: Psychology Press.

Hubbard, J. H., & West, B. H. (1991). *Differential equations: A dynamical systems approach.* New York: Springer-Verlag.

Kaplan, D., & Glass, L. (1995). *Understanding nonlinear dynamics.* New York: Springer-Verlag.

McArdle, J. J., & Boker, S. M. (1990). *Rampath.* Hillsdale, NJ: Erlbaum.

McArdle, J. J., & McDonald, R. P. (1984). Some algebraic properties of the reticular action model for moment structures. *British Journal of Mathematical and Statistical Psychology, 87,* 234–251.

Neale, M. C. (1994). *Mx: Statistical modeling* (2nd ed.). Richmond: Medical College of Virginia, Department of Psychiatry.

Nesselroade, J. R. (1991a). Interindividual differences in intraindividual changes. In J. L. Horn & L. Collins (Eds.), *Best methods for the analysis of change: Recent advances, unanswered questions, future directions* (pp. 92–105). Washington, DC: American Psychological Association.

Nesselroade, J. R. (1991b). The warp and woof of the developmental fabric. In R. Downs, L. Liben, & D. S. Palermo (Eds.), *Visions of aesthetics, the environment, and development: The legacy of Joachim F. Wohlwill* (pp. 213–240). Hillsdale, NJ: Erlbaum.

Nesselroade, J. R., & Boker, S. M. (1994). Assessing constancy and change. In T. F. Heatherton & J. L. Weinberger (Eds.), *Can personality change?* (pp. 121–147). Washington, DC: American Psychological Association.

Pezard, L., Nandrino, J., Renault, B., & Massioui, E. A. F. (1996). Depression as a dynamical disease. *Biological Psychiatry, 39,* 991–999.

Thelen, E. (1995). Motor development: A new synthesis. *American Psychologist, 50,* 79–95.

Thompson, J. M. T., & Stewart, H. B. (1986). *Nonlinear dynamics and chaos.* New York: Wiley.

Warren, W. (1990). The perception–action coupling. In H. Bloch & B. I. Bertenthal (Eds.), *Sensory–motor organization and development in infancy and childhood* (pp. 23–38). Dordrecht, The Netherlands: Kluwer.

Dynamical Models and "Differential Structural Equation Modeling of Intraindividual Variability"

Andrea M. Piccinin

Differential structural equation modeling is an innovative variation on methods for addressing dynamical processes. Developmentalists are interested in the (continuous) process of change. They are, however, able to measure only at discrete intervals. The dynamical models described by Steven M. Boker involve indicating process through variables constructed from discrete-occasion data.

What Are Dynamical Models?

A *dynamical system* has been defined as one whose state changes over time. Many recent applications of dynamical systems theory can be found in science and engineering, some of these in the context of chaos or other nonlinear analyses. The focus of much dynamical systems work is on iterative or self-regulating processes. The main goal is generally to characterize the mathematical relationship that describes how a system changes over time—ideally, to understand the behavior of the system. A dynamical model can be defined, as Boker does in his chapter, as one that includes change as a predictor or outcome variable.

Because these models are probably the most unfamiliar of those presented in this volume, it would seem useful to consider the features they share with more established methods. There is a history of simpler "dynamical" models with similar aims. A brief review may help readers see more clearly what differential models involve.

The most basic version of a model that includes change as a predictor or outcome variable could involve a simple change score. Change scores, obtained by subtracting the value of a variable at Time 1 from the value of the same variable at Time 2, are constructed from data collected at discrete points in time. Ignoring measurement error, if the value of this new variable is different than zero, one says that change has occurred. If one tries to predict the amount of change within an individual by using this new variable as an outcome variable in a regression equation, one is entering the world of dynamical models.

Growth curve, or slopes-as-outcomes models, which are incrementally more complex, estimate rate of change over three or more occasions and include it as a variable in the model. These models are currently very popular and are addressed in several chapters of this volume. One of their great selling points is that by using more measurement occasions to characterize change they may avoid some of the issues related to the potential unreliability of difference scores. On the principle that one can better measure constructs that are directly unobservable by including several indicators of one's construct, so does growth curve analysis better estimate rates of change.

In a simple growth curve analysis, three or more data points across time are summarized in terms of fewer parameters—for example, level and slope in the linear case—and then these summaries are used as outcomes (or predictors) in a regression equation. Although growth curves are far more complex than difference scores, they are based on the same principle: Aggregate information within a person to create a summary score characterizing change, then use this new variable in the analysis of interest.

What Are Differential Models?

The differential models Boker presents go one step further. Rather than using variables that characterize the entire curve, these models make use of hypothesized repeated patterns within a series of measurements. In, for example, the dampened linear oscillator model, a new variable—acceleration (i.e., the second derivative of any particular point in the curve, approximated here by the difference between successive slopes calculated from every pair of points measured in time)—is predicted by velocity (i.e., the first derivative [i.e., rate of change], another new variable) and the current value. Although these models are new and rather unfamiliar, and involve nonlinear variables, they are based on familiar regression equations.

Although it is possible to estimate slopes with curvatures in growth curve models, either through standard polynomial models (e.g., McArdle, 1988; Willett & Sayer, 1994) or by using Gompertz or logistic functions (e.g., Browne & Du Toit, 1991), the difference here is that acceleration in such models applies to the overall curve. In Boker's differential models acceleration is a function of smaller sections of the curve. In this way, differential models share features of time series analysis and generally have similar data requirements. Although it is possible to model piecewise sections of curves in the context of growth curve analysis, it is somewhat awkward, and of limited use. From difference scores to differential models, the common basic principle is that an attempt is made to characterize a process and then to ask whether people differ on this process.

Data Requirements and Limitations

Although, as Boker indicates, differential modeling may be possible with as few as three occasions of measurement, such an application is severely limited by the appropriateness of spacing and timing of the measurements (Cohen, 1991; Collins & Graham, 1991). If acceleration cannot be adequately estimated, the models cannot help answer the questions of interest. For example, although self-regulation may indeed characterize depressive episodes, one's ability to measure at appropriate intervals in order to illuminate this pattern may be rather limited. As in time series analysis, a substantial number of occasions would be necessary to explore questions regarding optimal time lags for identifying systematic patterns in data.

A second concern with differential models is that the assumption of homogeneity of attractor shape over individuals may not be tenable in psychological or other behavioral situations. For example, there may be individual differences in the progression of depression. Although this can be problematic, it is probably no more serious than the general assumption of ergodicity one makes whenever one aggregates across individuals in situations where one's questions are directed at within-individual change.

In situations with many measurements, as in Boker's example, differential models are useful mainly for processes that are not influenced by the act of measuring. The quality of measurement is important in the context of such derived variables. It must be possible to compute a reasonable approximation of acceleration before attempting to estimate models that depend on it.

As methods of analysis become more sophisticated, one must always remember that the best methods are unlikely to be useful in illuminating developmental or other processes without the foundation of good measurement. In this vein, it would be useful to report more extensive descriptive statistics for the differential variables, for example, some index of variability in the estimates of velocity and acceleration. How consistent are they within or across individuals? Are there some individuals for whom the model fits and others for whom R^2 is zero?

Finally, there is the question of whether it might be more appropriate to integrate and then fit the model to the integral. With Boker's method, in which the differentials are estimated by linear approximation, the modeling is much more straightforward and the parameters (velocity, acceleration) easier to interpret. Greater reassurance that the two methods produce the same results would be valuable.

Conclusion

For situations in which data can be collected to adequately identify the process of interest, these methods show great promise. They are an inventive solution to the challenge of characterizing processes of change. As Boker points out, these methods are appealing as well for allowing one to consider whether coupling of different change processes exists. This can help one along the path of understanding potentially complex relations among variables.

Boker should be applauded for presenting complex material in an accessible and straightforward manner. I look forward to seeing the imaginative and productive work that will surely emerge from this approach to the study of development.

References

Browne, M. W., & Du Toit, S. H. C. (1991). Models for learning data. In L. M. Collins & J. L. Horn (Eds.), *Best methods for the analysis of change* (pp. 47–68). Washington, DC: American Psychological Association.

Cohen, P. (1991). A source of bias in longitudinal investigations of change. In L. M. Collins & J. L. Horn (Eds.), *Best methods for the analysis of change* (pp. 18–25). Washington, DC: American Psychological Association.

Collins, L. M., & Graham, J. W. (1991). Comments on "A source of bias in longitudinal investigations of change." In L. M. Collins & J. L. Horn (Eds.), *Best methods for the analysis of change* (pp. 18–25). Washington, DC: American Psychological Association.

McArdle, J. J. (1988). Dynamic but structural equation modeling of repeated measures data. In J. R. Nesselroade & R. B. Cattell (Eds.), *Handbook of multivariate experimental psychology* (Vol. 2, pp. 561–564). New York: Plenum Press.

Willett, J. B., & Sayer, A. G. (1994). Using covariance structure analysis to detect correlations and predictors of individual change over time. *Psychological Bulletin, 116,* 363–381.

CHAPTER 2

Editors' Introduction

S tephen Raudenbush's chapter places the hierarchical linear models with which most readers are familiar into a much broader context. Arguing that restrictions imposed by software and estimation ought not to limit the researcher's imagination, Raudenbush discusses a variety of models for various types of change, in various metrics. This chapter is a compelling argument for thinking carefully about which model best expresses one's theory about the data and then choosing the best available approximation from available software, taking careful note of where the approximation deviates from the ideal. One topic of D. Wayne Osgood's penetrating commentary is the application of some of these ideas beyond growth curve models. Chapter 3, by Rovine and Molenaar, which illustrates how to estimate general linear mixed models using a structural equation modeling approach, makes an interesting companion piece.

Toward a Coherent Framework for Comparing Trajectories of Individual Change

Stephen W. Raudenbush

nthony Bryk once recounted a story from his graduate school days. He was taking an introduction to mathematical statistics course, taught by a new junior faculty member at Harvard. The blackboards along the perimeter of the classroom were covered with forbidding equations, when, just as class was starting, William Cochran, one of the eminent statisticians of the 20th century, walked in. Cochran looked around at the blackboard, slowly shook his head, and commented "I'm glad I'm not starting now as a graduate student."

The world of quantitative models for human development must look equally forbidding to anyone brave enough to enter, and I suspect even those who have been around the field for awhile are often bewildered at the array of terminology, models, and software packages for studying individual change. I have personally found it confusing, but I have been repeatedly asked to clarify how the approaches with which I am associated differ from other approaches. At several conferences (including those of the American Psychological Association and the Society for Research on Child Development), mini battles have been staged between hierarchical linear models (HLM) and structural equation models (SEM). This experience has motivated me to try to figure out what some of the language really means and what root principles can be educed that might be of use to those interested in estimating and comparing individual trajectories of change. My purpose in this chapter is to share what I have learned.

Part of the task is to try to demystify the rapidly exploding vocabulary associated with this field. Some of the labels for related models include (in alphabetical order) "covariance components models," "hierarchical models,"

The research reported in this chapter was supported by the Project on Human Development in Chicago Neighborhoods with funding from the John D. and Catherine T. MacArthur Foundation, the National Institute of Justice, and the National Institute of Mental Health.

35

HLM, "latent curve analysis," "latent growth models," "mixed models," "mixed linear models," "multilevel models," "multilevel linear models," "random effects models," "random coefficient models," and SEM. All of these terms can be shown to have some useful meaning, as I hope to show. However, I have concluded that the only way to understand the etymology is to realize that such labels tend to be associated with software packages.

Thus, there are HLMs associated with the package "HLM," mixed models associated with SAS Proc Mixed, multilevel models with MLWIN, and random coefficients models with VARCL and MixedReg; whereas terms such as *latent curve analysis, latent growth modeling,* and SEM tend to be associated with a set of related packages, including AMOS, EQS, LISCOMP, LISREL, and MPlus. At the risk of infuriating everyone, I tend to refer to these latter programs as *programs for mean and covariance structure analysis* because that longer phrase captures what these programs do.

The tendency of software development to drive vocabulary reflects the reality that, for most quantitative researchers, figuring out how to analyze data involves choosing a software package. This reality has a logistical basis, not a logical one. What makes sense logically is to ask the following questions, in order:

1. **What is my research question?** Attention in this chapter is confined to questions entailing a comparison of trajectories of individual change, for example, growth in vocabulary during the second year of life, growth in reading ability during the elementary-school years, change in propensity to use drugs or commit crimes during adolescence, or cognitive recovery from head injury. In each case, a participant's development can be represented by some curve or trajectory that summarizes change on a repeatedly measured outcome, and we want to understand why these trajectories vary.[1]

2. **How is the study designed?** Is each participant observed over a fixed set of measurement occasions? What defines those occasions? It could be age (as in the vocabulary study), grade or time of year (in the elementary-reading study), or time (since head injury). Once the data are collected, how discrepant are the collected data from the design, as a result of missing data or unexpected variation in the timing of observations?

---

[1]Longitudinal research has many other useful goals—for example, to ask how a variable measured at a given time is related to a different variable measured later. However, such goals are beyond the scope of this chapter, which concerns the study of trajectories with regard to repeated measures.

3. **What is the scale of the outcome data?** Possibilities include counts of words (vocabulary study), interval-scale data (e.g., reading test scores), binary data (whether drugs were used or a crime committed), or ordinal data (whether a given behavior occurred never, seldom, or often).

4. **What model makes sense?** The model has two parts: a *structural* part and a *probabilistic* part. The structural part should map onto the question and design; that is, the model should represent a theory for the process that is generating the data. It should be modified on the basis of visual inspection of the data. The probabilistic assumptions of the model should fit the character of the design and the scale of the data.

5. **How should the parameters of the model be estimated?** Maximum-likelihood (ML) estimates have good large-sample properties but require distributional assumptions and do not always have good small-sample properties. Bayes estimates are similar in regard to large-sample properties and assumptions about the data (because the data affect inference strictly through the likelihood). However, by imposing a prior distribution, the investigator buys useful small-sample properties. The price is that results may be sensitive to alternative reasonable priors. Other, less parametric possibilities include least squares, quasi-likelihood, and generalized estimating equations with robust standard errors (e.g., Zeger, Liang, & Albert, 1988).

6. **What algorithm is appropriate to compute the estimates?** Algorithms for ML estimates, such as expectation−maximization (EM; Dempster, Laird, & Rubin, 1977) or Fisher scoring, vary in computational speed, reliability of convergence, and generality of application. The same is true for Bayesian estimation (e.g., Gibbs sampling vs. numerical integration by means of Gauss−Hermite quadrature) and for less parametric approaches.

7. **What software, if any, can be used?** At this point the investigator might logically choose from available software packages, or, if none of the available packages meets the requirements of Steps 1–7, develop customized software.

Although presumably logical, this series of steps does not generally reflect practice. Few researchers have the means to customize software or the experience to know about all available software alternatives. People tend to use packages with which they are familiar, sometimes even when the assumptions of the approach in the package contradict the design and scale of the data. And sometimes the research question is fashioned to suit the use of the familiar software.

The purpose of my remarks is not to advocate a purist approach that would ignore the dependence of practice on available software. Instead, the purpose is to construct a framework for conceiving modeling alternatives, a framework that is substantially independent of currently available software. With such a framework in mind, one may be forced to compromise with limitations of available software, but one will know when one is compromising, and this knowledge may stimulate principled advances in applied statistics, including software development.

In the next section, I consider key similarities among modeling approaches currently in use, attempting to give some meaning to the vocabulary that alternative perspectives have generated. I then argue that a hierarchical modeling perspective can give substantial order to the seeming chaos, leading to a rather general framework for making key decisions about models for comparing developmental trajectories. As expected, the logic of the framework exceeds the capacity of any currently available computational software. My hope is that this framework will inform researchers' decisions and inspire advances in applied statistics, advances rooted in the needs of the field.

Models

Within a restricted class of models, all of the labels mentioned earlier describe the same model. Yet each label reflects some valuable insight about the nature of the model. To illustrate, consider a simple model for individual change and variation in change. Each person's status with respect to an outcome, Y, changes at a constant rate, and these rates vary randomly over a population of persons. More specifically, we have outcome Y_{ti} for person i at time t, with T_i time points ($t = 1, \ldots, T_i$) observed for person i. One might formulate a simple linear model for individual change:

$$Y_{ti} = \pi_{0i} + \pi_{1i}a_{ti} + e_{ti}, \; e_{ti} \sim N(0, \sigma^2), \tag{2.1}$$

where a_{ti} is the age of person i at time t. The parameters of individual i's trajectory are two: (a) π_{0i}, the status of that person at age 0, and (b) π_{1i}, that person's linear rate of change per unit increase in age.

Next I consider how these trajectories of change are distributed in the population of persons. For simplicity, I adopt an unconditional model (i.e., the model does not incorporate person-level covariates to account for variation in change). The model states that person-specific parameters (π_{0i}, π_{1i}) vary around their grand means (β_{00}, β_{01}) according to a bivariate normal distribution:

$$\tau_{0i} = \beta_{00} + u_{0i},$$

$$\pi_{1i} = \beta_{10} + u_{1i}, \tag{2.2}$$

with

$$\begin{pmatrix} u_{0i} \\ u_{1i} \end{pmatrix} \sim N \left[\begin{pmatrix} 0 \\ 0 \end{pmatrix}, \begin{pmatrix} \tau_{00} & \tau_{01} \\ \tau_{10} & \tau_{11} \end{pmatrix} \right].$$

The model described by Equations 2.1 and 2.2 is a *hierarchical model* because it specifies a model for Y_{ti} given first-level parameters (π_{0i}, π_{1i}), while these parameters, in turn, depend on second-level parameters (the βs and τs). Levels could be added: The second-level parameters could depend on third-level parameters, and so on.[2] Thus, it is the hierarchical dependence among the parameters that is decisive in making the model hierarchical, not necessarily the hierarchical structure of the data, although the two often go together.

This idea is central to this chapter. To generalize it, let the data Y_{ti}, $t = 1$, ... T_i; $i = 1, \ldots, n$, be collected in a vector Y, let the first-level parameters π_{0i}, π_{1i}, $i = 1, \ldots, n$ be collected in a vector π, and let the unsubscripted parameters (those that do not vary over cases i) be collected in a vector $\theta = (\beta_{00}, \beta_{10}, \tau_{00}, \tau_{01}, \tau_{11}, \sigma^2)$. One can then characterize the first-level model as $f(Y|\pi, \theta)$ and the second-level model as $p(\pi|\theta)$. All of the models considered in this chapter are hierarchical, and, of course, levels can be added. The essence of the decision framework I propose is to ensure that specification of the model fit the research question, design, and data.

The model described by Equations 2.1 and 2.2 is a hierarchical *linear* model because at the first stage Y is a linear function of π, whereas at the second stage π is a linear function of β. Note that all polynomial models at the first stage are linear. The model is *multilevel* because it describes data that vary at two levels: within persons and between persons. The model is a *random coefficients model* because the Level 1 model defines coefficients, π, that vary randomly at Level 2. It is a *latent curve model* because the trajectory or curve $\pi_{0i} + \pi_{1i}a_{it}$ is unobservable, depending, that is, on unobserved latent variables π. It may also be a *latent growth model,* although the use of the term *growth* implies a monotonic increasing trajectory, which may or may not be the case.

The model is also a *mixed model*. To see this, substitute Equation 2.1 into Equation 2.2, yielding the combined model

$$Y_{ti} = \beta_{00} + \beta_{01} + \varepsilon_{ti}, \tag{2.3}$$

---

[2]A Bayesian statistician would indeed specify a prior distribution for the βs and τs as an expression of prior uncertainty about the location of these unknowns. Thus, for the Bayesian, the model at hand would have three levels. Indeed, for the Bayesian, all models are hierarchical, having at least two levels, because a prior is always specified for the unknown parameters to be estimated.

where

$$\varepsilon_{ti} = u_{0i} + u_{1i}a_{ti} + e_{ti}. \tag{2.4}$$

Thus, the model has fixed effects (β_{00}, β_{01}) and random effects (u_{0i}, u_{1i}) as well as the elemental residual e_{ti}. It is a *covariance components model* because it includes variance components τ_{00}, τ_{11} and covariance τ_{01}.

The model is also an *SEM*. The first-stage model can be viewed as a measurement model with observed variable Y, latent variables π, and factor loadings 1 (for π_{0i}) and a_{ti} (for π_{1i}). The second-level model is an exceedingly simple SEM for π.

Given that all of the labels apply, what is all the fuss about? How are these models different? A common view, and one that I have voiced, is that the HLM approach (or multilevel approach, random coefficient approach, etc.) allows lots of flexibility in data structure for a limited class of models, whereas the SEM approach (or latent variable model, latent curve analysis, etc.) offers a broad class of models for a limited set of data structures. These ideas were illustrated with exceptional clarity by Willett and Sayer (1994). More specifically, HLM allows unequal numbers of time series data points per person and variable spacing of time points across persons, which are not generally allowed in SEM. In contrast, SEM routinely allows estimation of unknown factor loadings, a variety of covariance structures for Y (e.g., autocorrelated, Level 1 errors, Level 1 variances depending on time), and a variety of structural models (including simultaneous equations at the second stage). In terms of the general model, it might be said that HLM allows many structures for Y within a limited class of structures for θ, whereas SEM allows many choices of θ within a limited class of structures for Y.

Although this characterization of the difference in approaches may have been a reasonable description of differences in commercially available software packages, it is too superficial a view to guide one's thinking about models, primarily because model choice logically precedes software choice and because software packages are rapidly changing. So a deeper understanding is required, one that locates decisions about analysis in a framework that begins with questions, designs, and data and then considers estimation theory and algorithms, all of which logically precede choice of software.

In terms of my notation, the essence of the framework is as follows.

1. In light of the developmental theory at hand, the design, and the data, choose a model $f(Y|\pi, \theta)$ for individual development over time. The model has a structural part that specifies a trajectory in terms of π. It may be a linear structure (including polynomials), or it may be nonlinear. It also includes a probabilistic part that describes the random behavior of Y, given that π is held constant. The probability model may be normal, but it may not.

2. In light of key research questions and data, define $p(\boldsymbol{\pi}|\boldsymbol{\theta})$, that is, a model for the distribution of trajectories in the population. It also will have a structural part that describes the expected trajectory given the measured characteristics of persons and a probabilistic part that describes the random behavior of $\boldsymbol{\pi}$.

3. Continue to higher levels as necessary. One might, for example, have a three-level structure with $f_1(Y|\boldsymbol{\pi}_1, \boldsymbol{\theta})$ describing individual change; $f_2(\boldsymbol{\pi}_1|\boldsymbol{\pi}_2, \boldsymbol{\theta})$ describing interindividual variation within sites, such as schools; and $p(\boldsymbol{\pi}_2|\boldsymbol{\theta})$ describing variation between sites. A paradigm example is the use of repeated measures to study school effects on children's learning (Bryk & Raudenbush, 1992, chapter 8), although I have written about modifications needed to include joint effects of neighborhoods and schools on children's social and cognitive development (Raudenbush, 1993, 1995).

4. Assess alternative estimation methods, algorithms, and (one would hope) available software for making inferences about all unknowns.

Unfortunately, constraints in estimation theory, algorithms, and software often distort model choice. In particular, the convenience of linear models and normal distribution theory at each level, contrasted with the relative difficulty of constructing algorithms for nonlinear models and non-normal assumptions, have encouraged an unhealthy reliance on linearity and normality. Even within the normal framework, often untenable assumptions, such as homogeneity of dispersion, have constrained model choice.

Estimation Theory

For purposes of this chapter, I adopt the method of ML for estimating model parameters, $\boldsymbol{\theta}$. ML confers favorable large-sample properties, such as consistency and asymptotic efficiency, under widely applicable conditions. Lower level parameters, $\boldsymbol{\pi}$, can then be estimated by empirical Bayes methods given the ML estimates of $\boldsymbol{\theta}$. Of course, there are good arguments for adopting a fully Bayes perspective. However, in large samples Bayes and ML inferences converge, and there is little need in this chapter to consider the special problems that arise in small samples. In this section, I consider the two-level case, as all higher level cases follow the same principles.

The likelihood of observing the sample data Y for any possible value of $\boldsymbol{\theta}$ is $L(Y|\boldsymbol{\theta})$, where

$$L(Y|\boldsymbol{\theta}) = \int f(Y|\boldsymbol{\pi}, \boldsymbol{\theta})p(\boldsymbol{\pi}|\boldsymbol{\theta})d\boldsymbol{\pi}. \qquad (2.5)$$

The integrand is the joint distribution of Y and π, and the likelihood $L(Y|\theta)$ is therefore obtained by integrating (i.e., averaging) values of this joint distribution computed at every possible value of π. ML chooses as the point estimate of θ the value that maximizes this likelihood.

If both $f(Y|\pi, \theta)$ and $p(\pi|\theta)$ are multivariate normal densities and the model is linear at both levels, then the enormously convenient result $L(Y|\theta)$ is also a multivariate normal density. Moreover, the mean of Y also has a linear structure. Many applications of HLM and SEM make this assumption. In addition, SEM assumes that every Y_i from a given subpopulation has a common covariance matrix. This is not a limit on current software but is intrinsic to the method; that is, the covariance matrix cannot be unique for case i. This assumption sharply restricts the class of data and models that can sensibly be studied, but within that class the modeling options are generous.

Below I consider two classes of models. In the first, both the data Y (given π) and π are normal, with a linear structure. In the second class, either Y (given π) or π or both are non-normal (and possibly nonlinear). The first class of models is most familiar to psychology, and although it has many useful applications, it is often chosen more out of convenience than conviction. The second class is enormously broad and offers vast untapped potential for the modeling of developmental phenomena.

Normal Likelihoods

To understand similarities and differences between SEM and HLM in the normal case, it is important to consider three kinds of data: (a) the observed data are completely balanced; (b) the "complete data" are completely balanced, but time points are missing at random so that the number of time points per person varies; and (c) the "complete data" are unbalanced, as when Level 1 predictors have different distributions across people. Given the data at hand, one can then consider possible models for variation and covariation.

These differences can be illustrated in the context of the simple model of Equations 2.1–2.3. Recall that the combined model may then be written

$$Y_{ti} = \beta_{00} + \beta_{01} + \varepsilon_{ti}, \tag{2.6}$$

where

$$\varepsilon_{ti} = u_{0i} + u_{1i}a_{ti} + e_{ti}. \tag{2.7}$$

Thus, the likelihood for Y_i will be normal, with mean and covariance structure given by

$$E(Y_{ti}) = \beta_{00} + \beta_{01}a_{ti},$$

$$Var(Y_{ti}) = \delta_{ti}^2 = \tau_{00} + 2a_{ti}\tau_{01} + a_{ti}^2\tau_{11} + \sigma^2, \qquad (2.8)$$

$$Cov(Y_{ti}, Y_{t'i}) = \delta_{tt'i} = \tau_{00} + (a_{ti} + a_{t'i})\tau_{01} + a_{ti}a_{t'i}\tau_{11}.$$

Case 1: Observed Data Are Balanced

Suppose every person has T observations ($T_i = T$ for all i). Then the data Y_{ti} for person i will follow a T-variate normal distribution with variances δ_{ti}^2 at time t and covariance $\delta_{tt'i}$ between observations at time t and time t'. Suppose further that the age of person i at time t is the same for all people (e.g., every person is observed annually on his or her birthday and all people are the same age at the start of the study).[3] Thus, $a_{ti} = a_t$ for all i. In this case, the data follow the assumption of homogeneity of dispersion; that is, $\delta_{ti}^2 = \delta_t^2$ and $\delta_{tt'i} = \delta_{tt'}$ for all i. In sum, every person's data follows a T-variate normal distribution with a common covariance matrix having variances δ_t^2 and covariances $\delta_{tt'}$. In principle, the common covariance matrix has $T(T + 1)/2$ parameters: T variances (one for each time point) and $T(T - 1)/2$ covariances (one for each pair of time points). For example, if $T = 5$, as in the National Youth Survey (NYS; see Elliott, Huizinga, & Menard, 1989), there are 5 variances and 10 covariances. However, under the two-level model of Equations 2.1 and 2.2, these variances and covariances are functions of only four underlying parameters (τ_{00}, τ_{01}, τ_{11}, σ^2). Thus, in this case, the hierarchical model of Equations 2.1 and 2.2 is a special case of a more general T-variate normal model with restrictions imposed on the $T(T + 1)/2$ covariance parameters as specified in Equation 2.8. The HLM of Equations 2.1 and 2.2 can thus be viewed as a specific covariance structure model. Standard software for SEM can estimate this model and allow for a variety of other covariance structures (e.g., autocorrelated Level 1 residuals, Level 1 residuals having different variances at different times).

Case 2: Complete Data Are Balanced

Often overlooked in psychological and educational research is important work by Jennrich and Schluchter (1986), who developed a flexible approach to studying time series data having a multivariate normal distribution. Their approach is like SEM in that it allows estimation of several alternative covariance structures: "random effects" covariance structures identical to those normally specified in HLM as well as the autocorrelation models, models for heteroscedastic Level 1 variances, and models having a factor-analytic structure. Like the SEM

---

[3]Of course, it would never be true that every person is observed at exactly the same ages, but this may be approximately true.

approach, this approach assumes that the design is time structured (i.e., spacing between intended time points will not vary from person to person), but it does allow randomly missing time series data. This approach, popular in biomedical applications, thus combines advantages of flexibility in allowing missing data while also allowing a broad range of covariance structures. Thum (1997) extended this approach to three levels.

To illustrate, suppose now that although the aim of the study was to collect T observations for each person, data are missing at random. Thus, person i has T_i observations, with $T_i \leq T$. Now the data for person i is T_i-variate normal; that is, the distribution is person specific. Standard approaches to multivariate analysis for repeated measures and SEM no longer apply because these require a common covariance matrix for all persons in a given subpopulation. Thus, the HLM of Equations 2.1 and 2.2 can no longer be viewed as a special case of a T-variate normal distribution.

Following Jennrich and Schluchter (1986), one can solve this problem, however, by conceiving the Y_{ti} ($t = 1, \ldots, T$) as the "complete data," that is, the data one aimed to collect, whereas Z_{ri}, $r = 1, \ldots, R_i$ are the observed data, the subset of the Y values that one actually observes. Thus, Equations 2.1 and 2.2 constitute a hierarchical model for the "complete data" that is a special case of a T-variate normal model. Following Goldstein (1995), one can create a new Level 1 model that describes the pattern of missing data:

$$Z_{ri} = \sum_{t=1}^{T} m_{tri} Y_{ti}, \qquad (2.9)$$

where m_{tri} takes on a value of 1 if Z_{ri} is observed at time t and 0 otherwise. For example, consider a participant in the NYS who was observed at Times 1, 2, and 4 but was unavailable at Times 3 and 5. One would have, in matrix notation,

$$Z_i = M_i Y_i, \qquad (2.10)$$

or

$$\begin{pmatrix} Z_{1i} \\ Z_{2i} \\ Z_{3i} \end{pmatrix} = \begin{pmatrix} 1 & 0 & 0 & 0 & 0 \\ 0 & 1 & 0 & 0 & 0 \\ 0 & 0 & 0 & 1 & 0 \end{pmatrix} \begin{pmatrix} Y_{1i} \\ Y_{2i} \\ Y_{3i} \\ Y_{4i} \\ Y_{5i} \end{pmatrix}. \qquad (2.11)$$

Substituting Equation 2.6 into Equation 2.10 gives a combined model having matrix form

$$Z_i = M_i A X_i \boldsymbol{\beta} + M_i \boldsymbol{\varepsilon}_i, \qquad (2.12)$$

TABLE 2.1

Description of Sample: National Youth Survey, Cohort 1

AGE (YEARS)	n	MEAN TOLERANCE OF DEVIANT BEHAVIOR		NO. OBSERVATIONS	FREQUENCY
		MALES	FEMALES		
11	237	.24	.19	5	168
12	232	.27	.21	4	45
13	230	.36	.29	3	14
14	220	.45	.36	2	5
15	219	.49	.40	1	7

Where A is the Level 1 design matrix, X_i is the Level 2 design matrix, and ε_i is a $T \times 1$ vector of errors having a common T-variate normal distribution.

Let us consider several examples from the first cohort of NYS. These data, summarized in Table 2.1, were analyzed by Raudenbush and Chan (1993). Members of the first cohort were sampled in 1976 at age 11 and interviewed annually until 1980, when they were 15. The outcome is a measure of attitudes toward deviant behavior, with higher values indicating greater tolerance of pro-deviant activities, such as lying, cheating, stealing, vandalism, and drug use. I refer to this outcome as *tolerance* of deviant behavior. The table appears to indicate an increase in tolerance as a function of age during these early adolescent years; however, the means at each age based on different samples because of missing data. In fact, 168 people had a full complement of five time series measurements, whereas 45 had four, 14 had three, 5 had two, and 7 had only one time point. To illustrate the SEM approach to the study of change, Willett and Sayer (1994) analyzed the subset of 168 participants with complete data. The analysis below makes use of all available data from 239 participants. I show a series of models of increasing complexity.

Compound Symmetry

A covariance structure commonly assumed in univariate repeated-measures analysis of variance requires the variances to be the same at every time point and that all covariances be the same. This is equivalent to assuming that (a) all Level 1 random effects e_{ti}, $e_{t'i}$ are independent with homogeneous Level 1 variance σ^2 and (b) all participants have the same linear slope ($u_{1i} = 0$ for all i). In the case of the unconditional model, the Level 2 model becomes

$$\pi_{0i} = \beta_{00} + u_{0i}$$

$$\pi_{1i} = \beta_{10}.$$

(2.13)

The likelihood for Y_{ti} (i.e., the "complete data" likelihood) is thus normal, with the mean given by Equation 2.8 but with a simplified covariance structure that sets τ_{11} and τ_{01} to zero:

$$\varepsilon_{ti} = u_{0i} + e_{ti};$$

$$Var(Y_{ti}) = \delta_t^2 = \tau_{00} + \sigma^2; \tag{2.14}$$

$$Cov(Y_{ti}, Y_{t'i}) = \delta_{tt'} = \tau_{00}.$$

Thus, the compound symmetry model represents 15 variance–covariance parameters as functions of two underlying parameters (τ_{00} and σ^2).

First-Order Autoregressive

I now introduce a Markovian dependence of Level 1 residuals:

$$\varepsilon_{ti} = u_{0i} + (1 - p)e_{ti} + \rho e_{t-1i}, \tag{2.15}$$

where ρ is the autocorrelation parameter, leading to a marginal "complete-data" likelihood having the same mean as before but with covariance structure

$$\delta_t^2 = \tau_{00} + \sigma_t^2$$

$$\delta_{tt'} = \tau_{00} + \sigma_t^2 \rho^{|t-t'|}. \tag{2.16}$$

Thus, the model represents 15 possible variances and covariances as functions of three underlying parameters (τ_{00}, ρ, σ^2).

Random Slopes, Homogeneous Level 1 Variance

This is the widely used HLM of Equations 2.1 and 2.2. It represents the 15 variance–covariance parameters as a function of 4 underlying parameters (τ_{00}, τ_{01}, τ_{11}, σ^2).

Random Slopes, Heterogeneous Level 1 Variance

This elaborates the model of Equations 2.1 and 2.2 to allow a different variance at each time point. It therefore represents the 15 variance–covariance parameters as a function of 8 underlying parameters (τ_{00}, τ_{01}, τ_{11}, σ_1^2, σ_2^2, σ_3^2, σ_4^2, σ_5^2). A more parsimonious approach to heterogeneity at Level 1 models variation in variances, for example,

$$\sigma_t^2 = \exp\{\alpha_0 + \alpha_1 a_t\}. \tag{2.17}$$

This is a log linear model specifying a linear relationship between age and the log variance.

An Unrestricted Model

This model allows all 15 variance–covariance parameters to be estimated. Note that as T increases this model becomes inordinately complex. For example, an unrestricted model with 20 time points has 210 variance–covariance parameters. Nevertheless, with small T this model can serve as a standard to test the fit of more parsimonious submodels.

Results

Model fit can be assessed by examining the deviance, that is $-2 \times$ log likelihood, where the log likelihood is evaluated at the maximum. Under the null hypothesis that the simpler model fits as well as the more complex model, the difference between deviances is distributed approximately as chi-square with degrees of freedom equal to the difference between numbers of parameters estimated.

Inferences about the mean status, β_{00}, and the mean rate of change, β_{10}, are similar across models (see Table 2.2) except that the standard error for β_{10} is small when compound symmetry is assumed (notice $t = 16.17$ in that case). This small standard error appears to reflect the oversimplified covariance structure that assumes no autocorrelation (compare deviances of Models 1 and 2) or, alternatively, that assumes no variation in rates of change (compared with Model 3). Allowing variances to be heterogeneous (Model 4) slightly improves model fit, although no model fits as well as does the unrestricted model (Model 5). For example, under the null hypothesis that Model 4 fits as well as Model 5, the difference between deviances is $-348.598 - (-378.26) = 29.68$, $df = 17 - 10 = 7$, $p < .01$.

Case 3: Complete Data Are Unbalanced

Suppose now that the model includes a Level 1 predictor such as a_{ti}, having a random effect π_{1i}, and that a_{ti} takes on a different set of values for each participant. For example, in a large-scale field study, it is typically impossible to tightly control the time interval between observations, for a variety of reasons: Many participants are hard to find, or they will ask to reschedule appointments, and cost constraints may require a flexible deployment of data collectors. In this case, the age distribution is essentially unique to each participant. In fact, no 2 participants may have the same a_{ti} at time t. Even if the ages are nearly the same, other Level 1 predictors may have different values across participants. As illustrated below using the NYS as an example, the antisocial attitudes of one's peers may be a time-varying covariate having a random effect in the model; the set of values of this covariate tends to be different for each participant. In such cases, not even the complete data can be viewed as balanced,

TABLE 2.2

Estimates Based on Alternative Covariance Structure

MODEL	$\hat{\beta}_{00}$	SE	z	$\hat{\beta}_{10}$	SE	z	VARIANCE–COVARIANCE COMPONENT	DEVIANCE	NO. PARAMETERS
1. Compound symmetry	0.328	0.0132	24.84	0.064	0.0040	16.17	$\hat{\tau} = 0.0339$ $\hat{\sigma}^2 = 0.0323$	−229.00	4
2. AR(1)	0.328	0.0132	25.06	0.061	0.0048	12.71	$\hat{\tau} = 0.0243$ $\hat{\sigma}^2 = 0.0416$ $\hat{\rho} = 0.397$	−294.32	5
3. Random slopes	0.328	0.0131	25.07	0.065	0.0049	13.15	$\hat{\tau} = \begin{bmatrix} 0.0341 & 0.0078 \\ & 0.0025 \end{bmatrix}$ $\hat{\sigma}^2 = 0.0265$	−338.07	6
4. Random slopes, heterogeneous variances at Level 1	0.328	0.0131	25.28	0.063	0.0048	13.09	$\hat{\tau} = \begin{bmatrix} 0.0339 & 0.0077 \\ & 0.0029 \end{bmatrix}$ $\hat{\sigma}^2_1 = 0.0197$ $\hat{\sigma}^2_2 = 0.0282$ $\hat{\sigma}^2_3 = 0.0339$ $\hat{\sigma}^2_{-1} = 0.0250$ $\hat{\sigma}^2_5 = 0.0190$	−348.58	10
5. Unrestricted	0.321	0.0129	25.07	0.0594	0.0047	12.61	$\hat{\Delta} = \begin{bmatrix} 0.0351 & 0.0167 & 0.0189 & 0.0215 & 0.0249 \\ & 0.0446 & 0.0278 & 0.0247 & 0.0271 \\ & & 0.0727 & 0.0530 & 0.0480 \\ & & & 0.0857 & 0.0664 \\ & & & & 0.0899 \end{bmatrix}$	−378.26	17

Note. AR(1) = first-order autoregressive.

even if the number of time points per person is held constant at T. Thus, the variance δ_{ti}^2 varies continuously across participants as does each covariance $\delta_{tt'i}$. Such heteroscedastic models cannot be estimated within the framework of SEM or even the "complete-data" framework of Jennrich and Schluchter (1986). Thus, the standard HLM (mixed model, or random coefficient model) approach in such cases cannot be viewed as a simplified version of an unrestricted model.

In the NYS data, one has at each occasion a measure of the exposure of the participant to deviant peers, that is, a measure of the extent to which that person's peers are tolerant of deviant behavior (see Raudenbush & Chan, 1993, for details). This "exposure" variable has a different distribution over time for different participants. Suppose one specifies exposure as a predictor (a time-varying covariate) in the Level 1 model of HLM:

$$Y_{ti} = \pi_{0i} + \pi_{1i}a_{ti} + \pi_{2i}a_{ti}^2 + \pi_{3i}(expo)_{ij} + e_{ti}. \qquad (2.18)$$

The Level 1 variance is allowed to remain homogeneous. At Level 2, all coefficients are random:

$$\pi_{pi} = \beta_{p0} + u_{pi}, \ p = 0, 1, 2, 3. \qquad (2.19)$$

Thus, the Level 2 model has 14 parameters (4 βs and 10 τs), with 15 parameters overall. Compare this with the unrestricted model,

$$Y_{ti} = \beta_{00} + \beta_{10}a_{ti} + \beta_{20}a_{ti}^2 + \beta_{30}(expo)_{ti} + \varepsilon_{ti}, \qquad (2.20)$$

which involves 15 variance–covariance parameters along with 4βs—19 parameters in all. Results are displayed in Table 2.3. Note that inferences about the fixed effects are essentially identical. However, the deviance associated with the hierarchical model based on only 15 parameters is actually smaller than the deviance associated with the unrestricted model, which has 19 parameters. The models are not nested because the hierarchical model, which has fewer parameters, is not a submodel of the unrestricted model. The hierarchical model induces heterogeneous variance–covariance matrices across participants as a function of participant variation in exposure, whereas the unrestricted model is general only within the class of models assuming homogenous variance–covariance matrices. Only within that quite restricted class of models is it then possible to conceive a fit statistic based on a "gold standard" unrestricted model that measures the adequacy of a model's fit to the data.

Non-Normal Likelihoods

If either $f(Y|\pi, \theta)$ or $p(\pi|\theta)$ is non-normal, $L(Y|\theta)$ is also non-normal, and the covariance structure analysis described in the previous section does not apply. The integral of Equation 2.5 is, in general, challenging to evaluate and

TABLE 2.3

A Comparison Between an Unrestricted Model (Homogeneous Dispersion) and a Model With Heterogeneous Dispersion

FIXED EFFECTS	MODEL 1: COMPLETE DATA HAVE UNSTRUCTURED BUT HOMOGENEOUS DISPERSION			MODEL 2: DISPERSION DEPENDING ON EXPOSURE TO DEVIANT PEERS		
	COEFFICIENT	SE	RATIO	COEFFICIENT	SE	RATIO
Intercept, β_{00}	0.3252	0.0127	25.67	0.3251	0.0125	25.86
Linear, β_{10}	0.0487	0.0045	10.74	0.0466	0.0047	10.00
Quadratic, β_{10}	−0.0006	0.0030	−0.21	0.0006	0.0030	0.21
Exposure, β_{30}	0.3186	0.0244	13.07	0.3430	0.0295	11.62

Variance–covariance component

Model 1:

$$\hat{\tau} = \begin{bmatrix} 0.035 & 0.011 & 0.014 & 0.015 & 0.01 \\ & 0.035 & 0.018 & 0.016 & 0.01 \\ & & 0.054 & 0.034 & 0.02 \\ & & & 0.062 & 0.04 \\ & & & & 0.06 \end{bmatrix}$$

Model 2:

$$\hat{\tau} = \begin{bmatrix} 0.0236 & 0.0034 & -0.0016 & 0.0072 \\ & 0.0021 & 0.0000 & -0.0029 \\ & & 0.0000 & 0.0000 \\ & & & 0.0038 & 0.0457 \end{bmatrix}$$

$\hat{\sigma}^2 = 0.0210$

Model fit	MODEL 1	MODEL 2
Deviance	−517.26	−520.63
df	19	15

maximize.[4] Nevertheless, statisticians have made substantial progress in approximating the needed integral, using such approaches as Gauss–Hermite quadrature (Gibbons & Hedeker, 1997; Hedeker & Gibbons, 1994; Lillard & Farmer, 1998) and Monte Carlo integration (Chan, 1994; Karim, 1991; Wei & Tanner, 1990). My research group has developed an approach based on a LaPlace transform of the integrand, an approach we find especially appealing because of its accuracy and computational speed (Raudenbush, Yang, & Yosef, 2000; Yang, 1998).

As better computational approaches become available for nonconjugate mixtures (see footnote 4), vast new possibilities for modeling arise in studies of developmental trajectories (cf. Diggle, Liang, & Zeger, 1994). These modeling possibilities create opportunities to allow hierarchical models to be tailored better to fit the questions, theories, designs, and data yielded in studies using repeated measures. I organize consideration of these in terms of alternative Level 1 and Level 2 models and include possibilities for enriching developmental research by adding levels to the model.

Expanding the Class of Level 1 Models: $f(Y|\pi, \theta)$

To clarify the general modeling framework at Level 1, explicate key assumptions in the Level 1 model (Equation 2.1). Consider first the structural model at Level 1, that is, the model for the conditional mean of Y_{ti} given π:

$$E(Y_{ti}|\pi) = \mu_{ti} = \pi_{0i} + \pi_{1i}a_{ti}. \tag{2.21}$$

One can see from Equation 2.18 that the conditional mean μ_{ti} is equated to a linear model (i.e., a linear function of the πs). Second, now consider the probabilistic part of the model:

$$Y_{ti}|\mu_{ti} \sim N(\mu_{ti}, \sigma^2). \tag{2.22}$$

In words, given the conditional mean μ_{ti}, the outcome is normally distributed; the normal distribution has two parameters, a mean (here the mean is μ_{ti}) and a variance (here the variance is σ^2).

In sum, the Level 1 model has a linear structural model and a normal probability model. Such Level 1 models are so widely used in both HLM and

---

[4]The integral is comparatively simple to evaluate when $p(\pi|\theta)$ is chosen to be the conjugate prior for $f(Y|\theta)$. Conjugate pairs include, for example, the normal–normal, binomial–beta, Poisson–gamma, and gamma–inverse gamma. When π_i is multivariate (e.g., with dependence between π_{0i} and π_{1i}), the multivariate normal prior is particularly appealing. Thus, popular pairs for hierarchical models in repeated-measures studies include the binomial–normal for binary data, the Poisson–normal for count data, and the gamma–normal for duration times—all nonconjugate pairs, which makes the integration challenging.

SEM that these assumptions are rarely explicated. However, it would be a mistake to assume that such assumptions are always or even typically sensible or useful.

Consider Horney, Osgood, and Marshall's (1995) longitudinal study of high-rate offenders. Their interest focused on how changing life circumstances, such as getting a job or moving in with a spouse, are related to the propensity to commit crime. They therefore conceived each participant's propensity as having a trajectory over time that could be deflected by such changes in life circumstances. However, the data, collected by means of a life history calendar over 36 months, involved binary Y_{ti}; that is, $Y_{ti} = 1$ if person i committed a crime during time t, $t = 1, \ldots, 36$. The binary character of the data strongly suggests a Bernoulli probability model:

$$E(Y_{ti}|\pi) = \mu_{ti} = Prob(Y_{ti} = 1|\pi)$$

$$Var(Y_{ti}|\pi) = \mu_{ti}(1 - \mu_{ti}). \tag{2.23}$$

Note that unlike the normal model, the conditional variance at Level 1 is intrinsically heteroscedastic, depending on μ_{ti} and therefore varying over i at time t.

A linear structural model for μ_{ti} would make little sense in this case. A linear model would be inconsistent with the bounds $0 < \mu_{ti} < 1$ because a linear model could easily generate predicted values outside the unit interval. Thus, any effect sizes associated with such a model would be suspect. A more natural model, and that used by Horney et al. (1995), is the logit-linear structural model

$$\eta_{ti} = \log\left(\frac{\mu_{ti}}{1 - \mu_{ti}}\right) = \pi_{0i} + \sum_{p=1}^{P} \pi_{pti}a_{pti}. \tag{2.24}$$

Here $a_{pti}p = 1, \ldots, P$ are time-varying predictors, measured aspects of life circumstances, and π_{pi} can be thought of as a deflection in the propensity to commit crime associated with a change in a_{pti}. At Level 2 the πs can be viewed as having the same kind of model as before (Equation 2.2), that is, a linear structural model and a multivariate normal probability model.

In summary, the two-level model of Horney et al. (1995) is similar conceptually to the HLM/SEM of Equations 2.1 and 2.2, conceiving each participant to have a trajectory of development characterized by certain parameters π that, in turn, vary over a population of persons. However, the nature of the data calls for a nonlinear structural model at Level 1 and a non-normal sampling model.

Logit-linear (or probit-linear) structural models combined with Bernoulli or binomial probability models at Level 1 have many potentially important applications in developmental research. Consider, for example, a study using several binary items to represent a construct at each of several times. A three-level model would then be appropriate. At Level 1, item responses Y_{rti} would depend on item difficulty and person "ability" (the true latent trait of person i at time t), denoted as, say, ϕ_{ti}. At Level 2, ϕ_{ti} would change over time, given change parameters π_i, whereas at Level 3 π_i would vary over persons, depending on Level 3 parameters (βs and τs). Thus, Levels 2 and 3 would have the same structure as a standard HLM (Equations 2.1 and 2.2), except that a latent trait, ϕ_{ti}, would be the outcome. Raudenbush and Sampson (1999b) developed in detail the idea of a three-level model in which the first level of the model is an item response model.

Lillard and Farmer (1998) implemented such a model, except that the responses, rather than being binary, were ordinal. They modeled the ordinal responses using a cumulative probability model with logit-linear structural model at Level 1. At Level 2 the traits being measured followed a linear structural model and a multivariate normal probability model as in SEM.

In the language of the generalized linear model (McCullagh & Nelder, 1989), the logit transformation η_{ti} of the mean μ_{ti} is called the *link function for the binomial mean*. Other standard link functions are the log link for count data and the identity link for normal data. The link function is typically set equal to a linear model as in Equation 2.24; that is, η_{ti} is a linear function of the πs.

However, it will not always be the case that a linear model for the link function captures the interesting features of development. Consider now the age–crime curve, described by Gottfredson and Hirschi (1990) as one of the "brute facts" of criminology. Researchers have found that for many societies and many subgroups, the probability of committing a serious crime tends to be very small during preadolescence. However, this probability tends to increase at an accelerating rate early in adolescence, typically reaching a peak around ages 16–17 and then diminishing rapidly during late adolescence and early adulthood. This curve thus takes on a bell shape as a function of age, as displayed in Figure 2.1, based on an analysis of data from all seven cohorts of the NYS (Table 2.4 gives the sample sizes for each cohort at each age).

These curves describe the fitted values based on a two-level hierarchical model. At Level 1, the outcome Y_{ti} takes on a value of 1 if participant i commits serious theft during time interval t and 0 if he or she does not. One thus adopts a Bernoulli probability model, as did Horney et al. (1995) and, provisionally, a logit-linear structural model in which the log odds of committing serious theft is a quadratic function of age:

$$\eta_{ti} = \pi_{0i} + \pi_{1i}a_{ti} + \pi_{2i}a_{ti}^2, \tag{2.25}$$

Where a_{ti} is the age of person ti at time $t - 16$ (the median age of the sample during the 5 years of data collection). Ages range from 11 to 21 across the seven cohorts during the 5 years of the study. At Level 2, each of the three πs

FIGURE 2.1

Probability of theft during adolescence. These are expected probabilities for a "typical" participant and are smaller than the population-average probabilities.

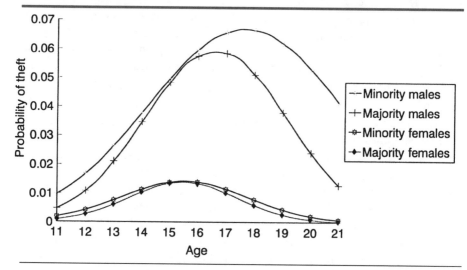

depends on gender (an indicator for female status), family income, and ethnicity (and indicator for minority status, with 1 = African American or Hispanic American and 0 = other):[5]

$$\pi_{pi} = \beta_{p0} + \beta_{p1}(\text{female})_i + \beta_{p2}(\text{minority})_i. \qquad (2.26)$$

The Level 2 probability model assumes the random effects associated with π_i to be normal in distribution with coefficients for linear and quadratic age fixed. However, the results in Table 2.5 are based on robust standard errors (Zeger et al., 1988). The curves in Figure 2.1 apply the results in Table 2.2 to the inverse logit transform

$$\hat{\mu}_{ti} = \frac{1}{1 + \exp\{-\hat{\eta}_{ti}\}}, \qquad (2.27)$$

that is, the predicted probability of committing serious theft for each of four groups (majority males, majority females, minority males, minority females).

Although the "picture" in Figure 2.1 is interesting, the results in Table 2.5 are not: It is difficult to interpret the polynomial coefficients. More inter-

---

[5]The vast majority of the sample in the NYS was either European American or African American. Sample sizes of other subgroups were too small for analysis, especially in light of the frequency of serious theft.

TABLE 2.4

Number of Participants Who Committed Theft Each Year From Ages 11–21 During 1976–1980

COHORT	AGE (YEARS)										
	11	12	13	14	15	16	17	18	19	20	21
Cohort 1	202	209	230	220	218	—	—	—	—	—	—
Cohort 2	—	218	218	234	225	219	—	—	—	—	—
Cohort 3	—	—	218	225	243	242	237	—	—	—	—
Cohort 4	—	—	—	217	212	225	212	202	—	—	—
Cohort 5	—	—	—	—	211	208	221	205	192	—	—
Cohort 6	—	—	—	—	—	186	194	219	194	189	—
Cohort 7	—	—	—	—	—	—	146	146	163	155	143
Overall	202	427	666	896	1,109	1,080	1,010	763	549	344	143

Note.   Dashes denote where combinations of cohort and age were not sampled.

TABLE 2.5

Correlates of Log Odds of Serious Theft

EFFECT	COEFFICIENT[a]	SE[a]	z
Intercept	−2.798	0.140	−19.97
Female	−1.501	0.236	−6.37
Minority	0.040	0.238	0.17
Age	0.101	0.046	2.18
Age × female	−0.241	0.097	−2.49
Age × minority	0.047	0.084	0.56
Age^2	−0.082	0.016	−5.02
Age^2 × female	−0.053	0.043	−1.25
Age^2 × minority	0.037	0.031	1.18

[a]Population average estimate with robust standard errors.

esting would be parameters that map onto a developmental theory linked to literature from the age–crime curve. First, one might be interested in the peak age of offending, that is, the age at which the expected probability of offending is a maximum. Second, one would be interested in the peak probability of offending, that is, the probability of offending at the peak age. Third, one would want to know about the persistence of offending, that is, the extent to which a person continues to offend rather than to desist from offending during the transition to young adulthood. The graph suggests, for example, that females "peak" earlier than males and that when they do, their offending rate is much lower than that of males. It also suggests that minority and majority youth have similar curves, except that minority males tend to peak later and to persist. Consistent with the results of Horney et al. (1995), one might expect that this persistence reflects the fact that minority males are having a harder time getting jobs and are more likely to remain single than are majority males, although one cannot test this hypothesis with the current data.

By taking the first derivative of Equation 2.27 with respect to a_{ti}, one defines the peak age of offending to be

$$\text{peak age of offending} = \alpha_i = -\frac{\pi_{1i}}{2\pi_{2i}}. \tag{2.28}$$

Next, by evaluating the predicted value (Equation 2.27) at the peak, one finds the log odds of offending at the peak to be

$$\text{probability of offending at peak} = C_i = \exp\left\{\pi_{0i} - \frac{\pi_{1i}^2}{2\pi_{2i}}\right\}, \tag{2.29}$$

and the persistence is the magnitude of the curvature near the peak, that is, the second derivative of Equation 2.24 with respect to a_{ti}:

$$\text{persistence} = V_i = -\frac{1}{2\pi_{2i}}. \tag{2.30}$$

Assuming π_{2i} to be negative, one can obtain ML point estimates of these quantities and their standard errors. The results are displayed in Table 2.6. The evidence suggests that males do peak later than females for both majority and minority youth (16.56 for majority males vs. 15.41 for majority females, $z = 4.48$; 17.73 for minority males vs. 15.47 for minority females, $z = 3.26$). The predicted probability of offending is significantly higher at peak for males than for females, $z = 13.18$ for majority youth, $z = 7.99$ for minority youth. There is also a tendency for minority males to persist longer than do majority males, $z = 1.84$. In terms of the more meaningful parameters, the structural model is

$$\eta_{ti} = \log(C_i) + \frac{\alpha_i}{V_i} a_{ti} - \frac{1}{2V_i} a_{ti}^2, \tag{2.31}$$

so that the logit link is a nonlinear function of the interesting parameters.

The example shows that the Level 1 structural model can be recast such that the parameters capture theoretically interesting properties of development. At the same time, the probabilistic part of the model is consistent with the binary nature of the data. A parallel analysis using the frequency of crime reached similar results. In this case, μ_{ti} is the event rate for person i at time t, the link function is the log link—that is, $\eta_{ti} = \log(\mu_{ti})$, and the structural model for η_{ti} is the same as in Equation 2.31.

Expanding the Class of Level 2 Models: $p(\pi \mid \theta)$

Thus far I have emphasized the importance of getting the model for individual development right. It is equally important to make sound choices about the model for individual variation in development.

Simultaneous-Equation Models

Applications of hierarchical models to date have nearly always specified multivariate regression models at Level 2. In terms of the paradigm example of Equations 2.1 and 2.2, this means expanding the Level 2 model, that is, in an especially simple case,

$$\pi_{0i} = \beta_{00} + \beta_{01}X_i + u_{0i}$$

$$\pi_{1i} = \beta_{00} + \beta_{11}X_i + u_{1i} \tag{2.32}$$

with

$$\begin{pmatrix} u_{0i} \\ u_{1i} \end{pmatrix} \sim N \left[\begin{pmatrix} 0 \\ 0 \end{pmatrix}, \begin{pmatrix} \tau_{00}, & \tau_{01} \\ \tau_{10} & \tau_{11} \end{pmatrix} \right].$$

TABLE 2.6

Translation of Polynomial Mood to Developmentally Meaningful Parameters

	MAJORITY			MINORITY			
PARAMETER	MALES (1)	FEMALES (2)	DIFFERENCE (1 − 2; z)	MALES (3)	FEMALES (4)	DIFFERENCE (3 − 4; z)	DIFFERENCE (3 − 1; z)
Peak age of serious theft	16.56	15.41	1.15 (4.48)	17.73	15.47	2.26 (3.26)	1.17 (1.84)
Probability of theft at peak age	.064	.013	.051 (13.18)	.068	.013	.055 (7.99)	.004 (1.84)
Persistence	5.64	3.43	2.21 (2.41)	10.70	4.80	5.90 (1.78)	5.06 (1.84)

Note. The probabilities given in this table are population averaged, and the z statistics are based on robust standard errors (Zeger et al., 1988).

Here the Level 1 parameters of individual change, π_{0i} and π_{1i}, become correlated outcomes predicted by person characteristic X_i. Raudenbush and Sampson (1999a) showed, however, how to specify and estimate simultaneous-equation models in which the random coefficient—say, π_{0i}—becomes a mediating variable. In the model below, X_i has both a direct effect on the rate of change, π_{1i}, given the intercept π_{0i}, and an indirect operating through the intercept. The model simply moves π_{0i} in Equation 2.32 to the right side of the equation for π_{1i}:

$$E(\pi_{1i}|\pi_{0i}) = \alpha_{10} + \alpha_{11}X_i + \alpha_{12}\pi_{0i}$$

$$= \beta_{10} - \alpha_{12}\beta_{00} + (\beta_{11} - \alpha_{12}\pi_{01})X_i + \alpha_{12}u_{0i}.$$

(2.33)

Here, $\alpha_{11} = \beta_{11} - \alpha_{12}\beta_{01}$ is the direct effect of X on π_1, $\alpha_{12}\beta_{01}$ is the indirect effect of X on π_1 operating through π_0, and $\alpha_{12} = \tau_{10}/\tau_{00}$. All the needed ML estimates are simple one-to-one transformations of ML estimates of the hierarchical model specified by Equations 2.1 and 2.32 and are thus readily available. Standard errors can be computed from a transformation of the information matrix. It is therefore possible to estimate a simultaneous-equation model for latent variables from intrinsically unbalanced data within the framework of the conventional HLM.

A Multinomial Prior

In many studies of growth, it is reasonable to assume that all participants are growing according to some common function but that the growth parameters vary in magnitude. For example, vocabulary growth curves in a normative sample of children invariably show upward curvature (acceleration) during the second year of life, and the interesting question about individual differences is the rate of acceleration (Huttenlocher, Haight, Bryk, & Seltzer, 1991). For many other repeated-measures studies, however, the situation is quite different.

Consider a study of changes in depression. It makes no sense to assume that everyone is increasing (or decreasing) with respect to depression. In a normative sample, many people are never high in depression, others are always high; some are recovering from serious depression, while others are becoming increasingly depressed. Perhaps another group oscillates between high and low levels of depression. Such "depression curves" can certainly be represented by a polynomial of sufficiently high degree, say three (cubic) in the Level 1 model. However, linear models for the polynomial coefficients, π, at Level 2 may not capture the qualitatively different types of trajectories found in the population.

To model these kinds of data, Nagin (1999) developed a two-level model in which the first level is similar to those discussed in this chapter. However, the second level of the model is reconceptualized such that the population is viewed as (approximately) falling into a fixed number of groups, where each group's development is characterized by a common set of change parameters (πs). The summary of evidence from this model is a set of conditional probabilities for each person: the probability that a person is in Group 1, the probability that the person is in Group 2, and so on. A multinomial regression model then can predict the probabilities of group membership. It may be, for example, that the predictors of being in the "always depressed" group are quite different from the predictors of being in the "becoming depressed" group. This model thus seems especially useful when trajectories of change involve sets of parameters that mark qualitatively different kinds of development. Nagin showed how to test the appropriateness of the assumed number of groups and thus to test alternative models for types of change.

Alternative Probabilistic Models

The vast majority of Level 2 models assume that departures of the change parameters (the πs) from their predicted values are multivariate normal. This is certainly a convenient assumption, as mentioned, but it may poorly fit the data, and results may not be robust to departures from it. In particular, outlier values of the growth parameters may be far more influential than one would desire, particularly in small-sample settings.

To develop more robust estimation, Seltzer (1993) adopted a multivariate t-prior distribution for the random effects (e.g., u_{0i}, u_{1i} in Equation 2.2). The t-prior anticipates more outliers than does the normal prior and, as a result, model estimates are more resistant to the influence of such outliers. Seltzer embedded this approach within a Bayesian framework—a three-level hierarchical model with the first two levels of the type given by Equations 2.1 and 2.2 and a third level specifying a prior for the parameters, θ. A key advantage of the Bayesian approach is that all inferences take into account the uncertainty about all other unknowns. This differs from ML, wherein, for example, inferences about π and β are conditional on point estimates of τ. However, the Bayesian approach is computationally intensive and is generally needed only for a small n. Thum (1997) also adopted a t-prior in his multilevel–multivariate model with estimation by means of ML. This model allows covariance structure analysis at each of two levels based on incomplete data.

Conclusion

Many researchers of developmental trajectories have adopted a basic two-level hierarchical model (cf. Equations 2.1 and 2.2). The first level of the model specifies a trajectory of change for person i and also a model for the random behavior of each time-series datum around that trajectory. The second stage of the model specifies how trajectories vary in the population of persons. If the structural models at both levels are linear, and if the probabilistic models at both levels are normal, one has a now-standard two-level (normal–normal) HLM for individual change and variation in change as described by Bryk and Raudenbush (1987). If, in addition, the observed data are balanced (equal numbers of time points for all people within a subpopulation and an invariant distribution of Level 1 predictors within each person), one has a simple SEM. Within the constraints of balanced data, current software for SEM offers a wide array of modeling possibilities.

The constraint on balance can be eased by viewing the complete data as balanced. Following Jennrich and Schluchter (1986) with extensions by Goldstein (1995) and Thum (1997), one can maximize the complete-data likelihood using incomplete data, assuming the missing data are missing at random (Little & Rubin, 1987). In essence, a level is added to the model that specifies the relationship between the observed data and the complete data. Within that framework the array of covariance structures that are standard in SEM become accessible.

However, if the incomplete data are unbalanced, then the two-level HLM, even with normality at both levels, falls outside the bounds of models having homogeneity of dispersion within subpopulations. Such models, estimable within the standard HLM framework, are not estimable within the statistical methods of SEM. There is no gold-standard unrestricted model that can be used to test the fit of simpler models.

However, the two-level linear normal–normal model, although useful, provides an extremely limited set of modeling possibilities when compared with the needs of developmental theory and data. It has been the purpose of this chapter to go beyond current debate about such models and to construct a more general framework for modeling of developmental trajectories based on repeated-measures data. Key elements of that framework include the following.

1. Within the core two-level model, expand the Level 1 model to include nonlinear structural models and non-normal probabilistic models. Such models incorporate binary data, or ordinal data, or count data with appropriate nonlinear link functions and probability models. This idea was illustrated with reference to Horney et al.'s (1995) work on a binary outcome. Such models can also estimate nonlinear transformations of parameters, providing more meaningful developmental interpretations, as illustrated with a reanalysis of data from the NYS.

2. Also within the core two-level model, expand possibilities at Level 2, where interest focuses on variation over persons. Examples include simultaneous-equation models and multinomial models for the case when qualitatively different kinds of trajectories are of

interest, as illustrated by Nagin (1999). Probabilistic assumptions can also be extended to include multivariate t-priors that are robust to outlier random effects, as illustrated by Seltzer (1993) and Thum (1997).

3. Expand the core two-level models "from below" by adding a model for missing data, measurement error, or both. The measurement models typically cope with items that are binary or ordinal. Thus, they become equivalent to the item–response models of educational testing. Such models define a person-specific latent trait or ability that can change over time at Level 2, with trajectories of change varying over persons at Level 3 (see Raudenbush & Sampson, 1999b). These item–response models can also underpin simultaneous-equation models of the type commonly estimated within SEM (see Lillard & Farmer, 1998; Raudenbush & Sampson, 1999a).

4. Expand the core two-level models "from above" to incorporate the clustering of persons within social settings such as schools or neighborhoods (see review by Raudenbush, 1995).

At each level of the model, the norm should be to specify structural models and probabilistic models that best fit developmental theory and data. It is time to wean ourselves as researchers from an adherence to normal–normal models that are assumed more for convenience than conviction. Outcomes, such as crime, substance use, and social behavior, as indicated by binary, ordinal, or count responses, do not lend themselves to linear link functions and normal probability models. We can, and should, do better.

We need a modeling framework that goes well beyond the capabilities of current software. Such a framework can bring modeling into line with developmental theory. In many cases, the ideal model requires methodological innovation. Of course, "the analysis must go on," even when current software is suboptimal, but let us not pretend in that case that our models are optimal. Instead, let the mismatch between the needs of developmental research and the limits of current software drive methodological innovation forward. In this way, developmental theory and methods will advance as the interplay between them enriches both.

References

Bryk, A., & Raudenbush, S. (1987). Application of hierarchical linear models to assessing change. *Psychological Bulletin, 101*, 147–158.

Bryk, A., & Raudenbush, S. (1992). *Hierarchical linear models in social and behavioral research: Applications and data analysis methods*. Newbury Park, CA: Sage.

Chan, W. (1994). *Toward a multilevel generalized linear model: The case for Poisson distributed data.* Unpublished doctoral dissertation, Michigan State University, East Lansing.

Dempster, A., Laird, N., & Rubin, D. (1977). Maximum likelihood from incomplete data via the EM algorithm. *Journal of the Royal Statistical Society, Series B(39)*, 1–8.

Diggle, P., Liang, K., & Zeger, S. (1994). *Analysis of longitudinal data.* New York: Oxford University Press.

Elliott, D. S., Huizinga, D., & Menard, S. (1989). *Multiple problem youth: Delinquency, substance abuse, and mental health problems.* New York: Springer-Verlag.

Gibbons, R. D., & Hedeker, D. (1997). Random effects probit and logistic regression models for three-level data. *Biometrics, 53*, 1527–1537.

Goldstein, H. (1995). *Multilevel statistical models* (2nd ed.). New York: Wiley.

Gottfredson, M., & Hirschi, T. (1990). *A general theory of crime.* Stanford, CA: Stanford University Press.

Hedeker, D., & Gibbons, R. D. (1994). A random effects ordinal regression model for multilevel analysis. *Biometrica, 50*, 933–944.

Horney, J., Osgood, D., & Marshall, I. (1995). Criminal careers in the short-term: Intra-individual variability in crime and its relation to local life circumstances. *American Sociological Review, 60*, 655–673.

Huttenlocher, J., Haight, W., Bryk, A., & Seltzer, M. (1991). Early vocabulary growth: Relation to language input and gender. *Developmental Psychology, 27*, 236–249.

Jennrich, R., & Schluchter, M. (1986). Unbalanced repeated-measures models with structured covariance matrices. *Biometrics, 42*, 805–820.

Karim, M. (1991). *Generalized linear models with random effects.* Unpublished doctoral dissertation, Johns Hopkins University, Baltimore, MD.

Lillard, L. A., & Farmer, M. M. (1998, April). *Functional limitations, disability and perceived health of the oldest old: An examination of health status in AHEAD.* Paper presented to a colloquium at the Survey Research Center, University of Michigan, Ann Arbor.

Little, R. J. A., & Rubin, D. B. (1987). *Statistical analysis with missing data.* New York: Wiley.

McCullagh, P., & Nelder, J. (1989). *Generalized linear models* (2nd ed.). London: Chapman & Hall.

Nagin, D. S. (1999). Analyzing developmental trajectories: A semi-parametric, group-based approach. *Psychological Methods, 4*, 139–157.

Raudenbush, S. W. (1993). A crossed-random effects model with applications in cross-sectional and longitudinal research. *Journal of Educational Statistics, 18*, 321–349.

Raudenbush, S. (1995). Hierarchical linear models to study the effects of social context on development. In J. Gottman (Ed.), *The analysis of change* (pp. 165–201). Hillsdale, NJ: Erlbaum.

Raudenbush, S., & Chan, W. (1993). Application of hierarchical linear model to the study appendix of adolescent deviance in an overlapping cohort design. *Journal of Clinical and Consulting Psychology, 61*, 941–951.

Raudenbush, S. W., & Sampson, R. (1999a). Assessing direct and indirect associations in multilevel designs with latent variables. *Sociological Methods and Research, 28*, 123–153.

Raudenbush, S. W., & Sampson, R. (1999b). Ecometrics: Toward a science of assessing ecological settings, with application to the systematic social observation of neighborhoods. *Sociological Methodology, 29*, 1–41.

Raudenbush, S., Yang, M., & Yosef, M. (2000). Maximum likelihood for hierarchical models via high-order, multivariate LaPlace approximation. *Journal of Computational and Graphical Statistics, 9*, 141–157.

Seltzer, M. (1993). Sensitivity analysis for fixed effects in the hierarchical model: A Gibbs sampling approach. *Journal of Educational Statistics, 18*, 207–235.

Thum, Y. (1997). Hierarchial linear models for multivariate outcomes. *Journal of Educational and Behavioral Statistics, 22*, 77–108.

Wei, G., & Tanner, M. (1990). A Monte Carlo implementation of the EM algorithm and the poor man's data augmentation algorithms. *Journal of the American Statistical Association, 83*, 37–42.

Willett, J., & Sayer, A. (1994). Using covariance structure analysis to detect correlates and predictors of individual change over time. *Psychological Bulletin, 116*, 363–380.

Yang, M. (1998). *Increasing the efficiency in estimating multilevel Bernoulli models.* Unpublished doctoral dissertation, Michigan State University, East Lansing.

Zeger, S., Liang, K.-Y., & Albert, P. (1988). Models for longitudinal data: A likelihood approach. *Biometrics, 44*, 1049–1060.

Editors' Introduction

M ichael Rovine and Peter Molenaar show that structural equation modeling (SEM) provides a broader statistical framework than has previously been thought. Among the models that can be estimated easily in this framework are the repeated-measures analysis of variance and multiple-groups growth curve models. It is true that the SEM approach is more restrictive than the hierarchical linear modeling (HLM) approach in terms of the structure of the input data. For example, all individuals involved in an SEM analysis must have been measured at approximately the same time. However, the SEM approach can be more flexible than the HLM approach when it comes to certain aspects of the model being tested, such as the structure of the error covariance matrix. In his commentary, Wayne Osgood discusses some of the benefits and limitations of the SEM approach. Raudenbush's chapter 2 makes an interesting comparison to this one.

A Structural Equations Modeling Approach to the General Linear Mixed Model

Michael J. Rovine

Peter C. M. Molenaar

In this chapter we present a method based on a structural equation modeling (SEM) framework for estimating models representing specific instances of the general linear mixed model (GLMM; Laird & Ware, 1982). We choose the GLMM as a starting point for two reasons. First, this model can be considered the basis of the general multilevel modeling approach (Bryk & Raudenbush, 1992; Goldstein, 1995), which has appeared in the psychometric, biostatistics, and education literatures under different names, including "random coefficients models" (Jennrich & Schluchter, 1986; Rosenberg, 1973), "random effects models" (Laird & Ware, 1982), "multilevel models" (Goldstein, 1986), "covariance component models" (Longford, 1993), and "hierarchical linear models" (HLM; Bryk & Raudenbush, 1992). We discuss some of the distinct advantages gained by estimating these popular models as SEM. Second, the GLMM appears in a form that can be directly translated into the SEM framework. Design matrices and error structures that result from specific instances of the model correspond directly to matrices in the SEM framework. This correspondence allows one to estimate many different models, including repeated-measures analysis of variance (ANOVA), with patterned residual matrices as SEM. Throughout this chapter, we refer to one particular SEM program, LISREL (Jöreskog & Sörbom, 1993), and to the matrices that compose that model. Because many different software packages are currently available, readers may be unfamiliar with LISREL notation. A number of excellent introductory explanations of the LISREL model and notation are available. These include Long (1983a, 1983b), Hayduk (1987), and Jöreskog and Sörbom (1993). Tabachnick and Fidell (1996) showed how to implement the same SEM using different programs, including LISREL and EQS (Bentler, 1995).

Because we can think of the GLMM as an extension of the more familiar general linear model, we begin with that model.

The general linear model is

$$y = X\boldsymbol{\beta} + \boldsymbol{\varepsilon}, \tag{3.1}$$

where $\boldsymbol{\beta}$ is a $k \times 1$ vector of regression weights, and $\boldsymbol{\varepsilon}$ is an $n \times 1$ vector of residuals that are assumed to be independent and distributed as $N(0, \sigma_\varepsilon^2)$. The design matrix, X (essentially the matrix of predictor variable values), can be used to include interval-level variables (regression predictors); dummy or effect-coded variables representing membership in a particular group, allowing ANOVA models to be estimated as regression; and combinations of interval and coded categorical variables allowing analysis of covariance (ANCOVA) models to be estimated as regression. In this model the regression weights, which are constant across all cases, can be described as *fixed*. The residuals, which are assumed to be sampled from a normal distribution, are described as *random*. Given the vector y of dependent variable values, and the design matrix X, we can obtain the least squares estimates of the regression weights as

$$\boldsymbol{\beta} = (X^T X)^{-1}(X^T y). \tag{3.2}$$

(Note: T indicates the transpose of a matrix.)

The GLMM (Laird & Ware, 1982) is

$$y_i = X_i \boldsymbol{\beta} + Z_i \boldsymbol{\gamma}_i + \boldsymbol{\varepsilon}_i, \tag{3.3}$$

where for the ith case, y_i is an $n_i \times 1$ vector of response values, X_i is an $n_i \times b$ design matrix for the fixed effects, Z_i is an $n_i \times g$ design matrix for the random effects, $\boldsymbol{\gamma}_i$ is a $g \times 1$ vector of random effects, and $\boldsymbol{\beta}$ is a $b \times 1$ vector of fixed effect parameters. The $\boldsymbol{\gamma}_i$ are assumed to be independently distributed across participants with a distribution $\boldsymbol{\gamma}_i \sim N(0, \sigma^2 D)$, where D is an arbitrary "between" covariance matrix, and the $\boldsymbol{\varepsilon}_i$, the within-subject errors, are assumed to have the distribution $\boldsymbol{\varepsilon}_i \sim N(0, \sigma_\varepsilon^2 W_i)$.

One can think of the GLMM as an extension of Equation 3.1 and as differing from Equation 3.1 in two ways. The first difference is that y_i is now a vector of n_i values for individual i. So, for example, if an individual is measured on four different occasions, the vector y_i would represent the four observed values for that individual. (Note that the index, i, allows different numbers of observations for different individuals although, in the models discussed below, we consider the case in which $n_i = n$; that is, each case has the same number of observations.) Similarly, each individual now has a vector of residuals, $\boldsymbol{\varepsilon}_i$. Within an individual one may expect these residuals to correlate. So unlike the general linear model, in which one assumes that all residuals (errors) are independent, we assume that residuals between any two different individuals are uncorrelated but that the residuals within an individual have a particular covariance structure. Part of our task in estimating the model is to select an appropriate structure for these residuals and estimate the parameters related to that structure.

If one collects longitudinal data on four occasions, one may expect a pattern such as the following: For the same variable measured on consecutive days, the closer together in time two measures are taken, the more highly correlated the residuals might be. Or one might expect a pattern such that the correlation between any pair of residuals is the same regardless of the separation between occasions. In addition to estimating parameters represented by these patterns, one could test the respective models to determine which pattern provided a better fit for the data.

The second difference has to do with what can be considered a different way of modeling "errors" in the model. This is related to the way the two different models allow for the possibility of random effects. In the general linear model the fixed effects are the βs. In a very simplistic sense, fixed-effect parameters are constant across individuals, whereas the random-effects parameters vary from individual to individual (they are, as a result, indexed). In the general linear model the only random effects are the errors, ε. The GLMM structures the random effects as $Z_i\gamma_i + \varepsilon_i$. Thus, in addition to the individual errors, we can model regression-type relations in which the values of the regression parameters vary from individual to individual.

One can most easily see the advantage of this structure through the use of an example, so consider the linear curve model shown in Figure 3.1. This

FIGURE 3.1

Imaginary data for three individuals measured on four occasions. Numbers indicate ith participant.

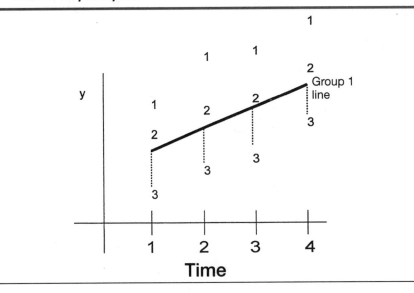

imaginary plot shows data for three individuals, each measured on four occasions.

These data are modeled hypothesizing a group straight line. If one were to model the data using the equation $y_i = X_i\beta + \varepsilon_i$, one would model each residual as the vertical distance between each data point and the line. In the figure, the dotted lines indicate the ε_i for the third individual. However, suppose that we consider each individual's four data points. It appears that each individual follows a straight line. We could then model the data by breaking the residual down into two components: (a) the degree to which the individual line differs from the group line and (b) the degree to which an individual's data points vary around the individual's line. This is tantamount to

$$\varepsilon_i^* = Z_i\gamma_i + \varepsilon_i, \tag{3.4}$$

where Z_i is a design matrix related to the γ_i, which are the degrees to which each individual slope and intercept differ from the group values.

Consider Figure 3.2. In this figure we again see data for three cases. A line has been drawn through each individual's four data points. We can think of each individual's line as having an intercept that differs from the group intercept by γ_{0i} and a slope that differs from the group slope by γ_{1i}. So the γ_i represent

FIGURE 3.2

A breakdown of the residuals into "between" and "within" components. Numbers indicate ith participant.

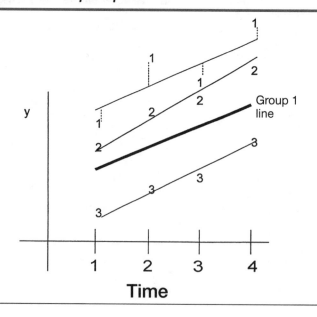

the differences between the individual curves and the group curve. The ε_i (again represented by the dotted lines) now represent the deviations of the observed data points around the individual's line.

For this straight-line growth model we can write the equation for each observed value as

$$y_i = \beta_0(1) + \beta_1 X_i + \gamma_{0i}(1) + \gamma_{1i} Z_i + \varepsilon_i, \tag{3.5}$$

where β_0 and β_1 represent the respective intercept and slope for a particular group. As the model is a straight line, and we assume equal spacing between occasions, we could select the values $X_i = \{1, 2, 3, 4\}$ and $Z_i = \{1, 2, 3, 4\}$; these values represent the occasions of measurement along the time axis; then, the set of equations for individual i becomes

$$
\begin{aligned}
y_{1i} &= (\beta_0 + 1\beta_1) + (\gamma_{0i} + 1\gamma_{1i}) + \varepsilon_{1i} \\
y_{2i} &= (\beta_0 + 2\beta_1) + (\gamma_{0i} + 2\gamma_{1i}) + \varepsilon_{2i} \\
y_{3i} &= (\beta_0 + 3\beta_1) + (\gamma_{0i} + 3\gamma_{1i}) + \varepsilon_{3i} \\
y_{4i} &= (\beta_0 + 4\beta_1) + (\gamma_{0i} + 4\gamma_{1i}) + \varepsilon_{4i}.
\end{aligned}
\tag{3.6}
$$

One can see how each observed data point is composed of (a) the degree to which an individual's straight line differs from the group's straight line, $\beta_0 + k\beta_1$, and (b) a deviation from the individual's straight line. The γ_i and the ε_i vary from person to person and can be described by their respective covariance matrices. Curves of any complexity can be approximated by choosing an appropriate set of design matrix coefficients. Coefficients can also be selected to reflect unequal spacing among occasions.

We now present the GLMM in a slightly more formal fashion and use it to model (a) a two-group repeated-measures ANOVA with a patterned covariance matrix and (b) a two-group linear growth curve model. We then show how to estimate each of these models as SEMs. These two examples are easily generalized to many different and useful models. To exemplify the method, we analyze two data sets: growth curve data presented by Potthoff and Roy (1964) and marriage data reported by Belsky and Rovine (1990).

A 2 Group × 4 Time Repeated-Measures ANOVA

If we assume that $Z_i = 0$, Equation 3.3 becomes

$$y_i = X_i \beta + \varepsilon_i. \tag{3.7}$$

If we observed each case repeatedly on 4 consecutive days, we could write Equation 3.7 for case i as

$$
\begin{bmatrix} y_{i1} \\ y_{i2} \\ y_{i3} \\ y_{i4} \end{bmatrix} = \begin{bmatrix} 1 & 1 & 0 & 0 \\ 1 & 0 & 1 & 0 \\ 1 & 0 & 0 & 1 \\ 1 & 0 & 0 & 0 \end{bmatrix} \begin{bmatrix} \beta_0 \\ \beta_1 \\ \beta_2 \\ \beta_3 \end{bmatrix} + \begin{bmatrix} \varepsilon_{i1} \\ \varepsilon_{i2} \\ \varepsilon_{i3} \\ \varepsilon_{i4} \end{bmatrix}, \tag{3.8}
$$

where the first column of X_i corresponds to the intercept, and the next three columns represent the dummy coded vectors for the Time effect.

We could determine which mean differences are tested by the parameters by using the fact that the expected value of y_i is the vector of observed variable means and thus solving the set of equations

$$
\hat{y}_i = X\beta \tag{3.9}
$$

as follows:

$$
\begin{aligned}
\overline{y_{i1}} &= \beta_0 + \beta_1 \\
\overline{y_{i2}} &= \beta_0 + \beta_2 \\
\overline{y_{i3}} &= \beta_0 + \beta_3 \\
\overline{y_{i4}} &= \beta_0.
\end{aligned} \tag{3.10}
$$

Substituting the last equation into the previous three gives:

$$
\begin{aligned}
\beta_1 &= \overline{y_{i1}} - \overline{y_{i4}} \\
\beta_2 &= \overline{y_{i2}} - \overline{y_{i4}} \\
\beta_3 &= \overline{y_{i3}} - \overline{y_{i4}} \\
\beta_0 &= \overline{y_{i4}}
\end{aligned} \tag{3.11}
$$

Because we wrote this model for a single individual, we would expect that the residuals would be correlated because the data were repeatedly measured. We must now consider how to model the covariance of those residuals. According to the model definition, the covariance matrix of the ε_i is assumed to be $\sigma_\varepsilon^2 W_i$. We also assume that the covariance matrix is the same for each case ($W_i = W$). Now we must hypothesize a structure. If we thought that the residuals would be independent, we could select $\sigma_\varepsilon^2 W = \sigma_\varepsilon^2 I$, where I is an identity matrix. The residuals would then have the following pattern:

$$
\sigma^2 \begin{bmatrix} 1 & 0 & 0 & 0 \\ 0 & 1 & 0 & 0 \\ 0 & 0 & 1 & 0 \\ 0 & 0 & 0 & 1 \end{bmatrix}.
$$

This would not be a likely outcome for repeatedly measured data. Were we to pattern all residual variances equal and all residual covariances equal ($\sigma_e^2 W = \sigma_b^2 \mathbf{1}\mathbf{1}^T + \sigma_a^2 \mathbf{I}$), where $\mathbf{1}$ represents an n_i vector of 1s, we would be hypothesizing compound symmetry. These residuals would have the following pattern:

$$
\begin{bmatrix}
\sigma^2 + \sigma_1 & \sigma_1 & \sigma_1 & \sigma_1 \\
\sigma_1 & \sigma^2 + \sigma_1 & \sigma_1 & \sigma_1 \\
\sigma_1 & \sigma_1 & \sigma^2 + \sigma_1 & \sigma_1 \\
\sigma_1 & \sigma_1 & \sigma_1 & \sigma^2 + \sigma_1
\end{bmatrix}.
$$

This pattern would probably be more appropriate for data from a repeated-measures experiment with randomized order of treatment presentation.

For longitudinal data we could assume that the residuals are stationary and the result of a first-order autoregressive (AR[1]) process, $\varepsilon_{1t} = \rho\varepsilon_{it-1} + v_i$, where ρ is the autocorrelation coefficient and v_i are the innovation errors (the difference between the predicted and observed values of ε_{it} under the time series model) assumed to be distributed as $v_i \sim N(0, \sigma^2)$. The assumption would result in the following pattern:

$$
\sigma^2
\begin{bmatrix}
1 & \rho & \rho^2 & \rho^3 \\
\rho & 1 & \rho & \rho^2 \\
\rho^2 & \rho & 1 & \rho \\
\rho^3 & \rho^2 & \rho & 1
\end{bmatrix},
$$

where ρ is the correlation between adjacent occasions and σ^2 is the variance of the residuals. Note that the pattern of this matrix is banded (Toeplitz) with values along each subdiagonal equivalent. This pattern corresponds to the notion described above that residuals taken from measures taken closer in times would be more highly correlated. With moderate or low values the ρ coefficients representing more distant occasions are required to drop off dramatically. An alternative would be a general autoregressive pattern:

$$
\begin{bmatrix}
\sigma_1 & \sigma_2 & \sigma_3 & \sigma_4 \\
\sigma_2 & \sigma_1 & \sigma_2 & \sigma_3 \\
\sigma_3 & \sigma_2 & \sigma_1 & \sigma_2 \\
\sigma_4 & \sigma_3 & \sigma_2 & \sigma_1
\end{bmatrix}.
$$

This pattern would allow the correlation to be smaller as the occasions became more distant while allowing the dropoff in the size of the correlation to be smaller. The cost would be the additional parameters that are estimated.

For any of these patterns we would estimate the β weights along with the parameters associated with the particular covariance structure of the residuals we assume (σ^2 and ρ for the AR[1] structure; σ_1, σ_2, σ_3, and σ_4 for the general autoregressive structure). It is, of course, possible to test and compare alternative patterns.

Now assume that in addition to the Time effect, we assigned members of our sample to one of two groups. For Group 1, the model is

$$
\begin{bmatrix} y_{i1} \\ y_{i2} \\ y_{i3} \\ y_{i4} \end{bmatrix} = \begin{bmatrix} 1 & 1 & 1 & 0 & 0 & 1 & 0 & 0 \\ 1 & 1 & 0 & 1 & 0 & 0 & 1 & 0 \\ 1 & 1 & 0 & 0 & 1 & 0 & 0 & 1 \\ 1 & 1 & 0 & 0 & 0 & 0 & 0 & 0 \end{bmatrix} \begin{bmatrix} \beta_1 \\ \beta_2 \\ \beta_3 \\ \beta_4 \\ \beta_5 \\ \beta_6 \\ \beta_7 \\ \beta_8 \end{bmatrix} + \begin{bmatrix} \varepsilon_{i1} \\ \varepsilon_{i2} \\ \varepsilon_{i3} \\ \varepsilon_{i4} \end{bmatrix}, \qquad (3.12)
$$

where the first column of X holds the coding vector values corresponding to the intercept, the second column has the coding vector values and represents the Group effect, and the next three columns represent the Time effect. The last three columns (the product of column 2 with columns 3, 4, and 5, respectively, are the coding vector values for the Time × Group interaction. The βs are the corresponding parameters.

For Group 2,

$$
\begin{bmatrix} y_{i1} \\ y_{i2} \\ y_{i3} \\ y_{i4} \end{bmatrix} = \begin{bmatrix} 1 & 0 & 1 & 0 & 0 & 0 & 0 & 0 \\ 1 & 0 & 0 & 1 & 0 & 0 & 0 & 0 \\ 1 & 0 & 0 & 0 & 1 & 0 & 0 & 0 \\ 1 & 0 & 0 & 0 & 0 & 0 & 0 & 0 \end{bmatrix} \begin{bmatrix} \beta_1 \\ \beta_2 \\ \beta_3 \\ \beta_4 \\ \beta_5 \\ \beta_6 \\ \beta_7 \\ \beta_8 \end{bmatrix} + \begin{bmatrix} \varepsilon_{i1} \\ \varepsilon_{i2} \\ \varepsilon_{i3} \\ \varepsilon_{i4} \end{bmatrix}. \qquad (3.13)
$$

Notice that column 2 is now a vector of 0s. As a result columns 6–8 are also 0s. Also notice that the predicted values of y_i for the second group will not be affected by β_2, β_6, β_7, and β_8 because these parameters are multiplied by 0 at each occasion. These parameters contain the differences between the two groups. When estimating this two-group model we constrain these "fixed" parameter values to be equivalent across groups. The values of the parameters are added in, contributing to the y_i of Group 1 but not of Group 2.

The parameter estimates contained in the βs represent tests of mean differences. For this set of dummy-coded vectors, the test represented by the parameters can be obtained in the same manner as described above and are:

$$\beta_1 = \overline{y_{24}}$$
$$\beta_2 = \overline{y_{14}} - \overline{y_{24}}$$
$$\beta_3 = \overline{y_{21}} - \overline{y_{24}}$$
$$\beta_4 = \overline{y_{22}} - \overline{y_{24}}$$
$$\beta_5 = \overline{y_{23}} - \overline{y_{24}}$$
$$\beta_6 = \overline{y_{11}} - \overline{y_{21}} + \overline{y_{24}} - \overline{y_{14}}$$
$$\beta_7 = \overline{y_{12}} - \overline{y_{22}} + \overline{y_{24}} - \overline{y_{14}}$$
$$\beta_8 = \overline{y_{13}} - \overline{y_{23}} + \overline{y_{24}} - \overline{y_{14}}$$

$$(3.14)$$

These parameters would be estimated along with the parameters representing the hypothesized residual covariance structure. A test of the fit of the model would indicate the adequacy of this representation.

A Linear Curve–Random Coefficients Model

Consider again Figure 3.2. Imagine that the thick line represents the slope and intercept for Group 1. In this figure, each individual, i, is a member of that group and has a slope and intercept (represented by a thin line) that differ from the group value. The random effect is represented by the difference between the individual and group slopes, γ_{1i}, and the difference between the individual and the group intercepts, γ_{0i}. The parameters related to the design matrix, X, are the fixed-effect parameters that are used to estimate the group differences, whereas the parameters related to the design matrix, Z, are the random effects (slopes and intercepts). We estimate the covariance matrix of the random effects and then use the estimates to predict the individual random effects (Henderson, 1990; Robinson, 1991).

In terms of Equation 3.3, X_i represents the respective design matrices that identify group membership. In this two-group illustration, the fixed-effects part of the model for Group 1 is

$$\begin{bmatrix} y_{i1} \\ y_{i2} \\ y_{i3} \\ y_{i4} \end{bmatrix} = \begin{bmatrix} 1 & 1 & 0 & 0 \\ 1 & 2 & 0 & 0 \\ 1 & 3 & 0 & 0 \\ 1 & 4 & 0 & 0 \end{bmatrix} \begin{bmatrix} \beta_1 \\ \beta_2 \\ \beta_3 \\ \beta_4 \end{bmatrix}, \qquad (3.15)$$

where the model is parameterized to describe the line representing Group 1 by the intercept β_1 and the slope β_2. The fixed-effects part of the model for Group 2 is

$$\begin{bmatrix} y_{i1} \\ y_{i2} \\ y_{i3} \\ y_{i4} \end{bmatrix} = \begin{bmatrix} 1 & 1 & 1 & 1 \\ 1 & 2 & 1 & 2 \\ 1 & 3 & 1 & 3 \\ 1 & 4 & 1 & 4 \end{bmatrix} \begin{bmatrix} \beta_1 \\ \beta_2 \\ \beta_3 \\ \beta_4 \end{bmatrix}, \qquad (3.16)$$

where the parameters β_3 and β_4 represent the differences in slope and intercept, respectively, between the groups. The parameters are fixed in that they are constant across all cases.

This random effect can be modeled by

$$Z\gamma_i + \varepsilon_i = \begin{bmatrix} 1 & 1 \\ 1 & 2 \\ 1 & 3 \\ 1 & 4 \end{bmatrix} \begin{bmatrix} \gamma_{i1} \\ \gamma_{i2} \end{bmatrix} + \begin{bmatrix} \varepsilon_{i1} \\ \varepsilon_{i2} \\ \varepsilon_{i3} \\ \varepsilon_{i4} \end{bmatrix}, \tag{3.17}$$

where γ_{i1} and γ_{i2} represent the respective differences in intercept and slope for the ith participant. The ε_i represent the differences between the estimated and observed y_{it} values. Because we now use the individual curves represented by the γ to account for the autocorrelations among the data, we can assume that the "within-subject" errors are uncorrelated ($W = I$). $\sigma^2 D$ is the covariance matrix of the γ_i, and the total covariance matrix for the ith participant is

$$\sigma^2 V_i = \sigma^2 (ZDZ^T + I), \tag{3.18}$$

which is the structure for the random coefficients model (Jennrich & Schluchter, 1986). For this linear growth curve model, one must estimate β, σ^2, and D. With those estimates one can predict the values of the individual random effects.

Estimating GLMM Parameters Through Covariance Structure Modeling

In this section, we describe how to estimate certain special cases of the GLMM as SEM. The primary difficulty stems from the problem of estimating both fixed and random effects in the same model. Using the LISREL model, we approach this problem by "tricking" LISREL into making the scores related to certain "factors" constant, thus defining them as fixed. Most typically in SEM, the η associated with the columns of Λ_y, the factor loading matrix, are random (they are the factor scores of the measurement model). However, in the proposed model we are using Λ_y as a design matrix in which the corresponding η_l are parameters related to the columns of Λ_y, either fixed or random regression weights. The fixed effects are constant across individuals. One can define a fixed effect η_f by giving it 0 variance, thus making it constant. We estimate the variance of each η_r that corresponds to a random effect column in Λ_y. We thus model the regression-type random effects by estimating the covariance structure of the corresponding η_r. As a result, two somewhat different analytic strategies are necessary depending on whether $Z_i = 0$. Because one can generalize these two basic strategies to represent many different models, we show an example of each: a repeated-measures ANOVA ($Z_i = 0$) and a linear growth curve model as an example of the random coefficients model ($Z_i \neq 0$). We (Rovine & Molenaar, 1998) provided more detail on how to use covariance structure modeling to estimate more complex repeated-measures ANOVA while imposing a number of different patterned structures, including compound symmetry, banded, and AR(1) on the covariance matrix of the errors.

The LISREL model to consider is

$$y = \tau_y + \Lambda_y \eta + \varepsilon, \tag{3.19}$$

where y is an $n \times 1$ vector of the response variables, τ_y is an $n \times 1$ vector of constant intercept terms, η is an $m \times 1$ random vector of latent variables, Λ_y is an $n \times m$ matrix of regression coefficients of y on η, and ε is an $n \times 1$ vector of measurement errors in y, and

$$\eta = \alpha + B\eta + \zeta, \tag{3.20}$$

where α is an $m \times 1$ vector of constant intercept terms, B is an $m \times m$ matrix of structural regression coefficients among the η, and ζ is an $m \times 1$ vector of equation errors.

The GLMM form of the one-way repeated-measures ANOVA model is described by Equation 3.6. As described above, we use Λ_y as a design matrix and model the covariance of the residuals, ε in Θ_ε.

If $B = 0$ and $\Psi = 0$ where $\Psi = \text{cov}(\zeta, \zeta^T)$, then η is a constant vector. With $\tau_y = 0$, Equation 3.19 now becomes

$$y = \Lambda_y \eta + \varepsilon. \tag{3.21}$$

The expectation of η is

$$E[\eta] = \alpha. \tag{3.22}$$

η are the direct estimates of the fixed-effect parameters, and ε is a vector of regression residuals one would get by regressing out the fixed-effect part of the mixed model. The covariance matrix of these within-subject errors is θ_ε. One can pattern θ_ε to represent a hypothesized covariance structure and test that structure as part of the model.

In words, by fixing Ψ to 0, one defines the η as constant. The residuals that remain after regressing out the fixed effects can then be patterned by applying the appropriate set of constraints.

A LISREL Model for the Repeated-Measures ANOVA

Consider a design that represents a two-way (4 Time × 2 Group) ANOVA. To model this design one would include vectors in the design matrix to represent Group membership, the Time effect, and the Time × Group interaction. For example,

$$
\Lambda_{y\,\text{Group 1}} = \begin{bmatrix} 1 & 1 & 1 & 0 & 0 & 1 & 0 & 0 \\ 1 & 1 & 0 & 1 & 0 & 0 & 1 & 0 \\ 1 & 1 & 0 & 0 & 1 & 0 & 0 & 1 \\ 1 & 1 & 0 & 0 & 0 & 0 & 0 & 0 \end{bmatrix};
$$

$$
\Lambda_{y\,\text{Group 2}} = \begin{bmatrix} 1 & 0 & 1 & 0 & 0 & 0 & 0 & 0 \\ 1 & 0 & 0 & 1 & 0 & 0 & 0 & 0 \\ 1 & 0 & 0 & 0 & 1 & 0 & 0 & 0 \\ 1 & 0 & 0 & 0 & 0 & 0 & 0 & 0 \end{bmatrix}
$$

$$
\alpha = \begin{bmatrix} \alpha_1 \\ \alpha_2 \\ \alpha_3 \\ \alpha_4 \\ \alpha_5 \\ \alpha_6 \\ \alpha_7 \\ \alpha_8 \end{bmatrix}; \quad \Theta_\varepsilon = \begin{bmatrix} \varepsilon_{11} & \varepsilon_{21} & \varepsilon_{31} & \varepsilon_{41} \\ \varepsilon_{21} & \varepsilon_{22} & \varepsilon_{32} & \varepsilon_{42} \\ \varepsilon_{31} & \varepsilon_{32} & \varepsilon_{33} & \varepsilon_{43} \\ \varepsilon_{41} & \varepsilon_{42} & \varepsilon_{43} & \varepsilon_{44} \end{bmatrix}. \tag{3.23}
$$

Notice that the parameters of the α vector and the Θ_ε matrix have the same values, regardless of the group.

If the data were observed monthly for 4 consecutive months, one might select the AR(1) pattern as appropriate to model the autocorrelation among the residuals. One could include this pattern using the following nonlinear constraints:

$$
\theta_{\varepsilon_{3,1}} = \theta_{\varepsilon_{2,1}}^2 / \theta_{\varepsilon_{1,1}}
$$
$$
\theta_{\varepsilon_{4,1}} = \theta_{\varepsilon_{2,1}}^3 / \theta_{\varepsilon_{1,1}}^2
$$
$$
\theta_{\varepsilon_{2,1}} = \theta_{\varepsilon_{3,2}} = \theta_{\varepsilon_{4,3}} \tag{3.24}
$$
$$
\theta_{\varepsilon_{3,1}} = \theta_{\varepsilon_{4,2}}
$$
$$
\theta_{\varepsilon_{1,1}} = \theta_{\varepsilon_{2,2}} = \theta_{\varepsilon_{3,3}} = \theta_{\varepsilon_{4,4}}.
$$

These constraints yield the patterned covariance matrix of residuals,

$$
\sigma^2 \begin{bmatrix} 1 & \rho & \rho^2 & \rho^3 \\ \rho & 1 & \rho & \rho^2 \\ \rho^2 & \rho & 1 & \rho \\ \rho^3 & \rho^2 & \rho & 1 \end{bmatrix},
$$

which is the AR(1) covariance structure.

To estimate this multiple-group model, one would specify this pattern for θ_ε and then constrain α and θ_ε equal across groups. Using this method, one can model a relatively broad range of ANOVA models in a fairly simple fashion.

A LISREL Model for the Random Coefficients Model

We now turn to an example of the random coefficients model, the linear curve model. We include the design matrix vectors related to both of the fixed (β) and random (γ_i) effects in the Λ_y matrix of the LISREL model. By doing this, we are able to estimate the covariance matrix of the random effects, D, and the variance of the "within-subject" errors, σ_ε^2.

We create the design matrix for this model by concatenating in Λ_y the vectors related to both the fixed and random effects. With both X_i and Z_i in the design matrix, Λ_y, we partition the Ψ matrix using a block diagonal structural in which a 0 matrix corresponds to the fixed-effects part of the model and a covariance matrix, Ψ_r, corresponds to the random-effects part of the model. Ψ and θ_ε can now be used to model the covariance structure of the random effects. The constraints necessary are those that when applied, yield the structure in Equation 3.18. This structure results if one (a) constrains the diagonal values in θ_ε equal and (b) freely estimates the elements in Ψ corresponding to the random effect vectors. In terms of Equation 3.18, the covariance for the ith participant then becomes

$$\sigma^2 V_i = Z\Psi_r Z^T + \Theta_\varepsilon. \tag{3.25}$$

The lower diagonal of Ψ, then, is $\sigma^2 \times D$. The diagonal elements of θ_ε equal σ^2, where Ψ and Θ_ε are the LISREL estimates. Because the design matrix is the same for all participants, we can drop the subscript i.

We now present a LISREL implementation for the covariance structure model described above. This model is used to estimate the linear growth curve model described above. For this model,

$$y_i = \Lambda_y \eta + \varepsilon = \begin{bmatrix} 1 & 1 & 0 & 0 & 1 & 1 \\ 1 & 2 & 0 & 0 & 1 & 2 \\ 1 & 3 & 0 & 0 & 1 & 3 \\ 1 & 4 & 0 & 0 & 1 & 4 \end{bmatrix} \begin{bmatrix} \eta_1 \\ \eta_2 \\ \eta_3 \\ \eta_4 \\ \eta_5 \\ \eta_6 \end{bmatrix} + \begin{bmatrix} \varepsilon_1 \\ \varepsilon_2 \\ \varepsilon_3 \\ \varepsilon_4 \end{bmatrix} \tag{3.26}$$

is the parameterization for Group 1. The first four columns of Λ_y represent the fixed effects, and the last two columns represent the random effects.

The means vector for this model is

$$\alpha^T = [\alpha_1 \ \alpha_2 \ \alpha_3 \ \alpha_4 \ 0 \ 0], \tag{3.27}$$

where $\alpha_1 - \alpha_4$ are the means for the fixed effects. The means for the random effects are 0.

For Group 2,

$$y_i = \Lambda_y \eta + \varepsilon = \begin{bmatrix} 1 & 1 & 1 & 1 & 1 & 1 \\ 1 & 2 & 1 & 2 & 1 & 2 \\ 1 & 3 & 1 & 3 & 1 & 3 \\ 1 & 4 & 1 & 4 & 1 & 4 \end{bmatrix} \begin{bmatrix} \eta_1 \\ \eta_2 \\ \eta_3 \\ \eta_4 \\ \eta_5 \\ \eta_6 \end{bmatrix} + \begin{bmatrix} \varepsilon_1 \\ \varepsilon_2 \\ \varepsilon_3 \\ \varepsilon_4 \end{bmatrix}. \tag{3.28}$$

To show how one obtains the covariance structure among the repeated measures, we first consider the expected covariance matrix for the first group, which is

$$\Sigma_{G_1} = \Lambda_y \Psi \Lambda_y^T + \Theta_\varepsilon = \begin{bmatrix} 1 & 1 & 0 & 0 & 1 & 1 \\ 1 & 2 & 0 & 0 & 1 & 2 \\ 1 & 3 & 0 & 0 & 1 & 3 \\ 1 & 4 & 0 & 0 & 1 & 4 \end{bmatrix}$$

$$\begin{bmatrix} 0 & 0 & 0 & 0 & 0 & 0 \\ 0 & 0 & 0 & 0 & 0 & 0 \\ 0 & 0 & 0 & 0 & 0 & 0 \\ 0 & 0 & 0 & 0 & 0 & 0 \\ 0 & 0 & 0 & 0 & \psi_{55} & \psi_{56} \\ 0 & 0 & 0 & 0 & \psi_{65} & \psi_{66} \end{bmatrix} \begin{bmatrix} 1 & 1 & 1 & 1 \\ 1 & 2 & 3 & 4 \\ 0 & 0 & 0 & 0 \\ 0 & 0 & 0 & 0 \\ 1 & 1 & 1 & 1 \\ 1 & 2 & 3 & 4 \end{bmatrix}$$

$$+ \begin{bmatrix} \theta_{\varepsilon 11} & 0 & 0 & 0 \\ 0 & \theta_{\varepsilon 22} & 0 & 0 \\ 0 & 0 & \theta_{\varepsilon 33} & 0 \\ 0 & 0 & 0 & \theta_{\varepsilon 44} \end{bmatrix}. \tag{3.29}$$

The covariances between the fixed and random effects in Ψ are fixed at 0. This has the effect of breaking down the covariance matrix (for Group 1) among the response variables as

$$\Sigma_{G_1} = \Sigma_{\text{fixed effects}} + \Sigma_{\text{random effects}} = 0 + \Sigma_{\text{random effects}}. \tag{3.30}$$

This implies that

$$\Sigma_{G_1} = \Lambda_y \Psi \Lambda_y^T + \Theta_\varepsilon = Z \Psi_r Z^T + \Theta_\varepsilon; \tag{3.31}$$

thus, according to Equation 3.24,

$$\sigma^2 V_i = \Sigma_{G_1}, \tag{3.32}$$

and the same results would hold for all other groups.

Figure 3.3 plots the data for Group 1 and indicates the fitted linear growth curve for that group. A graphical representation of the model is presented in Figure 3.4. The coefficients associated with the arrows linking the η to the y_i represent the fixed values from the design matrix Λ_y. Arrows are not drawn for

FIGURE 3.3

A plot of the individual data along with the group line for 11 girls (Group 1) from Potthof and Roy's (1964) data set. DEP = dependent.

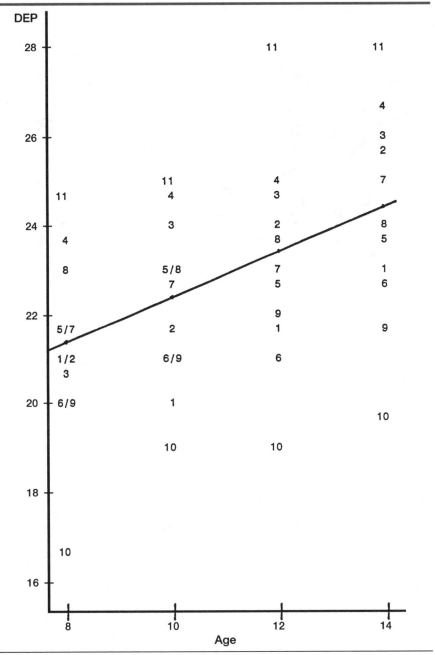

FIGURE 3.4

A graphical representation of the linear curve model for Group 1.

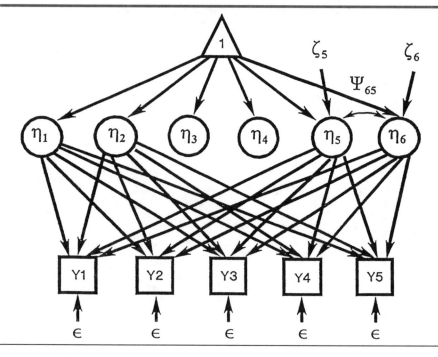

coefficients with values of 0. Because the variances related to the fixed effect η are all 0, only ζ_5 and ζ_6 are shown. Ψ_{65} is the covariance between ζ_5 and ζ_6, which is equal to the covariance between η_5 and η_6, because the latter are exogenous. The triangle in Figure 3.4 represents a constant. The path coefficients linking the constant to the η are the α. The variances of the ε are constrained equal.

The Group 2 model would differ from the Group 1 only in that nonzero coefficients linking η_3 and η_4 to the y_i would be included.

Predicting the Individual Random Effects

One can obtain the predicted values for each individual's curve using the estimates of σ^2 and D. First, best linear unbiased predicted values of the random effects (Harville, 1977; Jones, 1993; Robinson, 1991) can be obtained by

$$\hat{\gamma}_i = \hat{D}Z_i^T\hat{V}^{-1}(y_i - X_i\hat{\beta}). \tag{3.33}$$

These values are the deviations of each individual's slope and intercept from the group values. Given γ_i and β, one can predict each individual's curve values as

$$\hat{y}_i = X_i \hat{\beta} + Z_i \hat{\gamma}_i. \tag{3.34}$$

As an alternative, one can predict the individual random effects by treating the above model as a factor model and estimating factor scores. LISREL can be used to obtain the factor score regressions. A simple interactive FORTRAN program called FSCORE can be used to compute the individual factor scores (Molenaar, 1996). This program is available on request (Peter Molenaar: op_molenaar@macmail.psy.uva.edu).

Examples

Potthoff and Roy

As a first example, we analyze data presented by Pothoff and Roy (1964), who reported the measured distance from the center of the pituitary to the ptery-gomaxillary fissure for 11 girls and 16 boys at ages 8, 10, 12, and 14. We analyze the data hypothesizing a linear growth curve model and test whether the parameters of the straight lines representing growth differ according to gender.

The LISREL model for the first group (the girls) is

$$y_i = \Lambda_y \eta + \varepsilon_i = \begin{bmatrix} 1 & 8 & 0 & 0 & 1 & 8 \\ 1 & 10 & 0 & 0 & 1 & 10 \\ 1 & 12 & 0 & 0 & 1 & 12 \\ 1 & 14 & 0 & 0 & 1 & 14 \end{bmatrix} \begin{bmatrix} \eta_1 \\ \eta_2 \\ \eta_3 \\ \eta_4 \\ \eta_5 \\ \eta_6 \end{bmatrix} + \begin{bmatrix} \varepsilon_{i1} \\ \varepsilon_{i2} \\ \varepsilon_{i3} \\ \varepsilon_{i4} \end{bmatrix}, \tag{3.35}$$

and for the second group (boys) is

$$y_i = \Lambda_y \eta + \varepsilon_i = \begin{bmatrix} 1 & 8 & 1 & 8 & 1 & 8 \\ 1 & 10 & 1 & 10 & 1 & 10 \\ 1 & 12 & 1 & 12 & 1 & 12 \\ 1 & 14 & 1 & 14 & 1 & 14 \end{bmatrix} \begin{bmatrix} \eta_1 \\ \eta_2 \\ \eta_3 \\ \eta_4 \\ \eta_5 \\ \eta_6 \end{bmatrix} + \begin{bmatrix} \varepsilon_{i1} \\ \varepsilon_{i2} \\ \varepsilon_{i3} \\ \varepsilon_{i4} \end{bmatrix}. \tag{3.36}$$

Note that the coding vector values related to slope parameter represent the points along the time axis when the measures were taken. This easily allows unequal spacing between occasions to be included in the model. The vector of means, which is constrained equal across groups, is

$$\alpha^T = [\alpha_1 \ \alpha_2 \ \alpha_3 \ \alpha_4 \ 0 \ 0], \tag{3.37}$$

where the α_k are the direct parameter estimates of the fixed effects. The random coefficients structure is modeled in the Ψ and θ_ε matrices, respectively, with

$$\Psi = \begin{bmatrix} 0 & 0 & 0 & 0 & 0 & 0 \\ 0 & 0 & 0 & 0 & 0 & 0 \\ 0 & 0 & 0 & 0 & 0 & 0 \\ 0 & 0 & 0 & 0 & 0 & 0 \\ 0 & 0 & 0 & 0 & \psi_{55} & \psi_{65} \\ 0 & 0 & 0 & 0 & \psi_{65} & \psi_{66} \end{bmatrix}; \quad \Theta_\varepsilon = \begin{bmatrix} \theta_{\varepsilon 11} & 0 & 0 & 0 \\ 0 & \theta_{\varepsilon 22} & 0 & 0 \\ 0 & 0 & \theta_{\varepsilon 33} & 0 \\ 0 & 0 & 0 & \theta_{\varepsilon 44} \end{bmatrix}. \quad (3.38)$$

We now impose the following constraints: $\theta_{\varepsilon 11} = \theta_{\varepsilon 22} = \theta_{\varepsilon 33} = \theta_{\varepsilon 44}$.

The results of the LISREL analysis appear in Table 3.1, which includes the variances of the respective random effects, the covariance between random intercept and slope, and the fixed effects. These effects include $\beta_3 = \alpha_3$ and $\beta_4 = \alpha_4$, which are the tests of the respective differences in group intercepts and slopes. As one can see, there is no significant difference in the intercepts for boys and girls; there is, however, a significant difference in slope indicating that the boys are growing at a slower rate than the girls.

Figure 3.3 graphs the group line and some sample individual lines along with the original data. For each individual, one can see that the observed values are scattered around the individual lines, which are determined by the predicted values (Equation 3.34). Within a group, the individual lines deviate around the group line. The differences in slope and intercept are given by Equation 3.32.

In Appendixes 3A and 3B, we provide the best linear unbiased predicted estimates of the individual slopes and intercepts, the predicted values for each individual, and original data.

TABLE 3.1

Estimates for the Random Coefficients Model Using Pothoff and Roy's (1964) Data: LISREL Estimates

PARAMETER	ESTIMATE	SE	t( )	PARAMETER INTERPRETATION
σ^2	1.849	0.369	5.00	Residual variance
Ψ_{55}	4.951	5.241	0.94	Random intercept variance
Ψ_{65}	−0.217	0.425	−0.51	Random intercept–slope covariance
Ψ_{66}	0.026	0.038	0.67	Random slope variance
β_1	16.341	1.052	15.53	Intercept (girls' group)
β_2	0.784	0.089	8.83	Slope (girls' group)
β_3	1.032	1.663	0.62	Intercept difference (boys vs. girls)
β_4	−0.305	0.140	−2.17	Slope difference (boys vs. girls)

Note. Goodness of fit (LISREL): χ^2 (20, $N = 27$) = 31.514, $p = .048$, non-normed fit index = .89; critical $N = 30.80$.

Belsky and Rovine

Belsky and Rovine (1990) analyzed data collected on husbands and wives. Data were collected on four occasions: 3 months prior to having a baby and 3, 9, and 36 months after the fact. In attempting to model stability and change, they analyzed the data using a 2 Group (gender of the child) × 4 Time repeated-measures ANOVA under the assumption of sphericity. They also used transformed polynomial variables to attempt to describe patterns of change in the data.

To show how the models described above can be used and compared, we select the variable *love* as measured on husbands across the four occasions and analyze these data first with a repeated-measures ANOVA. We test three different residual covariance patterns on these data: compound symmetry (equal variances and covariances), and AR(1) structure, and a general autoregressive pattern. We then analyze the data, hypothesizing a linear curve model. For the two-group repeated-measures ANOVA, we use the following model (for couples who had boys):

$$
y_i = \Lambda_y \eta + \varepsilon =
\begin{bmatrix}
1 & 1 & 1 & 0 & 0 & 1 & 0 & 0 \\
1 & 1 & 0 & 1 & 0 & 0 & 1 & 0 \\
1 & 1 & 0 & 0 & 1 & 0 & 0 & 1 \\
1 & 1 & 0 & 0 & 0 & 0 & 0 & 0
\end{bmatrix}
\begin{bmatrix}
\eta_1 \\ \eta_2 \\ \eta_3 \\ \eta_4 \\ \eta_5 \\ \eta_6 \\ \eta_7 \\ \eta_8
\end{bmatrix}
+
\begin{bmatrix}
\varepsilon_{i1} \\ \varepsilon_{i2} \\ \varepsilon_{i3} \\ \varepsilon_{i4}
\end{bmatrix}.
\quad (3.39)
$$

For couples who had girls we use

$$
y_i = \Lambda_y \eta + \varepsilon =
\begin{bmatrix}
1 & 0 & 1 & 0 & 0 & 0 & 0 & 0 \\
1 & 0 & 0 & 1 & 0 & 0 & 0 & 0 \\
1 & 0 & 0 & 0 & 1 & 0 & 0 & 0 \\
1 & 0 & 0 & 0 & 0 & 0 & 0 & 0
\end{bmatrix}
\begin{bmatrix}
\eta_1 \\ \eta_2 \\ \eta_3 \\ \eta_4 \\ \eta_5 \\ \eta_6 \\ \eta_7 \\ \eta_8
\end{bmatrix}
+
\begin{bmatrix}
\varepsilon_{i1} \\ \varepsilon_{i2} \\ \varepsilon_{i3} \\ \varepsilon_{i4}
\end{bmatrix}.
\quad (3.40)
$$

The direct estimates of the fixed effects again appear in the α vector. The θ_ε matrix can be patterned to reflect the hypothesized covariance structure of the residuals. A comparison of the parameter estimates, along with the model fits, appears in Table 3.2.

Of the three models tested, the model representing compound symmetry seems best for these data. This result seems reasonable if one considers the

TABLE 3.2

Estimates (Est.) and Model Fit Indices for the Repeated-Measures Analysis of Variance: Belsky and Rovine's (1990) Data

PARAMETER	COMPOUND SYMMETRY		AR(1)		BANDED	
	EST.	SE	EST.	SE	EST.	SE
$\theta_{\varepsilon 11}$	101.51	9.84	106.34	9.50	102.71	10.01
$\theta_{\varepsilon 22}$	101.51	9.84	106.34	9.50	102.71	10.01
$\theta_{\varepsilon 33}$	101.51	9.84	106.34	9.50	102.71	10.01
$\theta_{\varepsilon 44}$	101.51	9.84	106.34	9.50	102.71	10.01
$\theta_{\varepsilon 21}$	63.11	9.62	70.15	9.14	66.25	9.93
$\theta_{\varepsilon 31}$	63.11	9.62	46.27	8.20	64.57	10.00
$\theta_{\varepsilon 32}$	63.11	9.62	70.15	9.14	66.25	9.93
$\theta_{\varepsilon 41}$	63.11	9.62	30.53	6.91	59.72	10.56
$\theta_{\varepsilon 42}$	63.11	9.62	46.27	8.20	64.57	10.00
$\theta_{\varepsilon 43}$	63.11	9.62	70.15	9.14	66.25	9.93
α_1	72.24	1.44*	72.24	1.47*	72.24	1.45*
α_2	−1.09	1.90	−1.09	1.94	−1.09	1.91
α_3	3.26	1.25*	3.26	1.76	3.26	1.32*
α_4	2.68	1.25*	2.68	1.57	2.68	1.25*
α_5	1.10	1.25	1.10	1.22	1.10	1.22
α_6	1.38	1.65	1.38	2.32	1.38	1.75
α_7	0.19	1.65	0.19	2.07	0.19	1.65
α_8	1.63	1.65	1.63	1.60	1.63	1.61
χ^2 (N = 117)	39.62	a	78.27	a	37.55	b
p		.0024		.0000		.0018
AIC		59.62		102.27		61.55

Note. AR(1) = first-order autoregression; AIC = Akaike information criterion. $^a df = 18.$ $^b df = 16.$ $*p = .05.$

pattern of correlation among the four variables (see Table 3.3). Notice that for the first three occasions of measurement, the pattern of expected correlation in the presence of an autoregressive model does not hold (in particular, note that the ρ_{23} correlation is actually smaller than the ρ_{13} correlation). The models used also do not consider the unequal spacing of the variables. In terms of the autoregressive model one would have to model that spacing in the Θ_ε matrix. The results suggest that there is no GROUP difference or Group × Time interaction. As a result, the degree to which husbands reported love for their wives did not appear to depend on whether their child was a boy or a girl. There are differences in the means across Time, and these differences show up as signif-

TABLE 3.3

Correlation Matrix and Simple Descriptive Statistics for the Variable Love

MEASUREMENT OCCASION	1	2	3	4
1. −3 months	—			
2. 3 months	.77	—		
3. 9 months	.64	.60	—	
4. 36 months	.63	.61	.53	—
M	75.84	74.66	73.52	71.15
Variance	94.22	80.96	79.76	153.76

icant contrasts between Occasions 1 and 4 (α_3) and Occasions 2 and 4 (α_4). Note that had we selected the AR(1) error structure, our Time difference would have disappeared.

We next modeled the data by fitting a two-group linear curve model. The model for families with boys is

$$y_i = \Lambda_y \eta + \varepsilon_i = \begin{bmatrix} 1 & -3 & 0 & 0 & 1 & -3 \\ 1 & 3 & 0 & 0 & 1 & 3 \\ 1 & 9 & 0 & 0 & 1 & 9 \\ 1 & 36 & 0 & 0 & 1 & 36 \end{bmatrix} \begin{bmatrix} \eta_1 \\ \eta_2 \\ \eta_3 \\ \eta_4 \\ \eta_5 \\ \eta_6 \end{bmatrix} + \begin{bmatrix} \varepsilon_{i1} \\ \varepsilon_{i2} \\ \varepsilon_{i3} \\ \varepsilon_{i4} \end{bmatrix}. \quad (3.41)$$

For families with girls, the model is

$$y_i = \Lambda_y \eta + \varepsilon_i = \begin{bmatrix} 1 & -3 & 1 & -3 & 1 & -3 \\ 1 & 3 & 1 & 3 & 1 & 3 \\ 1 & 9 & 1 & 9 & 1 & 9 \\ 1 & 36 & 1 & 36 & 1 & 36 \end{bmatrix} \begin{bmatrix} \eta_1 \\ \eta_2 \\ \eta_3 \\ \eta_4 \\ \eta_5 \\ \eta_6 \end{bmatrix} + \begin{bmatrix} \varepsilon_{i1} \\ \varepsilon_{i2} \\ \varepsilon_{i3} \\ \varepsilon_{i4} \end{bmatrix}. \quad (3.42)$$

The results of this analysis appear in Table 3.4. Under the assumption of a linear curve model, we chose coding coefficients that are centered around the time of birth. This has the effect of placing the intercept at the time of birth.

A comparison with ANOVA models suggests that the linear growth curve has the best fit to the data. In terms of the substantive results, love decreased slightly over the course of the study. There was, however, significant variability in the individual slopes (i.e., some people improved, some people got worse, some stayed the same). We are now in a position to predict the individual lines.

TABLE 3.4

Linear Individual Curve Analysis for Belsky and Rovine's (1990) Data

PARAMETER	EST.	SE	PARAMETER INTERPRETATION
σ^2	31.35	2.92*	Residual variance
ψ_{55}	58.04	9.34*	Random intercept variance
ψ_{56}	0.16	0.20	Random intercept–slope covariance
ψ_{66}	0.02	0.01*	Random slope variance
α_1	74.92	0.13*	Intercept (boys' group)
α_2	−0.11	0.03*	Slope (boys' group)
α_3	−0.02	1.58	Intercept difference (girls vs. boys)
α_4	0.03	0.04	Slope difference (girls vs. boys)
α_5	0.0		Random intercept mean (fixed to 0)
α_6	0.0		Random slope mean (fixed to 0)
χ^2 (20, N = 128)	25.38		
p	.1873		
AIC	41.37		

Note. AIC = Akaike information criterion. *p = .05.

A Comparison of SEM With Other Methods for Estimating GLMMs

As mentioned above, the model presented here translates the GLMM into the language of SEM. This results in what is a very general design matrix based model. Although it might take some effort to either determine the correct model specifications or to type in the design matrix, an array of models can be estimated. It may be that certain models are more easily estimated using other software. More equation-based programs, such as HLM (Bryk, Raudenbush, & Congdon, 1996) or ML3 (Goldstein, 1995), may be easier to use when the number of groups with different patterns of design matrix coefficients is large or for situations in which it becomes difficult for the user to specify the appropriate design matrices. Also, although some people are more comfortable with SEM modeling, others are more comfortable with some of the other approaches. However, although for many interesting models the methods described are presented as an alternative to other estimation strategies, we think that there are some distinct advantages to estimating certain models as SEM.

Advantages

We first mention some options available in SEM that are not available (or are more difficult to realize) in dedicated multilevel modeling software such as SAS

Proc Mixed (SPSS Inc., 1999), HLM, ML3, or VARCL (Longford, 1993). A more complete discussion comparing these SEM models with other methods (including other latent-variable models) appears in Rovine and Molenaar (2000).

Researchers are, in general, often interested in finding a model that fits their data well. SEM is a model-fitting approach that has a natural saturated model against which the fit of any other model can be judged. The result of this quantitative judgment is the chi-square value. This is not the case in multilevel modeling, which has no such saturated model. Consequently, only restrictions can be tested.

SEM seems to be more flexible in the number of patterns that can be used to model the covariance structure of the residuals. Programs designed specifically for the GLMM come with a preprogrammed set of error structures. As far as we are aware, SAS Proc Mixed, with 16 different error covariance structures, provides the most options. SAS Proc Mixed is designed as a general-purpose mixed-model program, so this would be expected. Multilevel modeling programs typically concentrate on the random coefficients error structure, although other options are sometimes available. In SEM, the number of patterns is essentially unlimited, with the possibility of estimating parameters related to any patterns that can be described by a set of nonlinear constraints.

ANCOVA can be modeling by explicitly including the assumptions; more important, one can still model the data even when the ANCOVA assumptions are not met. Below we describe the setup for modeling ANCOVA as SEM. The means structures and the covariance structure can be modeled separately. One can see the advantages of this by comparing the repeated-measures ANOVA model with the linear growth curve model for Belsky and Rovine's (1990) data.

If one looks at the residual means for the repeated-measures ANOVA model, one sees that they are zero. This is because this model is saturated in the means (i.e., all effects and all levels of interaction are included in the design matrix). As a result, any lack of fit in the model is due to the lack of fit to the residual covariance matrix. In comparison, the linear growth model has residual means other than zero. This is because we fit a straight line through the occasion means. The residual means represent the degree to which occasion means deviate from those predicted straight-line means. The lack of fit for this model is due to both the fit to the means structure and the fit to the residual covariance structure. One thus can determine the respective contributions of the means and covariance structures to the overall fit of the model. In addition, functional relations between the means and parameters related to the covariance structure can easily be modeled.

Other benefits derived from the use of any SEM approach also are gained. Because of the measurement model capabilities of SEM, it becomes possible to introduce fallible covariates into the model. Certain of the coefficients in Λ_y can be estimated rather than fixed (under appropriate constraints), leading to latent curve analysis (McArdle & Hamagami, 1991; Meredith & Tisak, 1990) with both fixed and random effects.

Similarities and Difficulties

The method described in this chapter is most similar in conception to the SAS Proc Mixed procedure. As in that procedure, one breaks down the error structure into the "within" and "between" covariance matrices. One also separates the models for the fixed and random effects by including them as separate columns (related to different parameters) in the Λ_y matrix. On the surface, this type of model looks much different than the Level 1–Level 2 type model of equation-based programs such as HLM or ML3, but one must remember that the same general principles underlie these different methods.

We are essentially breaking down the sample into groups with identical design matrix values and then weighting each group by the sample size. So in Group 1, for example, N_1 participants have this set of design matrix values. As a result, within each group all members have the same number of repeated measures and, in the models presented here, we assume that each member is measured on the same occasions (even though the occasions may be unequally spaced). We can model situations in which certain individuals are missing certain occasions and, with the proper constraints, model situations in which different groups are measured on different occasions. However, as the number of groups increases and the number of measurement patterns increases, these models require more effort to be correctly specified. Methods are also available to handle design-related problems such as unbalanced sampling designs (Lee & Poon, 1993); however, depending on the nature of the design, and especially for researchers who are less familiar with SEM, these problems are currently more easily handled with dedicated multilevel modeling software.

As with other SEM strategies, one can handle missing data either by turning to other software with general missing-data capabilities, such as AMOS (Arbuckle, 1996) or Mx (Neale, 1993); through the use of specific strategies based on the multiple-group capabilities of SEM (Rovine, 1994; see also chapter 5, this volume); or through the use of techniques such as multiple imputation (Schafer, 1997; chapter 12, this volume).

ANCOVA in SEM

To include a covariate in fitting the SEM variants of multilevel models, one must regress out the covariate not at the latent-variable level but at the level of the measurement model. Only then is the variable regressed out of the manifest dependent variables (as defined in ANCOVA). To accomplish this one must include an additional η factor related to the covariate. In contrast to the other fixed η factors of the design, this factor has a mean and a variance. This can be accomplished as follows: The loadings in Λ_y associated with the extra η factor are

$$\begin{bmatrix} 1 & 1 & 1 & 0 & 0 & \lambda_{15} \\ 1 & 0 & 0 & 1 & 0 & \lambda_{25} \\ 1 & 0 & 0 & 0 & 1 & \lambda_{35} \\ 1 & 0 & 0 & 0 & 0 & \lambda_{45} \\ 0 & 0 & 0 & 0 & 0 & 1 \end{bmatrix}$$

The variance, ψ_{55}, is estimated (or fixed to the variance of the covariate), and $\theta_{\varepsilon55} = 0$. In SPSS (1999) ANCOVA, an additional restriction is imposed that $\lambda_{15} = \lambda_{25} = \lambda_{35} = \lambda_{45}$. This restriction can now be tested. If it does not hold, it can be dropped without complicating the analysis. For the linear curve estimated above, a requirement is that the η associated with the manifest covariable is uncorrelated with the original two ηs associated with the level and slope ($\psi_{31} = \psi_{32} = 0$). We are not sure how this is treated in multilevel software, but the restriction of equal regression weights might be imposed there as well.

Discussion

In this chapter, we have presented a method for estimating specific instances of the GLMM through the use of SEM techniques. This method allows one to estimate a number of different models in what has become for many researchers a familiar and comfortable framework. Included are certain models that come under the general headings of multilevel or random coefficient models. The method presented allows a direct translation of the design matrices and parameter vectors into corresponding SEM matrices. When compared with other methods that have been suggested for the estimation of multilevel models, such as SEM (Muthén, 1994; Muthén & Satorra, 1989), one sees that this method requires no ad hoc programming and provides direct maximum-likelihood estimates of the parameters. The individual random effects can be obtained in a fairly easy fashion. In sum, the SEM approach to the GLMM brings all of the flexibility of covariance structure modeling to a set of interesting and important models that are of considerable interest and importance to researchers in the social sciences.

References

Arbuckle, J. L. (1996). Full information estimation in the presence of incomplete data. In G. A. Marcoulides & R. E. Schumacker (Eds.), *Advanced structural equation modeling: Issues and techniques* (pp. 243–278). Mahwah, NJ: Erlbaum.

Belsky, J., & Rovine, M. (1990). Patterns of marital change across the transition to parenthood. *Journal of Marriage and the Family, 52,* 5–19.

Bentler, P. M. (1995). *EQS structural equations program manual.* Los Angeles, CA: BMDP Statistical Software.

Bryk, A. S., & Raudenbush, S. W. (1992). *Hierarchical linear models.* Newbury Park, CA: Sage.

Bryk, A. S., Raudenbush, S. W., & Congdon, R. (1996). *HLM: Hierarchical linear and nonlinear modeling.* Chicago: SSI.

Goldstein, H. I. (1986). Multilevel mixed linear model analysis using interactive generalized least squares. *Biometrika, 73,* 43–56.

Goldstein, H. I. (1995). *Multilevel statistical modeling.* London: Arnold.

Harville, D. A. (1977). Maximum likelihood approaches to variance component estimation and to related problems. *Journal of the American Statistical Association, 72,* 320–340.

Hayduk, L. A. (1987). *Structural equation modeling with LISREL.* Baltimore: Johns Hopkins Press.

Henderson, C. R. (1990). Statistical methods in animal improvement: Historical overview. In D. Gianola & K. Hammond (Eds.), *Statistical methods for genetic improvement of livestock* (pp. 2–14). Berlin: Springer-Verlag.

Jennrich, R. I., & Schluchter, M. D. (1986). Unbalanced repeated measures models with structured covariance matrices. *Biometrics, 42,* 805–820.

Jones, R. H. (1993). *Longitudinal data with serial correlation: A state-space approach.* London: Chapman & Hall.

Jöreskog, K., & Sörbom, D. (1993). *LISREL user's reference guide.* Chicago: Scientific Software.

Laird, N. M., & Ware, J. H. (1982). Random effects models for longitudinal data. *Biometrics, 38,* 963–974.

Lee, S., & Poon, W. (1993). Structural equation modeling with hierarchical data. In K. Haagen, D. J. Bartholomew, & M. Deistler (Eds.), *Statistical modeling and latent variables* (pp. 203–227). Amsterdam: Elsevier Science.

Long, J. S. (1983a). *Confirmatory factor analysis: A preface to LISREL.* Beverly Hills, CA: Sage.

Long, J. S. (1983b). *Covariance structure models: An introduction to LISREL.* Beverly Hills, CA: Sage

Longford, N. T. (1993). *Random coefficient models.* Oxford, England: Clarendon Press.

McArdle, J. J., & Hamagami, F. (1991). Modeling incomplete longitudinal and cross-sectional data using latent growth curve structural models. In L. M. Collins & J. C. Horn (Eds.), *Best methods for the analysis of change* (pp. 276–304). Washington, DC: American Psychological Association.

Meredith, W., & Tisak, J. (1990). Latent curve analysis. *Psychometrika, 55,* 107–122.

Molenaar, P. C. M. (1996). *FSCORE: A FORTRAN program for factor scores estimation in LISREL models* (Tech. Rep. Series No. 96-6. University Park: Pennsylvania State University, Methodology Center).

Muthén, B. O. (1994). Multilevel covariance structure analysis. *Sociological Methods and Research, 22*, 376–398.

Muthén, B. O., & Satorra, A. (1989). Multilevel aspects of varying parameters in structural models. In R. D. Bock (Ed.), *Multilevel analysis of educational data* (pp. 87–99). San Diego, CA: Academic Press.

Neale, M. C. (1993). *Mx: Statistical modeling*. Richmond: Medical College of Virginia.

Potthoff, R. F., & Roy, S. N. (1964). A generalized analysis of variance model used especially for growth curve problems. *Biometrika, 51*, 313–326.

Robinson, G. K. (1991). That BLUP is a good thing: The estimation of random effects. *Statistical Science, 6*, 15–51.

Rosenberg, B. (1973). Linear regression with randomly dispersed parameters. *Biometrika, 60*, 61–75.

Rovine, M. J. (1994). Latent variable models and missing data analysis. In A. von Eye & C. C. Clogg (Eds.), *Latent variables analysis* (pp. 181–225). Thousand Oaks, CA: Sage.

Rovine, M. J., & Molenaar, P. C. M. (1998). A LISREL model for the analysis of repeated measures with a patterned covariance matrix. *Structural Equation Modeling, 5*, 318–343.

Rovine, M. J., & Molenaar, P. C. M. (2000). A structural modeling approach to a multilevel random coefficients model. *Multivariate Behavioral Research, 35*, 51–88.

Schafer, J. L. (1997). *Analysis of incomplete multivariate data*. London: Chapman & Hall.

SPSS Inc. (1999). *Advanced models 10.0*. Chicago: Author.

Tabachnick, B. G., & Fidell, L. S. (1996). *Using multivariate statistics*. New York: HarperCollins.

Appendix 3A

LISREL Program for Estimating the Random Coefficients Model
(Potthoff & Roy's, 1964, data)

```
lisrel random coefficients pothoff and roy data
da ni=4 no=16 ma=cm ng=2
cm sy fi=spotroy.dat
me fi=ampotroy.dat
mo ny=4 ne=6 ly=fu,fi ps=sy,fi te=di,fr al=fr ty=ze
pa ps
0
0 0
0 0 0
0 0 0 0
0 0 0 0 1
0 0 0 0 1 1
pa al
1 1 1 1 0 0
ma ly
1 8 0 0 1 8
1 10 0 0 1 10
1 12 0 0 1 12
1 14 0 0 1 14
ma ps
0
0 0
0 0 0
0 0 0 0
0 0 0 0 4
0 0 0 0 -.1 1
eq te 1 1 te 2 2 te 3 3 te 4 4
st .5 te(1,1)
ou ns ad=off rs nd=4 xm fs it=200
group2
da no=11
cm sy fi=spotroy.dat
me fi=ampotroy.dat
mo ly=fu,fi ps=in te=in al=in ty=ze
ma ly
1 8 1 8 1 8
1 10 1 10 1 10
1 12 1 12 1 12
1 14 1 14 1 14
```

ou

spotroy.dat:
    6.016666667
    2.291666667   4.562500000
    3.629166667   2.193750000   7.032291667
    1.612500000   2.810416667   3.240625000   4.348958333
    4.513636364
    3.354545455   3.618181818
    4.331818182   4.027272727   5.590909091
    4.356818182   4.077272727   5.465909091   5.940909091
ampotroy.dat
    22.8750000   23.8125000   25.7187500   27.4687500
    21.1818182   22.2272727   23.0909091   24.0909091

Appendix 3B

Random Effects Predicted and Observed Values
for the Pothoff and Roy (1964) Data

SUBJECT I	GAMMA		PREDICTED				OBSERVED			
	γ_1	γ_2	Y_1	Y_2	Y_3	Y_4	Y_1	Y_2	Y_3	Y_4
1	−0.682	−0.039	20.206	21.085	21.964	22.844	21.0	20.0	21.5	23.0
2	−0.459	0.071	21.324	22.427	23.530	24.633	21.0	21.5	24.0	25.5
3	−0.031	0.093	21.922	23.067	24.212	25.357	20.5	24.0	24.5	26.0
4	1.611	0.030	23.067	24.088	25.109	26.129	23.5	24.5	25.0	26.5
5	0.438	−0.042	21.303	22.176	23.049	23.922	21.5	23.0	22.5	23.5
6	−0.862	−0.043	19.998	20.870	21.742	22.614	20.0	21.0	21.0	22.5
7	0.096	0.019	21.463	22.462	23.460	24.259	21.5	22.5	23.0	25.0
8	1.200	−0.053	21.984	22.836	23.689	24.542	23.0	23.0	23.5	24.0
9	−0.640	−0.064	20.053	20.883	21.714	22.544	20.0	21.0	22.0	21.5
10	−2.917	−0.065	17.769	18.597	19.426	20.544	16.5	19.0	19.0	19.5
11	2.245	0.093	24.206	25.353	26.500	27.647	24.5	25.0	28.0	28.0
12	1.631	0.074	24.841	26.558	28.275	29.993	26.0	25.0	29.0	31.0
13	−1.125	−0.024	21.292	22.812	24.331	25.850	21.5	22.5	23.0	26.5
14	−0.440	−0.017	22.035	23.569	25.103	26.637	23.0	22.5	24.0	27.5
15	2.546	−0.103	24.333	25.695	27.057	28.419	25.5	27.5	26.5	27.0
16	−1.561	−0.014	20.938	22.478	24.018	25.558	20.0	23.5	22.5	26.0
17	1.254	−0.002	23.848	25.411	26.974	28.537	24.5	25.5	27.0	28.5
18	−0.911	−0.014	21.591	23.131	24.672	26.212	22.0	22.0	24.5	26.5
19	−0.123	−0.101	21.931	23.297	24.664	26.031	24.0	21.5	24.5	25.5
20	−0.311	0.041	22.640	24.292	25.945	27.598	23.0	20.5	31.0	26.0
21	3.335	0.057	26.410	28.094	29.778	31.461	27.5	28.0	31.0	31.5
22	0.055	−0.115	21.750	23.089	24.428	25.766	23.0	23.0	23.5	25.0
23	−0.996	0.034	21.897	23.535	25.173	26.811	21.5	23.5	24.0	28.0
24	−3.108	0.232	21.370	23.404	25.439	27.474	17.0	24.5	26.0	29.5
25	0.509	−0.055	22.681	24.149	25.597	27.054	22.5	25.5	25.5	26.0
26	−0.105	0.083	23.181	24.918	26.655	28.392	23.0	24.5	26.0	30.0
27	−0.894	−0.076	21.105	22.519	23.934	25.349	22.0	21.5	23.5	25.0

COMMENT (on Chapters 2 and 3):
Advances in the Application of Multilevel Models to the Analysis of Change

D. Wayne Osgood

In recent years, interest in using multilevel models to analyze change has grown rapidly. The chapters by Michael Rovine and Peter Molenaar and by Stephen Raudenbush are both valuable contributions to this approach to analyzing change. I am glad to have been asked to comment on these chapters, and I use this opportunity to offer some general observations about multilevel modeling of longitudinal data as well. I begin with my view of the main contributions of each chapter.

Chapter 3

Rovine and Molenaar use covariance structure analysis to implement multilevel models of change. Thus, their work falls within a general approach initiated by McArdle and Epstein (1987) and presented to a broader audience by Willett and Sayer (1994). Rovine and Molenaar's chapter lays out a promising path for expanding the range of applications for this approach by segregating fixed effects from random effects in their structural equation models. Fixed effects characterize mean levels as they differ over repeated observations and between groups, whereas random effects characterize the systematic patterning of the residual variance around these means. Combining this separation of fixed and random effects with the multiple-group feature of covariance structure models, Rovine and Molenaar provide readers with a framework for adding between-group comparisons to covariance structure models of within-individual change. I think that their approach will prove to be influential because it is flexible and straightforward and because they have presented it so clearly.

Rovine and Molenaar's chapter demonstrates some important points about multilevel modeling of change in general and about the covariance structure approach in particular. Their work shows how the covariance structure approach is built on a layout of categorical independent variables, much like analysis of variance (ANOVA). A separate outcome variable defines each level of a within-subject factor, whereas a separate group defines each level of a between-subject factor. They use the factor pattern matrix (lambda in LISREL) to specify a design matrix that captures the effects of interest.

By developing both repeated-measures ANOVA and random coefficient growth curves models within their framework, Rovine and Molenaar show readers the essential similarity of two models that are often treated as dissimilar. A linear growth curve simply corresponds to a linear contrast among means of repeated observations. Unlike repeated-measures ANOVA, their approach does not require restrictive assumptions about the pattern of covariances among residuals. The framework can incorporate random coefficients, which generate certain types of patterns, or one can model the residual covariances directly.

It is interesting that the primary limitations of covariance structure models of change stem from the same source as their major advantages. Treating repeated observations as separate variables underlies the detailed specification of the structure of residual variance provided by this approach. Yet this treatment of occasions of measurement is poorly suited to some research designs that present no special problem for regression-based multilevel modeling approaches such as hierarchical linear modeling (HLM; Bryk & Raudenbush, 1992). Consider, for instance, a study in which the number of observations differs widely across individuals, by design or because of missing data. In a covariance structure model this would present the substantial difficulty that the number of variables in the model would differ across individuals. In a regression-based multilevel model it merely implies that the number of Level 1 observations varies across Level 2 units, which is entirely permissible.

A second limitation is that the covariance structure strategy for defining random effects applies to effects defined by comparisons among occasions, so these effects must be direct functions of time. Thus, this strategy does not provide a means of specifying random effects for measured time-varying variables, such as individual differences in responsiveness to support or stress. This is a point that Raudenbush develops in his chapter. Thus, where the covariance structure models allow a greater variety of patterns of covariance among residuals, the regression-based multilevel models are suited to a broader range of research designs and allow random effects for a greater variety of variables.

Chapter 2

In his chapter, Raudenbush develops a strategy for choosing a model that is well suited to one's needs. I think that this chapter has great value for practicing researchers. It addresses their primary concern, which is completing sound analyses that address their substantive questions, not becoming expert on the statistics for their own sake.

I appreciate Raudenbush's emphasis on putting issues before software in designing an analysis. Indeed, it is sobering to think about how often analysis choices are driven by personal experience using one program rather than another. Before turning to the choice of software, Raudenbush wants readers to think through all of the features of their studies that have important implications for their statistical models. This is important not only for pressing researchers to understand the choices they are making, but also for prodding statisticians and software developers to identify and fill the gaps where needs are greatest.

Readers should find Raudenbush's exercise in demystifying the vocabulary of multilevel modeling especially valuable. The variety of terminology is a great source of confusion, and it presents a substantial barrier to understanding the similarities and differences among available approaches. The primary lesson I gained from his review and explanation of the terms is that the title of a statistical approach or software package does not necessarily denote what is unique about that approach. More often than not, these titles designate features that are common to many, if not all, of the approaches to multilevel modeling. Thus, a good understanding of these terms is especially helpful for appreciating the similarities.

I am impressed with the decision framework that Raudenbush develops in his chapter. It identifies the important issues, and organizes them in a logical order. Researchers should find it quite useful. I am not convinced that this is necessarily the best decision framework, but that is just fine. What is critical is the recognition of the need for a coherent framework for attacking the task of choosing a model. His effort opens the door for further discussion about how one should design a multilevel model of change, which is at least as important to the field as mathematical and software development.

Expanding the Model of Within-Individual Change

Growth curves have been the primary basis for applying multilevel statistical models to the study of within-subject change. Rogosa, Brandt, and Zimowski (1982) first presented the idea of individual growth curves as an improved version of change scores. These curves would be polynomial functions characterizing individual patterns of change over time. Bryk and Raudenbush (1987) applied their multilevel modeling framework to these ideas by treating the coefficients of the polynomial terms as randomly varying across individuals. The value of the growth curve conception of change is readily apparent in the explosion of work on this topic, both in Bryk and Raudenbush's HLM framework and in other frameworks, such as covariance structure modeling (e.g., Willett & Sayer, 1994).

One of the things I like best about the chapters by Rovine and Molenaar and by Raudenbush, however, is that they show readers that multilevel statistical models of individual change are not limited to growth curves. I think this is critically important for understanding the full potential of multilevel models for studying within-subject change. Thus, although neither chapter gives this point any special emphasis, I would like to do so here.

In applying their multilevel framework to repeated-measures ANOVA, Rovine and Molenaar demonstrate that the within-subject component of multilevel models need not be limited to the continuous change implicit in growth curves. As they show, multilevel models are amenable to categorical contrasts among occasions, which are necessary for substantive questions that inherently imply discontinuous change. For instance, consider a program evaluation that uses multiple pretest and posttest observations to compare treatment and control groups. The contrast between the pretest period and the posttest period cannot be captured by a continuous growth curve, but it can be captured by a simple categorical coding of time (e.g., 0 for pretest, 1 for posttest). Furthermore, interactions between categorical and continuous codings of time are effective for capturing more complex patterns, such as gradual growth or decline in the program effect (Osgood & Smith, 1995). Categorical codings of time are also essential for modeling the impact of important life transitions, such as entering school, parental divorce, getting married, or retiring (Horney, Osgood, & Marshall, 1995).

Another distinctive feature of growth curve models is that change is solely a function of time itself. Raudenbush shows that multilevel models are not limited in this fashion but rather are also amenable to modeling change as a function of measured explanatory variables that vary over time. In particular, he models an individual's changing levels of tolerance for deviance as a function not only of age but also of that individual's recent exposure to delinquent peers. This requires no special elaboration of the HLM approach, for all time-varying explanatory variables are treated the same.

Yet the use of time-varying explanatory variables has profound implications for explanations of development and change. In growth curve models, coefficients for polynomials of time express an individual's pattern of change. Thus, to explain change, one seeks variables that account for variation in those coefficients across individuals. Unlike the original observations, which reflect single occasions, those coefficients characterize the person for the entire period under study. Therefore, the variables that would appear relevant to explaining these coefficients are stable factors, such as sex, race, or genetics, that characterize the person for the entire period, rather than variables that change, such as physical development, peer group norms, or exposure to opportunities. In other words, restricting the model of change to growth curves corresponds to conceiving of development as an unfolding of predetermined patterns, rather than as an open-ended process shaped by experience.

Our analyses need not be restricted in this fashion. One can model effects of experience by adding time-varying explanatory variables to the within-individual component of the model, as Raudenbush demonstrates for exposure to delinquent peers. If such a variable closely tracks within-individual subject change in the outcome variable, then it may account for much of the change that would be captured by the individual growth curves and for residual variance around those growth curves. Growth curves have no reality independent of the original, time-specific observations, so explaining variance in the time-specific observations can explain variance in the growth curves. It is an error of reification to assume that trajectories of change must be explained by time-constant variables. Multilevel models offer a range of options for analyzing change that is much broader than the basic growth curve formulation.

Modeling Dependence Over Time

Why does one need multilevel models of change? Why not use ordinary least squares statistics to answer questions about patterns of change over time? The reason is that longitudinal data, with multiple observations for a single sample of individuals, are almost sure to violate the assumption of independence of residuals. No matter how good one's explanatory model, there is little chance it will account for all of the within-individual similarity over time. Statistical theory tells us that violating the independence assumption does not bias estimates of the relationships of interest, but it does reduce the precision of those estimates, and it produces inaccurate significance tests, because of biased estimates of standard errors (Hanushek & Jackson, 1977, pp. 141–146).

Multilevel models solve these problems by explicitly modeling dependence among the residuals. This not only leads to valid significance tests but also may provide other useful information. For instance, consider a linear growth curve model that treats individual intercepts and slopes as random coefficients. Both Raudenbush's and Rovine and Molenaar's chapters show that individual differences in growth curve coefficients generate correlated residuals across waves of data. Because multilevel models include residual variance terms to capture those individual differences, they can yield appropriate significance tests. Furthermore, those variance components are informative in their own right, summarizing the degree to which individuals systematically differ in their average levels and their rates of change.

Rovine and Molenaar's and Raudenbush's chapters both show that multilevel methods have developed to the point that there is now a great variety of choices for modeling dependence. As a result, an analyst may choose among an extensive set of alternatives to arrive at an accurate and parsimonious model of dependence.

I think that researchers have now arrived at the point that they need a better understanding of the consequences of these choices for modeling dependence. Rovine and Molenaar suggest that researchers may gain power with a parsimonious model that accurately characterizes dependence with few parameters. Raudenbush indicates that the perfect model of dependence often may not exist, so compromises are necessary. How much can be gained by a parsimonious model, and how problematic are compromises? Practicing researchers need guidance about these choices. Statistical researchers could help in this regard by investigating the sensitivity of results to variations in models of dependence.

If the results presented in these chapters are any indication, perhaps this matter need not be so troublesome. In both chapters, the authors apply a variety of alternative specifications of dependence to the same data and find that many produce essentially equivalent estimates and standard errors. With a little luck, maybe future work in this area will show that a "perfect" model of dependence is not so critical and that a variety of "pretty good" models serve quite well.

Multilevel Models and Within-Individual Change

For my last point, I raise a question that does not come up in these two chapters but that I think needs more attention in the use of multilevel models to analyze change: Do multilevel models produce analyses of change? Although this question may seem superfluous in a volume titled *New Methods for the Analysis of Change*, the answer may be surprising to many readers. The standard multilevel model is no more or less an analysis of change than is an ordinary least squares analysis that ignores the longitudinal nature of the data.

Consider Rovine and Molenaar's analysis of data on physical growth of boys and girls for ages 8–14. Because the entire sample is observed at each age, age differences necessarily reflect within-subject change. Rovine and Molenaar's analysis qualifies as an analysis of change—but so would any other analysis relating age to this physical measurement, given this research design. This would not be the case if the sample varied in age at the beginning of the study or if one were interested in change produced by a measured explanatory variable, such as marriage or exposure to delinquent peers. In these cases, mean differences do not strictly reflect change because there is both within- and between-subject variance on the explanatory variable.

Even though one may allocate time-varying variables to the within-subject portion of a multilevel model, the resulting estimate pools the within- and between-subject relationships, just as would an ordinary least squares analysis. This is a simple fact about random coefficient models that is well recognized in analyses of context effects (Bryk & Raudenbush, 1992, pp. 121–123) and in the econometrics literature, where tests for consistency of within- and between-subject relationships are a standard part of the analysis (Greene, 1993). What one gains from a multilevel model are powerful tools for addressing dependence, but those are not tools to separate within-subject change from stable characteristics. I suspect that considerable confusion on this score stems from the emphasis on the growth curves, which have been promoted as an improved type of change score.

Am I claiming that multilevel models are not useful for studying change? Not at all. Fortunately, adding a term to the between-subject model (specifically, the individual mean on the variable of interest) is all that is necessary to convert a multilevel model to an analysis of change (Bryk & Raudenbush, 1992, pp. 121–123). My point is simply that there is widespread misunderstanding about the connection between multilevel models and the analysis of within-subject change. It is critical that this be clarified because interest in change is the primary reason for the trouble and expense of collecting longitudinal data. I think that this issue would be a good addition to Raudenbush's decision framework: An additional step in designing an analysis should be to determine whether additional elements are necessary to isolate change from stable individual differences.

Conclusion

I am pleased to have had the opportunity to comment on these two chapters. They represent important advances in the multilevel modeling approach to analyzing change, and I learned a great deal from them. They also stimulated me to think about the current state of this field, which led me to offer some observations of my own about areas that need more attention. The first area is that multilevel models are far more useful for analyzing change than is widely recognized because they are not limited to analyzing growth curves. Instead, they are equally useful for making categorical contrasts among time periods and for estimating effects of all time-varying explanatory variables. Second, now that multilevel models have developed to the point that they offer a wide range of options for specifying the dependence among repeated observations, the field would greatly benefit from work to identify consequences of greater and smaller misspecifications of the dependence. Finally, because I think that most researchers come to these models with an interest in analyzing change, I thought that it was important to point out that multilevel models of longitudinal data are not, inherently, analyses of change. Researchers need to be aware of the extra steps necessary to segregate change from stable individual differences.

References

Bryk, A., & Raudenbush, S. W. (1987). Application of hierarchical linear models to assessing change. *Psychological Bulletin, 101*, 147–158.

Bryk, A. S., & Raudenbush, S. W. (1992). *Hierarchical linear models: Applications and data analysis methods.* Newbury Park, CA: Sage.

Greene, W. (1993). *Econometric analysis* (2nd ed.). New York: Macmillan.

Hanushek, E. A., & Jackson, J. E. (1977). *Statistical methods for social scientists.* New York: Academic Press.

Horney, J., Osgood, D. W., & Marshall, I. H. (1995). Criminal careers in the short-term: Intra-individual variability in crime and its relation to local life circumstances. *American Sociological Review, 60*, 655–673.

McArdle, J. J., & Epstein, D. (1987). Latent growth curves within developmental structural equation models. *Child Development, 58*, 110–133.

Osgood, D. W., & Smith, G. (1995). Applying hierarchical linear modeling to extended longitudinal evaluations: The Boys Town Follow-Up Study. *Evaluation Review, 19*, 3–38.

Rogosa, D., Brandt, D., & Zimowski, M. (1982). A growth curve approach to the measurement of change. *Psychological Bulletin, 92*, 726–748.

Willett, J., & Sayer, A. (1994). Using covariance structure analysis to detect correlates and predictors of individual change over time. *Psychological Bulletin, 116*, 363–380.

Editors' Introduction

utoregressive models and growth curve models represent the two most frequently used approaches to analyzing longitudinal data in a structural equation modeling framework. Until recently, these were seen as mutually exclusive data analysis options. In fact, as David Kenny and Alex Zautra point out, the autoregressive models have fallen out of favor in recent years, branded as unsophisticated in comparison to latent growth curve models. Yet each of these models has advantages and disadvantages, and there might be occasions in which a phenomenon might contain elements of both autoregressive and growth curve models. For example, in addition to systematic growth over time, there might also be deviations from this systematic growth that have an autoregressive structure. In an exceptionally clearly presented chapter, Patrick Curran and Kenneth Bollen show how to weave the autoregressive and growth curve models together to address questions about the relation between development of antisocial behavior and depressive symptomatology in children. Then compare the Curran and Bollen approach to the latent difference score approach presented by John McArdle and Fumiaki Hamagami (chapter 5) and to the state-trait work of Kenny and Zautra (chapter 8).

The Best of Both Worlds

Combining Autoregressive and Latent Curve Models

Patrick J. Curran
Kenneth A. Bollen

There are various approaches to both the theoretical conceptualization and the statistical analysis of panel data. Two analytic approaches that have received a great deal of attention are the *autoregressive model* (or "fixed effects Markov simplex model") and random coefficient *growth curve models*. Researchers have attempted to identify the conditions under which the growth curve and autoregressive approaches do or do not provide useful results when applied to empirical longitudinal data (see, e.g., Bast & Reitsma, 1997; Curran, 2000; Kenny & Campbell, 1989; Marsh, 1993; and Rogosa & Willett, 1985). This critical comparative approach has tended to foster a polarization of views that has led many proponents of one modeling approach to reject the methods of the other, and vice versa.

However, what has become increasingly apparent is that there is not necessarily a "right" or "wrong" approach to analyzing repeated-measures data over time. The proper choice of a statistical model varies as a function of the theoretical question of interest, the characteristics of the empirical data, and the researcher's own philosophical beliefs about issues such as causation and change. Despite the more tempered view that different analytic approaches can reveal different things about the same data, the autoregressive and growth curve modeling approaches remain competing analytic viewpoints. A moderate position sees these two models as equally viable options in which the autoregressive model is more appropriate under some conditions and the growth

This work was funded in part by Grant DA13148 awarded by the National Institute on Drug Abuse. Additional information about this chapter and other related work can be found at http://www.unc.edu/~curran.

curve model works best under other conditions. Although this approach tends to be less adversarial than the correct–incorrect distinction, the result still remains an either–or scenario; that is, one adopts the autoregressive approach or the growth modeling approach, but not both.

Given that the autoregressive and growth curve models are each associated with certain key advantages and disadvantages, it seems logical to work toward synthesizing these approaches into a more unified general framework. If successful, this would allow for drawing on the strengths of both approaches that might provide even greater information than either approach taken alone. Our goal is to work toward developing such a synthesized longitudinal model of change.

In this chapter, we present an extended empirical example to illustrate our ongoing efforts to synthesize these models. Although we provide the basic equations and assumptions for the models that we estimate, our emphasis here is on the application of these techniques to an empirical example. A more technical treatment of our models is presented elsewhere (Bollen & Curran, 1999, 2000). We open this chapter with a description of a theoretical substantive question that motivates the development of the synthesized model. This is followed by a brief introduction to the data for the empirical example. We then present a review of the univariate and bivariate autoregressive simplex models followed by a general description of the univariate and bivariate latent curve models. In the next section, we propose the synthesis of the simplex and latent curve model for both the univariate and bivariate cases. The simplex, latent curve, and synthesized models are then systematically applied to the empirical data set to evaluate a series of questions relating to the developmental relation between antisocial behavior and depressive symptomatology in children over time. We conclude with model extensions on which we are currently working as well as directions for future research.

Developmental Relation Between Antisocial Behavior and Depressive Symptomatology

There has been a great deal of interest in the developmental relation between antisocial behavior and depressive symptomatology over time, both in terms of predictors of change in these constructs and potential bidirectional relations between them over time. Better understanding of these complex developmental processes are important not only for establishing the etiology of these disorders but also for helping inform prevention and intervention programs targeted at internalizing and externalizing symptomatology. Recent empirical evidence suggests that antisocial behavior and depressive symptomatology in childhood are related to one another, both cross-sectionally (e.g., Capaldi, 1991) and longitudinally (e.g., Capaldi, 1992). Despite these important findings, the specific nature of this developmental relation remains unclear. Specifically, it is not clear if the continuous underlying developmental trajectories of these constructs are related to one another or if instead the underlying trajectories are rather independent of one another but the time-specific levels of symptomatology are related over time.

For example, it may be that a steeply increasing developmental trajectory of antisocial behavior across time may influence the corresponding underlying trajectory of depressive symptomatology. Thus, the time-specific measures of these behaviors do not relate directly to one another but instead the relation is solely at the level of the continuous trajectory. Alternatively, these two underlying developmental trajectories may be relatively independent, but an elevated level of antisocial behavior at a particular time point might be associated with a subsequent elevation of depressive symptomatology at a later time point. In this case, there are two sources of influence on the repeated measures over time. The first is the influence from the underlying growth trajectory for that particular construct (e.g., antisociality), and the second is the influence from the time-specific preceding measures on the other construct (e.g., depression). So the time-specific observed measures of antisocial behavior are due to a combination of the continuous underlying developmental trajectory of antisociality and time-specific influences of depressive symptomatology.

Although it is rather straightforward to hypothesize a theoretical model such as this, current statistical methods are not well suited for empirically evaluating this model using sample longitudinal data (Curran & Hussong, in press). It is ironic that there are two well-developed analytic approaches that can be used to examine one component of the theoretical model or of the other but not of both. The Markov simplex modeling approach is well suited for examining the time-specific relations between two constructs over time, and the growth modeling approach is well suited for examining relations in individual differences in continuous developmental trajectories over time. At this point, there is no well-developed strategy for examining both of these components simultaneously (but see chapter 5, by McArdle and Hamagami, in this volume, for an important alternative approach to dealing with a similar type of problem). The development of such a model serves two key purposes. First, this technique allows for a comprehensive empirical evaluation of the developmental relation between antisocial behavior and depressive symptomatology over time. Second, this technique can be generalized and applied to many other types of longitudinal settings to evaluate similar types of questions.

Data for an Applied Example

The empirical data come from the National Longitudinal Survey of Youth (NLSY). The original 1979 panel included a total of 12,686 respondents, 6,283 of whom were women. Beginning in 1986, an extensive set of assessment instruments was administered to the children of the original NLSY female respondents and was repeated every other year thereafter. The data used here are drawn from the children of the NLSY female respondents, and three key criteria determined inclusion in the sample. First, children must have been 8 years of age at the first wave of measurement, a sampling design that helps control for developmental heterogeneity. Second, children must have data on all measures we use for all four waves of measurement. Finally, the sample includes only one biological child from each mother. On the basis of these three criteria, the final sample consisted of 180 children (57% were male).

Although there are a variety of powerful options currently available for estimating models with missing data (e.g., Arbuckle, 1996; Graham, Hofer, & MacKinnon, 1996; Little & Rubin, 1987; B. O. Muthén, Kaplan, & Hollis, 1987; L. K. Muthén & Muthén, 1998), for purposes of simplicity we ignore this complication to better focus on the proposed models. Of the initial 282 cases that met the selection criteria with valid data at Time 1, 29 (10%) were missing at Time 2; 76 (27%) were missing at Time 3; 79 (28%) were missing at Time 4; and 102 (36%) were missing one or more assessments at Times 2, 3, and 4. Thus, the final sample consisted of 180 (64%) of those children eligible at Time 1 and with complete data at Times 2, 3, and 4, and subsequent modeling results should be interpreted with this in mind.

Children's antisocial behavior and children's depressive symptomatology are the two constructs we consider. Antisocial behavior was operationalized using the mother's report on six items that assessed the child's antisocial behavior as it had occurred over the previous 3 months. The three possible response options were "not true" (scored 0), "sometimes true" (scored 1), or "often true" (scored 2). We summed these six items to compute an overall measure of antisocial behavior that ranged from 0 to 12. Depressive symptomatology was operationalized using the mother's report on five items that assessed the child's internalizing and depression symptoms having occurred over the previous 3 months using the same response options as for antisocial behavior. We summed the five items to compute an overall measure of depressive symptomatology with a range from 0 to ten. The means, standard deviations, and correlations for the four repeated measures of antisocial behavior and depressive symptomatology are presented in Table 4.1.

The Longitudinal Markov Simplex Model

One of the most important approaches developed for the analysis of panel data is the autoregressive or Markov simplex model. Its earliest development dates back to the seminal work of Guttman (1954), who proposed a model to examine the simplex structure of correlations derived from a set of ordered tests.

TABLE 4.1

Means, Variances, Covariances, and Correlations for Four Repeated Measures of Antisocial Behavior and Four Repeated Measures of Depressive Symptomatology

MEASURE	1	2	3	4	5	6	7	8
1. Time 1 antisocial	2.926	1.390	1.698	1.628	1.240	0.592	0.929	0.659
2. Time 2 antisocial	0.394	4.257	2.781	2.437	0.789	1.890	1.278	0.949
3. Time 2 antisocial	0.466	0.633	4.536	2.979	0.903	1.419	1.900	1.731
4. Time 4 antisocial	0.402	0.499	0.591	5.605	1.278	1.004	1.000	2.420
5. Time 1 depression	0.405	0.214	0.237	0.301	3.208	1.706	1.567	0.988
6. Time 2 depression	0.173	0.458	0.333	0.212	0.477	3.994	1.654	1.170
7. Time 3 depression	0.287	0.327	0.471	0.223	0.462	0.437	3.583	1.146
8. Time 4 depression	0.202	0.241	0.426	0.535	0.289	0.306	0.317	3.649
M	1.750	1.928	1.978	2.322	2.178	2.489	2.294	2.222

Note. Correlations are below the diagonal, covariances are above the diagonal, and variances are on the diagonal. All statistics are based on $N = 180$.

Anderson (1960), Humphreys (1960), Heise (1969), and Jöreskog (1970, 1979) further developed these univariate panel data models. The key characteristic of the simplex model is that correlations decrease in magnitude as a function of distance from the diagonal of the correlation matrix. When applied to longitudinal data, this means that later measures have progressively lower correlations with earlier measures as a function of increasing time. Furthermore, change in the construct over time is an additive function of the influence of the immediately preceding measure of the construct plus a random disturbance. The path diagram for the model is presented in Figure 4.1. The equation for the measured variable y at initial time period $t = 1$ is

$$y_{i1} = \alpha_1 + \varepsilon_{i1},\qquad(4.1)$$

and for subsequent time periods is

$$y_{it} = \alpha_t + \rho_{t,t-1}y_{i,t-1} + \varepsilon_{it},\qquad(4.2)$$

where $E(\varepsilon_{it}) = 0$ for all i and t and $COV(\varepsilon_{it}, y_{i,t-1}) = 0$ for all i and $t = 2, 3,$ ..., T. Furthermore, the variance of the measured y for all i at the initial time period is

$$V(y_{i1}) = \theta_{\varepsilon_1}\qquad(4.3)$$

and at subsequent time periods is

$$V(y_{it}) = \rho_{t,t-1}^2 V(y_{i,t-1}) + \theta_{\varepsilon_1},\qquad(4.4)$$

with the expected value for the initial time period

$$E(y_{i1}) = \alpha_1\qquad(4.5)$$

and for subsequent time periods

$$E(y_{it}) = \alpha_t + \rho_{i,t-1}\alpha_{t-1}.\qquad(4.6)$$

Each measure is only a function of the immediately preceding measure plus

FIGURE 4.1
Univariate Markov simplex model.

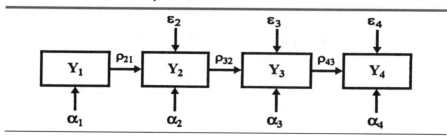

a random disturbance. This is the source of the term *autoregressive*—the measure at each time point is regressed onto the same measure at the previous time point. Variables assessed at times earlier than the immediately prior time have no direct impact on the current value. An implication of this model is that the correlation between time t and time $t + 2$ is zero when controlling for the effects of time $t + 1$; the influence of the measure at time t on the measure at time $t + 2$ is entirely mediated by the measure at time $t + 1$.

Another term for this autoregressive model is the *univariate simplex model* because of the focus on only a single variable. This model can be directly extended to the multivariate case with two or more distinct variables over time. These panel data models that include additional explanatory variables received considerable attention and development from several sources (e.g., Bohrnstedt, 1969; Campbell, 1963; O. D. Duncan, 1969; Heise, 1969; Jöreskog, 1979). We extend Equation 4.2 to include both the autoregressive parameters and the *crosslagged* coefficients that allow for influences across constructs (see Figure 4.2). These crosslags represent the longitudinal prediction of one construct from the other above and beyond the autoregressive prediction of that construct from itself. The initial measures remain as before, but subsequent measures on y are

$$y_{it} = \alpha_{yt} + \rho_{yt,yt-1} y_{i,t-1} + \rho_{zt,zt-1} z_{i,t-1} + \varepsilon_{y_{it}}, \qquad (4.7)$$

indicating that the measure of y at time t is a function of an intercept, the weighted influence of y at time $t - 1$, the weighted influence of z at time $t - 1$, and a random time-specific error, $\varepsilon_{y_{it}}$, that has a mean of zero and is uncorrelated with $y_{i,t-1}$ and $z_{i,t-1}$. An analogous equation holds for z_{it}, and the disturbances for these two equations are allowed to correlate. The substantive interpretations of the crosslagged parameter is that an earlier measure of z

FIGURE 4.2
Bivariate Markov simplex model with correlated disturbances.

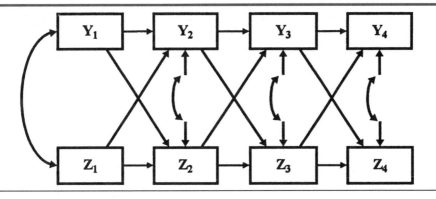

predicts a later measure of y above and beyond the previous measure of y. This is often referred to as an *autoregressive crosslagged* model.

Latent Curve Analysis

The preceding autoregressive univariate and bivariate models consider change over time in terms of each variable depending on its immediately prior value but not on its values for earlier periods. In addition, the autoregressive and crosslagged effects are the same for each individual. Although advantageous in many settings, this approach can be somewhat limiting when studying theoretical questions about individual differences in continuous developmental trajectories over time. Growth models approach the question of change from a different perspective. Instead of examining the time-adjacent relations of antisocial measures, we use the observed repeated measures to estimate a single underlying growth trajectory for each person across all time points. We can think of this as fitting a short time series trend line to the repeated measures for each individual. The x variable is time (where x equals 0, 1, 2, 3 in the case of four waves), the y variable is antisocial behavior, and we consider only 1 participant at a time. This line of best fit is an estimate of the individual's *growth trajectory* of antisociality over time. When a trajectory is fit to each individual in the sample, a researcher can compute an average intercept and average slope (sometimes called *fixed effects*) as well as the variability around these averages (sometimes called *random effects*).

Such developmental trajectories have long been hypothesized from substantive theory, but it has historically been quite difficult to properly estimate these trajectories statistically. There are several different approaches available for the estimation of these types of models, and one important example is latent curve analysis. Latent curve analysis is a direct extension of the structural equation model (SEM) that is common in the social sciences. The SEM approach simultaneously estimates relations between observed variables and the corresponding underlying latent constructs, and between the latent constructs themselves (Bentler, 1980, 1983; Jöreskog, 1971a, 1971b; Jöreskog & Sörbom, 1978). However, unlike the standard SEM approach, latent curve analysis explicitly models both the observed mean and covariance structure of the data (McArdle, 1986, 1988, 1989, 1991; McArdle & Epstein, 1987; Meredith & Tisak, 1984, 1990; B. Muthén, 1991).

From the SEM framework, the factor analytic model relates the observed variables y to the underlying latent construct η such that

$$y = v + \Lambda\eta + \varepsilon, \tag{4.8}$$

where v is a vector of measurement intercepts, Λ is a matrix of factor loadings (or measurement slopes), and ε is a vector of measurement residuals. The latent variable equation is

$$\eta = \alpha + \beta\eta + \zeta, \tag{4.9}$$

where α is a vector of structural intercepts, β is a matrix of structural slopes, ζ is a vector of structural residuals, and $V(\zeta) = \Psi$ represents the covariance structure among the latent factors. The model-implied mean structure is given as

$$E(y) = \mu = \nu + \Lambda(I - \beta)^{-1}\alpha, \tag{4.10}$$

and the covariance structure is given as

$$V(y) = \hat{\Sigma} = \Lambda(I - \beta)^{-1}\Psi(I - \beta)^{-1\prime}\Lambda' + \Theta. \tag{4.11}$$

Given that latent curve models are a direct extension of SEMs, one can use standard software such as AMOS, EQS, LISREL, or MPlus to estimate these models.

To estimate the variance components associated with the random growth coefficients, the latent curve analysis imposes a highly restricted factor structure on η through the Λ matrix. Consider an example in which there are $T = 4$ yearly measures of antisocial behavior collected from a sample of children. Two latent factors are estimated, one representing the intercept of the antisocial behavior growth trajectory (η_α), and the second representing the slope (η_β). This model is presented in Figure 4.3. The factor loadings relating the four antisocial measures to the intercept factor are fixed to 1.0 to define the intercept of the antisocial growth trajectory. The factor loadings relating the observed repeated measures to the slope factors are a combination of fixed and free loadings that best capture the functional form of the growth trajectory over the four time points. The initial approach is to fix the factor loadings to 0, 1, 2, and 3 to represent straight-line growth. The estimated mean of the intercept factor (μ_α) represents the initial status of the antisocial growth trajectory averaged across all individuals; the estimated variance of the intercept factor (ψ_α) represents the individual variability in initial levels of antisociality. Similarly, the estimated mean of the slope factor (μ_β) represents the slope of the antisocial trajectory averaged across all individuals, and the estimated variance of the slope factor (ψ_β) represents individual variability in rates of change in antisociality over time. Finally, the covariance between the intercept and slope factors is denoted $\psi_{\alpha\beta}$. Thus, the observed repeated measures are expressed as

$$y_{it} = \eta_{\alpha_i} + \lambda_t\eta_{\beta_i} + \varepsilon_{it}, \tag{4.12}$$

where $\lambda_t = 0, 1, 2, 3$ and

$$\eta_{\alpha_i} = \mu_\alpha + \zeta_{\alpha_i} \tag{4.13a}$$

$$\eta_{\beta_i} = \mu_\beta + \zeta_{\beta_i}. \tag{4.13b}$$

FIGURE 4.3

Univariate latent curve model.

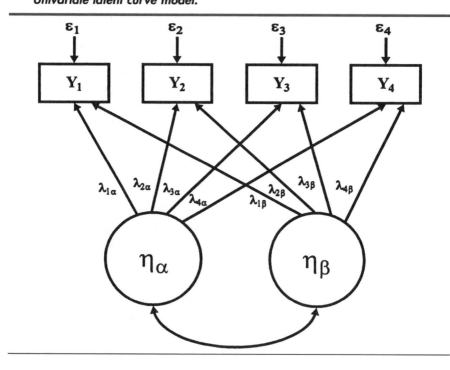

Substituting Equations 13a and 13b into Equation 12 leads to

$$y_{it} = (\mu_\alpha + \lambda_t\mu_\beta) + (\zeta_{\alpha_i} + \lambda_t\zeta_{\beta_i} + \varepsilon_{it}), \qquad (4.14)$$

where the first parenthetical term represents the fixed effect and the second term represents the random effect. The variance and expected value can then be expressed as

$$V(y_{it}) = \psi_\alpha + \lambda_t^2\psi_\beta + 2\lambda_t\psi_{\alpha\beta} + \theta_{\varepsilon_t} \qquad (4.15)$$

$$E(y_{it}) = \mu_\alpha + \lambda_t\mu_\beta. \qquad (4.16)$$

The latent curve model described above is considered *univariate,* given that growth in a single construct is considered. However, this model can easily be extended to a *multivariate* situation to consider change in two or more constructs over time. Technical details of this procedure were presented by MacCallum, Kim, Malarkey, and Kiecolt-Glaser (1997) and McArdle (1989), and sample applications include Curran and Hussong (in press); Curran, Stice, and Chassin (1997); S. C. Duncan and Duncan (1996), and Stoolmiller (1994). Conceptually, the multivariate growth model is simply the simultaneous estimation of two univariate growth models. A researcher estimates growth factors for each construct, and typically the relation between changes in the construct over time is modeled at the level of the growth factors. That is, we allow covariances among the factors across constructs, or, alternatively, one growth factor might be regressed onto another growth factor to examine unique predictability across constructs. Regardless of how an analyst estimates these, it is important to note that the relations across constructs are typically evaluated at the level of the growth trajectories, not at the level of the repeated measures over time.

Each of these modeling approaches is uniquely suited to examining a particular form of change over time. The autoregressive simplex explicitly models the time-specific relations within and between repeated measures of one or more constructs, whereas the latent curve model explicitly models these relations strictly at the level of the continuous trajectory believed to underlie these same repeated measures. It would be valuable in many areas of applied research to be able to simultaneously take advantage of the strengths of each of these approaches. Furthermore, it also would be useful to know whether the autoregression, the latent curve model, or some combination of these models best describes the data. To address these issues, we now work toward combining the autoregressive simplex and latent curve modeling strategies into a single comprehensive model of change over time.

Combined Autoregressive Latent Curve Model

This synthesis proceeds in a straightforward manner, and we begin with the univariate case presented in Figure 4.4. The model includes a random intercept and slope factor from the latent curve model to capture the continuous underlying growth trajectories over time. It also incorporates the standard autoregressive simplex parameters to allow for the time-specific influences between the repeated measures themselves. Whereas the means and intercepts are part of the repeated measures in the simplex model, the mean structure enters solely through the latent growth factors in the synthesized model. This parameterization results in the expression of the measure of construct y for individual i at time point t as

$$y_{it} = \eta_{\alpha_i} + \lambda_t \eta_{\beta_i} + \rho_{t,t-1} y_{i,t-1} + \varepsilon_{it}, \qquad (4.17)$$

which highlights that the time-specific measure of y is an additive function of the underlying intercept factor, the underlying slope factor, a weighted contribution of the prior measure of y, and a time-specific random error term that has a mean of zero and that is uncorrelated with the righthand side variables. Viewing the model from this equation one sees that the simplex and latent curve models are not necessarily in competition as to which is proper or im-

FIGURE 4.4

Univariate simplex latent curve model.

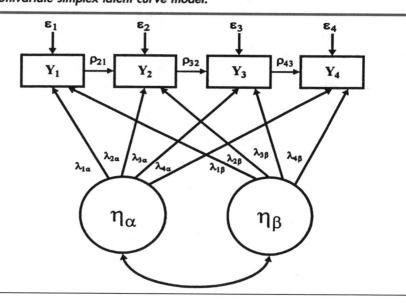

proper, but instead each is a restricted variation of a more comprehensive model.

Some implications of Equation 4.17 that are not immediately obvious concern the "factor loadings" of y_{i1} on $\eta_{\alpha i}$ and $\eta_{\beta i}$. In the usual latent curve model these loadings are fixed to 1 and 0, respectively. However, in the presence of an autoregressive structure for y, this is no longer true. The reason is that implicit in this model is that y_{i1} depends on y_{i0}, which in turn depends on $y_{i,-1}$, on back to the earliest possible value of y. Furthermore, each of these earlier (unavailable) ys would be influenced by $\eta_{\alpha i}$ and $\eta_{\beta i}$. Figure 4.5 represents these omitted earlier measures of y and their positions in the model in gray and the positions of the observed measures in black. As a result of these omitted ys, the factor loadings of y_{i1} on $\eta_{\alpha i}$ and on $\eta_{\beta i}$ depart from their values in a standard latent curve model. More specifically, the factor loading for y at time $t = 1$ on $\eta_{\alpha i}$ is

$$\lambda_{1\alpha} = \frac{1}{1 - \rho},$$
(4.18)

and the factor loading for y at time $t = 1$ on $\eta_{\beta i}$ is

$$\lambda_{1\beta} = -\left(\frac{\rho}{(1 - \rho)^2}\right),$$
(4.19)

FIGURE 4.5

Univariate simplex latent curve model with omitted measures preceding Time 1.

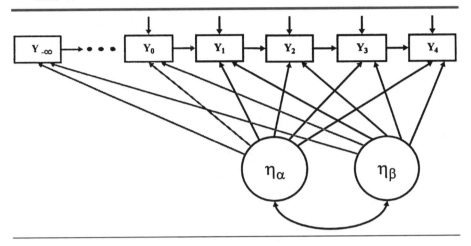

for which we assume that the autoregressive parameter is equal for all t ($\rho_{t,t-1}$ = ρ) and that $|\rho| < 1$. As $\rho \to 0$, then $\lambda_{1\alpha} \to 1$ and $\lambda_{1\beta} \to 0$, which corresponds precisely to the values imposed in the standard latent curve model. However, as the value of ρ departs from zero, then fixing these factor loadings to 1.0 and 0 becomes increasingly restrictive and likely leads to bias elsewhere in the model. The technical developments that lead to these results are presented in Bollen and Curran (2000) in which we also propose a form of this model that treats the y_{i1} as "predetermined" so that these nonlinear constraints are not needed.

We can extend this univariate combined model to the multivariate case to examine these relations both within and across constructs. Here, the measure of y at time t for individual i is composed of the influence from the growth factors underlying y, the prior measure of y, and now the prior measure of, say, z. This leads to

$$y_{it} = \eta_{\alpha_i} + \lambda_t \eta_{\beta_i} + \rho_{yt,yt-1} y_{i,t-1} + \rho_{zt,zt-1} z_{i,t-1} + \varepsilon_{it}. \qquad (4.20)$$

This combined bivariate autoregressive latent curve model is presented in Figure 4.6, in which the omitted lagged measures described above are portrayed in gray and the observed measures are portrayed in black. This model highlights that a given measure of y is an additive combination of the continuous growth process underlying y, the weighted influence of the preceding measure of y,

FIGURE 4.6

Multivariate simplex latent curve model with omitted measures preceding Time 1.

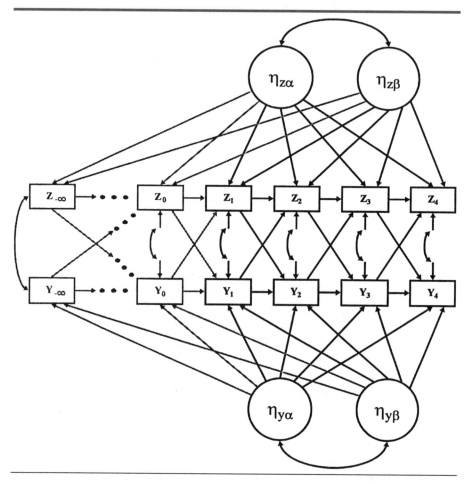

the weighted influence of the preceding measure of z, and a time-specific random disturbance.[1] The model simultaneously and explicitly incorporates the strengths of both the autoregressive simplex and the latent curve model and

---

[1]Several colleagues have suggested that instead of modeling autoregressive structure among the observed measures we instead model these effects directly among the time-specific residuals. We do not pursue this strategy given our desire to more explicitly combine the autoregressive (simplex) and growth curve modeling traditions. See Goldstein, Healy, and Rasbash (1994) for an example of autoregressive structures among residuals.

allows for a more comprehensive evaluation of change in one or more constructs over time.

To demonstrate this approach, we will now apply a series of simplex and latent curve models to an empirical data set to evaluate the developmental relation between antisocial behavior and depressive symptomatology over time.

An Applied Example of the Autoregressive, Latent Curve, and Synthesized Models

We now incrementally illustrate the univariate and multivariate models that we presented in the previous sections. We apply these to the relation between antisocial behavior and depressive symptomatology in the sample of $N = 180$ eight-year-old children.

Tests of Equality of Means Over Time: Antisocial Behavior

Although the summary statistics presented in Table 4.1 suggest that both the means and variances of antisocial behavior are increasing as a function of time, a more formal test of this relation is necessary. There are a variety of methods for executing such a test (e.g., paired t test, repeated-measures analysis of variance), but we evaluate the mean structure using an SEM approach. The advantage of this technique is that an extension of this mean difference model allows the estimation of both the simplex model and the latent curve model. We fit this model of equal means to the four antisocial-behavior measures. We did not constrain the variances and covariances of the repeated measures, and we placed no equality constraints on the means of the four measures. This model is just identified and thus has a chi-square value of zero. Next we imposed equality constraints on the four means, which resulted in $\chi^2(3, N = 180) = 11.1$, $p = .011$; incremental fit index (IFI) = .96, root mean square error of approximation (RMSEA) = .12, 90% confidence interval (CI) = .05, .20 (see Steiger & Lind, 1980, and Browne & Cudeck, 1993, for a description of the RMSEA; and Bollen, 1989, for a description of the IFI). On the basis of this poor model fit (e.g., although the IFI exceeded .95, this was in the presence of a significant chi-square and an RMSEA exceeding .10), the null hypothesis that all means are equal over time is rejected. In a moment, we will use a latent curve model to examine the patterning of these means as a function of time.

The Simplex Model With Means: Antisocial Behavior

We now fit the univariate simplex model to the four repeated measures of antisocial behavior. Given the findings of the mean difference model, we begin by including means in the simplex model. Although in the traditional simplex modeling approach the mean structure is usually omitted, this is not necessary. The baseline simplex model has each variable at a given time regressed onto its immediately preceding variable value. We estimate the mean and variance for the Time 1 measure and the intercepts and disturbance variances for the Times 2, 3, and 4 measures without any equality constraints. The model fit the data quite poorly, $\chi^2(3, N = 180) = 29.04$, $p < .001$; IFI = .88; RMSEA = .22; 90% CI = .15, .30. Next we include a series of equality constraints starting with the three autoregressive parameters, then on the variances of the three disturbances and, finally, on the three intercepts. None of these constraints led to statistically significant decrements in model fit relative to the baseline model, yet the final model still fit the observed data poorly, $\chi^2(9, N = 180) = 40.58$, $p < .001$; IFI = .86; RMSEA = .14; 90% CI = .10, .19. These results strongly suggest that the simplex model does not provide an acceptable reproduction of the observed covariances and mean structure of antisocial behavior over time.

The One-Factor Latent Curve Model: Antisocial Behavior

Given the clear rejection of the autoregressive simplex structure of the relations among the four antisocial measures over time, we turn to a one-factor random intercept model. This one-factor model is an intercept-only latent curve model and is functionally equivalent to a one-factor repeated-measures analysis of variance with random effects (Bryk & Raudenbush, 1992). Unlike the simplex model, in which each later measure is influenced only by the immediately preceding measure, the random-intercept model hypothesizes that all repeated measures are equally influenced by a single underlying latent factor and that it is this shared influence that is responsible for the observed covariance and mean structure. This model also implies that there is a stable component underlying the repeated measures over time that is not changing as a function of time. Given the earlier rejection of the equal-means model, we do not expect this model to fit well. Consistent with this prediction, the one-factor intercept model fit the observed data poorly, $\chi^2(8, N = 180) = 41.8$, $p < .001$; IFI = .85; RMSEA = .15; 90% CI = .11, .20). The latent intercept was characterized by both a significant mean ($\hat{\mu}_\alpha = 1.96$) and variance ($\hat{\psi}_\alpha = 2.12$), suggesting an important underlying stable component of the four measures. However, given the poor model fit, additional components of growth are likely necessary.

The Two-Factor Latent Curve Model: Antisocial Behavior

We re-estimated the random intercept model with the addition of a second latent factor to account for potential systematic change as a function of time. This second factor is a *slope* factor in latent curve analytic terms. The addition of this second factor led to a significant improvement in model fit over the one-factor model, $\chi^2(6, N = 180) = 14.8$, $p = .022$; IFI = .96; RMSEA = .09; 90% CI = .03, .15. The intercept and slope factors had significant means ($\hat{\mu}_\alpha = 1.73$ and $\hat{\mu}_\beta = .17$, respectively) and variances ($\hat{\psi}_\alpha = 1.67$ and $\hat{\psi}_\beta = .20$, respectively), indicating that there not only is evidence for a meaningful starting point and positive rate of linear change in antisocial behavior over time but also substantial individual variability in these growth factors.

The Two-Factor Latent Curve Model With Autoregressive Parameters: Antisocial Behavior

Up to this point, we have treated the autoregressive simplex and latent curve models as independent approaches to modeling the relations among the repeated measures of antisocial behavior over time. However, given that both modeling strategies analyze the observed covariance matrix and mean vector, it seems logical to expect that these apparently separate models may share a common parameterization. As a first step in working toward the synthesizing of the autoregressive and latent curve model, we estimated the two-factor latent curve model with the inclusion of the autoregressive parameters between the time-adjacent measures of antisocial behavior. This model is meant to simultaneously capture two components of change over time. The latent variable parameters represent individual variability in continuous rates of change over time, whereas the autoregressive parameters represent group-level influences present at the prior time point. We freely estimated the factor loadings between the Time 1 measure of antisocial behavior and the intercept and slope factors because of the possibility that the loadings may take on values other than 0 and 1 as described in Equations 4.18 and 4.19.[2] The estimated model with the autoregressive parameters did not result in a significant improvement in model fit, $\chi^2(1, N = 180) = 3.12$, $p = .08$; IFI = .99; RMSEA = .11; 90% CI = 0, .25, beyond that for the latent curve model only. Equality constraints on all three autoregressive parameters did not significantly degrade model fit, $\chi^2(3, N = 180) = 3.3$, $p = .35$; IFI = .99; RMSEA = .02; 90% CI = 0, .13, and none of the individual autoregressive estimates significantly differed from zero ($p > .10$). On the basis of these results, we concluded that the observed covariance and mean structure are best captured with the two-factor latent curve model without autoregressive structure.

---

[2]In the presence of a significant ρ parameter, a more formal evaluation of these factor loadings would include the imposition of a nonlinear constraint on λ as a function of ρ. Given the near-zero estimates of ρ, we did not proceed with the imposition of these nonlinear constraints.

Tests of Equality of Means Over Time: Depressive Symptomatology

Before estimating the full multivariate model, we must repeat the above uni-variate analyses for the four repeated measures of depressive symptomatology. We begin by testing for the equality of the means of depressive symptomatology across the four time periods using the same model we used for antisocial behavior. The first model had all parameters freely estimated and fit the data perfectly given the model is just identified. A re-estimated model had an equal-ity constraint placed on the observed means over the four time points. Unlike antisocial behavior, the restriction of equal means for the four depression mea-sures was not rejected, $\chi^2(3, N = 180) = 4.89$, $p = .18$; IFI = .99; RMSEA = .06; 90% CI = 0, .15, indicating a single mean estimate for all four time points.

The Simplex Model With Means: Depressive Symptomatology

Next, we estimated the autoregressive simplex model. The baseline model had no imposed equality constraints and fit the observed data poorly, $\chi^2(3, N = 180) = 28.7$, $p < .001$; IFI = .80; RMSEA = .22; 90% CI = .15, .29. Equality constraints on the regression parameters, then on the disturbances and finally on the intercepts, did not result in a significant decrement in model fit, although the final model still fit the data poorly, $\chi^2(9, N = 180) = 37.7$, $p < .001$; IFI = .77; RMSEA = .13; 90% CI = .09, .18. So even though the means of depressive symptomatology were equal over time, the simplex model still resulted in a poor fit to the observed data.

The One-Factor Latent Curve Model: Depressive Symptomatology

Given the poor fit of the simplex model, we then tested a one-factor latent variable model in which the factor mean and variance were freely estimated but all factor loadings were fixed to 1. This model fit the data quite well, $\chi^2(8, N = 180) = 11.51$, $p = .17$; IFI = .97; RMSEA = .05; 90% CI = 0, .11, suggesting that the observed covariance and mean structure are well replicated given the presence of a single random-intercept factor. There was a significant mean of the latent factor, suggesting meaningful levels of depressive symptomatology in the sample, and there was a significant variance, suggesting meaningful indi-vidual variability in these levels of depression.

The Two-Factor Latent Curve Model: Depressive Symptomatology

To test if an additional factor was necessary to account for systematic change over time, we added a linear slope factor to the above model. The addition of this factor did not significantly improve the overall model fit, and the mean and variance of the slope factor did not significantly differ from zero. This suggests that although there is a random-intercept component underlying the four depressive symptomatology measures, there is no corresponding random-slope component. Indeed, this finding is consistent with the initial equal-means model that suggests that the means did not vary as a function of time. Thus, there is no evidence to retain the linear slope factor.[3]

The Bivariate Autoregressive Crosslagged Model: Antisocial Behavior and Depressive Symptomatology

The motivating goal of these analyses is to empirically examine the relation between antisocial behavior and depressive symptomatology over time. Now that we better understand the characteristics of stability and change within each construct, we can proceed to the simultaneous evaluation of these constructs across the four time periods. We start by combining the two simplex models described above; this allows for the introduction of the important crosslagged parameters across construct and across time. Although this model was built in a series of sequential steps (see Curran et al., 1997, for more details), only the final model is presented here, which was found to fit the data poorly, $\chi^2(26, N = 180) = 95.1$, $p < .001$; IFI = .86; RMSEA = .12; 90% CI = .10, .15. The model includes all imposed equality constraints with the exception of equalities on the intercepts within each construct at Times 2, 3, and 4. Findings indicate that there were large and significant positive regression parameters between time-adjacent measures within each construct. Furthermore, there were positive significant covariances of the disturbances within each time across the two constructs. Finally, whereas earlier depressive symptomatology did not predict later antisocial behavior, earlier antisocial behavior did significantly and positively predict later depressive symptomatology. Both of these crosslagged effects are evident even after controlling for the previous measure of each construct. For example, Time 1 antisocial behavior predicted Time 2 depressive symptomatology above and beyond the effects of Time 1 depressive symptomatology.

These results thus suggest that there is a relation between depressive symptomatology and antisocial behavior over time, but only in that earlier antisocial behavior predicts later depressive symptomatology, not vice versa. However, two important issues remain. First, although these crosslagged parameters were significant, these are drawn from a model that fits the observed data quite poorly, and biased parameter estimates and standard errors are likely (e.g., Kaplan, 1989). Second, previous analyses indicated that both antisocial behavior

---

[3]Given the pattern of means that first increased and then decreased as a function of time, we estimated an additional model that included three growth factors: an intercept, a linear slope, and a quadratic slope. However, there was a nonsignificant mean and variance for the quadratic factor, indicating that there was not a meaningful curvilinear component to changes in depression over time.

and depressive symptomatology are characterized by one or more random growth parameters, influences that are not incorporated into this bivariate fixed-effects simplex model. To address these issues, we will now turn to a bivariate latent curve model.

The Bivariate Latent Curve Model: Antisocial Behavior and Depressive Symptomatology

We first estimated our baseline bivariate latent curve model that consisted of the combination of the two univariate latent trajectory models from above (see Figure 4.7). Additional parameters included the three covariances among the latent growth factors and within time covariances for the time-specific residuals. As expected, this baseline model did not reflect adequate fit, $\chi^2(23, N = 180)$ = 54.45, $p < .001$; IFI = .94; RMSEA = .09; 90% CI = .06, .12. We introduced a series of equality constraints on the variances of the disturbances across time and within construct, as well as the covariances within time and across construct. None of these equality constraints resulted in a significant deterioration in model fit, and the final model fit the data moderately well, $\chi^2(32, N = 180)$ = 62.9, $p < .001$; IFI = .94; RMSEA = .07; 90% CI = .05, .10. Parameter estimates indicated that the three latent factors were positively and significantly correlated with one another (correlations ranged between .44 and .53), indicating that there was meaningful overlapping variability in the components of growth underlying the repeated measures of antisocial behavior and depressive symptomatology. Of greatest interest was the significant positive relation between the depressive symptomatology intercept and the antisocial slope. This correlation suggests that individual differences in the stable component of depressive symptomatology are positively associated with increases in antisociality over time. That is, on average, children with a higher stable component of depressive symptomatology tended to report steeper increases in antisocial behavior relative to children who reported lower stable levels of depressive symptomatology.

This finding has direct implications for our research hypotheses of interest. Namely, there does appear to be a relation between antisocial behavior and depressive symptomatology over time. However, this finding highlights one of the limitations of this model. Although empirical evidence suggests these two constructs are related over time, this relation holds only for the stable continuous component underlying antisociality and depression over time—that is, it is difficult to infer temporal ordering or a possible direction of influence; we can only observe that these two constructs are related in a potentially important way. To allow for the simultaneous influence of both the random underlying components of change with the time-specific fixed components of change, we now combine the crosslagged effects from the simplex model with the growth factors of the latent trajectory model.

FIGURE 4.7

Standard bivariate latent curve model without lagged effects between indicators. Dep = depression; Anti = antisocial behavior.

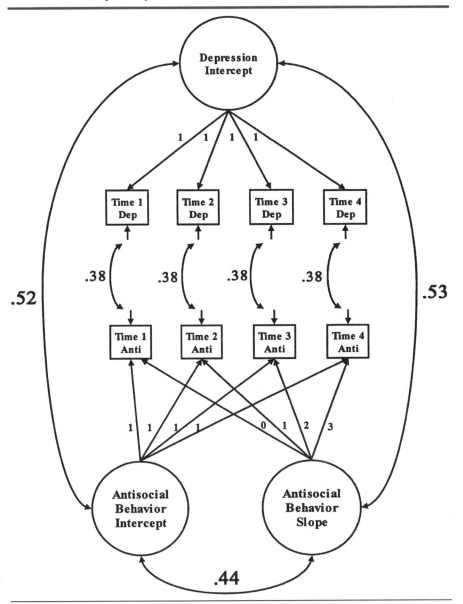

The Bivariate Crosslagged Latent Curve Model: Antisocial Behavior and Depressive Symptomatology

We extended the latent curve model by adding crosslagged effects in which we regressed a later measure of one variable onto the prior measure of the other variable. These parameters resulted in a significant improvement in model fit, $\chi^2(26, N = 180) = 54.9$, $p < .001$; IFI = .94; RMSEA = .08; 90% CI = .05, .11. Before interpreting the final model, we imposed additional equality constraints on the lagged effects, and none of the constraints resulted in a significant decrement to model fit. The final model fit the data moderately well, $\chi^2(30, N = 180) = 55.3$, $p = .003$; IFI = .95; RMSEA = .07; 90% CI = .04, .10, and is presented in Figure 4.8. All three growth factors were positively and significantly correlated with one another. Furthermore, although earlier measures of depression did not predict later levels of antisocial behavior, earlier levels of antisocial behavior did significantly predict later levels of depressive symptomatology. Note that this prospective lagged prediction is evident after the influences of the underlying latent growth processes have been partialed out. Thus, this bivariate latent trajectory model with lagged effects allows for the estimation of both the stable component of development over time (as captured in the latent factors) and time-specific differences in antisocial behavior or depressive symptomatology at any given time point. This is an extremely important combination of influences that neither the simplex nor the latent trajectory model allows when taken alone.

Summary of Substantive Findings Relating to Antisocial Behavior and Depressive Symptomatology

The series of simplex and latent curve models provides a great deal of insight into the relations between antisocial behavior and depressive symptomatology over an 8-year period in this sample of children. First, we found developmental changes in antisocial behavior to be positive and linear for the overall group. In addition, there was a significant amount of variability in both the starting point and the rate of change of antisociality over time; some children were increasing more steeply, some less steeply, and some not at all. Second, a similar systematic developmental trajectory over time did not exist for depressive symptomatology. There was a stable component of depressive symptomatology that was characterized by significant individual variability indicating that some children were reporting higher levels of depression over time whereas others were reporting lower levels or none at all. However, there was not a significant relation between depressive symptomatology and time. Third, both modeling approaches indicated that antisocial behavior and depressive symptomatology

FIGURE 4.8

Bivariate simplex latent curve model including lagged effects between indicators. Dep = depression; Anti = antisocial behavior.

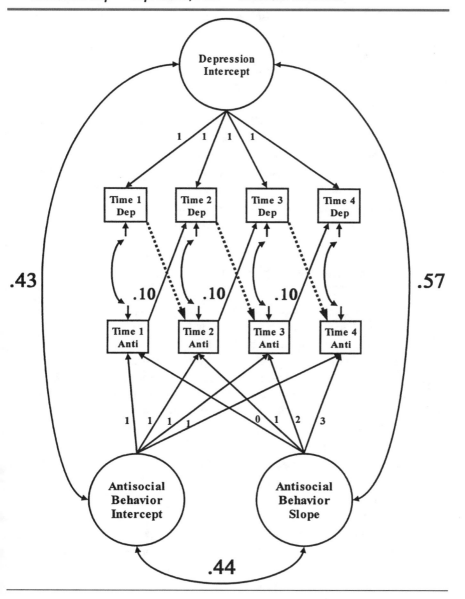

were related over time in important ways. The latent curve model suggests that children who report higher baseline levels of depression tend to report steeper increases in antisocial behavior over time. However, the crosslagged models suggest that earlier levels of antisocial behavior are associated with later levels of depression but not vice versa.

It was only the synthesized autoregressive latent curve model that allowed for a simultaneous estimation of both of these stable and time-specific effects. The latent curve component of the model estimated the portion of variability in the repeated measures that was associated with a continuous underlying developmental trajectory of antisocial behavior or depressive symptomatology. At the same time, the simplex crosslagged effects indicated that, after controlling for the variability associated with the developmental trajectories, earlier antisociality predicted later depression, but earlier depression did not predict later antisociality. Taken together, these models provide important information that helps further our understanding about these complicated developmental issues.

Extensions of the Crosslagged Latent Curve Model

The proposed modeling strategy is expandable in a variety of ways. For example, one could regress the latent growth factors onto exogenous explanatory variables to better understand individual differences in change over time. In analyses not presented here because of space constraints, we regressed the growth factors defining antisocial behavior and depressive symptomatology onto family-level measures of emotional and cognitive support in the home (see Curran & Bollen, 1999, for details). The results suggest intriguing relations between these home support measures and individual differences in developmental trajectories over time. Additional explanatory variables could be incorporated to model variability both in the latent growth factors as well as directly in the repeated measures over time.

A second important extension uses the strength of the SEM framework for analyzing interactions as a function of discrete groups. An important example of this would be the examination of potential interactions between a child's gender and the relation between antisociality and depression over time. Again, in additional analyses not reported here, we evaluated gender differences in these models using a multiple-group estimation procedure, and the results suggest that the relation between antisociality and depression may interact as a function of gender (see Curran & Bollen, 1999). These techniques could be extended further by combining the synthesized models discussed here with the analytic methods proposed by Curran and Muthén (1999) and B. O. Muthén and Curran (1997), which would allow for the evaluation of whether two developmental processes could be "unlinked" from one another over time because of the implementation of a prevention or treatment program.

A third extension would be to further capitalize on the strengths of the SEM approach and to use multiple-indicator latent factors to define the constructs of interest within each time point. For example, instead of using a single scale score to measure antisocial behavior or depressive symptomatology, analysts could use latent factors to estimate these constructs and would thus be theoretically free from measurement error. Given the difficulty of measuring many constructs in the social sciences, incorporating the presence of measurement error is an important aspect in any modeling approach; Sayer and Cumsille (chapter 6, this volume) explore this issue.

Finally, although we found that earlier antisocial behavior was related to later depressive symptomatology, little is known about precisely why this effect exists. To better understand the relation between these two constructs over time, it would be very important to include potential mediators that might account for this observed effect. For example, it may be that higher levels of antisocial behavior are associated with greater rejection from positive social groups, and this social rejection is associated with greater isolation and depression. These models could be directly extended to include the influences of social rejection given the availability of appropriate data.

Conclusion

The simplex model and the latent curve model are both important tools for understanding change over time. However, each approach is limited in key ways that preclude drawing comprehensive inferences about change and development from observed empirical data. Although these limitations are difficult to overcome when considering only one modeling approach or the other, we believe that significant improvements are possible by combining elements drawn from each analytic approach to create a more general model of development and change. Of course, there are a variety of situations in which the simplex model or the latent curve model taken alone is well suited to evaluate the particular research hypotheses at hand. An advantage of the proposed framework is that under such conditions, the synthesized model directly simplifies to either the standard simplex model or the latent curve model (Bollen & Curran, 2000). However, under conditions in which there is interest in both continuous underlying trajectories and time-specific influences across constructs, we believe that the proposed modeling approach provides a powerful and flexible tool to help elucidate these complex relations over time.

References

Anderson, T. W. (1960). Some stochastic process models for intelligence test scores. In K. J. Arrow, S. Karlin, & P. Suppes (Eds.), *Mathematical methods in the social sciences, 1959* (pp. 205–220). Stanford, CA: Stanford University Press.

Arbuckle, J. L. (1996). Full information estimation in the presence of incomplete data. In G. A. Marcoulides & R. E. Schumacker (Eds.), *Advanced structural equation modeling: Issues and techniques* (pp. 243–278). Mahwah, NJ: Erlbaum.

Bast, J., & Reitsma, P. (1997). Matthew effects in reading: A comparison of latent growth curve models and simplex models with structured means. *Multivariate Behavioral Research, 32,* 135–167.

Bentler, P. M. (1980). Multivariate analysis with latent variables: Causal modeling. *Annual Review of Psychology, 31,* 419–456.

Bentler, P. M. (1983). Some contributions to efficient statistics for structural models: Specification and estimation of moment structures. *Psychometrika, 48,* 493–517.

Bohrnstedt, G. W. (1969). Observations on the measurement of change. In E. F. Borgatta (Ed.), *Sociological methodology 1969* (pp. 113–133). San Francisco: Jossey-Bass.

Bollen, K. A. (1989). *Structural equations with latent variables.* New York: Wiley.

Bollen, K. A., & Curran, P. J. (1999, June). *An autoregressive latent trajectory (ALT) model: A synthesis of two traditions.* Paper presented at the 1999 meeting of the Psychometric Society, Lawrence, KS.

Bollen, K. A., & Curran, P. J. (2000). *Autoregressive latent trajectory models: A synthesis of two traditions.* Manuscript submitted for publication, University of North Carolina, Chapel Hill.

Browne, M. W., & Cudeck, R. (1993). Alternative ways of assessing model fit. In K. A. Bollen & J. S. Long (Eds.), *Testing structural equation models* (pp. 136–162). Newbury Park, CA: Sage.

Bryk, A. S., & Raudenbush, S. W. (1992). *Hierarchical linear models: Applications and data analysis methods.* Newbury Park, CA: Sage.

Campbell, D. T. (1963). From description to experimentation: Interpreting trends as quasi-experiments. In C. W. Harris (Ed.), *Problems in measuring change* (pp. 212–242). Madison: University of Wisconsin Press.

Capaldi, D. M. (1991). Co-occurrence of conduct problems and depressive symptoms in early adolescent boys: I. Familial factors and general adjustment at Grade 6. *Development and Psychopathology, 3,* 277–300.

Capaldi, D. M. (1992). Co-occurrence of conduct problems and depressive symptoms in early adolescent boys: II. A 2-year follow-up at Grade 8. *Development and Psychopathology, 4,* 125–144.

Curran, P. J. (2000). A latent curve framework for studying developmental trajectories of adolescent substance use. In J. Rose, L. Chassin, C. Presson, & J. Sherman (Eds.), *Multivariate applications in substance use research* (pp. 1–42). Mahwah, NJ: Erlbaum.

Curran, P. J., & Bollen, K. A. (1999, June). *Extensions of the autoregressive latent trajectory model: Explanatory variables and multiple group analysis.* Paper presented at the 1999 meeting of the Society for Prevention Research. New Orleans, LA.

Curran, P. J., & Hussong, A. M. (in press). Structural equation modeling of repeated measures data. In D. Moskowitz & S. Hershberger (Eds.), *Modeling intraindividual variability with repeated measures data: Methods and applications.* Mahwah, NJ: Erlbaum.

Curran, P. J., & Muthén, B. O. (1999). The application of latent curve analysis to testing developmental theories in intervention research. *American Journal of Community Psychology, 27,* 567–595.

Curran, P. J., Stice, E., & Chassin, L. (1997). The relation between adolescent and peer alcohol use: A longitudinal random coefficients model. *Journal of Consulting and Clinical Psychology, 65,* 130–140.

Duncan, O. D. (1969). Some linear models for two-wave, two-variable panel analysis. *Psychological Bulletin, 72,* 177–182.

Duncan, S. C., & Duncan, T. E. (1996). A multivariate latent growth curve analysis of adolescent substance use. *Structural Equation Modeling, 3,* 323–347.

Goldstein, H., Healy, M., & Rasbash, J. (1994). Multilevel time series models with applications to repeated measures data. *Statistics in Medicine, 13,* 1643–1655.

Graham, J. W., Hofer, S. M., & MacKinnon, D. P. (1996). Maximizing the usefulness of data obtained with planned missing value patterns: An application of maximum likelihood procedures. *Multivariate Behavioral Research, 31,* 197–218.

Guttman, L. A. (1954). A new approach to factor analysis. The radex. In P. F. Lazarsfeld (Ed.), *Mathematical thinking in the social sciences* (pp. 258–348). New York: Columbia University Press.

Heise, D. R. (1969). Separating reliability and stability in test–retest correlation. *American Sociological Review, 34,* 93–101.

Humphreys, L. G. (1960). Investigations of the simplex. *Psychometrika, 25,* 313–323.

Jöreskog, K. G. (1970). A general method for analysis of covariance structures. *Biometrika, 57,* 239–251.

Jöreskog, K. G. (1971a). Simultaneous factor analysis in several populations. *Psychometrika, 36,* 409–426.

Jöreskog, K. G. (1971b). Statistical analysis of sets of congeneric tests. *Psychometrika, 36,* 109–133.

Jöreskog, K. G. (1979). Statistical estimation of structural models in longitudinal developmental investigations. In J. R. Nesselroade & P. B. Baltes (Eds.), *Longitudinal research in the study of behavior and development* (pp. 303–352). New York: Academic Press.

Jöreskog, K. G., & Sörbom, D. (1978). *Advances in factor analysis and structural equation models.* Cambridge, MA: Abt Books.

Kaplan, D. (1989). A study of the sampling variability and z-values of parameter estimates from misspecified structural equation models. *Multivariate Behavioral Research, 24,* 41–57.

Kenny, D. A., & Campbell, D. T. (1989). On the measurement of stability in over-time data. *Journal of Personality, 57,* 445–481.

Little, R. J. A., & Rubin, D. B. (1987). *Statistical analysis with missing data.* New York: Wiley.

MacCallum, R. C., Kim, C., Malarkey, W., & Kiecolt-Glaser, J. (1997). Studying multivariate change using multilevel models and latent curve models. *Multivariate Behavioral Research, 32,* 215–253.

Marsh, H. W. (1993). Stability of individual differences in multiwave panel studies: Comparison of simplex models and one-factor models. *Journal of Educational Measurement, 30,* 157–183.

McArdle, J. J. (1986). Latent growth within behavior genetic models. *Behavioral Genetics, 16,* 163–200.

McArdle, J. J. (1988). Dynamic but structural equation modeling of repeated measures data. In J. R. Nesselroade & R. B. Cattell (Eds.), *Handbook of multivariate experimental psychology* (2nd ed., pp. 561–614). New York: Plenum Press.

McArdle, J. J. (1989). Structural modeling experiments using multiple growth functions. In P. Ackerman, R. Kanfer, & R. Cudeck (Eds.), *Learning and individual differences: Abilities, motivation and methodology* (pp. 71–117). Hillsdale, NJ: Erlbaum.

McArdle, J. J. (1991). Structural models of developmental theory in psychology. In P. Van Geert & L. P. Mos (Eds.), *Annals of theoretical psychology* (Vol. 7, pp. 139–160). New York: Plenum.

McArdle, J. J., & Epstein, D. (1987). Latent growth curves within developmental structural equation models. *Child Development, 58,* 110–133.

Meredith, W., & Tisak, J. (1984, July). *"Tuckerizing" curves.* Paper presented at the annual meeting of the Psychometric Society, Santa Barbara, CA.

Meredith, W., & Tisak, J. (1990). Latent curve analysis. *Psychometrika, 55,* 107–122.

Muthén, B. (1991). Analysis of longitudinal data using latent variable models with varying parameters. In L. M. Collins & J. L. Horn (Eds.), *Best methods for the analysis of change: Recent advances, unanswered questions, future directions* (pp. 1–17). Washington, DC: American Psychological Association.

Muthén, B. O., & Curran, P. J. (1997). General longitudinal modeling of individual differences in experimental designs: A latent variable framework for analysis and power estimation. *Psychological Methods, 2,* 371–402.

Muthén, B. O., Kaplan, D., & Hollis, M. (1987). On structural equation modeling with data that are not missing completely at random. *Psychometrika, 52,* 431–462.

Muthén, L. K., & Muthén, B. O. (1998). *MPlus user's guide.* Los Angeles, CA: Author.

Rogosa, D., & Willett, J. B. (1985). Satisfying simplex structure is simpler than it should be. *Journal of Educational Statistics, 10,* 99–107.

Steiger, J. H., & Lind, J. M. (1980, June). *Statistically based tests for the number of common factors*. Paper presented at the annual meeting of the Psychometric Society, Iowa City, IA.

Stoolmiller, M. (1994). Antisocial behavior, delinquent peer association, and unsupervised wandering for boys: Growth and change from childhood to early adolescence. *Multivariate Behavioral Research, 29*, 263–288.

Editors' Introduction

In their chapter, McArdle and Hamagami present an innovative approach to integrating autoregressive and latent growth models, based on the idea of a latent difference score. The latent difference score approach allows tremendous flexibility in modeling change and stability. In addition, McArdle and Hamagami show how to deal with missing data, and they illustrate this using a data set in which participants were present for anywhere from a single observation to all four observations. This chapter is an excellent example of the power and flexibility of structural equation modeling for longitudinal data. For a slightly different approach to the integration of autoregressive and growth curve models, see chapter 4, by Curran and Bollen. For a general discussion of disentangling change and stability, see chapter 8, by Kenny and Zautra. Readers may find it interesting to compare McArdle and Hamagami's latent difference score ideas with Boker's (chapter 1) approach to expressing change.

Latent Difference Score Structural Models for Linear Dynamic Analyses With Incomplete Longitudinal Data

John J. McArdle

Fumiaki Hamagami

The creation of "best methods" for the analysis of change has been a continuing concern in longitudinal and developmental research (e.g., Bayley, 1956; Bell, 1953; Harris, 1963; Horn & Little, 1966; Nesselroade & Baltes, 1979; Tanner, 1960). Some common goals of these methods were outlined by Baltes and Nesselroade (1979) as "five key objectives for longitudinal research":

- direct identification of intraindividual change
- direct identification of interindividual differences in intraindividual change
- analysis of interrelationships in change
- analysis of causes (determinants) of intraindividual change
- analysis of causes (determinants) of interindividual differences in intraindividual change.

These latent difference score analyses were previously presented to the International Society for Behavioral Development, Bern, Switzerland, in July 1998, and at the American Psychological Association conference "New Methods for the Analysis of Change," Pennsylvania State University, in October 1998. This research was supported by Grants AG02695, AG04704, and AG07137 from the National Institute on Aging. These National Longitudinal Survey of Youth (NLSY) data were selected by Patrick Curran of Duke University for a presentation on comparative longitudinal analyses at the Society for Research on Child Development in April 1997. All NLSY data used here are publicly available, and the computer program scripts used here are available from John J. McArdle, so all analyses should be relatively easy to reproduce from the available files or from the original data. We thank our colleagues John R. Nesselroade, Paolo Ghisletta, and Patrick Curran for their comments on drafts of this chapter.

The kind of longitudinal data we deal with in this chapter are multiple measures from a reasonably large number of participants repeated on at least a few occasions. Figure 5.1 is a plot of longitudinal data selected from the publicly available archives of the *National Longitudinal Survey of Youth* (NLSY; see Baker, Keck, Mott, & Quinlan, 1993). Figure 5.1A is a plot of repeated scores on reading (assessed with the Peabody Individual Achievement Test [PIAT]; American Guidance, 2000) data for each individual that is drawn as a connected line representing an individual growth curve for each child (N = 405) as a function of age. This plot includes data on all participants, even if they missed one or more occasions of measurement. The same kind of longitudinal information is

FIGURE 5.1

Individual growth curves from the National Longitudinal Survey of Youth.

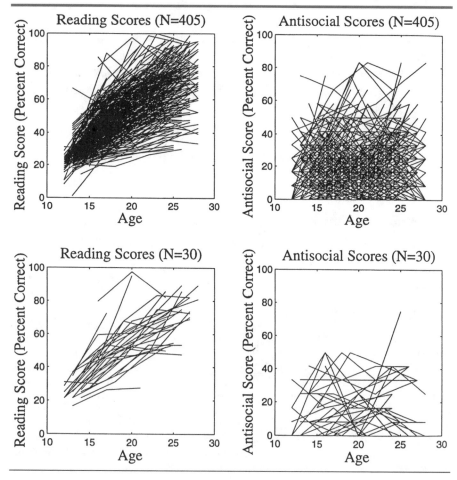

presented for a set of antisocial scores (from the Behavior Problems Inventory [BPI], developed for the National Health Interview Survey; Peterson & Zill, 1986) in Figure 5.1B. Our analyses of these longitudinal data are designed to provide information about the five goals listed above.

To clarify some of these features we also include Figures 5.1C and 5.1D, which include data for only the first 30 participants; the different patterns of growth and incomplete data are more obvious. We can see that not everyone has four time points of measurement and, even for those who were measured on four occasions, the participants were measured at different ages. Even though Figures 5.1C and 5.1D show data from the same participants, the plots paint decidedly different pictures: The growth trends in reading are clear, but the antisocial variable has no discernable trend over time, there are dramatic ups and downs throughout the individual vectors, and there are many children whose scores are close to zero over all time periods. Given these practical limits, we still hope to use these longitudinal data to help understand the sequential development of these kinds of behaviors; that is, we are interested in whether lower reading ability leads to increases in antisocial behaviors or whether more engagement in antisocial behaviors leads to a lowering of reading abilities (see Patterson & Bank, 1989).

Many recent innovations in mathematical and statistical models for the analysis of longitudinal data have been focused on these kinds of data and objectives (e.g., Collins & Horn, 1991; Diggle, Liang, & Zeger, 1994; Dwyer, Feinleib, Lippert, & Hoffmeister, 1992; Jones, 1993; Lindsey, 1993). Some recent approaches to longitudinal data analysis have used linear structural equation modeling (SEM; Bollen, 1989; Jöreskog & Sörbom, 1979, 1993; Loehlin, 1992; McDonald, 1985). The original SEM for longitudinal data was based on a stationary autoregressive change model (see Jöreskog & Sörbom, 1979; and McArdle & Aber, 1990). Other aspects of these questions are derived from dynamic systems modeling, which usually is used with time series data with more measurement occasions (e.g., see chapter 1, Boker, this volume). In seminal work, Arminger (1986) developed a way to reinterpret standard LISREL results from panel data using differential equations, and Gollob and Reichardt (1987) considered alternative ways to deal with inferences about the time lag between occasions in longitudinal data. At about the same time, these well-known SEMs were expanded on by Meredith and Tisak (1990) to include latent growth curve model (LGM) components (also see Browne & Du Toit, 1991; Curran & Bollen, chapter 4, this volume; McArdle, 1988; McArdle & Anderson, 1990; McArdle & Epstein, 1987; McArdle & Hamagami, 1991, 1992; Muthén, chapter 10, this volume; Sayer & Cumsille, chapter 6, this volume; and Willett & Sayer, 1994, 1996).

In a related area of statistical research there has been much innovation in dealing with incomplete data analyses (see Graham, Taylor, & Cumsille, chapter

11, this volume; Little & Rubin, 1987; McArdle, 1994; Rubin, 1987; and Schafer, 1997, chapter 12, this volume). Some aspects of these analyses provide a direct solution to classical problems in self-selection and longitudinal attrition (Allison, 1987; Berk, 1983; Heckman, 1979). In the context of growth models, this strategy has often been used to examine correlates of change (e.g., Rogosa & Willett, 1985) or in what are now popularly termed *multilevel models, hierarchical models,* or *random coefficients models* (see Bryk & Raudenbush, 1992; Goldstein & McDonald, 1988; Longford, 1993; McArdle & Hamagami, 1996; and Raudenbush, chapter 2, this volume). Other aspects of his incomplete data analyses can be used to formalize the concept of convergence analyses for combining longitudinal and cross-sectional data in earlier work by Bell (1953; Duncan & Duncan, 1995; Horn & McArdle, 1980; McArdle & Hamagami, 1991, 1992; McArdle & Woodcock, 1997). In any case, dealing with incomplete data is an important practical issue in real longitudinal data (see, e.g., Figure 5.1).

In this chapter, we present a relatively new way to approach SEM-based analyses of longitudinal data. The specific approach we use in this chapter is termed *latent difference score* (LDS) analysis (McArdle & Hamagami, 1995, 1998; McArdle & Nesselroade, 1994), and we aim to integrate many aspects of prior approaches using principles derived from linear difference models (e.g., Arminger, 1986; Goldberg, 1958; Pankratz, 1991; Sandefur, 1993). This integration of some prior longitudinal SEMs permits evaluations of different types of change, for example, additive change over time (α), multiplicative change over time (β), and change coupled from one variable to another over time (γ). This version of LDS modeling is also designed to be practical and easy to use with available SEM software (e.g., LISREL, Mx, RAMONA) and permits features of incomplete-data analyses. The well-known latent growth and multilevel models can be used to describe group and individual differences in change within a variable, but the structural models presented here provide an opportunity to examine the sequential dependency among variables based on dynamic principles.

We begin this chapter with a basic description of the available data, give some basic foundations of the LDS methods, and provide references to recent research on these topics. We then illustrate a variety of LDS models using the available NLSY data (see Figure 5.1).

Models

A brief description of the dynamic models to be used here can be organized around two path diagrams: Figure 5.2 is a structural model of a univariate path diagram, Figure 5.3 is the same model including an additional "extension" variable, and Figure 5.4 is a structural model of a bivariate dynamic system. In

FIGURE 5.2

A latent variable path diagram of a dual change score model. Squares represent observed variables; circles represent latent variables; triangles represent constants; one-headed arrows represent regression coefficients; double-headed arrows represent a correlation, a covariance, or a crossproduct; dots represent an implied repetition of a time series.

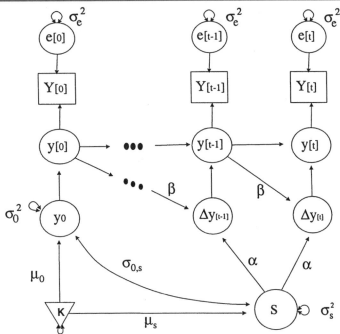

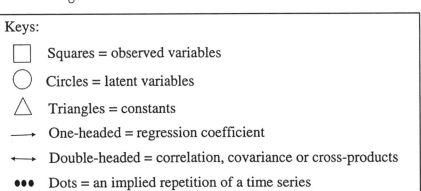

Keys:

☐ Squares = observed variables

◯ Circles = latent variables

△ Triangles = constants

⟶ One-headed = regression coefficient

⟷ Double-headed = correlation, covariance or cross-products

●●● Dots = an implied repetition of a time series

FIGURE 5.3

Adding an extension variable (x) into a dual change score model. Squares represent observed variables; circles represent latent variables; triangles represent constants; one-headed arrows represent regression coefficients; double-headed arrows represent a correlation, a covariance, or a crossproduct; dots represent an implied repetition of a time series.

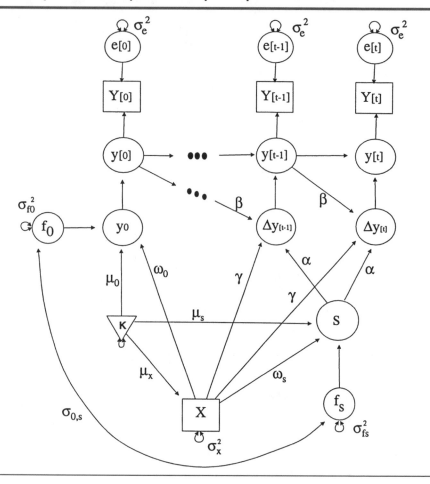

the graphic notation used here (RAM; McArdle & McDonald, 1984; see also McArdle & Boker, 1990), we can describe any linear system of equations using only three parameter matrices: **A, S,** and **F.** Although these three model matrices are not intended to have any substantive meaning independent of each other, they are each directly related to the graphic elements in a path diagram: (a) all one-headed arrows, representing regression or deviation coefficients, are in-

FIGURE 5.4

A latent variable path diagram of bivariate dual change score model. Squares represent observed variables; circles represent latent variables; triangles represent constants; one-headed arrows represent regression coefficients; double-headed arrows represent a correlation, a covariance, or a crossproduct; dots represent an implied repetition of a time series. * = standardized latent scores.

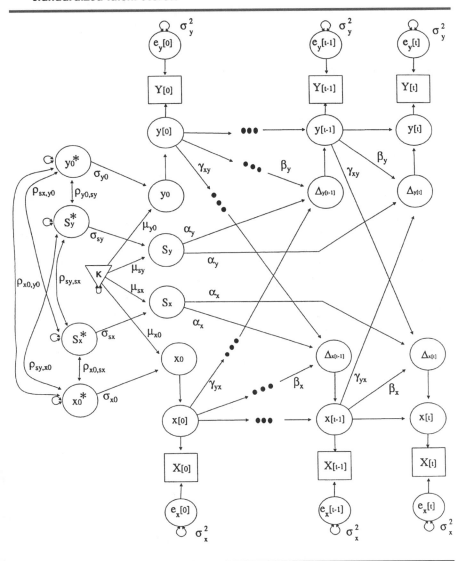

cluded in matrix **A**; (b) all two-headed arrows, representing variance, covariance, or correlations, are included in matrix **S**; and (c) the separation of the manifest variables (squares) from the latent variables (circles) is included in matrix **F**. To simplify this presentation, this notation is used in all subsequent algebraic derivations and in the computer input scripts that follow.

Latent Difference Scores

Many traditional statistical models start by assuming that one has measured a homogeneous sample of persons, N, independently drawn from a population of interest. Many traditional longitudinal models further assume one has repeatedly measured the same variable $Y(t)$ using the same procedures of measurement on at least two different occasions ($T > 1$). Other traditional models deal with the possibility of measurement error by following classical *true score theory*, according to which each observed raw score Y measured can be decomposed into the sum of a *latent score* y plus some kind of independent error or unique score e. For the observed score at any time point t, one can write

$$Y(t)_n = y(t)_n + e(t)_n \qquad (5.1)$$

(e.g., McArdle & Woodcock, 1997). This first algebraic equation is depicted in the path diagram of Figure 5.2 by having the latent variables $y(t)$ and the error scores $e(t)$ add (with implied unit weights) to form the observed variables $Y(t)$. We further assume that these error scores: (a) have a zero mean ($\mu_e = 0$), (b) have a nonzero variance (σ_e^2), (c) are uncorrelated with any other scores in the model, and (d) have the same variance at each time point. These restrictive assumptions about random or unique errors may need to be altered in later analyses.

We are next interested in representing the latent difference score as a *rate of change*, $\Delta y(t)/\Delta(t)$, given a time lag [$\Delta(t)$]. This means we can define a first difference in the latent scores by simply writing

$$\Delta y(t)_n = y(t)_n - y(t - 1)_n,$$

or

$$y(t)_n = y(t - 1)_n + \Delta y(t)_n. \qquad (5.2)$$

This latent difference score ($\Delta y[t]$) is defined in Figure 5.2 by the unit-weighted formation of the latent scores $y(t)$. More specifically, the latent score at the second occasion ($y[2]$) is formed as the unit-weighted sum of the latent score at the first occasion $y(1)$ plus the latent score $\Delta y(2)$, so the latter score $\Delta y(2)$ is interpreted as a *first difference* at the second occasion (as in McArdle & Nesselroade, 1994). Notice that in this picture the difference score $\Delta y(2)$ is not a new manifest variable calculated from the data but a latent variable implied from the structural relationships. This use of a latent difference score rather than a manifest difference score has useful properties in later aspects of this model.

To simplify the rest of this presentation, we always assume the times between all pairs of latent scores $y(t)$ and $y(t - j)$ have a constant interval (i.e., $\Delta[t] = 1$). As it turns out, this simplifying assumption of equal latent intervals is not a testable feature of the model. However, this model does not require equal observed intervals of time as long as any unequal intervals are taken into account (see McArdle & Bell, 2000; and McArdle & Woodcock, 1997).

Models of Latent Difference Scores

One can now write any basic model for the rate of change at any time point by assuming the *latent rate score* $\Delta y[t]_n/\Delta[t]$, where $(\Delta[t] = 1)$ is a dependent variable in some substantive equation. Although there are many alternatives possible now, the specific kind of change model drawn in Figure 5.2 can be written as

$$\Delta y(t)_n = \alpha \times s_n + \beta \times y(t - 1)_n. \qquad (5.3)$$

In this model changes in the score (Δy) as a function of changes in time $(\Delta[t] = 1)$ are both (a) constantly related to some alternative but fixed slope $(\alpha \times s)$ and (b) proportional to the previous state $(\beta \times y[t - 1])$. The group coefficients to be estimated are the constant α and the proportion β, but individual differences are permitted in the difference scores $\Delta y(t)$, the constant score s, and the previous score $y(t - 1)$. Because of the use of two additive components, we term this a *dual change score* (DCS) model.

The coefficient β is included as a predictor of the latent difference score $\Delta y(t)$ from the prior score $y(t - 1)$ at Lag 1, and this coefficient is assumed to apply for all pairs of consecutive occasions. The coefficient α is included as a predictor of the latent difference score $(\Delta y[t])$ from a new common latent variable (s), and this coefficient is repeatedly used for all occasions. In SEM estimation the numerous α and β parameters in the path model (as in Figure 5.2) are estimated using equality constraints (so there is only one estimate for α and one for β).

This SEM is now completed, adding several parameters for the latent variable covariances and latent means. There are many ways to do this, but for now we simply assume the existence of a nonzero (a) variance of the initial scores (σ_0^2), (b) variance of the slope scores (σ_s^2), and (c) covariance among the initial levels and slope scores (σ_{0s}). These are depicted as two-headed arrows in Figure 5.3 and represent standard parameters in these models. In addition, we assume a possibly nonzero value for (d) the mean at the initial occasion (μ_0), and (e) the mean of the slopes (μ_s). A constant score $(K_n = 1)$ is added to the path diagram of Figure 5.3 because the mean at the initial occasion (μ)

and the mean of the slopes (μ_s) are included as regression weights in the equation for the specific variable (see McArdle & Boker, 1990). We also note that the variance of the latent difference scores (σ_Δ^2) is not a specific parameter in this model, but it can be constructed as a function of these other parameters. We also do not include specific residual terms on the difference scores in this model, but these parameters can be identified in more complex versions of these models (e.g., McArdle & Hamagami, 1998).

Generating Model Expectations

This DCS model (Equation 5.3) is only one kind of model for the righthand side of Equation 5.2. However, even these kinds of dynamic structural models have proven difficult to empirically evaluate in past research (e.g., Arminger, 1986; Coleman, 1964; Tuma & Hannan, 1984). Most recent work includes the use of standard factor model expressions with nonlinear constraints on the factor loadings (as in Browne & Du Toit, 1991; McArdle & Hamagami, 1996). To illustrate the potential complexity of these results, we can rewrite this dynamic equation model as a trajectory over time for two consecutive time points as

$$
\begin{aligned}
Y(1)_n &= y(0)_n + \Delta y(1)_n/\Delta(t) + e(1)_n \\
&= y(0)_n + \alpha \times s_n + \beta \times y(0)_n + e(1)_n \\
&= (1 + \beta) \times y(0)_n + \alpha \times s_n + e(1)_n, \\
&= \lambda_{01} \times y(0)_n + \lambda_{s1} \times s_n + e(1)_n
\end{aligned}
$$

and

$$
\begin{aligned}
Y(2)_n &= y(1)_n + \Delta y(2)_n/\Delta(t) + e(2)_n \\
&= y(1)_n + \beta \times y(1)_n + \alpha \times s_n + e(2)_n \\
&= [(1 + \beta) \times y(0)_n + \alpha \times s_n] + [\beta \times (1 + \beta) \times y(0)_n + \alpha \times s_n] \\
&\quad + \alpha \times s_n + e(2)_n \\
&= [(1 + 2\beta + \beta^2) \times y(0)_n + (1 + 2\beta \times \alpha) \times s_n] + e(2)_n \\
&= \lambda_{02} \times y(0)_n + \lambda_{s2} \times s_n + e(2)_n.
\end{aligned}
\tag{5.4}
$$

It follows that this expected value expression for each score increases in complexity with more time points ($t > 2$), but it follows the same factorial structure defined by the initial change model; that is, with nonlinear factor loadings λ_0 and λ_S, latent factor scores $y(0)_n$ and s_n, and unique or error scores $e(t)_n$. These dynamic models can be fitted by using standard factor model expressions with nonlinear constraints on the factor loadings (as in Browne & Du Toit, 1991; McArdle & Hamagami, 1996).

In general, we somehow need to write and evaluate these kinds of nonlinear constraints on the trajectories. However, this is done implicitly simply by specifying structural model matrices based on the path diagram of Figure 5.2. These LDS algebraic and graphic specifications provide a restrictive structure for means and covariances of the observed data, and we do not need to explicitly write the nonlinear constraints on the trajectories. This is important because it means these LDS models can be easily introduced into any standard SEM technique (e.g., LISREL, Mx, etc.) to estimate the model parameters and assess the goodness of fit. Detailed examples are presented in the next section.

The resulting parameters of the dual-change model imply a variety of dynamic trajectories, and some means of comparing alternative propositions is important. Following standard SEM logic we can fit a variety of alternative DCS models simplified in different ways. For example, (a) if we set parameter $\beta = 0$, we obtain a *constant change score model* [CCS; $\Delta y(t)/\Delta(t) = \alpha \times s$]; (b) if we set parameter $\alpha = 0$, we obtain a *proportional change score* model [PCS; $\Delta y(t)/\Delta(t) = \beta \times y(t - 1)$]; (c) if we set both parameters $\alpha = \beta = 0$, we obtain a *no-change score* model [$\Delta y(t)/\Delta(t) = 0$]. These choices of dynamic forms may now be made on substantive or empirical considerations.

Bivariate Dynamic Structural Models

By avoiding some of the usual complexity in defining standard expectations, we can now rapidly expand these models for effectively dealing with more than one dynamic variable. In some applications, an additional observed variable (X) might be used as an "extension variable" (Horn, 1976). In this notation, one could write

$$\Delta y(t)_n = \alpha \times s_n + \beta \times y(t - 1)_n,$$

with

$$y_{0n} = \omega_0 \times X_n + f_{0n},$$

and

$$s_n = \omega_s \times X_n + f_{sn} \tag{5.5}$$

with regression coefficients (ω_0, ω_s) and residual terms (f_0, f_s). This model permits the new extension variable (X) to account for the variation initially presumed to be a predictor of the constant level (y_0), constant slope (s), or both. These LDS coefficients and error terms can now be interpreted as multilevel or random coefficients (Bryk & Raudenbush, 1992; McArdle & Epstein, 1987; McArdle & Hamagami, 1996; Willett & Sayer, 1996).

In a different kind of dynamic extension we can expand the original univariate model as

$$\Delta y(t)_n = \alpha \times s_n + \beta \times y(t-1)_n + \gamma \times X_n, \tag{5.6}$$

so the change in one variable is a function of both itself and another variable (X). This $\Delta y(t)$ equation implies both a constant impact (α), an autoproportional dynamic coefficient (β), and a constant regression γ effect of variable X over all times. This is not the same as the prior models because here the extension variable directly affects the latent change scores at each time.

A single diagram introducing both kinds of parameters (ω, γ) is presented in Figure 5.3. This is used to illustrate how the two previous models may also be considered in various combinations, each used to identify a different approach to the inclusion of an extension variable. Any expansion of these models might include other assumptions about the new variable, such as that it is measured with error (i.e., $X = x + e_x$) or that it is used as an independent grouping variable ($\beta^{[x]}$).

A variety of different models emerge when one considers the additional variable as being time dependent; that is, $X(t)$ is measured. The previous dynamic logic now leads naturally to the consideration of a bivariate dynamic model, where one writes

$$\Delta y(t)_n = \alpha_y \times s_{yn} + \beta_y \times y(t-1)_n + \gamma_y \times x(t-1)_n,$$

and

$$\Delta x(t)_n = \alpha_x \times s_{xn} + \beta_x \times x(t-1)_n + \gamma_x \times y(t-1)_n, \tag{5/7}$$

so the change in one variable is a time-based function of both itself and another variable. The first equation suggests both an autoproportional effect of the variable on itself, together with a coupling γ_y effect of variable $x(t)$ on $\Delta y(t)$ over time. Here, as part of the same model, we include both an autoproportional effect of the variable $x(t)$ on itself and a coupling γ_x effect of variable $x(t)$ on $\Delta y(t)$ over time.

This kind of *bivariate dual change score* (BDCS) model is drawn as a structural path diagram in Figure 5.4. This model includes most of the previous LDS assumptions, including (a) the separation of individual scores from group parameters, (b) the assumption of a constant time interval ($\Delta[t] = 1$), and (c) the separation of the true scores ($y[t]$) from the measurement error scores ($e(t)$). This diagram includes the same kinds of parameters for the means (μ), variances (σ^2), and covariances among the initial scores. In addition, this BDCS model includes (d) two simultaneous equations in which a latent rate of change $\Delta y(t)$ is governed by a first equation and a latent rate of change $\Delta x(t)$ is governed by a second equation. In this dynamic model it is clear that the predictors of one model are embedded in the outcomes of the other variable and vice versa.

In this SEM formulation we deal with dynamic hypotheses about coupling or lead–lag relationships by means of restrictions on the model parameters.

Alternative models may be used to examine hypotheses in which: (a) there is no dynamic coupling among both variables ($\gamma_y = 0$ and $\gamma_x = 0$), (b) $x(t)$ is a leading indicator of $y(t)$ (e.g., only $|\gamma_y| > 0$), (c) $y(t)$ is a "leading indicator" of $x(t)$ (e.g., only $|\gamma_y| > 0$), and (d) a form of dynamic coupling exists among both variables ($|\gamma_y| > 0$ and $|\gamma_x| > 0$). These alternatives can now be examined as dynamic structural hypotheses in combination with restrictions on the univariate α and β dynamic parameters of each variable. The expected values of this kind of bivariate model can be expressed in terms of a set of bivariate predictions about the score changes from one point to another in a *statistical vector field plot* (for details, see Boker & McArdle, 1995; and McArdle & Hamagami, 1995, 1998).

The specific models presented above are only a few of a wide class of difference equations that can be written using SEM form. More important, these time-dependent dynamic equations and hypotheses may be considered in the presence of individual differences in constant growth and change, and this can be useful for behavioral data. These LDS models are applied to the data of Figure 5.1 in the sections that follow.

Method

All of the following illustrations are based on a selected set of raw longitudinal data from the NLSY (Baker et al., 1993; Chase-Lansdale, Mott, Brooks-Gunn, & Phillips, 1991).

Participants

The NLSY data set we use here includes repeated measurements of up to 405 children measured at various locations in the United States. These children and other family members were initially measured as part of the NLSY in 1986. At this initial testing, the children were about 6–8 years of age, and they were measured on a wide variety of individual and group variables. Many of these same children ($N = 405$) were then measured again at approximately 2-year intervals up to four times over 8 years as part of the NLSY follow-ups.

Variables

A variety of cognitive and noncognitive variables are available, but we use only two of these variables in these illustrations. The key variables we use here include

- *reading achievement*: We use the composite scores from the NLSY administration of the PIAT, a broad measure of current levels of reading comprehension. The original PIAT reading scores ranged from 0 to 84, but we have converted these raw scores into a percentage-correct metric that ranges from 0 to 100. The individual growth data on reading are plotted in Figure 5.1.

- *antisocial behavior:* We use the composite scores from the NLSY administration of the BPI. This is a broad measure of the recent level of antisocial behavior directed at the home, friends, school, and society in general. The original BPI Antisocial scores ranged from 0 to 120, but we converted these raw scores into a percentage-correct metric that ranges from 0 to 100. The individual growth data on antisocial behavior are plotted in Figure 5.1.

In both cases the original scale of measurement was not used. However, this scaling is equivalent to the use of the raw score metric, it does not enhance or alter any of the psychometric or statistical comparisons we make, and it does facilitate presentation and interpretation (Cohen, 1996; McArdle, 1988, 1994). Also, the implicit zero point on each scale is not altered by this kind of rescaling. This also means that model comparisons are not affected by this rescaling, and interested researchers can always convert the estimated model parameters back into the original metric.

A variety of additional NLSY data are available, including a wide variety of demographic and family characteristics (e.g., mother's rating of the "cognitive support" in the child's home). Other variables are not introduced at this time, but these data are available from the original sources (for details, see McArdle & Bell, 2000; and Baker et al., 1993).

Statistical Summaries

In Table 5.1 we present the same data using a simple incomplete-data display technique originally devised by J.-B. Lohmoeller (personal communication, June 1981, 1989; for programming details see Rovine & Delaney, 1991). In this display a variable is created to define the pattern of complete data for each participant across an array of other variables, and the frequency counts on this new variable yield the size of each pattern. Among the four Reading scores the number of people measured only on the first occasion (the pattern 1000) included 16 people (4.0% of the total). Next the number of people measured on the first and second occasions (1200) is large, including 83 people (20.5%). In contrast, the number of people measured only on the first and third occasions (the pattern 1030) is small, including only 5 people (1.2%). This approach shows that there are only eight distinct patterns of incompleteness in these data. These participants were selected because they had complete data at the first occasion; otherwise, we would probably have many more patterns (e.g., 0204, 0300, etc.).

Standard statistical summaries, such as means, deviations, and correlations,

TABLE 5.1

Initial Patterns of Complete and Incomplete Data in the National Longitudinal Survey of Youth Measurements (Using Lohmoeller's, 1989, Method)

PATTERN OF RETESTING (1234)	FREQUENCY	PERCENTAGE
1234	233	57.5
1230	5	1.2
1204	28	6.9
1200	83	20.5
1034	6	1.5
1030	3	0.7
1004	31	7.7
1000	16	4.0
Totals	405	100.0

can be a bit misleading with so many patterns of incomplete data. However, an initial statistical summary of some of this raw information is presented in Table 5.2. The statistics presented in the table are based on an accumulation of scores into nearest half-year age categories (i.e., $Age[t] = [6.0, 6.5, 7.0, 7.5, \ldots, 14.0]$). For both variables we list the number of people measured and the mean and standard deviation of the scores in that category. As can be seen in Table 5.2, there are slightly different numbers of available data points at each time for each person, so we use a statistical technique that accounts for this complexity.

This age grouping approach also permits us to create a relatively large and sparse (17×17) matrix of pairwise correlations among all scores over all ages, and most of these correlations are positive (e.g., the correlation between the first and fourth occasions is $r[1, 4] = .45$, $N = 233$; see McArdle & Bell, 2000). However, this pairwise correlation matrix is not included here because it could be misleading: Each correlation would be based on largely incomplete information, the standard errors would vary depending on the common sample size, and these interrelations would not be used in further modeling analyses. Further interpretation of these kinds of statistics are considered based on the model guiding the analyses.

Model Fitting Computer Programs

There are now many different SEM computer programs that can carry out such analyses, including some with friendly and colorful names (see Hamagami, 1997). All such computer programs have common technical features, and many

TABLE 5.2

Summary Statistics for PIAT–Reading and BPI–Antisocial Scores From the NLSY Data Set Using Data From All Measured Occasions

AGE CATEGORY (YEARS)	PIAT-READING			BPI-ANTISOCIAL		
	N	*M*	*SD*	*N*	*M*	*SD*
6.0	68	20.8	3.4	68	11.4	12.0
6.5	107	25.7	8.4	107	14.0	14.1
7.0	87	29.5	6.7	87	12.4	12.7
7.5	79	36.3	10.6	79	16.9	14.8
8.0	127	41.5	11.8	128	16.1	15.8
8.5	101	46.1	12.6	100	16.8	16.1
9.0	81	47.2	11.5	81	14.0	15.3
9.5	70	53.7	11.4	72	19.4	17.2
10.0	109	54.2	13.6	110	15.2	17.5
10.5	66	59.0	14.5	76	16.1	17.4
11.0	69	59.8	12.8	70	13.0	14.1
11.5	47	61.6	13.3	52	18.3	15.5
12.0	93	65.1	13.6	96	16.6	15.8
12.5	70	67.3	16.0	79	18.7	19.4
13.0	68	68.9	14.4	73	17.6	19.2
13.5	47	73.5	14.0	49	16.3	15.3
14.0	36	69.7	16.2	43	14.5	18.0

Note. $N = 405$. All scores were initially rescaled into a 0–100 percentage-correct form. All statistics are from Mx-96/1.04 based on incomplete-data convergence models. PIAT = Peabody Individual Achievement Test; BPI = Behavior Problems Inventory; NLSY = National Longitudinal Survey of Youth.

of these programs can be used for analysis of the present set of data. The longitudinal analyses we present here were initially carried out using the LISREL 8 computer program (Jöreskog & Sörbom, 1979, 1993), but the fitting of individual raw data was accomplished by using the current version of the Mx computer program by Neale (1993). These input scripts include the SEM algebra needed for the automatic generation of mean and covariance expectations.

This numerical technique was used because it allowed us to simultaneously evaluate hypotheses about both the covariances and the mean structures (for further details, see Browne & Arminger, 1995; McArdle, 1988; Meredith & Tisak, 1990; and Sörbom, 1974). All analyses to follow are based on maximum-likelihood estimation (MLE). In typical cases, these MLEs can be obtained from an *augmented-moments matrix* (e.g., an average sums of squares and crossproducts or a central moments matrix; for further details, see Browne & Arminger,

1995; and McArdle & Aber, 1990). Because of the incomplete raw data, we use slightly more complex statistical approaches for dealing with estimation and goodness of fit. However, in these analyses we report an approximate likelihood ratio test (LRT) statistic, the differences, the associated degrees of freedom, and a root mean square error of approximation (RMSEA) statistic. This minimal statistical information permits the calculation of several alternative indices of goodness of fit (e.g., Bollen, 1989).

Using any standard SEM program we could introduce the latent difference score model of, say, Figure 5.2, by using a few basic steps:

1. Define the vector of three manifest variables by ordering $m = [Y(0)$, $Y(t − 1), Y(t)]$, and the vector of 14 total variables $v = [Y(0), Y(t − 1), Y(t), e(0), e(t − 1), e(t), y(0), y(t − 1), y(t), y_0, \Delta y(t − 1), \Delta y(t), s, K]$.

2. Distinguish between these vectors by writing a 3×14 *filter* matrix **F** with fixed nonzero entries only at locations defined by $F[Y(0), Y(0)] = 1$, $F[Y(t − 1), Y(t − 1)] = 1$, and $F[Y(t), Y(t)] = 1$.

3. Include the one-headed arrows in this model: (a) Define an initially null 14×14 arrow matrix **A**. (b) Add fixed unit entries at locations defined by $A[Y(0), y(0)]$, $A[Y(t − 1), y(t − 1)]$, $A[Y(t), y(t)]$, $A[Y(0), e(0)]$, $A[Y(t − 1), e(t − 1)]$, $A[Y(t), e(t)]$, $A[y(0), \Delta y_0]$, $A[y(t − 1), \Delta y(t − 1)]$, $A[y(t), \Delta y(t)]$. (c) Add free but equal parameters defined at locations $A[\Delta y(t − 1), y(0)] = \beta$, $A[\Delta y(t), y(t − 1)] = \beta$, $A[\Delta y(t − 1), s] = \alpha$, $A[\Delta y(t), s] = \alpha$. (d) Add free latent means defined at locations $A[y(0), K] = \mu_0$, $A(s, K) = \mu_s$.

4. Include the *two-headed arrows* in this model: (a) Define an initially null 14×14 *sling* matrix **S**. (b) Add free nonzero entries defined at locations $S[e(0), e(0)] = \sigma_e^2$, $S[e(t − 1), e(t − 1)] = \sigma_e^2$, $S[e(t), e(t)] = \sigma_e^2$, $S(y_0, y_0) = \sigma_0^2$, $S(s, s) = \sigma_s^2$, $S(y_0, s) = \sigma_{0s}$. (c) Add one fixed unit crossproduct at the location defined by $S(K, K) = 1$.

5. Identify the DCS model parameters: In the univariate case this can be done by either setting (a) slope loading $\alpha = 1$ or (b) slope variance $\sigma_s^2 = 1$ and estimating one and only one error variance σ_e^2 (as in a quasi-Markov model; see Jöreskog & Sörbom, 1979).

This notation for structural algebra and graphics permits models with covariances and means or raw data, and this same logic can be used to represent the models of Figures 5.3 and 5.4. In most actual applications the choice of an algebraic representation is arbitrary but because of the complexity of the longitudinal models, this simplified algebraic approach seems to be useful (for examples, see McArdle & Hamagami, 1996; McArdle, Prescott, Hamagami, & Horn, 1998; and McArdle & Woodcock, 1997).

Dealing With Incomplete Data

A multiple-group SEM approach presented by us (McArdle & Hamagami, 1991, 1992) was initially used to account for initial participant self-selection and participant dropout (attrition). In this approach participant vectors are assigned to groups on the basis of having a common pattern of complete and incomplete data. The identical latent growth model is assumed to account for these data, but the number of manifest variables in the **Y** vector differs across groups— that is, different groups have different patterns of circles and squares. Each group is specified with one invariant **A** regression matrix and one invariant **S** moment matrix, but the observed variables are "filtered" using different **F** matrices (i.e., where the F_g is a matrix of 1s and 0s defining the pattern of observed data within each group). On a conceptual basis this multiple-group approach is appealing and requires no new SEM software.

One technical problem is that very small sample sizes in some of the groups are likely to lead to a singular-moment matrix, and full MLE is not possible (e.g., participants with longitudinal pattern 1234 number $n = 233$, but pattern 1230 includes only $n = 5$). These problems are even more severe if one wishes to estimate a model based on the age at testing. If one uses the same technique listed above but makes a slot for each age (in, say, half-year increments), one has 17 possible ages at measurement that range from 6.0 years to 14.0 years (see Table 5.2). Because any individual can fill a maximum of four of these age slots (i.e., the ages at which he or she was measured), one can end up with a large number of age patterns. The 405 participants measured here have more than 50 different patterns of ages at measurement, and many of these patterns have very small sample sizes.

The complexity of this problem led us to use a nonstandard approach to model fitting: estimating the parameters using all individual raw data using a *pedigree analysis* technique (i.e., Lange, Westlake, & Spence, 1976; Neale, 1993). This maximum-likelihood technique is just one of a class of incomplete-data analysis techniques, and it should give the same results as other computer programs (e.g., HLM, AMOS, etc.). In this approach, a structural model is defined, and a set of parameters are iteratively estimated to maximize the likelihood (L) of the raw data (Y). To do so here we have fit the LGM using the (405 × 4) raw data matrix as input to the Mx program (using the "raw" data option). This matrix includes 1,620 possible data points, but only 1,325 of these data points are complete (81.2%; see Tables 5.1 and 5.2). These data were set up to include only 17 possible ages at testing (i.e., $Age[t] = [6.0, 6.5, 7.0, 7.5, \ldots, 14]$). This grouping by half-year ages was not strictly necessary, and certainly not optimal, but it was easy to implement. This approach seemed to work well, so the results using all available information for any participant on any data point (i.e., any variable measured at any occasion) are presented next.

Results

In this illustration, we are mainly interested in describing the time-to-time sequential relationships among the reading and antisocial behavior scores. We start with a univariate analysis of each variable separately. Four models are fitted to describe the interdynamic sequence of each variable, and we interpret the coefficients of these models as a description of the trajectory of each variable over time. Next we fit a bivariate model to describe the dynamic relationships across the variables. We interpret the coefficients of these models in terms of a description of the coupling, or lead–lag relationships, among reading and antisocial behavior.

The Univariate Latent Difference Model

In Table 5.3 we present results from four models fitted to the raw data on PIAT–Reading. The first model is a no-growth model that includes three parameters (μ_0, σ_0, σ_e) and a fit to the raw data (with a likelihood of $L_0 = 11,615$). The size of this initial likelihood is dependent on the raw scale scoring of the data, but this likelihood can be used as a constant baseline to judge the improvement in fit of the other models. This simple three-parameter model posits an equal mean, equal variance, and equal correlation over all occasions, and these restrictions generally yield a poor fit compared to the other models, which are discussed next.

The second model fitted is a PCS model, and this model adds a multiplicative parameter β to the prior model. The resulting model has four estimated parameters, including an initial mean ($\mu = 30.7$) and standard deviation ($\sigma_0 = 6.1$) at age 6, an autoproportion coefficient ($\beta = .06$) for one-half year of age, and an error deviation ($\sigma_e = 8.5$). This PCS model fits the raw data ($L_1 = 10,103$) and, by comparison with the baseline model ($L_0 = 11,615$), we obtain a substantial change in fit ($L_0 - L_1 = \text{LRT} = 1,512$ on $df = 1$). The inclusion of this single parameter represents a relatively large improvement over the no-growth model for these data.

The third model is a CCS model, and it forms a linear basis for all possible ages at testing. This model was identified by adding a common slope variable (s) with a fixed parameter $\alpha = 1$ to the structural model. The model includes six estimated parameters, including an initial level ($\mu = 25.6$) and deviation ($\sigma_0 = 4.7$) at age 6, a mean slope ($\mu_s = 3.4$) and standard deviation ($\sigma_s = 0.8$) for one-half year of age, an error deviation ($\sigma_e = 7.2$), and a latent correlation ($\rho_{0s} = .9$). This CCS model fits the raw data ($L_2 = 9,790$) and, by comparison with the baseline model ($L_0 = 11,615$), we obtain a substantial change in fit ($L_0 - L_2 = \text{LRT} = 1,825$ on $df = 3$). This CCS model is a large improvement over the no-growth model.

TABLE 5.3

Numerical Results From Alternative Change Score Models Fitted to the All Incomplete Longitudinal NLSY–Reading Composite Raw Data Vectors

PARAMETER AND FIT INDEX	ε_0 NO CHANGE SCORE BASELINE (NCS)	ε_1 PROPORTIONAL CHANGE SCORE (PCS)	ε_2 CONSTANT CHANGE SCORE (CCS)	ε_3 DUAL CHANGE SCORE
Additive loading α	0[a]	0[a]	1[a]	1[a]
Multiplicative proportion β	0[a]	.06[b]	0[a]	-.09[b]
Initial mean μ_0	49.0[b]	30.7[b]	25.6[b]	19.7[b]
Slope mean μ_s	0[a]	0[a]	3.4[b]	7.7[b]
Initial deviation σ_0	6.5[b]	6.1[b]	4.8[b]	3.9[b]
Slope deviation σ_s	0[a]	0[a]	0.8[b]	1.7[b]
Correlation $\rho_{0,s}$	0[a]	0[a]	.90[b]	-.79[b]
Error deviation ψ	18.4[b]	8.5[b]	7.2[b]	6.3[b]
Parameters	3	4	6	7
Degrees of freedom	V-3	V-4	V-6	V-7
Likelihood ratio	11,615	10,103	9,790	9,560
Differences between models ΔLRT/Δdf		NCS–1,512/1	NCS–1,825/3	NCS–2,055/4 PCS–543/3 CCS–230/1

Note. All scores were rescaled into 0–100% correct form. Interval of time was set to $\Delta t = 1/2$ years. Moments-based maximum-likelihood estimation was obtained from Mx-96/1.04 for $N = 405$ and $V = 1,325$. NLSY = National Longitudinal Survey of Youth; LRT = likelihood ratio test; V = total number of observations. [a]Fixed parameter. [b]Parameter is at least twice its own SE.

The fourth and final model fitted here is a DCS model. This model was identified by estimating both the multiplicative parameter β and including a slope score with a fixed $\alpha = 1$. The resulting model has seven estimated parameters, including an initial mean ($\sigma = 19.7$) and standard deviation ($\mu_0 = 3.9$) at age 6, a mean slope ($\mu_s = 7.7$) and deviation ($\sigma_s = 1.7$), a one-half year autoproportion coefficient ($\beta = -.09$), an error deviation ($\sigma_e = 6.3$), and a latent correlation ($\rho_{0s} = -.79$). This DCS model fits the raw data ($L_3 = 9,560$) better than all other models. This result is different from (a) the baseline model ($L_0 - L_3 = \text{LRT} = 2,055$ on $df = 4$), (b) the CCS model ($L_1 - L_3 = \text{LRT} = 230$ on $df = 1$), and (c) the PCS model ($L_2 - L_3 = \text{LRT} = 543$ on $df = 3$). On a statistical basis this DCS model for reading seems much better than the other models fitted here.

The same four models were fitted to the BPI–Antisocial scores, and the results are listed in Table 5.4. Here the alternative models fit only slightly better than the baseline models. The best model was again the DCS, including an initial mean ($\mu = 11.8$) and standard deviation ($\sigma_0 = 5.9$) at age 6, a mean slope ($\mu_s = 4.2$) and deviation ($\sigma_s = 3.4$), a one-half year autoproportion coefficient ($\beta = -.24$), an error deviation ($\sigma_e = 11.0$), and a latent correlation ($\rho_{0,s} = .68$). This DCS model fits the raw data ($L_3 = 11,102$) slightly better than all other models. This result is different from (a) the baseline model ($L_0 - L_3 = \text{LRT} = 72$ on $df = 4$), (b) the CCS model ($L_1 - L_3 = \text{LRT} = 14$ on $df = 1$), and (c) the PCS model ($L_2 - L_3 = \text{LRT} = 27$ on $df = 3$). On a statistical basis this DCS model for antisocial behavior scores seems only slightly better than the other models fitted here.

Other analyses were completed to provide a direct comparison of some of the model fits when using the complete and incomplete data sets. An important issue here is the individual analysis of the misfit. The individual likelihood indices (L_n) were calculated for all 405 participants on all models (using an Mx-OUTPUT option). This procedure allowed the numerical results from the LDS model *individual misfits* to be plotted sequentially for each of the participants. Although no notable outliers were found here, the analysis of individual misfits certainly provides some useful information (as used in McArdle, 1997).

The Bivariate Model

Several bivariate DCS models were fitted using all raw data from the NLSY data for both reading scores and antisocial scores. Just in terms of dynamic parameters, we can fit many different combinations of the three model parameters (i.e., α, β, and γ) using both variables $y(t)$ and $x(t)$ (see McArdle & Hamagami, 1999). To simplify these issues here, we report on only three models: (a) a baseline model, (b) a fully saturated bivariate model based on Figure 5.4, and (c) the same model with no slopes. Figure 5.4 was directly specified using a

TABLE 5.4

Numerical Results From Alternative Change Score Models Fitted to the All Incomplete Longitudinal NLSY–Antisocial Composite Raw Data Vectors

PARAMETER AND FIT INDEX	ε_0 NO CHANGE SCORE BASELINE (NCS)	ε_1 PROPORTIONAL CHANGE SCORE (PCS)	ε_2 CONSTANT CHANGE SCORE (CCS)	ε_3 DUAL CHANGE SCORE
Additive loading α	0^a	0^a	1^a	1^a
Multiplicative proportion β	$.00^a$	$.03^b$	$.00^a$	$-.24^b$
Initial mean μ_0	15.8^b	13.1^b	13.7^b	11.8^b
Slope mean μ_s	0.0^a	0.0^a	0.3^b	4.2^b
Initial deviation σ_0	11.2^b	9.5^b	8.2^b	5.9^b
Slope deviation σ_s	0.0^a	0.0^a	0.6^b	3.4^b
Correlation $\rho_{0,s}$	$.00^a$	$.00^a$	$.63^b$	$.68^b$
Error deviation ψ	11.6^b	11.3^b	11.1^b	11.0^b
Parameters	3	4	6	7
Degrees of freedom	V-3	V-4	V-6	V-7
Likelihood ratio	11,174	11,129	11,116	11,102
Differences between models ΔLRT/Δdf	—	NCS–45/1	NCS–58/3	NCS–72/4 PCS–27/3 CCS–14/1

Note. All scores were rescaled into 0–100% correct form. Interval of time was set to $\Delta t = 1/2$ years. Moments-based maximum-likelihood estimation was obtained from Mx–96/1.04 for $N = 404$ and $V = 1,325$. NLSY = National Longitudinal Survey of Youth; LRT = likelihood ratio test; V = total number of observations. [a] Fixed parameter. [b] Parameter is at least twice its own SE.

three-matrix expression, and the incomplete and unequal time lag spacing between these occasions was handled in the same way as described before. Selected numerical results from the Mx program are presented in Table 5.5.

The initial no-change baseline model used required seven parameters (μ_{y0}, μ_{x0}, σ_{y0}, σ_{x0}, σ_{ey}, σ_{ex}, σ_{ey}, and σ_{xy}). This longitudinal model required equal means, equal variances, equal within-variable correlations, and an equal within-variable correlation at all occasions. This restrictive model led to a very poor fit to the raw data of Table 5.2 ($L_0 = 21,327$).

The results listed in the first two columns of Table 5.5 come from a fully saturated BDCS model. As starting values for this SEM we used the MLE obtained in the previously separate univariate DCS models (see Tables 5.3 and 5.4). The results for antisocial raw scores ($Y[t]$) yielded a small constant slope (μ_{sy} or $\alpha_y = 4.2$), a large autoproportion ($\beta_y = -.27$), and a nontrivial coupling parameter from $x(t)$ to $y(t)$ ($\gamma_y = -.11$). In contrast, the model for the reading raw scores [$X(t)$] includes a large positive mean slope (μ_{sx} or $\alpha_x = 9.1$), a small autoproportion ($\beta_x = -.08$), and a trivial coupling parameter from $x(t)$ to $y(t)$ ($\gamma_x = -.008$). The initial levels and slopes are all correlated (e.g., $\rho_{sy,sx} = .65$). This fully saturated model includes 21 parameters, and the fit is a large improvement over the baseline no-change model ($L_0 - L_4 = \text{LRT}_{14} = 2,690$).

The substantive interpretation of a bivariate coupling can now be evaluated on a statistical basis by fitting a few additional models. First we fit an omnibus test of the impact of coupling by restricting both parameters to zero ($\gamma_y = \gamma_x = 0$), and this led to a small but significant loss of fit ($\text{LRT}_1 = 6$). Second, we fit a model restricting the "x as leader" to be zero ($\gamma_x = 0$), and this led to a small but significant loss of fit ($L_3 - L_1 = \text{LRT}_1 = 5$). Third, we fit a model restricting the "y as leader" to be zero ($\gamma_y = 0$), and this led to a nonsignificant loss of fit ($\text{LRT}_1 = 1$). Taken as a whole, these model comparisons imply that antisocial behavior is not a leading indicator of reading, but reading may be a small leading indicator of antisocial behavior. Careful readers will notice that this lead–lag interpretation is based strictly on the dynamic coefficients (γ_y, γ_x) and not on the correlations among the levels and slopes.

The final model fitted is presented in the last two columns of Table 5.5. Here we have eliminated all 10 parameters dealing with the constant change slopes. The results show the parameters of this multiple-occasion crosslagged model including autoproportions ($\beta_y = -.03$ $\beta_x = -.03$) that may be translated into standard autoregressions ($B_{yy} = .97$, $B_{xx} = .97$). This model also includes crosslags ($\gamma_y = .30$, $\gamma_x = .001$) that may be interpreted in a way similar to the dynamic coupling of the previous BDCS model. However, in contrast to the previous BDCS model, this no-slope model does not fit the data well ($L_5 - L_4 = \text{LRT}_9 = 601$). Although several alternative models may be fitted using this logic (i.e., growth in $y[t]$ but not in $x[t]$), this general result means that the

TABLE 5.5

Numerical Results From Bivariate Dual Change Score (BDCS) Models Fitted to the Longitudinal NLSY Statistics

PARAMETER AND FIT INDEX	ε_4 FULLY SATURATED MODEL		ε_5 NO-SLOPE MODEL	
	ANTISOCIAL EQ. (Y[f] =)	READING EQ. (X[f] =)	ANTISOCIAL EQ. (Y[f] =)	READING EQ. (X[f] =)
Loading α	1[a]	1[a]	0[a]	0[a]
Proportion α	−.27[b]	−.08[b]	−.03[b]	−.03[b]
Coping γ	−.11[b]	−.008[c]	.30[b]	.001[b]
Initial mean μ_0	12.5[b]	19.6[b]	19.0(7)[b]	21.5[b]
Mean slope μ_s	4.2[b]	9.1[b]	1[a]	1[a]
Initial deviation σ_0	7.1[b]	4.0[b]	3.6(7)[b]	5.5[b]
Slope deviation σ_s	3.7[b]	1.8[b]	0[a]	0[a]
Correlation $\rho_{0,s}$	.65[b]	−.41[b]	0[a]	0[a]
Correlations $\rho_{y0,x0}$, $\rho_{sy,sx}$,	−.90[b]	.65[b]	.76[b]	0[a]
$\rho_{sy,x0}$, $\rho_{sx,y0}$	−.35[b]	−.21[b]	0[b]	0[a]
Error deviation ψ and $\rho_{ex,cy}$	11.0[b]	6.1[b]	16.9(5)[b]	6.4[b]
	.20[b]		.20[b]	
Parameters	21		12	
Degrees of freedom	V-21		V-12	
Likelihood ratio	20,637		21,238	
Differences between models	NCS-2,690/14		NCS-2,089/5	
ΔLRT/Δdf			BDCS-601/9	

Note. Moments-based maximum-likelihood estimation (and *SE*) were obtained from RAMONA, LISREL-8, and Mx-96/1.04 for *N* = 405 and *V* = 2,695. The fit function for the no-change baseline model was LE_0 = 21,327. NLSY = National Longitudinal Survey of Youth; NCS = no-change score; LRT = likelihood ratio test; *V* = total number of observations. [a]Fixed parameter. [b]Parameter is at least twice its own *SE*. [c]Numerically improper solution.

standard crosslagged assumptions (i.e., no growth) are not a viable alternative for these NLSY data.

Plotting Trajectories Over Time

The expectations about the trajectory over time can be plotted from the parameters of any model, and these trajectories may facilitate interpretation of the results (see McArdle & Woodcock, 1997; Rogosa & Willett, 1985; and Willett, 1989). Plots of this type are presented in Figure 5.5.

FIGURE 5.5

Expected dynamic trajectories from the dual change score (DCS) and bivariate dual change score (BDCS) models of the National Longitudinal Survey of Youth data.

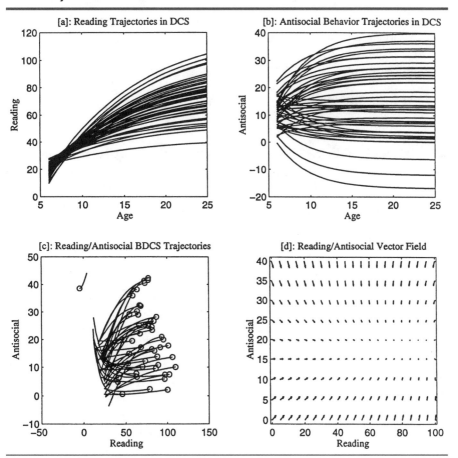

The resulting DCS equation for the PIAT–Reading scores can be written for the overall group curve from the model parameters as

$$E[\Delta \text{Reading}(t)_n] = \alpha \times \mu_s + \beta \times E[\text{Reading}(t - 1)_n]$$

$$= 7.7 - .09E[\text{Reading}(t - 1)_n], \qquad (5.8)$$

which shows that for each one-half year of age, the expected group mean of reading increases additively by 7.7 points and, at the same time, also decreases proportionally by −.09 points. The simple substitution of specific time points ($t = 1-16$) into this equation results in a nearly straight average group curve that could be added to Figure 5.5A. The projected values past age 14 (i.e., the limit of these data) illustrate forecasts about the future trajectory of these means. To produce individual latent curves we generated the expected individual latent curves based on the repeated application of the difference equation yielding curves that follow the particular solution. The resulting individual latent curves (for $N = 50$) seem to show more upward curvature than the means. This collection of curves also shows increasing variance in the well-known shape of a "fan spread" (see Cook & Campbell, 1979, pp. 184–185).

The resulting DCS equation for the BPI–Antisocial scores can be written for the overall group curve from the model parameters as

$$E[\Delta \text{Antisocial}(t)_n] = \alpha \times \mu_s + \beta \times E[\text{Antisocial}(t - 1)_n]$$

$$= 4.2 - .24E[\text{Antisocial}(t - 1)_n], \qquad (5.9)$$

which shows that for each one-half year of age, the expected group mean of antisocial increases additively by 4.2 points and, at the same time, also decreases proportionally by −.24 points. This function is plotted in Figure 5.5B as a group trajectory and as a set of individual latent curves based on these model parameters. This more extreme positive–negative (increase–decrease) dynamic also leads to a curve with an asymptote with an equilibrium point (e.g., where the increases equal the decreases).

These graphic illustrations show only one small sampling of the family of curves that can be generated from the few DCS model parameters. These group curves show the mean-structure contributions to the model, and the individual curves add the covariance-structure contributions to the model. The individual reading and antisocial scores may be of interest on a substantive basis (as in Patterson & Bank, 1989; see also McArdle, 1989), but these latent scores are common factor score estimates, so they should be considered indeterminant at the individual level (see McDonald, 1985; and Saris, de Pijper, & Mulder, 1978).

The resulting dynamic structural equations for the bivariate DCS model can be written as

$$E[\Delta\text{Reading}(t)_n] = \alpha_y \times \mu_{sy} + \beta_y \times E[\text{Reading}(t - 1)_n]$$

$$+ \gamma_y \times E[\text{Antisocial}(t - 1)_n]$$

$$= 4.2 - .27E[\text{Reading}(t - 1)_n]$$

$$- .11E[\text{Antisocial}(t - 1)_n]$$

$$E[\Delta\text{Antisocial}(t)_n] = \alpha_x \times \mu_{sx} + \beta_x \times E[\text{Antisocial}(t - 1)_n]$$

$$+ \gamma_x \times E[\text{Reading}(t - 1)_n]$$

$$= 9.1 - .08E[\text{Antisocial}(t - 1)_n]$$

$$- .008E[\text{Reading}(t - 1)_n], \tag{5.10}$$

and fitting these simultaneous latent difference equations yielded some new estimates (e.g., $\beta_y \, \mu_{sy} = 4.2$ vs. 7.7 in Equation 5.7). One interpretation of these expressions is drawn in Figure 5.5C. This is a different kind of time sequence plot because here, for each individual, is drawn the expected reading latent curve scores paired against the expected antisocial latent curve scores for the same occasions. This "state-space" pairing of latent growth curves seems to show that most individuals follow rapid increases in both variables, with a few individuals dropping off toward lower reading scores but higher antisocial scores. The correlations among the latent components are not dynamic (i.e., time dependent), but they are informative because they describe the location of the individual dynamic curves in the time sequence plots.

The final picture of Figure 5.5D is a *statistical vector field* (see Boker & McArdle, 1995) version of the same bivariate curves in Figure 5.5C. Each arrow in Figure 5.5D shows the general direction of all curves within that specific region (equal-sized cells) of these curves. That is, for any pair of latent scores at time t (i.e., $x[t]$, $y[t]$) the small arrow points to where the pair of latent scores are expected to be at Time $t + 1$ (i.e., $x[t + 1]$, $y[t + 1]$). This final figure was calculated from only the model coefficients, and it seems to emphasize the increases in the upper quadrant of the bivariate field. Of course, these patterns are relatively weak because of the sizes of the parameters described. A more detailed evaluation of the robustness of the salient features of this plot is now needed.

Overview of the LDS Approach

The approach we used in this chapter is based on a model for a set of variables measured over time in terms of a prediction equation for first differences in latent variables (true scores). In these models we assumed that some dynamic process can be identified over some well-defined intervals of time and explained by a structural expression including a set of unknown parameters and variables. We made some practical choices, added individual differences to the scores, and demonstrated how we could fit a variety of alternative models using standard SEM algebra.

Our broad goal was to use these models to make some sensible dynamic statements about longitudinal data. The success or failure of this approach may come from the reasonableness of some of the broad LDS model features used here:

1. apply to latent variables but only indirectly to observed variables.

2. use a latent difference score as the key dependent variable.

3. written for differences over discrete periods of time and not as differentials for continuous periods of time.

4. written as deterministic over time within an individual.

5. allow individual differences between people.

6. may be estimated and fit using standard structural equation algorithms.

7. lead to some useful theoretical relationships among all kinds of structural and dynamic models.

Each of these features was added for practical or theoretical reasons, and each can be altered as needed.

In practice, the raw data model fitting approach (using Mx) seemed useful. In this approach one does not attempt to impute the scores that are missing, but one does attempt to *compute* the model parameters using all available data. These raw data techniques were used here to both (a) provide an equal latent interval and (b) not require complete data on all participants and look at likelihood-based outliers. Unfortunately, this estimation approach relies on some untestable assumptions about the data, including that the incomplete data are missing at random (Little & Rubin, 1987) and subgroup metric factorial invariance (Meredith, 1993). The raw data approach was a bit tedious to set up and is computationally slower than the standard block-matrix approach to incomplete data analysis (e.g., McArdle, 1994; McArdle & Bell, 2000; McArdle & Hamagami, 1992, 1998; McArdle & Woodcock, 1997).

Model Extensions and Future Research

This LDS approach naturally allows far more complexity in dynamic models of change. For example, one could allow the parameters of the model to be time dependent simply by permitting parameters $\alpha(t)$ and $\beta(t)$ (as in Meredith & Tisak, 1990; see also McArdle, 1988). In any model one may wish to consider the inclusion of a disturbance term at the latent variable level by adding some unique time-dependent disturbance score (as in Guttman, 1955; see also Jöreskog, 1970, 1974). Even more complex lagged effects and the "moving averages" or "random shocks" can be considered as part of a model (e.g., Pankratz, 1991). When these bivariate models are extended for use with multivariate longitudinal data, a variety of alternative models can be considered (as in McArdle, 1988, 1989; McArdle & Woodcock, 1997; Nesselroade & McArdle, 1997).

The final LDS illustrations presented here dealt with the central problem of interrelations among different growth variables. In previous work, McArdle (1989, 1991) outlined some of these issues and fit a model where the levels and slopes (y_0, s_y) of one series ($y[t]$) were correlated with, or regressed onto, the levels and slopes (x_0, s_x) of a different series ($x[t]$). A similar kind of LGM analysis was recently presented by Willett and Sayer (1996); Walker, Acock, Bowman, and Li (1996); and Raykov (1997). Of most importance in these kinds of analyses is the idea that the correlation among the slopes of two different variables may reflect something about the common changes (Griffiths & Sandland, 1984; McArdle & Nesselroade, 1994). However, it is also important to recognize that models of individual-differences relationships among dynamic variables do not necessarily reflect dynamic processes for the group. In this way the bivariate dynamic model of Figure 5.4 is different than its predecessors. The substantive differences that can result because of different models can be seen in the latent growth curve analyses of the same NLSY data presented by Curran and Hussong (in press).

Another useful feature of this SEM strategy is that multivariate extensions follow naturally. We could, for example, use the dynamic latent variables together with additional external predictors (as in McArdle & Epstein, 1987). In the context of growth models, this strategy has often been used to examine correlates of change (e.g., Rogosa & Willett, 1985) or in what are now popularly termed "multilevel models," "hierarchical models," or "random coefficients models" (see Bryk & Raudenbush, 1992; Goldstein & McDonald, 1988; Longford, 1993; and McArdle & Hamagami, 1996), and now we can add "multivariate dynamic parameters" (McArdle, 1988; McArdle & Woodcock, 1997). Other, more qualitative questions can be answered by extending a model of multiple-group factorial invariance to dynamic processes (see Horn & McArdle, 1980, 1992; Jöreskog, 1971; McArdle & Cattell, 1994; Meredith & Horn, chapter 7, this volume; and Sörbom, 1974). In a multiple-group dynamic model one initially writes a separate dynamic model for independent subgroups of persons, and then one can evaluate hypotheses about the equality of group dynamics by means of models fit with equality constraints in the group parameters (e.g., $\alpha^{[g]}$, $\beta^{[g]}$, and $\gamma^{[g]}$).

This also leads us to consider even more complex nonlinear models of change (e.g., Boker, 1997, chapter 1, this volume; Brown, 1988; Nesselroade

& Boker, 1994; Vallacher & Nowak, 1994). Although many of these nonlinear models have additional requirements for lengthy time series, the basic equations used here can be extended to deal with some of the variations on this same general theme. Here, however, further exploration is required to examine the sensitivity of LDS model estimates and fit to various assumptions. The assumption of an equal time interval among latent variables requires some accurate assessment of the interval of time between manifest variables, and this is often a practical problem (Gollob & Reichardt, 1987). The additional assumption about equal interval scaling seems most crucial when a difference score of any kind is used, and the assessment of item-based measurement models may be needed in advance of any dynamic system model (e.g., McArdle & Woodcock, 1997). The measurement issues involved in using each of these variables—reading (see Schawitz, Escobar, Shawitz, Fletcher, & Makuch, 1992) and antisocial behavior (see Patterson & Bank, 1989)—are complex. A focus on measurement of timing and the scaling of variables is critical to future work (Nesselroade, 1993).

Final Comments

In practice, the LDS models presented here offer a practical way to formalize and evaluate some of the dynamic features between different variables measured over time, and this approach is required by contemporary psychological theory (e.g., Baltes, 1987; Horn, 1972; Tanner, 1960). We have illustrated how the LDS approach is a practical use of available SEM techniques and how the resulting estimates can tell us something about change or dynamic features within a variable measured over time. This LDS approach also permits combinations of the useful features of many prior repeated-measures models, such as multivariate analysis of variance or crosslagged regression, but it is also far more flexible. However, as with any other model, LDS can offer a next approximation that is only as good as the data and the theory being evaluated.

In theory, the LDS models just described can be a reasonable match to the goals of longitudinal data analysis proposed by Baltes and Nesselroade (1979):

1. The direct identification of intraindividual change was organized and evaluated by the parameters of the original difference model.
2. Interindividual differences in change were permitted by the parameters representing the means and the variances around the means.
3. The analysis of interrelations in change included parameters related to both levels and slopes.
4. The analysis of causes (determinants) of intraindividual change was reflected in the dynamic coupling parameters of the bivariate model.

5. The analysis of causes (determinants) of interindividual differences in intraindividual change was not fully considered here but can be seen as a natural extension of these LDS models.

A most informative aspect of future LGM analyses will be based on differences between groups in the fundamental dynamic processes. Historians of developmental psychology and behavioral science will be pleased to find that there are now some improved formal ways to deal with the kinds of questions that are routinely asked but rarely answered (e.g., Featherman, Lerner, & Perlmutter, 1994; Wohwill, 1973). In future work we may even begin an analysis by asking, "What is your model for $\Delta Y(t)/\Delta(t)$?" It will be intriguing to find out if future modeling analyses will have the accuracy and power to let us know when our dynamic theories are wrong.

References

Allison, P. D. (1987). Estimation of linear models with incomplete data. In C. C. Clogg (Ed.), *Sociological methodology* (Vol. 17, pp. 71–103). San Francisco: Jossey-Bass.

American Guidance. (2000). *Peabody Individual Achievement Test.* Circle Pines, MN: Author.

Arminger, G. (1986). Linear stochastic differential equation models for panel data with unobserved variables. In N. B. Tuma (Ed.), *Sociological methodology* (Vol. 16, pp. 187–213). San Francisco: Jossey-Bass.

Baker, P. C., Keck, C. K., Mott, F. L., & Quinlan, S. V. (1993). *NLSY child handbook: A guide to the 1986–1990 National Longitudinal Survey of Youth child data* (rev. ed.). Columbus: Ohio State University, Center for Human Resources Research.

Baltes, P. B. (1987). Theoretical propositions of life-span developmental psychology: On the dynamics between growth and decline. *Developmental Psychology, 23,* 611–626.

Baltes, P. B., & Nesselroade, J. R. (1979). History and rationale of longitudinal research. In J. R. Nesselroade & P. B. Baltes (Eds.), *Longitudinal research in the study of behavior and development* (pp. 1–40). New York: Academic Press.

Bayley, N. (1956). Individual patterns of development. *Child Development, 27,* 45–74.

Bell, R. Q. (1953). Convergence: An accelerated longitudinal approach. *Child Development, 24,* 145–152.

Berk, R. A. (1983). An introduction to sample selection bias in sociological data. *American Sociological Review, 48,* 386–398.

Boker, S. M. (1997). *Linear and nonlinear dynamical systems data analytic techniques and an application to developmental data.* Unpublished doctoral dissertation, University of Virginia, Charlottesville.

Boker, S. M., & McArdle, J. J. (1995). Statistical vector field analysis applied to mixed cross-sectional and longitudinal data. *Experimental Aging Research, 21,* 77–93.

Bollen, K. A. (1989). *Structural equations with latent variables.* New York: Wiley.

Brown, C. (1988). *Ballots of tumult.* Ann Arbor: University of Michigan Press.

Browne, M., & Arminger, G. (1995). Specification and estimation of mean and covariance-structure models. In G. Arminger, C. C. Clogg, & M. E. Sobel (Eds.), *Handbook of statistical modeling for the social and behavioral sciences* (pp. 185–250). New York: Plenum Press.

Browne, M., & Du Toit, S. H. C. (1991). Models for learning data. In L. M. Collins & J. L. Horn (Eds.), *Best methods for the analysis of change: Recent advances, unanswered questions, future directions* (pp. 47–68). Washington, DC: American Psychological Association.

Bryk, A. S., & Raudenbush, S. W. (1992). *Hierarchical linear models: Applications and data analysis methods.* Newbury Park, CA: Sage.

Chase-Lansdale, P. L., Mott, F. L., Brooks-Gunn, J., & Phillips, D. A. (1991). Children of the National Longitudinal Survey of Youth: A unique research opportunity. *Developmental Psychology, 27,* 919–931.

Cohen, P. A. (1996, October). *Enhancing the clarity of presentation of multivariate data.* Paper presented at the annual meeting of the Society of Multivariate Experimental Psychology, Bellingham, WA.

Coleman, J. S. (1964). *Introduction to mathematical sociology.* New York: Free Press.

Collins, L. M., & Horn, J. L. (Eds.). (1991). *Best methods for the analysis of change.* Washington, DC: American Psychological Association.

Cook, T. D., & Campbell, D. T. (1979). *Design and analysis issues for field settings.* Boston, MA: Houghton Mifflin.

Curran, P., & Hussong, A. M. (in press). Structural equation modeling of repeated measures data. In D. Moskowitz & S. L. Hershberger (Eds.), *Modeling intraindividual variability with repeated measures data: Methods and applications.* Mahwah, NJ: Erlbaum.

Diggle, P. J., Liang, K.-Y., & Zeger, S. L. (1994). *Analysis of longitudinal data.* New York: Oxford University Press.

Duncan, S. C., & Duncan, T. E. (1995). Modeling the processes of development via latent variable growth curve methodology. *Structural Equation Modeling: A Multidisciplinary Journal, 2,* 187–213.

Dwyer, J. H., Feinleib, M., Lippert, P., & Hoffmeister, H. (1992). *Statistical models for longitudinal studies of health.* New York: Oxford University Press.

Featherman, D. L., Lerner, R. M., & Perlmutter, M. (Eds.). (1994). *Life-span development and behavior* (Vol. 12). Hillsdale, NJ: Erlbaum.

Goldberg, S. (1958). *Introduction to difference equations with illustrative examples from economics, psychology, and sociology.* New York: Wiley.

Goldstein, H., & McDonald, R. P. (1988). A general model for the analysis of multilevel data. *Psychometrika, 53,* 435–467.

Gollob, H. F., & Reichardt, C. S. (1987). Taking account of time lags in causal models. *Child Development, 58,* 80–92.

Griffiths, D., & Sandland, R. (1984). Fitting generalized allometric models to multivariate growth data. *Biometrics, 40,* 139–150.

Guttman, L. (1955). A generalized simplex for factor analysis. *Psychometrika, 20,* 173–182.

Hamagami, F. (1997). A review of the Mx computer program for structural equation modeling. *Structural Equation Modeling, 4,* 157–175.

Harris, C. W. (Ed.). (1963). *Problems in measuring change.* Madison: University of Wisconsin Press.

Heckman, J. J. (1979). Sample selection bias as a specification error. *Econometrica, 47,* 153–161.

Horn, J. L. (1972). State, trait, and change dimensions of intelligence. *British Journal of Educational Psychology, 42,* 159–185.

Horn, J. L. (1976). On extension analysis and its relation to correlations between variables and factor scores. *Multivariate Behavioral Research, 11,* 320–331.

Horn, J. L., & Little, K. B. (1966). Isolating change and invariance in patterns of behavior. *Multivariate Behavioral Research, 1,* 219–228.

Horn, J. L., & McArdle, J. J. (1980). Perspectives on mathematical and statistical model building (MASMOB) in research on aging. In L. Poon (Ed.), *Aging in the 1980's: Psychological issues* (pp. 503–541). Washington, DC: American Psychological Association.

Horn, J. L., & McArdle, J. J. (1992). A practical and theoretical guide to measurement invariance in aging research. *Experimental Aging Research, 18*(3–4), 117–144.

Jones, R. H. (1993). *Longitudinal data with serial correlation: A state–space approach.* London: Chapman & Hall.

Jöreskog, K. G. (1970). Estimation and testing of simplex models. *British Journal of Mathematical & Statistical Psychology, 23*(2), 121–145.

Jöreskog, K. G. (1971). Simultaneous factor analysis in several populations. *Psychometrika, 36,* 409–426.

Jöreskog, K. G. (1974). Analyzing psychological data by structural analysis of covariance matrices. In R. C. Atkinson (Ed.), *Contemporary developments in mathematical psychology* (Vol. 2, pp. 1–56). San Francisco: Freeman.

Jöreskog, K. G., & Sörbom, D. (1979). *Advances in factor analysis and structural equation models.* Cambridge, MA: Abt Books.

Jöreskog, K. G., & Sörbom, D. (1993). *LISREL 8: Structural equation modeling with the SIMPLIS command language.* Hillsdale, NJ: Erlbaum.

Lange, K., Westlake, J., & Spence, M. A. (1976). Extensions to pedigree analysis: III. Variance components by the scoring method. *Annals of Human Genetics, 39,* 485–491.

Lindsey, J. K. (1993). *Models for repeated measurements*. New York: Oxford University Press.

Little, R. J. A., & Rubin, D. B. (1987). *Statistical analysis with missing data*. New York: Wiley.

Loehlin, J. C. (1992). *Latent variable models: An introduction to factor, path, and structural analysis* (2nd ed.). Hillsdale, NJ: Erlbaum.

Lohmoeller, J-B. (1989). *Latent variable path modeling with partial least squares*. Heidelberg, Germany: Physica-Verlag.

Longford, N. T. (1993). *Random coefficients models*. Oxford, England: Clarendon Press.

McArdle, J. J. (1988). Dynamic but structural equation modeling of repeated measures data. In J. R. Nesselroade & R. B. Cattell (Eds.), *The handbook of multivariate experimental psychology* (Vol. 2, pp. 561–614). New York: Plenum Press.

McArdle, J. J. (1989). Structural modeling experiments using multiple growth functions. In P. Ackerman, R. Kanfer, & R. Cudeck (Eds.), *Learning and individual differences: Abilities, motivation, and methodology* (pp. 71–117). Hillsdale, NJ: Erlbaum.

McArdle, J. J. (1991). Structural models of developmental theory in psychology. In P. Van Geert & L. P. Mos (Eds.), *Annals of theoretical psychology* (Vol. 7, pp. 139–160). New York: Plenum Press.

McArdle, J. J. (1994). Structural factor analysis experiments with incomplete data. *Multivariate Behavioral Research, 29*, 409–454.

McArdle, J. J. (1997). Recent trends in modeling longitudinal data by latent growth curve models. In G. Marcoulides (Ed.), *New statistical models with business and economic applications* (pp. 359–406). Mahwah, NJ: Erlbaum.

McArdle, J. J., & Aber, M. S. (1990). Patterns of change within latent variable structural equation modeling. In A. von Eye (Ed.), *New statistical methods in developmental research* (pp. 151–224). New York: Academic Press.

McArdle, J. J., & Anderson, E. (1990). Latent variable growth models for research on aging. In J. E. Birren & K. W. Schaie (Eds.), *The handbook of the psychology of aging* (pp. 21–43). New York: Plenum Press.

McArdle, J. J., & Bell, R. Q. (2000). Recent trends in modeling longitudinal data by latent growth curve methods. In T. D. Little, K. U. Schnabel, & J. Baumert (Eds.), *Modeling longitudinal and multiple-group data: Practical issues, applied approaches, and scientific examples* (pp. 69–108). Mahwah, NJ: Erlbaum.

McArdle, J. J., & Boker, S. M. (1990). *RAMpath: A computer program for automatic path diagrams*. Hillsdale, NJ: Erlbaum.

McArdle, J. J., & Cattell, R. B. (1994). Structural equation models of factorial invariance applied to parallel proportional profiles and confactor problems. *Multivariate Behavioral Research, 29*, 63–113.

McArdle, J. J., & Epstein, D. B. (1987). Latent growth curves within developmental structural equation models. *Child Development, 58*, 110–133.

McArdle, J. J., & Hamagami, F. (1991). Modeling incomplete longitudinal and cross-sectional data using latent growth structural models. *Experimental Aging Research, 18*, 145–166.

McArdle, J. J., & Hamagami, F. (1992). Modeling incomplete longitudinal data using latent growth structural equation models. In L. Collins & J. L. Horn (Eds.), *Best methods for the analysis of change* (pp. 276–304). Washington, DC: American Psychological Association.

McArdle, J. J., & Hamagami, F. (1995, June–July). *A dynamic structural equation modeling analysis of the theory of fluid and crystallized intelligence.* Paper presented at the annual meeting of the American Psychological Society and the European Congress of Psychology, Athens, Greece.

McArdle, J. J., & Hamagami, F. (1996). Multilevel models from a multiple group structural equation perspective. In G. Marcoulides & R. Schumacker (Eds.), *Advanced structural equation modeling: Issues and techniques* (pp. 89–124). Mahwah, NJ: Erlbaum.

McArdle, J. J., & Hamagami, F. (1998). *Dynamic structural equation analyses of longitudinal data based on a latent difference score approach.* Manuscript submitted for publication, University of Virginia, Charlottesville.

McArdle, J. J., & Hamagami, F. (1999). *Multivariate dynamic analyses of longitudinal data based on a latent difference score approach.* Manuscript submitted for publication, University of Virginia, Charlottesville.

McArdle, J. J., & McDonald, R. P. (1984). Some algebraic properties of the reticular action model for moment structures. *British Journal of Mathematical and Statistical Psychology, 37*, 234–251.

McArdle, J. J., & Nesselroade, J. R. (1994). Structuring data to study development and change. In S. H. Cohen & H. W. Reese (Eds.), *Life-span developmental psychology: Methodological innovations* (pp. 223–267). Mahwah, NJ: Erlbaum.

McArdle, J. J., Prescott, C. A., Hamagami, F., & Horn, J. L. (1998). A contemporary method for developmental–genetic analyses of age changes in intellectual abilities. *Developmental Neuropsychology, 14*, 69–114.

McArdle, J. J., & Woodcock, J. R. (1997). Expanding test–rest designs to include developmental time-lag components. *Psychological Methods, 2*, 403–435.

McDonald, R. P. (1985). *Factor analysis and related methods.* Hillsdale, NJ: Erlbaum.

Meredith, W. (1993). Measurement invariance, factor analysis and factorial invariance. *Psychometrika, 58*, 525–543.

Meredith, W., & Tisak, J. (1990). Latent curve analysis. *Psychometrika, 55*, 107–122.

Neale, M. C. (1993). *Mx statistical modeling.* Unpublished program manual, Virginia Commonwealth University, Richmond, Department of Human Genetics, Medical College of Virginia.

Nesselroade, J. R. (1993). Whether we Likert or not, personality measurement and the study of development and change are demanding activities. *Psychological Inquiry, 4*(1), 40–42.

Nesselroade, J. R., & Baltes, P. B. (Eds.). (1979). *Longitudinal research in the study of behavior and development*. New York: Academic Press.

Nesselroade, J. R., & Boker, S. M. (1994). Assessing constancy and change. In T. F. Heatherton & J. L. Weinberger (Eds.), *Can personality change?* (pp. 121–147). Washington, DC: American Psychological Association.

Nesselroade, J. R., & McArdle, J. J. (1997). On the mismatching of levels of abstraction in mathematical–statistical model fitting. In M. D. Franzen & H. W. Reese (Eds.), *Life-span developmental psychology: Biological and neuropsychological mechanisms* (pp. 23–49). Mahwah, NJ: Erlbaum.

Pankratz, A. (1991). *Forecasting with dynamic regression models*. New York: Wiley.

Patterson, G. R., & Bank, L. (1989). Some amplifying mechanisms for pathological processes in families. In M. R. Gunnar & E. Thelen (Eds.), *Systems and development: The Minnesota Symposia on Child Psychology* (Vol. 22, pp. 167–209). Hillsdale, NJ: Erlbaum.

Peterson, J. L., & Zill, N. (1986). Marital disruption, parent–child relationships, and behavior problems in children. *Journal of Marriage and the Family, 48*, 295–307.

Raykov, T. (1997). Disentangling intervention and temporal effects in longitudinal designs using latent curve analysis. *Journal of Biometrics, 39*, 239–259.

Rogosa, D., & Willett, J. B. (1985). Understanding correlates of change by modeling individual differences in growth. *Psychometrika, 50*, 203–228.

Rovine, M. J., & Delaney, M. (1991). Missing data estimation in developmental research. In A. von Eye (Ed.), *Statistical methods in longitudinal research* (pp. 35–79). Cambridge, MA: Academic Press.

Rubin, D. B. (1987). *Multiple imputation for nonresponse in surveys*. New York: Wiley.

Sandefur, J. T. (1993). *Discrete dynamic modeling*. New York: Oxford University Press.

Saris, W. E., de Pijper, W. M., & Mulder, J. (1978). Optimal procedures for the estimation of factor scores. *Sociological Methods and Research, 7*, 85–106.

Schafer, J. L. (1997). *Analysis of incomplete multivariate data*. London: Chapman & Hall.

Schawitz, S. E., Escobar, M. D., Shawitz, B. A., Fletcher, J. M., & Makuch, R. (1992). Evidence that dyslexia may represent the lower tail of a normal distribution or reading ability. *New England Journal of Medicine, 326*, 280–281.

Sörbom, D. (1974). A general method for studying differences in factor means and factor structures between groups. *British Journal of Mathematical and Statistical Psychology, 27*, 229–239.

Tanner, J. M. (Ed.). (1960). *Human growth*. New York: Pergamon Press.

Tuma, N., & Hannan, M. (1984). *Social dynamics*. New York: Academic Press.

Vallacher, R. R., & Nowak, A. (Eds.). (1994). *Dynamical systems in social psychology*. San Diego, CA: Academic Press.

Walker, A. J., Acock, A. C., Bowman, S. R., & Li, F. (1996). Amount of care given and caregiving satisfaction: A latent growth curve analysis. *Journal of Gerontology: Psychological Sciences, 51B*, 130–142.

Willett, J. B. (1989). Some results on reliability for the longitudinal measurement of change: Implications for the design of studies of individual growth. *Educational & Psychological Measurement, 49*, 587–602.

Willett, J. B., & Sayer, A. G. (1994). Using covariance structure analysis to detect correlates and predictors of individual change over time. *Psychological Bulletin, 116*, 363–381.

Willett, J. B., & Sayer, A. G. (1996). Cross-domain analyses of change over time: Combining growth modeling and covariance structure analysis. In G. Marcoulides & R. Schumacker (Eds.), *Advanced structural equation modeling: Issues and techniques* (pp. 125–157). Mahwah, NJ: Erlbaum.

Wohwill, J. F. (1973). *The study of behavioral development*. New York: Academic Press.

Editors' Introduction

One shortcoming of latent growth curve models has been that they do not take full advantage of the structural equation model's ability to model measurement error. In an ordinary first-order latent growth curve model, any deviation from the growth curve is considered an error. This confounds measurement error with true deviation from the growth curve. Aline Sayer and Patricio Cumsille address this in their chapter with a discussion of second-order growth curve models. These models simultaneously construct latent variables based on manifest indicators, using ordinary factor analysis methods, and estimate a growth model for these latent variables. The residual variance associated with the latent variables is then not attributable to the growth curve; in other words, this is a method for disentangling stability and change. It is interesting that this approach facilitates the testing of factorial invariance across occasions of measurement. Readers may be interested in comparing this chapter with those by Curran and Bollen (chapter 4), McArdle and Hamagami (chapter 5), and Kenny and Zautra (chapter 8). Another highly relevant chapter is chapter 7, by Meredith and Horn.

Second-Order Latent Growth Models

Aline G. Sayer

Patricio E. Cumsille

The assessment of change over time is fundamental to answering important research questions in the social sciences, including the study of psychological and social development, the process of learning, and the behavior of individuals in organizations. If researchers have panel data (repeated measurements taken on a relatively large group of individuals on a small number of occasions), if the phenomenon of interest changes systematically rather than fluctuating randomly, and if the variable of interest is measured on a continuous scale, then growth curve analysis is an appropriate and powerful method for drawing correct inferences about change.

This strategy is based on fitting a model to the repeated measures that allows for the description of systematic interindividual differences in intraindividual change. The individual growth modeling framework uses a hierarchical model to represent simultaneously individual status as a function of time (the *Level 1 model*, in random coefficient terminology) and interindividual differences in true change (the *Level 2 model*). Typically, the simplest forms of these models include parameters that describe individual growth, population average change, and the heterogeneity around the average change. If interindividual differences in change are present, covariates can be added to the model to predict such variability.

One of the most popular approaches to estimating the model parameters is to use mean and covariance structure analysis, as implemented in a variety of structural equation modeling (SEM) software packages, such as LISREL, AMOS, or EQS. A key feature of these structural equation models is the capacity to describe the relation of manifest (observed) indicators to the underlying latent construct that is assumed to drive the responses on these indicators. What is noteworthy is that this feature has been ignored in the SEM parameterization

This research was supported by National Institute on Drug Abuse Center Grant 1 P50DA10075.

of latent growth curve models; that is, the SEM growth model uses a first-order factor structure to investigate change in an observed score across time. The model is fit to the vector of means and covariance matrix among single observed scores measured at each assessment occasion. Often, these scores are composites of a set of ratings, questionnaire items, and other multiple indicators that are summed or averaged in some way to create an index for use in first-order latent growth modeling. Taking such an approach does not capitalize on the benefits inherent in modeling the relations between the indicators and the composite. Aside from ignoring important information about the psychometric properties of the items, this approach has the obvious disadvantage of incorporating the measurement errors of the various indicators into the observed composite score.

By contrast, a second-order latent growth model uses a second-order factor structure to investigate growth over time. It incorporates the multiple indicators directly into the model—that is, several items or scales represent the latent composite at each time. In the terminology of confirmatory factor analysis, these latent composites are *first-order factors*. Change is modeled in the repeated latent composites rather than in the observed scores. The growth parameters are the *second-order factors* that capture the shared variation among the latent composites.

Second-order latent growth modeling is a relatively new approach that has not been used to any great extent, although the theory underlying the approach has been available for some time (Duncan and Duncan, 1996; McArdle, 1988). The second-order latent growth model has several key advantages over the first-order model. First, it allows for the decomposition of the variance in the latent composites that is not attributable to growth. In a first-order model, the unique variance associated with each indicator (sometimes called *measurement error*) is confounded with time-specific variance (variance not dependent on time). The second-order model provides separate estimates for these sources of variance. Second, the model provides information about the measurement characteristics of the indicators. For example, when creating manifest composites using a summation procedure, the items are assumed to have equal, or unit weights. In a second-order model it is possible to test this assumption by fitting a first-order factor structure with unequal within-time factor loadings.

Perhaps most important, the second-order model permits a test of the factorial invariance of the composites over time. In the growth modeling context, the researcher must be convinced that it is the phenomenon that is changing rather than the scale used to measure the construct. Chan (1998) referred to this as *alpha* change, or change in absolute level given a constant conceptual domain and a constant measuring instrument. It is typical for researchers using the same indicator over time to implicitly assume both constant measurement (that the numerical values across waves are on the same scale) and constant conceptualization (that the construct retains the same interpretation across waves). However, this assumption is rarely tested in practice. This issue has great relevance for developmental science, where the time metric is typically age and change is measured over relatively long intervals. For example, many researchers are interested in charting trajectories of aggressive behavior from childhood to early adolescence. What is common, particularly in survey research, is the repeated use of the same questionnaire items at very different ages (e.g., does the child bully others?). The implicit assumption is that the question is tapping the same underlying construct on each occasion of measurement. Second-order growth modeling asks explicitly if indicators with the same face validity (identical scaling and wording) relate to the underlying construct in the same fashion over time. The second-order model allows the researcher to test directly for invariance by investigating individual item functioning across waves.

In this chapter, we are guided by the general framework provided by Meredith's (1993; see also Meredith & Horn, chapter 7, this volume) definition of *invariance*, although we recognize that it was developed for the purpose of determining invariance across populations rather than across time. An interesting issue is what forms of invariance are necessary in the growth modeling context. Meredith distinguishes between nonmetric (configural) and metric invariance, a distinction we retain in our analyses. We assume configural invariance when we can demonstrate that the pattern of the factor loadings is equivalent across time. Within the domain of metric invariance, Meredith described a taxonomy of weak, strong, and strict invariance. Weak invariance is present when the relations between the indicators and the construct, as represented by the magnitude of the factor loadings, are equivalent across time. This is the basic test of factorial invariance and is included in our models.

More stringent forms of invariance involve consideration of the means on both the measured and latent variables. In this chapter, we investigate the hypothesis of strong invariance by fitting models with constraints on the measurement intercepts, that is, the intercepts in the regression models that relate each indicator to the latent composite. Constraints on the latent composite means are not applicable to the growth modeling context, which assumes that there is change in the mean levels over time. Strict factorial invariance involves an additional constraint, that the measurement uniquenesses for each item (i.e., item residual variances) are equivalent across time. This test of invariance is likely to fail when applied to the modeling of change. Heterogeneous variance across time is often observed in developmental research—that is, time-related increases in mean level are accompanied by time-related increases in the variance, resulting in what Rogosa and Willett (1985) termed the *fanspread* appearance of a collection of growth trajectories. Even if the reliability of the indicator remains constant across time, the error variance will increase in concert with the increase in reliable construct variance. For completeness of presentation, we test the hypothesis of equivalent uniquenesses but expect that it will not be supported.

Willett and Sayer (1994) provided a technical framework for representing interindividual differences in intraindividual change and gave examples of how model parameters can be estimated by maximum-likelihood methods. Several recent articles provide empirical examples using that framework (e.g., Curran, Harford, & Muthén, 1997; MacCallum, Kim, Malarkey, & Kiecolt-Glaser, 1997). In each case, the analysis was based on the restricted case of a first-order latent growth model. The goal of this chapter is to provide a description of the model parameterization necessary for incorporating multiple indicators into latent growth models and provide a worked example, with empirical data on alcohol expectancies drawn from a school-based alcohol prevention trial. We use second-order latent growth models to address two sets of research questions. The first addresses the issue of measurement invariance: Does the construct show full factorial invariance over time? If not, what aspects of invariance can be substantiated? The second is descriptive: Do expectancies change during the course of early adolescence? What is the average pattern of change? Is there heterogeneity in change?

This chapter has three sections and a concluding discussion. In the first section, we introduce the data example we use to illustrate our approach to second-order growth modeling. In the second section, we introduce the parameterization necessary to fit a second-order latent growth model using the LISREL structural modeling program. We show how the y-measurement model, which in the Willett and Sayer (1994) parameterization represents the individual (Level 1) growth model, can be used to represent a measurement model for the first-order latent composites. The growth model representing how first-order composites are related to second-order growth factors is relegated to the structural part of the LISREL model. In the third section, we fit the second-order model to the data and provide information on tests of invariance hypotheses, interpret the parameters of the unconditional growth model, and discuss some of the measurement characteristics of individual items across waves. In the concluding section, we summarize the advantages of this method and suggest possible extensions.

An Application of a General Latent Growth Model to Adolescent Alcohol Expectancies

Alcohol expectancies are cognitive variables that describe an individual's beliefs about the effects of alcohol consumption on social, cognitive, and physical functioning. Positive alcohol expectancies are beliefs that alcohol facilitates social interaction and enhances personal well-being. The importance of studying positive alcohol expectancies in childhood and adolescence is based on evidence that suggests that expectancies play a role in the initiation and maintenance of alcohol consumption (Critchlow, 1989) and are particularly potent predictors in samples of middle-school adolescents. For example, Christiansen, Smith, Roehling, and Goldman (1989) found that scores on the Positive Expectancies subscale of the Alcohol Expectancies Questionnaire were the strongest concurrent and prospective (1 year) predictor of quantity and frequency of alcohol consumption, problem drinking, and transition to problem drinking in a sample of 871 eighth graders. In a similar vein, Killen et al. (1996) examined a set of individual-level variables, including temperament characteristics, depression, and self-esteem in a ninth-grade sample and reported that expectancy for enhanced social behavior was the only significant predictor of drinking onset.

Evidence from cross-sectional studies strongly suggest that there are age-related differences in expectancy scores, with older children having greater positive expectancies than younger children (Christiansen, Goldman, & Inn, 1982). Other evidence suggests that because of social-learning influences, young children develop expectancies prior to pharmacological experience with alcohol. These beliefs tend to consolidate by early adolescence into a form similar to those held by adults (Miller, Smith, & Goldman, 1990). It is likely that children's attitudes toward alcohol consumption undergo substantial change during the transition from early to mid-adolescence, especially in light of the large changes in perspective taking that permit adolescents to consider the multiple consequences of their actions.

There is some empirical evidence to suggest that the form of this attitudinal change may be discontinuous with time during early adolescence, particularly over the transition from elementary to middle school. Eccles, Lord, Roeser, Barber, and Jozefowicz (1997) reviewed the empirical literature on school transitions and noted the radical changes in the school environment encountered by young adolescents during the transition from sixth to seventh grade. They argued that a lack of fit between the need for experimentation and identity development and the more structured, impersonal, and bureaucratic organization of the school environment places adolescents at risk for negative motivational outcomes. They presented evidence of a sharp disjuncture in the trajectories of achievement, school engagement, and self-esteem, all of which decline rapidly after the shift to junior high school (usually during the seventh-grade year).

Throughout this article, we illustrate second-order models using panel data drawn from the Adolescent Alcohol Prevention Trial (AAPT), a longitudinal investigation of children enrolled in school-based prevention programs (Hansen & Graham, 1991). The AAPT study was designed to assess the relative impact of four different school-based alcohol-prevention curricula for young adolescents in southern California. The data set includes four panels of data, each one corresponding to a sample of children followed for several years. The sub-sample on which these analyses are based is drawn from Panel 1, which followed children from fifth through 10th grades. This sample includes 610 children who were measured for the first time in 1986–1987 and then assessed annually for a period of 6 years. The distribution of boys and girls was approximately equal at each time of measurement. The ethnic distribution of the sample in fifth grade was approximately 51% White, 28% Latino, 9% Asian, and 4% African American, and it remained relatively unchanged over time.

At Grades 5, 6, 7, 9, and 10, children were administered a survey containing questions on alcohol beliefs. Positive alcohol expectancy was assessed with three items tapping the social consequences of drinking alcohol. They include "Does drinking alcohol make it easier to be part of a group?" (GROUP), "Does drinking alcohol make parties more fun?" (PARTIES), and "Does drinking make it easier to have a good time with friends?" (GOODTIME). Adolescents had to indicate the extent of their agreement with each item using a 4-point Likert format, with anchors at 1 (*strongly disagree*) and 4 (*strongly agree*).

In a prior analysis of these data (Sayer & Willett, 1998) these items were summed within grades using principal-components analysis to form a composite score. Thus, positive alcohol expectancy was represented as a linear composite of the three expectancy items at each occasion of measurement, and a first-order latent growth model was fit to the observed composite scores. For purposes of comparison, we present here some descriptive information about modeling growth in the composite scores.

Choosing an appropriate mathematical function to represent true individual change is an important first step in any growth-modeling project. If theory guides a rational choice of model, individual growth parameters will have powerful substantive interpretations, On the basis of the work of Eccles et al. (1997), we had some theoretical basis for expecting that the positive expectancy trajectories would be discontinuous with time. Initial exploratory plots and later confirmatory data analyses indicated that change in positive expectancies could be represented well by a "piecewise" growth model, which allowed a discontinuity in the trajectory at Grade 7. Thus, the following Level 1 model was selected to represent the positive alcohol expectancy Y_{ti} of the ith child on the tth occasion of measurement ($t = 5, 6, 7, 9, 10$):

$$Y_{ti} = \pi_{0i} + \pi_{1i}x_t + \pi_{2i}a_t + \varepsilon_{ti}. \tag{6.1}$$

In this model, the metric of the time variable x_t has been rescaled by the subtraction of a constant from each grade, so that x_1 through x_5 take on values -2, -1, 0, 2, and 3, respectively. The shape of the hypothesized trajectory depends on the particular parameterization of time chosen and on the specific values of the individual growth parameters. Thus, the slope parameter π_{1i} represents change in true positive expectancies per unit time for the ith child. This can be considered the baseline rate of change throughout the entire time period under consideration. Adolescents whose expectancies increased the most rapidly between grades 5 and 10 have the largest values of this parameter. The intercept parameter π_{0i} represents the predicted expectancy score of child i when x_t is equal to zero, that is, at Grade 7; children whose positive expectancies are higher in early adolescence possess higher values of this parameter. The third parameter, π_{2i}, represents the increment to the growth rate beginning at Grade 7. Here, the variable a_t represents a second parameterization of time. Its presence in the model ensures that the slope of the trajectory is not constrained to be identical prior to and after Grade 7. It measures linear time after Grade 7 and is set equal to zero up to and including Grade 7, so that a_1 through a_5 take on values 0, 0, 0, 2, and 3 (see Bryk & Raudenbush, 1992, for alternative coding of piecewise linear growth models). Adolescents who experience a large positive increment to their growth rate after Grade 7 have high positive values of this parameter, whereas adolescents who experience a decrement in growth have negative values.

In preliminary exploratory analyses, we fitted the models of Equation 6.1 using "within-child" ordinary least squares (OLS) regression analysis to the observed composite scores of all children in the sample. Figure 6.1 presents these OLS-fitted trajectories for a random subsample. It is easy to see from Figure 6.1 that observed change can be either positive or negative, that individuals are

FIGURE 6.1

OLS-fitted trajectories summarizing discontinuous linear growth in positive expectancies between Grades 5 and 10. These are displayed by gender for a subsample of 15 randomly selected children.

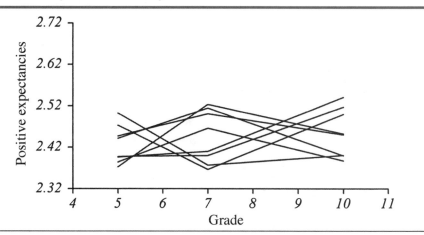

diverging over time (fanspread) and that there is heterogeneity in status, rate of change, and increments to rate across children.

Specifying the Second-Order Latent Growth Model

The First-Order Parameterization

As a basis for comparison we review briefly the parameterization of a first-order latent growth model, as described by Willett and Sayer (1994). In this formulation the hypothesized individual growth model in Equation 6.1 plays the role of the LISREL measurement model for the vector of endogenous variables Y,

$$Y = \tau_y + \Lambda_y \eta + \varepsilon, \tag{6.2}$$

with LISREL score vectors Y, η, and ε that contain the empirical growth record, the three individual growth parameters, and the five errors of measurement, respectively. The elements of the LISREL τ_y and Λ_y parameter matrices in Equation 6.2 are constrained to contain only known values and constants, rather than a collection of unknown parameters to be estimated. This specification acts to "pass" the critical Level 1 individual growth parameters (π_{0i}, π_{1i}, π_{2i}) from the Level 1 growth model into the LISREL endogenous construct vector η, which we have then referred to as the *latent growth vector*. In other words, our fully constrained specification of Λ_y has forced the η vector to contain the individual-level parameters whose Level 2 distribution must become the focus of our subsequent between-person analyses. The error vector ε is distributed with zero mean vector and covariance matrix Θ_ε.

These required Level 2 analyses are conducted in the "structural" part of the general LISREL model. The particular population means, variances, and covariances that we select as parameters of the structural model are those that we have hypothesized are the important parameters in the joint distribution of the latent growth vector. The latent growth vector has the form of the reduced LISREL structural model:

$$\eta = \alpha + B\eta + \zeta. \tag{6.3}$$

We removed the population averages of the individual growth parameters—a true intercept, slope, and increment—into the LISREL α-vector. This permits these important mean parameters to be estimated explicitly. The elements of the LISREL latent residual vector, ζ, in Equation 2.3 contain deviations of π_{0i}, π_{1i}, and π_{2i} from their respective population means. The ζ vector of latent residuals is of special interest because it is distributed with zero mean vector and covariance matrix Ψ—the latter matrix containing the variance and covariance parameters in which we are most interested in an investigation of interindividual differences in change. Note that in Equation 6.3 the B matrix containing the regression coefficients is constrained to zero, thus permitting the relations among the growth parameters to be expressed exclusively as covariances in the Ψ matrix.

To summarize, the individual growth modeling framework provides baseline Level 1 (within-person) and Level 2 (between-person) models that represent our initial hypotheses about the growth structure underlying the five waves of panel data in our data example. Then, in Equations 6.2 and 6.3 we showed that these Level 1 and Level 2 models can be rewritten using the format and notation of the LISREL model with mean structures. By carefully choosing our specification of the various standard LISREL parameter matrices we have forced the LISREL Y-measurement model to become our original Level 1 individual growth model (including all existing assumptions on the distribution of the measurement errors), and we have forced a reduced form of the LISREL structural model to become our Level 2 model for interindividual differences in true change.

Rewriting the Measurement Model as a Second-Order Latent Growth Model

To incorporate multiple indicators of the latent composites into the model, the LISREL Y-measurement model is reparameterized as follows:

$$
\begin{bmatrix} Y_{1i} \\ Y_{2i} \\ Y_{3i} \\ Y_{4i} \\ Y_{5i} \\ Y_{6i} \\ Y_{7i} \\ Y_{8i} \\ Y_{9i} \\ Y_{10i} \\ Y_{11i} \\ Y_{12i} \\ Y_{13i} \\ Y_{14i} \\ Y_{15i} \end{bmatrix}
=
\begin{bmatrix} 0 \\ \tau_2 \\ \tau_3 \\ 0 \\ \tau_5 \\ \tau_6 \\ 0 \\ \tau_8 \\ \tau_9 \\ 0 \\ \tau_{11} \\ \tau_{12} \\ 0 \\ \tau_{14} \\ \tau_{15} \end{bmatrix}
+
\begin{bmatrix}
1 & 0 & 0 & 0 & 0 & 0 & 0 & 0 \\
\lambda_{21} & 0 & 0 & 0 & 0 & 0 & 0 & 0 \\
\lambda_{31} & 0 & 0 & 0 & 0 & 0 & 0 & 0 \\
0 & 1 & 0 & 0 & 0 & 0 & 0 & 0 \\
0 & \lambda_{52} & 0 & 0 & 0 & 0 & 0 & 0 \\
0 & \lambda_{62} & 0 & 0 & 0 & 0 & 0 & 0 \\
0 & 0 & 1 & 0 & 0 & 0 & 0 & 0 \\
0 & 0 & \lambda_{83} & 0 & 0 & 0 & 0 & 0 \\
0 & 0 & \lambda_{93} & 0 & 0 & 0 & 0 & 0 \\
0 & 0 & 0 & 1 & 0 & 0 & 0 & 0 \\
0 & 0 & 0 & \lambda_{114} & 0 & 0 & 0 & 0 \\
0 & 0 & 0 & \lambda_{124} & 0 & 0 & 0 & 0 \\
0 & 0 & 0 & 0 & 1 & 0 & 0 & 0 \\
0 & 0 & 0 & 0 & \lambda_{145} & 0 & 0 & 0 \\
0 & 0 & 0 & 0 & \lambda_{155} & 0 & 0 & 0
\end{bmatrix}
\begin{bmatrix} \eta_{1i} \\ \eta_{2i} \\ \eta_{3i} \\ \eta_{4i} \\ \eta_{5i} \\ \pi_{0i} \\ \pi_{1i} \\ \pi_{2i} \end{bmatrix}
+
\begin{bmatrix} \varepsilon_{1i} \\ \varepsilon_{2i} \\ \varepsilon_{3i} \\ \varepsilon_{4i} \\ \varepsilon_{5i} \\ \varepsilon_{6i} \\ \varepsilon_{7i} \\ \varepsilon_{8i} \\ \varepsilon_{9i} \\ \varepsilon_{10i} \\ \varepsilon_{11i} \\ \varepsilon_{12i} \\ \varepsilon_{13i} \\ \varepsilon_{14i} \\ \varepsilon_{15i} \end{bmatrix}.
$$

$$(6.4)$$

It still has the format of the LISREL measurement model for endogenous variables Y:

$$Y = \tau_y + \Lambda_y \eta + \varepsilon. \tag{6.5}$$

However, as illustrated in Equation 6.4, the score vectors are partitioned differently. As before, Y is a response vector that contains the scores on the 15 observed items. On the basis of our data example, this vector contains the 3 observed items repeated on the five occasions of measurement. For example, Y_{1i}, Y_{4i}, U_{7i}, Y_{10i}, and Y_{13i} represent the responses on the GROUP item measured at Grades 5, 6, 7, 9, and 10, respectively. Now η is a combined vector that contains the scores on eight latent variables: the five composite variables, or first-order factors, in the upper partition and the three growth parameters, or second-order factors, in the lower partition; ε is a score vector that contains the measurement error associated with each item. In the first-order parameterization, the error score confounded occasion-specific and unique variance as measurement error. By contrast, in the second-order parameterization the error score can be interpreted as unique variance in the factor-analytic sense: It is a mixture of (a) nonrandom specific item variance that is not attributable to the common factor and (b) random measurement error. We refer to it as the *measurement uniqueness*.

The Λ_y parameter matrix in Equation 6.4 now contains the regression coefficients (factor loadings) that capture the relation of each indicator to its composite. The first indicator for each composite serves as a reference variable to set the scale of the latent variable, with a loading value constrained to 1. The LISREL τ_y parameter vector, constrained to zero in a first-order growth model, is no longer completely constrained. It contains the measurement intercepts relating each item to its composite. For purposes of model identification the intercept for the indicator that serves as a reference variable for the construct is constrained to zero. All other elements in this vector are free to be estimated.

Alternative Error Covariance Structures

As in the original growth formulation, the error vector ε is distributed with zero mean vector and covariance matrix Θ_ε. The imposition of the assumptions of independence and homoscedasticity on the measurement uniquenesses is common but, with measurements being obtained repeatedly on the same adolescent over time, these assumptions may not be tenable. For example, as mentioned previously, it is likely that error variance increases in concert with true score variance over time. This heterogeneity would be reflected by permitting the variances of the measurement uniquenesses to be unequal or heteroscedastic across time. Because the uniquenesses contain nonrandom variance in each item that is not shared with other indicators of the same construct, they contain reliable variance and may covary over time. These covariances are modeled by permitting the off-diagonal elements of Θ_ε to be estimated under various autocorrelation structures (for a general discussion of the growth processes that may give rise to different patterns for the covariance matrix of the errors, see chapter 3, this volume, by Rovine and Molenaar). One specification that permits

FIGURE 6.2

Path diagram of a second-order growth model. Expect. = expectancies.

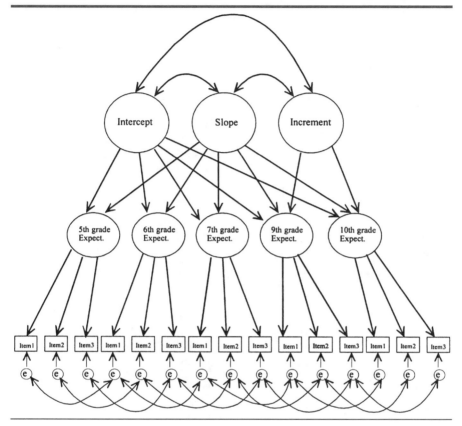

both heteroscedastic measurement error variances and allows temporally adjacent pairs of measurement errors to be mutually autocorrelated is the specification we used in fitting our models to data. A path diagram of the second-order model under this specification is presented in Figure 6.2.

Rewriting the Structural Model as a Second-Order Latent Growth Model

All information about the Level 1 individual growth model is now represented in the structural part of the model, as follows:

$$\eta = \alpha + B\eta + \zeta \qquad (6.6)$$

and

$$
\begin{bmatrix} \eta_{1i} \\ \eta_{2i} \\ \eta_{3i} \\ \eta_{4i} \\ \eta_{5i} \\ \pi_{0i} \\ \pi_{1i} \\ \pi_{2i} \end{bmatrix} = \begin{bmatrix} 0 \\ 0 \\ 0 \\ 0 \\ 0 \\ \alpha_6 \\ \alpha_7 \\ \alpha_8 \end{bmatrix} + \begin{bmatrix} 0 & 0 & 0 & 0 & 0 & 1 & -2 & 0 \\ 0 & 0 & 0 & 0 & 0 & 1 & -1 & 0 \\ 0 & 0 & 0 & 0 & 0 & 1 & 0 & 0 \\ 0 & 0 & 0 & 0 & 0 & 1 & 2 & 2 \\ 0 & 0 & 0 & 0 & 0 & 1 & 3 & 3 \\ 0 & 0 & 0 & 0 & 0 & 0 & 0 & 0 \\ 0 & 0 & 0 & 0 & 0 & 0 & 0 & 0 \\ 0 & 0 & 0 & 0 & 0 & 0 & 0 & 0 \end{bmatrix} \begin{bmatrix} \eta_{1i} \\ \eta_{2i} \\ \eta_{3i} \\ \eta_{4i} \\ \eta_{5i} \\ \pi_{0i} \\ \pi_{1i} \\ \pi_{2i} \end{bmatrix} + \begin{bmatrix} \zeta_{1i} \\ \zeta_{2i} \\ \zeta_{3i} \\ \zeta_{4i} \\ \zeta_{5i} \\ \zeta_{6i} \\ \zeta_{7i} \\ \zeta_{8i} \end{bmatrix}. \quad (6.7)
$$

Note that the elements of the η score vector represent the latent variables as centered variables, that is, as deviated from their respective means. This changes the specification of the α-vector, in which elements α_1 through α_5 are now constrained to zero. As before, the population averages of the individual growth parameters are estimated in elements α_6 through α_8.

The **B** parameter matrix serves a different function in the second-order model. It becomes a design matrix with fixed regression coefficients that represent known constants and the spacing of the occasions of measurement that underlie the individual growth model. Thus, in our example the piecewise model is specified in the upper partition, last three columns, as follows:

$$
\mathbf{B} = \begin{bmatrix} 0 & 0 & 0 & 0 & 0 & 1 & -2 & 0 \\ 0 & 0 & 0 & 0 & 0 & 1 & -1 & 0 \\ 0 & 0 & 0 & 0 & 0 & 1 & 0 & 0 \\ 0 & 0 & 0 & 0 & 0 & 1 & 2 & 2 \\ 0 & 0 & 0 & 0 & 0 & 1 & 3 & 3 \\ 0 & 0 & 0 & 0 & 0 & 0 & 0 & 0 \\ 0 & 0 & 0 & 0 & 0 & 0 & 0 & 0 \\ 0 & 0 & 0 & 0 & 0 & 0 & 0 & 0 \end{bmatrix} \quad (6.8)
$$

The distribution of the elements of the vector of latent residuals ζ continues to be expressed in the parameter matrix $\mathbf{\Psi}$:

$$
\mathbf{\Psi} = Cov(\zeta) = \begin{bmatrix} \sigma^2_{\eta_1} \\ 0 & \sigma^2_{\eta_2} \\ 0 & 0 & \sigma^2_{\eta_3} \\ 0 & 0 & 0 & \sigma^2_{\eta_4} \\ 0 & 0 & 0 & 0 & \sigma^2_{\eta_5} \\ 0 & 0 & 0 & 0 & 0 & \sigma^2_{\pi_0} \\ 0 & 0 & 0 & 0 & 0 & \sigma_{\pi_1\pi_0} & \sigma^2_{\pi_1} \\ 0 & 0 & 0 & 0 & 0 & \sigma_{\pi_2\pi_0} & \sigma_{\pi_2\pi_1} & \sigma^2_{\pi_2} \end{bmatrix}. \quad (6.9)
$$

Note that in Equation 6.9 all covariances among the five latent composites are constrained to zero, because relations among the first-order factors are assumed to be explained completely by the second-order latent variables, the growth parameters. However, similar to the first-order growth model, the important relations among the growth parameters continue to be expressed as covariances in Ψ. They are shown in the triangular submatrix (last three rows) in the lower right.

The residual variances of both the first- and second-order latent variables, the diagonal entries of the matrix, are interesting to interpret. For the (centered) latent composites η_1 through η_5 the residual variance is occasion-specific factor variance that is not attributable to growth. Because measurement error has been removed from these composites by means of the first-order part of the model, σ_η^2 represents random variance attributable to fluctuations unique to each time of measurement. This may reflect state variance (see Kenny & Zautra, chapter 8, this volume) or, in the language of sociologists, *random shocks* that disturb the underlying growth process (Kowaleski-Jones & Duncan, 1999). The ability to decompose error variance into systematic and random variance is one of the nice features of a second-order model. For the latent growth factors π_0 through π_2 the residual variance continues to represent the (centered) growth parameters deviated from their respective population means and is important for describing the heterogeneity in growth.

Fitting the Models to Data

Testing Invariance Hypotheses

As noted previously, the researcher wishes to ascertain that the measurement properties of the construct are stable over time to draw the correct inferences regarding change. This is typically accomplished by fitting a longitudinal confirmatory factor model to the covariance matrix among the items over time (Nesselroade, 1983). The model is similar to the formulation in Equation 6.4, with the following modifications: The τ_y vector is constrained to zero, and the η vector contains only the latent composites (η_1 through η_5). Interest lies in the magnitude of the factor loadings that are common across time as well as the correlations among the latent composites. A series of equivalence constraints can be applied to the factor loadings, item uniquenesses, and factor variances and covariances to test various hypotheses regarding across-time measurement stability. It is important to note that these hypotheses are tested independently of the specific growth model underpinning the across-time covariance matrix. In contrast, the measurement model for the indicators and the individual growth model are fit simultaneously in a second-order latent growth model. This method relies heavily on the assumption that the researcher has specified the Level 1 growth model correctly, so that any lack of fit can be attributed to the measurement process alone.

We fitted the taxonomy of models presented in Table 6.1. In practice, one would begin with the most restrictive model (Model 4), systematically freeing constraints until the best fit is achieved. For pedagogical reasons these models (and their accompanying fit statistics) are displayed in reverse order in Table 6.1, from least to most restrictive, to conform to Meredith's (1993) taxonomy of weak to strong invariance. We discuss these models so that comparisons among the goodness-of-fit statistics of nested models can be used to test hypotheses concerning increasingly stringent forms of invariance.

A test of configural invariance is represented by Model 1. The τ_y, Λ_y, Θ_ε, α, B, and Ψ parameter matrices for all adolescents were patterned as described in Equations 6.4 and 6.7, but the unknown matrix elements in Λ_y and τ_y were free to vary over time. The goodness of fit of this model was good—the chi-square statistic is small relative to its degrees of freedom, and the values of the various incremental fit indices are close to .95 (see Bollen, 1989, for a discussion of the use of summary statistics in model evaluation). This model serves as a baseline and suggests that the same pattern of constrained and free factor loadings are invariant across time; that is, one factor appears to underlie the three expectancy scores, and there is simple structure (no cross-factor loadings).

Models 2, 3, and 4 provided further tests of the invariance hypotheses. To test whether the relations of the indicators to the composites remained invariant (weak metric invariance) we fit a model in which the τ_y, Λ_y, Θ_ε, α, B, and Ψ parameter matrices for all adolescents were patterned as described in Equations 6.4 and 6.7, but the loadings for indicators common across time in Λ_y were constrained to take on identical values. The goodness of fit of this model is summarized in Table 6.1 (Model 2). In an absolute sense, Model 2 fits moderately well—the chi-square statistic is a little large relative to its degrees of freedom, but the values of the various incremental fit indices are greater than .9. The test of invariance is carried out by comparing the fit of this model with the less restrictive Model 1. Note there is a change in chi-square of 71.71 relative to a gain of 8 *df*. This suggests that the less restricted model is a better fit, indicating that we reject the hypothesis that the factor loadings are invariant over time. Byrne, Shavelson, and Muthén (1989) argued that measurement invariance is a matter of degree. It may be that a form of partial factorial invariance, in which only some indicators are constrained to be equal, would provide a better fit. That test was not carried out with these data because we had no hypotheses regarding which items would be invariant over time, but it remains an option for researchers with strong hypotheses regarding item functioning at different ages.

Because Model 2 is a poorer fit to the data, in practice one would not continue to add restrictions to an already-unsatisfactory model. We do so here

TABLE 6.1

Model Comparisons: Comparing Covariance and Mean Structures Across Time

MODEL NUMBER AND DESCRIPTION	χ^2	df	GOODNESS-OF-FIT STATISTICS			
			GFI	NNFI	CFI	RMSEA
1: λ unequal across time τ unequal across time Θ_ε unequal across time	217.72	84	.95	.933	.947	.052
2: λ equal across time τ unequal across time Θ_ε unequal across time	289.43	92	.939	.91	.92	.060
3: λ equal across time τ equal across time Θ_ε unequal across time	652.08	104	.933	.779	.781	.088
4: λ equal across time τ equal across time Θ_ε equal across time	853.72	116	.891	.733	.705	.099

Note. $N = 610$; GFI = goodness-of-fit index; NNFI = non-normed fit index; CFI = comparative fit index; RMSEA = root mean square error of approximation.

for illustrative purposes only. In the third model fitted in the taxonomy (Model 3), we retained the equality constraints on Λ_y and added constraints in τ_y, so that the intercepts common across time are constrained to be invariant. This is a test of strong metric invariance, which holds that the entire linear model relating each indicator to its composite must be invariant. Compared with Model 2, this was a worse fit to the data (change in chi-square of 362.65 relative to a change of 12 df). We reject the invariance hypothesis of equivalent measurement intercepts over time.

In the final model in the series (Model 4), we test the most stringent invariance hypothesis, that of equal measurement error variances over time. In this model, we retained the equality constraints on τ_y and Λ_y and constrained the corresponding elements of Θ_ε. As expected, this hypothesis received no support. The decrement-to-chi-square test indicated that this model, compared with Model 3, was a much worse fit. It suggests that the indicators measured the construct with varying precision at different points during adolescence or, conversely, that true scores (and corresponding error scores) are more heterogeneous at older ages.

Average Trajectories of Change in Positive and Negative Expectancies

To obtain estimates of the average growth trajectory and the heterogeneity in growth, we fit a second-order model similar to that expressed in Equations 6.4 and 6.7. In Table 6.2, we provide maximum-likelihood estimates of the population means and variances of the true growth parameters in positive expec-

TABLE 6.2

Estimated Average Expectancy Trajectories and Heterogeneity in Growth

PARAMETER	PARAMETER ESTIMATE
Average true status at Grade 7	1.332*
Average base rate of true change	0.039*
Average increment to base rate	0.070*
Variance of true status at Grade 7	0.066*
Variance of base rate of true change	0.017*
Variance of increment to base rate	0.046*
Covariance of true status and base rate	0.028*
Covariance of true status and increment	−0.037*
Covariance of base rate and increment	−0.023*

*$p < .001$.

tancies, along with approximate p values.[1] Inspection of the estimates of the population means indicates that, on average, true status on the positive expectancy composite at Grade 7 is approximately 1.3 on a scale that ranges from 1 to 4. Thus, in Grade 7 the population average expectancy score is not yet elevated. The estimate of the base rate of true change is .039, indicating that, on average, positive expectancies increase at a rate of four-tenths of a point over 10 years. Of greatest interest is the estimate of the increment to the base rate. It is positive and relatively large, indicating that, on average, there is a marked upward shift in growth in positive expectancies beginning in Grade 7.

The model provides estimates of the heterogeneity around the average trajectory and of the relationships among the growth parameters. Inspection of the estimates of the residual variances (Rows 3–6) indicates that there is heterogeneity in all growth parameters, indicating individual differences in the growth trajectories. The covariances displayed in the last three rows of Table 6.2 are interesting to interpret. The positive covariance between true status and base rate suggests that children with higher expectancy scores in Grade 7 are also increasing in expectancy beliefs at a rate faster than those with lower scores; the opposite holds for children with low expectancy scores. The negative covariances of true status and base rate with the increment suggest that children with higher expectancy scores and faster rates of baseline change present a smaller shift upward in expectancy beliefs. It is always a possibility that this represents a ceiling effect and that the expectancy measure does not discriminate well among children at the top of the scale. However, it may also be a true picture of the developmental timing of the underlying expectancy process. With the exception of the first occasion of measurement, all residual variances associated with the latent composites are significantly different from zero, indicating that a substantial amount of score variance is time specific.

Measurement Characteristics of the Items

Table 6.3 presents the estimates that can be obtained when multiple indicators are incorporated into the model. These are maximum-likelihood estimates from Model 1, which was retained as the best-fitting and most reasonable representation of the data. The estimates represent the measurement characteristics of the items. Focus first on the factor loadings presented in the top half of the table. Reading down the columns, we note that the within-time loadings vary substantially, indicating that unequal weights are necessary to create the composite variables. Reading across the rows, the across-time loadings reveal the

---

[1] The approximate p value tests the null hypothesis that the value of a parameter is zero in the population, using a test statistic that is the ratio of the parameter estimate to its asymptotic standard error (see Bollen, 1989, p. 286).

TABLE 6.3

Measurement Characteristics for the Alcohol Expectancy Items

			GRADE			
ITEM	**5**	**6**	**7**	**9**	**10**	
			Factor loadings			
GROUP	1.000	1.000	1.000	1.000	1.000	
PARTIES	.878**	1.542**	1.729**	2.052**	2.253**	
GOODTIME	.565**	.697**	1.306**	1.371**	1.730**	
			Measurement error variance			
GROUP	.614**	.399**	.455**	.519**	.630**	
PARTIES	.179**	.113*	.172**	.235**	.328**	
GOODTIME	.155**	.164**	.133**	.231**	.282**	

*p < .05. **p < .001.

extent of the lack of metric invariance. There is a trend for all the items to have a stronger relation to the latent factor at the later grades, suggesting that these are relatively poor indicators for younger children. In addition, we note that with the exception of Grade 5, the PARTIES item is consistently the strongest indicator of the composite variable. Next, focus on the measurement error variances presented in the lower half of the table. Reading down the columns, we note that the GROUP item appears to have the largest measurement error variance at each time. One interpretation of the greater specific variance in this item is that it measures the construct with less precision than the other two items; again, this result is consistent across time. The general point is that these types of inferences could not be made using a first-order latent growth model, which provides no information on individual item functioning.

Discussion

In recent years, methodologists have demonstrated how individual growth modeling can be accommodated within the general framework offered by covariance and mean structure analysis (McArdle & Epstein, 1987; Meredith & Tisak, 1990; Muthén, 1991). In this chapter we have extended the earlier work of Willett and Sayer (1994) to incorporate multiple indicators of growth and describe the parameterization of the second-order latent growth model. We show how this model provides a convenient technique for addressing research questions about measurement invariance as well as continuing to provide estimates of the important growth parameters needed in any study of change. We summarize the major advantages here:

- The model permits the separation of observed score variance into reliable construct variance, reliable unique variance, and random occasion-specific variance.[2] These sources are confounded in first-order latent growth modeling. Because measurement error has been removed from the latent growth parameters we would expect that the regression coefficients representing relations among the growth parameters and other covariates to be disattenuated and the accompanying standard errors to be smaller. In other words, we obtain a more precise estimate of the relation between change and its correlates using a second-order model.

- A by-product of modeling the measurement structure of the indicators

---

[2]In a recent paper, Hancock, Stapleton, and Berkovits (1999) provided formulas for estimating the variance decomposition in a multisample covariance and mean structure model.

directly is the provision of information on individual item character-istics.

▪ By comparing the goodness of fit of explicitly specified and nested models, the investigator can test complex hypotheses about the nature of measurement invariance. One benefit of fitting a covariance structure to data using a flexible software package such as LISREL is that selected model parameters can be individually or jointly constrained during analysis to particular values. This allows the investigator to conduct a variety of nested tests. For example, multiple-group analysis could be conducted to answer questions not just about invariance over time but also about invariance across time and across populations simultane-ously.

One goal of this chapter is to provide details on model parameterization in the hopes of encouraging applied researchers to adopt this method. However, there are many unanswered questions. For example, can we accept partial rather than full measurement invariance? If so, how many items need to be invariant in their functioning across time? And under what conditions? What if the func-tional form of growth is different for different indicators (e.g., PARTIES shows linear growth, GOODTIME shows quadratic growth)? How does that affect interpretation and model fit? Should a first-order growth model be fit separately to the repeated responses of each item prior to fitting the second-order model? Can growth models with time intervals estimated by the data rather than spec-ified a priori be accommodated in second-order latent growth models (cf. McArdle & Epstein, 1987; Meredith & Tisak, 1990)? Many other extensions to second-order latent growth models can be considered that increase the capacity of applied researchers to answer complex questions about the measurement of change over time.

References

Bollen, K. (1989). *Structural equations with latent variables.* New York: Wiley.

Bryk, A. S., & Raudenbush, S. W. (1992). *Hierarchical linear models: Applications and data analysis methods.* Newbury Park, CA: Sage.

Byrne, B. M., Shavelson, R. J., & Muthén, B. (1989). Testing for the equivalence of factor covariance and mean structures: The issue of partial measurement invariance. *Psychological Bulletin, 105,* 456–466.

Chan, D. (1998). The conceptualization and analysis of change over time: An integrative approach incorporating longitudinal mean and covariance structures analysis (LMACS) and multiple indicator latent growth modeling (MLGM). *Organizational Research Methods, 1,* 421–483.

Christiansen, B., Goldman, M., & Inn, G. (1982). Development of alcohol-related expectancies in adolescents: Separating pharmacological from social-learning influences. *Journal of Consulting and Clinical Psychology, 50,* 336–344.

Christiansen, B., Smith, G., Roehling, P., & Goldman, M. (1989). Using alcohol expectancies to predict adolescent drinking behavior after one year. *Journal of Consulting and Clinical Psychology, 57,* 93–99.

Critchlow, B. (1989). In search of the seven dwarves: Issues of measurement and meaning in alcohol expectancy research. *Psychological Bulletin, 105,* 361–373.

Curran, P. J., Harford, T., & Muthén, B. (1997). The relation between heavy alcohol use and bar patronage: A latent growth model. *Journal of Studies of Alcohol, 57,* 410–418.

Duncan, S. C., & Duncan, T. E. (1996). A multivariate growth curve analysis of adolescent substance use. *Structural Equation Modeling, 3,* 323–347.

Eccles, J. S., Lord, S. E., Roeser, R., Barber, B., & Jozefowicz, D. M. (1997). The association of school transitions in early adolescence with developmental trajectories through high school. In J. Schulenberg, J. Maggs, & K. Hurrelmann (Eds.), *Health risks and developmental transitions during adolescence* (pp. 283–320). New York: Cambridge University Press.

Hancock, G. R., Stapleton, L., & Berkovits, I. (1999). *Loading and intercept invariance within multisample covariance and mean structure models.* Manuscript in preparation, University of Maryland, College Park.

Hansen, W., & Graham, J. (1991). Preventing alcohol, marijuana, and cigarette use among adolescents: Peer pressure resistance training versus establishing conservative norms. *Preventive Medicine, 20,* 414–430.

Killen, J., Hayward, C., Wilson, D., Farish Haydel, K., Robinson, T., Barr Taylor, C., Hammer, L., & Varady, A. (1996). Predicting onset of drinking in a community sample of adolescents: The role of expectancy and temperament. *Addictive Behaviors, 21,* 473–480.

Kowaleski-Jones, L., & Duncan, G. (1999). The structure of achievement and behavior across middle childhood. *Child Development, 70,* 930–943.

MacCallum, R. C., Kim, C., Malarkey, W. B., & Kiecolt-Glaser, J. K. (1997). Studying multivariate change using multilevel models and latent curve models. *Multivariate Behavioral Research, 32,* 215–254.

McArdle, J. J. (1988). Dynamic but structural equation modeling of repeated measures data. In R. B. Cattell & J. Nesselroade (Eds.), *Handbook of multivariate experimental psychology* (2nd ed., pp. 561–614). New York: Plenum Press.

McArdle, J. J., & Epstein, D. (1987). Latent growth curves within developmental structural equation models. *Child Development, 58,* 110–133.

Meredith, W. (1993). Measurement invariance, factor analysis, and factorial invariance. *Psychometrika, 58,* 525–543.

Meredith, W., & Tisak, J. (1990). Latent curve analysis. *Psychometrika, 55,* 107–122.

Miller, P., Smith, G., & Goldman, M. (1990). Emergence of alcohol expectancies in childhood: A possible critical period. *Journal of Studies on Alcohol, 51,* 343–349.

Muthén, B. O. (1991). Analysis of longitudinal data using latent variable models with varying parameters. In L. M. Collins & J. L. Horn (Eds.), *Best methods for the analysis of change* (pp. 1–17). Washington, DC: American Psychological Association.

Nesselroade, J. R. (1983). Temporal selection and factorial invariance in the study of development and change. In P. B. Baltes & O. G. Brim, Jr. (Eds.), *Life-span development and behavior* (pp. 59–87). New York: Academic Press.

Rogosa, D. R., & Willett, J. B. (1985). Understanding correlates of change by modeling individual differences in growth. *Psychometrika, 50,* 203–228.

Sayer, A. G., & Willett, J. B. (1998). A cross-domain model for growth in adolescent alcohol expectancies. *Multivariate Behavioral Research, 33,* 509–543.

Willett, J. B., & Sayer, A. G. (1994). Using covariance structure analysis to detect correlates and predictors of individual change over time. *Psychological Bulletin, 116,* 363–381.

Editors' Introduction

actorial invariance has emerged as a critically important issue for the analysis of change. It has been recognized for some time that to make quantitative comparisons between groups, one must establish that the factor structure is comparable in each group. More recently, with the advent of models for intraindividual change, such as growth curves, it has become clear that establishing factorial invariance is necessary for a model of change to be meaningful. We are fortunate indeed to have in this volume a contribution from William Meredith and John Horn, two senior statesmen in the area of longitudinal methods, who offer a perspective on factorial invariance derived from decades of experience. Their chapter shows clearly that factorial invariance is not as simple a concept as it appears. This chapter reveals the startling fact that subgroup structure within a sample can profoundly affect the resulting factor structure. Even when invariance is established across groups, the "invariant" structure may not emerge when the groups are combined. Meredith and Horn explore this and other interesting aspects of factorial invariance. This chapter invites consideration of the implications of factorial invariance—or lack thereof—for the work presented elsewhere in this volume by Muthén (chapter 10), Curran and Bollen (chapter 4), Kenny and Zautra (chapter 8), McArdle and Hamagami (chapter 5), Raudenbush (chapter 2), Rovine and Molenaar (chapter 3), and Sayer and Cumsille (chapter 6).

The Role of Factorial Invariance in Modeling Growth and Change

William Meredith
John Horn

cience requires invariance. Relationships that represent scientific principles must be identifiable under different conditions of measurement and sampling. The law specifying that objects attract each other with a force that is directly proportional to their mass and indirectly proportional to their distance applies both to feathers drawn by the gravitational force of the earth and to the sun drawn by the gravitational force of the Milky Way. These examples illustrate that it may be very difficult to establish the conditions under which invariance can be found. Scientists are confronted with the equivalent of feathers. How can it be demonstrated that the same laws of development of human abilities apply to privileged suburban children and underprivileged inner city children? But difficult though it may be, still the requirement is that to establish a scientific principle it is necessary to demonstrate that principle under the diverse conditions in which it is expected to apply.

In this chapter, we describe factor analytic models that behavioral scientists can adapt to substantive theories about development and use to investigate the invariance of principles of development. Derivations from developmental theory can be framed in terms of these models, and the models can be tested for fit to data. We describe what can and cannot be invariant in such models and, in some cases, what probably should and should not (in most applications) be invariant. We outline features of the kinds of data one would need to gather to provide adequate realization of the models. In particular, we report on conditions needed to establish common factor measurement invariance across separate, cross-sectional samples of participants (Horn & McArdle, 1992; Meredith, 1993, 1997). We contrast and compare these conditions with those required

We thank J. Jack McArdle for his insightful and helpful comments on a draft of this chapter.

for invariance across longitudinal and repeated-measures samples. We specify conditions that must obtain to support a hypothesis of invariance of simplex patterns of change across different groups, and we describe how these conditions can be combined with the conditions of invariant models of growth.

In examining the requirements for invariance of different models we find that it is very important to attend to the fact that specific factors (in the parlance of factor analysis) are real sources of variation. They do not behave as error in analyses aimed at testing hypotheses of invariance. Disregard of specific factors can have grave consequences. When different kinds of participants (e.g., male, female, young, old) are aggregated or combined into a single group for purposes of analyses, differences in specific factor means may appear as common factors. Specific factors may coalesce into common factors under conditions of selection of subgroups or may coalesce into common factors arising from replication induced by the choice of manifest variables in the design of a study. We describe difficulties in establishing invariance under these conditions. Note that what is often referred to as *uniqueness* (unique variance), or in the somewhat ludicrous parlance of structural equation modeling (SEM) programs as *error variance*, is the sum of the variances of a specific factor and measurement error.

We also examine the role played by specific factors in longitudinal factor analysis and related methods. Certain failures of invariance can occur in connection with aggregation even when it is reasonable to assume that specific factors are not present but measurement error is. This situation arises when development change or growth in a single variable is the subject of analysis. We discuss difficulties in establishing invariance under conditions of aggregation and error of measurement for developmental change (growth) of a single variable.

The developments in this chapter are principally theoretical. We do not dwell much on the details of methods of estimation, identification, fit evaluation, and related practical aspects of establishing, or disestablishing, invariance.

Factor Analysis, Linear Composite Measurement, and Factor Invariance

The fundamental concepts of behavioral science often can be regarded as latent variables underlying sets of manifest variables. There are good reasons for conceptualizing concepts in this manner, not the least being that the phenomena to which behavioral science concepts refer often do have many manifestations. In this chapter we confine our attention to latent variables conceptualized as linear common factors, although it is clearly possible to develop nonlinear alternatives, as in item response theory.

It is common in the behavioral sciences that operationally defined measurements are linear composites, most typically sums of indicators—that is, combinations of responses to a number of stimuli (items) or linear combinations of a number of subtests of responses to stimuli. Reliability of measurement of such composites arises through the replication of the common (true score) component inherent in each indicator. Because the common parts of items being aggregated are correlated, whereas the error components are not, the "true" variance increases much more rapidly than measurement error variance, hence high reliability can be attained as a result of compositing. Measurements thus have the character of a common factor model regardless of whether this assumption is made explicit. Selection of indicators in such measurement usually is not random from a universe of indicators: Rather selection is thought to be logically or theoretically or conceptually representative of the concept.

The indicators are assumed to measure the "same thing" when used with different samples of participants, or with the same people at different times. However, this assumption is not necessarily warranted; it is really a hypothesis that should be tested. The same indicator stimuli used with different samples of people, or with the same people on different occasions, do not necessarily relate to concepts in the same way. The stimuli can mean different things to different people and to the same people in different circumstances. This was illustrated concretely in Mussen, Eichorn, Honzick, Beiber, and Meredith's (1980) study of observer ratings of personality characteristics. The authors found that raters of women observed as young mothers and observed again 40 years later attributed different meanings to what were ostensibly the same behaviors. For example, the rating "talkative" in young mothers related positively to a factor deemed to be "poise," but in these same women at a later stage of development the word related negatively to a similar (identical?) factor. Other examples of this kind were discussed by Horn, McArdle, and Mason (1983).

Although Thurstone (1947) pointed to the need to establish invariance of measurement under different conditions such as those in which means or variances or intercorrelations are compared, this advice seems to have been ignored by the vast majority of researchers in the behavioral sciences. In most research it was simply assumed that if the same test was used in different samples or at different times with the same people, the same attribute was measured. Rarely was there any mention of the possibility that this might not be true. In those few cases where this possibility was mentioned, usually there was no mention of the idea that the assumption of invariance was a hypothesis for which there should be a test. However, this situation now seems to be changing, at least gradually—as evidenced by the present chapter in a book, expected to be popular, on advice for conducting developmental research (and by other writings, such as those of Cunningham, 1982, 1991; Horn & McArdle, 1992; Horn et al., 1983).

Thurstone's (1947) advice may have been ignored largely because researchers believed that there was no way to test the assumption of invariance of measurement. In fact, however, the assumption can be formulated as a hypothesis and tested. The test can be incorporated into SEM analyses designed to compare differences in means, variances, correlations, and models, generally, over occasions and groups. Under the assumptions of validity of a factor model of measurements, a test of invariance of the factor pattern provides objective evidence indicating whether the linear composites assumed to measure a given set of concepts in different groups, or at different times, are indeed measuring those concepts in the same way in the different circumstances. We now consider these tests in some detail.

Formulating the Factor Analytic Model

Although the factor analytic model is well known, it is desirable to review it here to bring the concepts of specific factor and measurement error into clear focus. Often, as in computing programs, these two concepts are lumped together as "error." This creates a conceptual trap for the unwary.

We specify the model first in scalar form as follows. Let x denote a manifest variable, w a common factor variable, s a specific factor variable, e an error-of-measurement variable, and τ an intercept. The model, then, can be stated simply as

$$x_i = \sum \lambda_{ik} w_k + s_i + e_i + \tau_i; \quad i = 1, 2, \ldots p; \quad k = 1, 2, \ldots q; \quad p > q. \quad (7.1)$$

To see the model in matrix form, let the vector variables corresponding to x, w, s, e, and τ be denoted by $\mathbf{X}$, $\mathbf{W}$, $\mathbf{S}$, $\mathbf{E}$, and $\mathbf{T}$ and write the model as

$$\mathbf{X} = \Lambda\mathbf{W} + \mathbf{S} + \mathbf{E} + \mathbf{T}. \quad (7.2)$$

The matrix Λ, with elements λ_{ik}, is the factor pattern matrix of regression weights for predicting $\mathbf{X}$ from $\mathbf{W}$. The vector $\mathbf{T}$, with elements τ_i, is a vector of arbitrary intercepts typically chosen to be the mean of $\mathbf{X}$, which sets the means of the common and specific factors to zero. Alternative choices for $\mathbf{T}$ are possible and, in connection with invariance, are essential.

We assume that the conditional expectation of $\mathbf{E}$ is a null vector for every fixed value of $(\mathbf{W}, \mathbf{S})$. This means that $\mathbf{E}$ is expected to be uncorrelated (i.e., correlated zero) with $\mathbf{W}$ and $\mathbf{S}$ in any population of individuals (not chosen by inspection of $\mathbf{E}$—which is in principle impossible) whatsoever. This assumption is a special (slightly stronger) form of what has become known as *weak true score theory* (Lord & Novick, 1968; Novick, 1966). In accordance with this theory, the vector of true scores, $\Lambda\mathbf{W} + \mathbf{S}$, is uncorrelated with $\mathbf{E}$.

It is desirable, if not completely essential, that measurement errors be mutually uncorrelated in any subpopulation. One can ensure this by requiring experimental independence of measures (Lord & Novick, 1968). Experimental dependence can arise in a variety of ways. For an elementary example, consider any pair of variables. Their sum, difference, product, or ratio are variables that are experimentally dependent on them. However, there are more insidious forms of dependence. In a questionnaire a given answer to an item may constrain the possible choices of answers to one or more subsequent items in such a way as to induce correlation between the associated measurement errors. In some situations multiple measures may be taken as behavioral responses to a single "stimulus" as perceived on a single presentation, of reading. Any "error" in the "perception" of that stimulus would propagate through the variates. A similar way that dependence may arise is when a test yields two or more scores based on the same material, as in reading speed and comprehension assessed by the same device. Item overlap in the scale of personality tests is a well-known source of experimental dependence.

We note that repeated measurements with the same scales, as in longitudinal research, usually do not lead to violations of the assumption of experimental dependence, although it sometimes seems to be thought that such is the case. In retesting, the same operations of measurement are used with the same people on separate and disparate occasions. Thus there is no operational or mathematical relationship between the scales that induces dependency.

When merely the same operations are used in retest, the errors at each testing are likely to be independent. There may be high statistical relationships—but this is not mathematical dependence. Correlated specific variates may contribute substantially to strong relationships over occasions, but this is not correlated error. The assumption of experimental independence rules out the possibility of correlated measurement error over repeated observations—which is not to say that the assumption always holds and that correlated errors can never occur. Throughout this chapter experimental independence is assumed.

Homogeneity of error variance is not assumed in our factor model, which means that error variances may be different for different individuals and may be dependent on the values of W and S. For example, it is known that for most tests composed of binary items, the measurement error variance approaches zero as the true score approaches either its maximum or minimum (Nunnally, 1967). Thus, the average error variance of a group near the maximum or minimum could be expected to differ nontrivially from that of another group scoring near the middle of a distribution, and there are other ways in which the error variances for groups can differ.

The factor model to be considered first requires that the following conditions hold in any population of interest, but not necessarily in subpopulations within a population:

- *Assumption 1*: The correlations between **W** and **S** are all (expected value) zero.

- *Assumption 2*: The correlations among the variables of **S** are (expected value) zero.

From these conditions we derive the following statements about, first, the means,

$$\mu = \Lambda\xi + \eta + T, \tag{7.3}$$

in which μ, ξ, and η are the mean vectors of **X**, **W**, and **S**, respectively and, second, the dispersion matrices,

$$\Sigma = \Lambda\Phi\Lambda' + \Omega + \Theta = \Lambda\Phi\Lambda' + \Psi, \tag{7.4}$$

in which Σ and Φ are the dispersion matrices of **X** and **W**, and Ω and Θ are the diagonal dispersion matrices of **S** and **E**.

Because the means of **E** are always null, e terms do not appear in Equation 7.3. Usually, as in specifying the factor model for a single occasion and not considering questions of invariance, both ξ and η are taken to be null as well, but it turns out that in considering invariance it is important to recognize that these means could be non-null parameters.

It is common, too, that it is convenient to collapse $\Omega + \Theta$ into Ψ, as in the second equality of Equation 7.4. This is especially true when considering the factor model for the case in which there are no replicate measures. Even in this situation, however, a good case can be made for using parallel or linearly equivalent pairs of every manifest variable and incorporating the design feature of separating specific and error variance into the model.

We now lay down a theoretical basis for describing and evaluating factorial invariance. This enables us to demonstrate how factorial invariance plays an important role in the study of change and development.

It is not our intention to describe how statistical theory can be invoked for this purpose, although we refer to the fact that multiple-group SEM analyses can be used to test different models of invariance. However, we do not make statistical distinctions between sample and population or deal with issues of statistical estimation and evaluation of fit. In considering multiple groups, we may refer to them as *subpopulations* and speak of the union of such groups— that is, the group composed of all subgroups, usually weighted by the proportion of participants in a subgroup relative to the number of participants in the union of all groups. With these provisos, the reader can usually substitute the term *sample*, as it would be used in statistical estimation, for the words *subgroup* and *subpopulation*. Also, when we say a factor model "fits" or "does not fit" we mean that reasonable scientists, examining the evidence for fit and failure of fit, would generally agree.

We should make clear at this point that one should have no illusions about the validity of a factor analytic model. Factor models can be extremely useful approximations, but one should maintain good awareness of the unlikelihood that such models truly represent reality. Fitting the equations should include provision for some degree of acceptable misfit. In most applications misfit is due in part to departures from linearity, but it also almost surely depends on the fact that the causes of behavior are myriad and complex and probably not, in the last analysis, linear. For an interesting discussion of these matters see MacCallum and Tucker's (1991) article.

Also there should be more to a factor analysis than merely establishing that Equation 7.4 describes a dispersion matrix. The model should be theoretically informed, even in cases regarded as largely exploratory. This means that in general the number of common factors anticipated is specified in advance; at worst, a range of reasonable values should be specified (Horn & Engstrom, 1979). This also means that the values of more elements in Λ and Φ than are required to merely identify a solution should be specified, which is to say that the model should be overdetermined. Overdetermination is often attained by use of the simple structure principles first elucidated by Thurstone (e.g., 1947), but there are other reasonable models—alternatives to simple structure—for establishing overdetermination.

Thurstone (1947) pointed out that insofar as its "null" elements are concerned, a simple-structure factor pattern can be expected to be invariant across different samples even when these samples are not drawn to be representative of a specified population, provided the factor intercorrelations and variances are able to vary, for these capture the nonrandom differences between samples. McArdle and Cattell (1994) found that this would be true if the variables in the hyperplanes (i.e., the near-zero elements) of a simple structure genuinely had only random relationships with the factors. However, if any nonchance relationships were reflected in even very small pattern coefficients, these relationships would need to be accounted for in the tests for invariance. It seems that in most sets of data in the behavioral sciences small but nonchance factor pattern relationships are the rule even when studies are well designed to indicate a simple structure. The magnitudes of small latent roots of obtained dispersion matrices do not decrease in the manner of error (Horn & Engstrom, 1979). Given this situation, McArdle and Cattell suggested that investigators should probably seek evidence of factorial invariance by evaluating saturated factor patterns rather than considering only the most simple of simple structures.

Cross-Sectional Factorial Invariance

Factorial invariance, whether cross-sectional or longitudinal, is essentially an empirical issue, albeit an issue of fundamental importance. The failure of invariance to hold is, in most situations, prima facie evidence that the manifest variables fail to measure the same latent attributes in the same way in different situations. There is nothing in the factor analytic model itself that guarantees invariance or its absence.

Suppose the existence of multiple subpopulations, such as males and females; 9-, 10-, and 11-year-olds; and so on, each subpopulation representing a crossing of categories of age, gender, ethnicity, and other such designators of population characteristics. It seems reasonable to suppose that the simplest, most direct, and best way to establish that the same factor model (the same equations specifying the model) holds for every individual in every subpopulation is to combine the subpopulations and analyze the dispersion matrix for that union. If the equality specified in Equation 7.4 holds with the anticipated number of common factors and the theoretically expected structure on Λ, then it seems reasonable to conclude that there is an invariant law of composition represented by Equations 7.1 and 7.2 and that this law can be used to correctly characterize the subpopulations. This seemingly reasonable approach is fraught with difficulties, however. The main problem is that the anticipated model can hold in subpopulations but not hold in the union. The reason for the failure of a factor model to fit in the union of populations usually has to do with the role played by specific factors.

The most basic requirement of factorial invariance is *pattern invariance*, namely that given a set of populations indexed by $g = 1, 2, \ldots m$, there exists a pattern matrix such that

$$\Sigma_g = \Lambda \Phi_g \Lambda' + \Psi_g = 1, 2, \ldots, m. \tag{7.5}$$

Notice that this implies that Assumptions 1 and 2 hold in every group—Ω and Θ are collapsed into one matrix, Ψ_g because all correlations of S are zero and correlate zero with all W. If there were no specific factors, only measurement error, Assumptions 1 and 2 would hold, for a consequence of the fundamental nature of error is that it is uncorrelated with all variables of the universe. Thus, E (erstwhile S) and W are uncorrelated in every population, as are the components of E. Under such conditions pattern invariance would be easier to obtain than if, as is likely, non-error specific factors are present.

The matrix Φ_g need not be of full rank, which is to say that certain factors may have zero variance and hence not appear in some subpopulations. Another way to look at this matter is to assume that

$$\Sigma_g = \Lambda_g \Lambda_g' + \Psi_g, \quad \Lambda_g = \Lambda R_g, \quad \Phi_g = R_g R_g', \tag{7.6}$$

in which R_g is not necessarily a square rotation or transformation matrix. These conditions thus allow that some of the common factors identified in a given subpopulation appear to be different from some of the common factors identified in other subpopulations or in the union of all subpopulations. The order of Λ in the aggregate population $(p \times q)$ need not be the same as the order of Λ_g in any subpopulation $(p \times d,$ with $d < q)$, and the order in any one subpopulation may differ from the order in others. Also a given common factor of an aggregate need not appear in any of the subgroups in the form it appears in the aggregate, although any common factors that occur in any of the separate subgroups are in the union of all subgroups in some form. This all sounds more complex in words than it actually is. What we are trying to describe is what the rotation matrix $\mathbf{R}_g$ can do.

Although these conditions are possible, it should be recognized that because a common factor is defined within the context of other common factors, and therefore is a function of this company that it keeps, it is no easy matter to specify conditions under which common factors appear in some samples of participants but not in others. To see this concretely, recall that a common factor coefficient is, in effect, a beta weight for estimating an observed variable from that factor in a multiple regression equation involving other common factors. Next consider what happens in a multiple regression equation when a variable —now factor—is left out of the equation in one sample and put into the equation in another sample. If the factor is correlated with other factors, then when it is put into the equation the beta weights for the factors with which it is correlated are reduced in magnitude relative to what they are when it is not included in the equation. Then consider that for each variable there is such a regression equation, and for invariance to obtain the weights for a given factor in one subpopulation must remain proportional to the comparable weights in that factor in other subpopulations. If each of the weights of a factor were reduced by the same amount as other common factors were included and excluded in going across different subpopulations, there would no be problem for obtaining invariance, for this requires only that the factor pattern weights be proportional from one sample to another. However, the weights are not likely reduced by the same or proportional amounts in all the regression equations for estimating variables from factors (as predictor factors are left in and taken out of the equations, certainly not as some are left out of the equation in one sample and others are left out in another sample). An exception would be if the common factors were correlated to zero in the population of the union and in the subpopulations. This is unlikely. Even if the factors were uncorrelated in the population of the union, they would not be expected to be uncorrelated in nonrandom subpopulations.

Hence, although in theory invariance can occur when the number of common factors in the subpopulations and the union of the subpopulations can vary—and this can be true even when the factors are not orthogonal—it is a difficult condition to obtain in the practice of finding and demonstrating factor invariance. To test for invariance when there is evidence of different numbers of factors in subpopulations, multiple-dispersion matrices should be analyzed with (a) the number of factors specified and forced to be invariant over groups, (b) the free elements in Λ constrained to be invariant over groups, and (c) specification to allow the Φ matrices to be of less than full rank as necessary.

The variances of the specifics, Ω, and the error variances, Θ, in separate samples need not be equal for invariance to obtain; that is, the variables may not be as well described in terms of common factors in some samples as in others or in the union of all samples. In this case, for example, the factor pattern coefficients in one sample could be small relative to what they were in another sample. Necessary for factorial invariance in this example, however, is that the vector of coefficients in one sample be perfectly proportional to the vector of coefficients in the other sample.

The general principle to be aware of here is that evaluation of invariance of a common factor should take account of the context in which the factor is identified: The factor pattern is affected by the context in which the factor is identified. The context includes the indicator variables of the factor, other common factors, and error and specific factors. In evaluating the conditions that allow for and detract from a finding of invariance, specific factors are most often neglected—by, in effect, being assumed to be error. We examine the role of specific factors in some detail in the sections that follow.

Alternatives to factor pattern invariance also should be considered. As we have noted, the factor model is only an approximation to the laws of nature. There are almost certainly nonlinearities of relationships and minor factors that enter into lack of fit as well as many uncontrollable influences. Thurstone, following the early work of Thomson and Lederman (see Thomson, 1951), believed that pattern invariance was not possible and proposed that study design to indicate simple structure solved the problem. In this case the "same" simple structure solution would be found in multiple groups, but with variation in the magnitude of the "non-zero" elements. Essentially this meant that the same manifest variables would appear in the same hyperplanes over groups. Thurstone (1947) called this *configurational invariance*, and this idea was revived by Horn and McArdle (1980, 1992; Horn et al., 1983). This notion merits more attention and study than it has received, as does the concept of "partial pattern invariance"—namely, the idea that many, but not all, elements of the pattern matrix may be invariant over groups (Byrne, Shavelson, & Muthén, 1989). Partial pattern invariance is a special case of configurational invariance.

Factorial Invariance and Selection Theory

The question of the feasibility of cross-sectional factorial invariance has typically been approached from the point of view of selection theory, which affords a unique and interesting perspective (Ahmavaara, 1954; Meredith, 1964; Muthén,

1989a, 1989b; Thomson, 1951; Thurstone, 1947). In this approach a parent population is postulated in accordance with Equations 7.1, 7.2, 7.3, and 7.4, under Assumptions 1 and 2, and a selection variable (e.g., sex, age) is thought to provide a basis for selecting subpopulations from a parent population. The question then is "How does selection affect factor analysis results?" Without loss of generality it can be assumed that the common and specific factor means are null vectors in the parent population.

Now if $\mathbf{X} = \Lambda\mathbf{W} + \mathbf{S} + \mathbf{E} + \mathbf{T}$ in the parent population, it must be the case that $\mathbf{X} = \Lambda\mathbf{W} + \mathbf{S} + \mathbf{E} + \mathbf{T}$ in any subpopulation of the parent no matter how the subpopulations are chosen. Selective choice of subpopulations cannot alter the basic rule of composition of $\mathbf{X}$. What may happen, however, is that Assumptions 1, 2, or both, fail to obtain in a selected subpopulation. Selection can produce correlation among specific factors or between specific and common factors. It would then be impossible to express the dispersion matrix of $\mathbf{X}$ in terms of common factors that are uncorrelated with specific factors, mutually uncorrelated specifics, or both. Indeed, a factor model might fit with more "common factors" than are present in the parent population. Two interesting results can be considered to indicate conditions under which factor invariance can obtain if the assumptions are somewhat stronger than those invoked above to define the factor model. In Case 1, the model assumptions are

- *Assumption 1A*: For every fixed value of $\mathbf{W}$ the conditional expectation of $\mathbf{S}$ is null;

- *Assumption 2A*: For every fixed value of $\mathbf{W}$ the conditional dispersion of $\mathbf{S}$ is diagonal.

Also it is assumed that the selection variable affects only $\mathbf{W}$ (i.e., is independent of $\mathbf{S}$). Then, in any subpopulation selected from the parent population by the use of the selection variable,

$$\Sigma_s = \Lambda\Phi_s\Lambda' + \Omega_s + \Theta_s \quad \text{and} \quad \mu_s = \Lambda\xi_s + \mathbf{T}. \qquad (7.7)$$

The assumption that selection is independent of $\mathbf{S}$ means that the only consequence of selection is an alteration in the distribution of $\mathbf{W}$. Recall our assumptions about measurement error and notice that Assumptions 1A and 2A imply that $(\mathbf{S} + \mathbf{E})$ behaves with respect to $\mathbf{W}$ in the fashion that $\mathbf{E}$ behaves with respect to true score. Thus, altering the distribution of $\mathbf{W}$ has no effect on the linear relation of the elements of $(\mathbf{S} + \mathbf{E})$ to $\mathbf{W}$ or to each other. In Case 2, the assumptions are stronger:

- *Assumption 1B*: $\mathbf{W}$ and $\mathbf{S}$ are independent;

- *Assumption 2B*: The elements of $\mathbf{S}$ are mutually independent.

Also it is assumed that selection is sequential and independent, taking place first on $\mathbf{W}$, then on s_h, followed by selection on s_i, and so on. Then, in a subpopulation so chosen,

$$\Sigma_s = \Lambda\Phi_s\Lambda' + \Omega_s + \Theta_s \quad \text{and} \quad \mu_s = \Lambda\xi_s + \eta_s + \mathbf{T}. \tag{7.8}$$

(It can be shown that there exists a multivariate selection variable whose use in selection would have precisely the same result as the sequential process described above.) The difference between the two results lies in the fact that if selection depends only on $\mathbf{W}$ (Case 1) the mean μ_s differs from the parent population mean only by means of the fact that ξ_s differs from ξ, whereas in the second case there are mean differences in the specific factors—that is, "intercept" differences, for the specific factor means can be absorbed into an intercept term as $\mathbf{T}_s = (\eta_s + \mathbf{T})$.

The proof of the first of the foregoing results can be found in Meredith's (1993) article. Proof of the second is unpublished (Meredith, 1997).

These two cases illustrate the severity of the restrictions that must obtain if invariance is to be found under conditions of selection. The selection approach presupposes that a factor model characterizes some parent population. If so, then in any subpopulation of that population the model (see Equation 7.2) holds. However, what need not be true in a subpopulation is that $\mathbf{W}$ and $\mathbf{S}$ are uncorrelated and/or that the elements of $\mathbf{S}$ are mutually uncorrelated. The conditions under which pattern invariance occurs with exactly the same number of factors and pattern matrix that characterize the parent are stringent. Either the selection variable can affect only the common factors, as in Case 1, or an unusual form of selection must occur in the presence of mutual statistical independence of $\mathbf{W}$ and $s_1, s_2, \ldots, s_p$, as in Case 2. These strictures seem to be unlikely in practice. One would expect the selection variate to affect both $\mathbf{W}$ and $\mathbf{S}$ in such a way that correlations are induced between the elements of $\mathbf{W}$ and those of $\mathbf{S}$ and among the elements of $\mathbf{S}$. These matters have had insufficient discussion in the literature (but see Bloxom, 1972).

Typically a selection variable would be sex, ethnicity, or educational level. Selection of a subgroup using such a variable is likely to affect specific factors and common ones, with the consequence that the basic assumptions of factor analysis fails in subpopulations. One can see that if there were no specific factors, selection would affect only common factors, and invariance could obtain. However, it turns out that if one fits a pattern-invariant model to multiple selected groups with different specific factor means (η_g), then the common and specific factors may not be uncorrelated in their union, that is, in the parent population. If no such specific factor differences are needed to attain fit, then the common and specific factors are uncorrelated in the union. We take up this matter in the next section without reference to selection.

Aggregation and the Role of Means in Factor Invariance

One reason for fitting cross-sectional invariant models across multiple groups is that group differences in specific factors can lead to violations of Assumptions 1 and 2 in a population that is a union of heterogeneous subpopulations. For example, suppose that an investigator had assembled a set of cognitive tests, each one of which measured a single primary factor, in such a way that the factors of Fluid Reasoning (Gf) and Crystallized Knowledge (Gc) should emerge as the primary factors in the selected battery. Now suppose there are sex differences on two of the tests, say 1 and 2, such that $\eta_{1,f} < \eta_{1,m}$ and $\eta_{2,f} > \eta_{2,m}$. The result would be a negative correlation between s_1 and s_2 in the combined population that would not be present if males and females were modeled separately. Similarly, imagine using this battery with 11-, 12-, 13-, and 14-year-old children. One would expect growth, leading to increases in both common and specific factor means—for example, $\xi_{1,11} < \xi_{1,12} < \xi_{1,13} < \xi_{1,14}$ and $\eta_{1,11} < \eta_{1,12} < \eta_{1,13} < \eta_{1,14}$. This would result in a positive correlation between w_1 and s_1 in the combined population, but again such a correlation could be largely absent in subpopulations in which age did not vary.

To see this formally in detail, suppose there are m subpopulations of different sizes and a population that is their union. Let π_g denote the proportionate contribution of group g to the union. The variable means then are $\mu = \sum \pi_g \mu_g$. Using a standard result (e.g., one-way multivariate analysis of variance), the dispersion matrix of $\mathbf{X}$ in the union can be obtained as

$$\Sigma = \sum \pi_g \Sigma_g + \sum \pi_g (\mu_g - \mu)(\mu_g - \mu)'. \tag{7.9}$$

The common and specific factor means in the population are $\xi = \sum \pi_g \xi_g$, $\eta = \sum \pi_g \eta_g$, respectively. Let Ξ be a $q \times m$ matrix whose columns consist of the common factor mean differences $\xi_g - \xi$, and let Y be a $p \times m$ matrix whose columns are specific factor mean differences $\eta_g - \eta$. Finally, let Π be a diagonal matrix of the π_g. Now the dispersion matrix of the common factors in the union is

$$\Phi = \sum \pi_g \Phi_g + \Xi \Pi \Xi'. \tag{7.10}$$

Next, simplify notation by letting $\Lambda_\eta = Y \Pi^{1/2}$ and $\Phi_\xi = \Xi \Pi^{1/2}$. With these terms, then, the dispersion matrix of the manifest variables in the union can be seen to be

$$\Sigma = [\Lambda | \Lambda_\eta] \begin{bmatrix} \Phi & \Phi_\xi \\ \Phi_\xi' & I \end{bmatrix} [\Lambda | \Lambda_\eta]' + \sum \pi_g \Psi_g. \tag{7.11}$$

This makes it clear that there are $m - 1$ additional factors in the union of groups unless the common factor mean vectors ξ_g and specific factor mean vectors η_g have the property that $\Lambda_\eta \Phi'_\xi = 0$ and $\Lambda_\eta \Lambda'_\eta$ = diagonal (which would then be absorbed into $\Sigma \, \pi_g \Psi_g$).[1]

One can see that it would make matters simple if Y were null, thus trivially satisfying both conditions. However, a requirement that all $\eta_g - \eta = 0$ is just what generally cannot be assumed. And if these differences are not zero, the conditions under which $\Lambda_\eta \Phi'_\xi = 0$ and $\Lambda_\eta \Lambda'_\eta$ = diagonal are extremely restrictive and unlikely to be satisfied in practice. For example, if all $\eta_g - \eta$ are not zero, then for the off-diagonals in $\Lambda_\eta \Lambda'_\eta$ to be zero it is necessary either that all crossproducts of the form $(\eta_{jg} - \eta_j) (\eta_{kg} - \eta_k)\pi_g = 0$ over p variables, j and k, and m groups, or that those crossproducts that are positive sum to precisely the same value as the crossproducts that are negative. More simply, the requirement is that there be no correlation among any of the specifics in any of the groups. Now the number of groups is typically small (judging by research up to the present time), and the ranks of $\Lambda_\eta \Lambda'_\eta$ and Φ_ξ do not exceed $m - 1$, so there is a sense in which there are few opportunities for additional factors to enter.[2] The main point, however, is that even if an invariant model with q factors exists within groups that model likely will not obtain in a union that might be formed by combining groups.[3]

The following rather contrived example illustrates these points. The data consist of scores on a subset of 5 of the "twenty-four psychological tests" (Holzinger & Swineford, 1939) that have been used so frequently in factor analysis articles and textbooks. The 5 tests were chosen to access one of each of the different domains defining a common factor in the original study, namely, Lozenges (representing spatial ability), Word Meaning (a verbal comprehension test), Coding (representing perceptual speed), Object–Number (a short-term memory test) and Woody–McCall (an arithmetical reasoning test). The participants were 301 students. A one-factor model, F1, might be expected to fit these data (to represent the positive manifold among all the tests), but it does not (root mean square error of approximation [RMSEA] = .10, confidence interval [CI] = .05–.14).

However, the sample can be thought of as comprising subpopulations. The children, boys and girls, were sampled from two schools in which the average economic level (i.e., socioeconomic status [SES]) of the parents of the students was markedly different. To represent the idea of subpopulations we divided the total sample into four groups based on sex and school attended. The partition-

---

[1] There are no more than $m - 1$ additional factors because the ranks of both Ξ and Y are at most $m - 1$.

[2] If the rank of Φ_ξ is $m - 1$, there being $m - 1$ additional common factors, the only "diagonal" form of $\Lambda_\eta \Lambda'_\eta$ is a null matrix.

[3] Priority in this observation is probably due to Gibson (1959), but Muthén (1989b) also noted that heterogeneous subpopulation means could induce artifactual factors.

TABLE 7.1

A Spearman Model With Specific Factor Group Differences

VARIABLE	F1	LG	LB	HG	HB
Spatial ability	0.42	−0.01	0.31	−0.25	−0.06
Verbal comprehension	0.59	−0.15	0.01	0.08	0.07
Perceptual speed	0.58	0.18	−0.04	−0.02	−0.12
Short-term memory	0.41	0.28	0.00	−0.09	−0.20
Arithmetic reasoning	0.65	−0.11	−0.10	0.12	0.10
G factor means	—	−0.07	−0.37	0.10	0.12

Note. F1 = one-factor model; L = low socioeconomic status; G = girls; B = boys; H = high socioeconomic status.

ing yields 83 girls and 74 boys from the low-SES school, and 73 girls and 72 boys from the high-SES school. For these groupings a one-factor, pattern-invariant model with no group differences in intercepts does not fit (RMSEA = .19, CI = .16−.22), but a one-factor pattern-invariant model with group differences in intercepts fits very well (RMSEA = .00, CI = .00−.06). (The Ψ_g varied across groups in these solutions, as, of course, did the Φ_g.)

The augmented matrix $[\Lambda | \Lambda_\eta]$ of Equation 7.11 for the good-fit solution is given in Table 7.1. The row labels indicate the expected primary common factor affiliation of the tests in an analysis of all the variables. The column labels indicate first the common factor, Λ, followed by specific factor effects, Λ_η, attributable to low-SES girls, high-SES girls, low-SES boys, and high-SES boys, respectively. The common factor means for the four groups are provided at the foot of the table. The last four (specific factor) columns were computed from the intercept terms in the analysis. Because any one of them can be expressed as a linear combination of the other three, one can be eliminated in expressing a four-factor solution.[4]

What seems to be going on here is that there is a complex interaction between gender and social class that is manifested as group differences in the means of specific factors. Notice that in this interpretation, however, we have implicitly assumed that $\mu_g = \Lambda\xi_g + \eta_g + T$ rather than $\mu_g = \Lambda\xi_g + T_g$, which is to say that we think the group differences in manifest means that fail to pass through the common factor—that is, that are not accounted for by the general factor—should be attributed to group differences in specific factor means. It is well nigh impossible to empirically distinguish this assumption from an assumption that there are group differences in arbitrary intercepts T_g. The differences in assumption do pertain to meaning, however. To attribute group mean

---

[4]Parenthetically we remark that, of course, it would be practically impossible to fit a four-factor model to the five-variable dispersion matrix based on the aggregate sample.

differences that are not accounted for by differences in common factor means to intercepts is to assert bias in measurement, whereas to assert that they are specific factors is to suggest that with better study design—that is, better choice of manifest variables—the factors could either be eliminated or be shown to be common factors. It is interesting in this respect that when all of the available variables of the Holzinger–Swineford data are used in multiple-group invariance analysis most, but not all, of the group differences in specific factor means that appear in this example are absorbed into common factors and consequently disappear.

Practical Aspects of Determining Means

The method typically suggested for identifying common factor means and intercepts (which are implicitly equal to $\eta_g + T$) in the application of multiple-group applications of SEM programs is to set suitably chosen elements of intercepts to zero. However, this confounds group differences in common and specific factors. We illustrate this using the example presented in the previous section. If one minimally identifies the common factor means and intercepts by setting the intercept terms for, say, Lozenges, all equal to zero, the common factor means become -0.05, 1.17, -0.88, and -0.25, respectively, but if instead we set intercepts for Word Meaning to zero, the common factor means become -0.51, -0.31, 0.61, and 0.28, respectively. The means in each case are notably different from those obtained with the solution we presented, which were obtained by a method described shortly, that we think should be preferred.

To deal with this problem of arbitrariness, one approach has been to equate intercepts over groups and impose the q restrictions entailed in $\Sigma \, \pi_g \xi_g = 0$ (or equate intercepts and set the common factor means to zero for one group). The hoped-for outcome is that a satisfactory fit of the model then will be attained. Whatever the outcome, this choice for common factor means forces these means to "account for as much of group differences in manifest means as possible." If the fit of the model is not good, one encounters a problem as to how best to proceed unless a satisfactory result can be attained by freeing up a few sensibly chosen elements in the intercept vectors.

Part of the problem here lies in the fact that this approach affects the numerical values of elements of Λ as it is determining the common factor means and intercepts. The approach works well only if a relatively simple and theoretically informed "fixup" is sufficient. The common factor means obtained by equating intercepts in this manner in our example are $-.18$, -0.43, 0.49, and 0.15, respectively. However, with this approach we find that one or more of the model modification indices for every variable but the Woody–McCall exceed 12 and range to as large as 27, and the modification indices for the

Woody–McCall average 6. Inspecting these indices gives no real clue as to how to proceed. We have some ideas that could be invoked based on what is known about sex and class differences in cognitive variables, but it turns out that these ideas are not consistent with the pattern of large modification indices. In particular, an attempt to model group differences as a function of additive sex and school "effects" failed (RMSEA = .12 ; CI = .09–.16).

Our recommendation is to first carry out a multigroup-invariant factor analysis ignoring means. Then set $\mathbf{T}$ equal to the average of the μ_g and compute common factor means by the equation $\xi_g = (\Lambda'\Psi_g^{-1}\Lambda)^{-1}\Lambda'\Psi_g^{-1}(\mu_g - \mathbf{T})$. The matrix $(\Lambda'\Psi_g^{-1}\Lambda)^{-1}\Lambda'\Psi_g^{-1}$ is the matrix of Bartlett weights for predicting factor scores in subpopulation g. This choice for ξ_g minimizes the Euclidean distance between $(\Lambda\xi_g)$ and $(\mu_g - \mathbf{T})$ in the metric of Ψ_g, and the underlying logic is that the matrix Ψ_g is nearly proportional to the sampling dispersion of the specific factor means. This method was used in calculating the common factor means and specific factor means reported in the good-fit solution in the previous section. Note that fixing common factor means in this way does not alter the degrees of freedom. It is precisely the same as for the analysis ignoring means, and the various goodness-of-fit statistics are unaffected. To completely carry out this procedure one needs a matrix manipulation program such as SAS/IML or MATLAB.

These common factor means could subsequently be entered as fixed values in an analysis with intercepts allowed to be free over groups. Examination of the results might then suggest some simplification in the pattern of specific factor means by equating or zeroing certain elements. After imposing enough restrictions on intercepts it would be desirable to free up the formerly fixed common factor means in further analyses. Care needs to be exercised in such an endeavor not to capitalize on chance to get a good fit.

An alternative would be to minimize the Euclidean distance between $(\Lambda\xi_g)$ and $(\mu_g - \mathbf{T})$ in the metric of $\Sigma_g = \Lambda\Phi_g\Lambda' + \Psi_g$. The logic underlying this approach is that the sampling dispersion matrix of the manifest means in group g is proportional to Σ_g. It can be shown that this leads to $\xi_g = (\mathbf{W}_g'\Lambda)^{-1}\mathbf{W}_g'(\mu_g - \mathbf{T})$, where $\mathbf{W}_g$ is the usual matrix of "least square" regression weights for predicting factor scores, that is, $\mathbf{W}_g = (\Phi_g^{-1} + \Lambda'\Psi_g^{-1}\Lambda)^{-1}\Lambda'\Psi_g^{-1}$.

Of course, another possibility would be to use $\mathbf{W}_g$ itself in $\xi_g = \mathbf{W}_g'(\mu_g - \mathbf{T})$, but this seems to be less desirable than the other methods suggested, because it implicitly assumes that the subgroup means for specific variables are all zero.

The user of these approaches should recognize that the fixing of common factor means in these ways does not increase the degrees of freedom. Whatever degrees of freedom appeared in the output listing should be reduced by $q(m - 1)$, the number of free means fixed. It should be emphasized that freeing up specific factor means (i.e., intercepts) should be done cautiously, and one would expect that the process would be informed by theoretical considerations about the nature of the variables involved.

Factorial Invariance and Methods for Studying Univariate Development

In this section, we take up two essentially univariate models for development: (a) the simplex, or first-order autoregression and (b) latent curve analysis, which includes multilevel modeling (hierarchical linear models). The basic theoretical developments of these models can be found in publications by Browne (1993); Duncan et al. (1999); Jöreskog (1970); MacCallum, Kim, Malarkey, and Kiecolt-Glaser (1997); McArdle and Hamagami (1996); Meredith (1984); Meredith and Tisak (1990); and Rogosa and Willett (1985). Early interesting applications were described by McArdle (1988, 1989).

Suppose a variable x is measured on occasions $j = 1, \ldots, r$. Arrange x_1, $x_2, \ldots, x_r$ into a vector $\mathbf{X}$. Now, in a simplex model describing the evolution of x over time, the basic equation is

$$x_j = \delta_j(w_1 + w_2 + \ldots + w_j) + e_j, \tag{7.12}$$

in which the w_i are assumed to be uncorrelated and e_j is measurement error. In this formulation $w_2, w_3, \ldots, w_r$ represent latent increments. In many applications δ_j is taken to be unity. The mean vector and dispersion matrix can be expressed as (Jöreskog & Sörbom, 1979)

$$\mu = \Delta \mathbf{L} \xi \quad \text{and} \quad \Sigma = \Delta \mathbf{L} \Phi \mathbf{L}' \Delta + \Theta, \tag{7.13}$$

where Δ, Φ, and Θ are diagonal matrices and $\mathbf{L}$ is a lower triangular matrix whose nonzero elements are all unity. The elements of ξ and Φ are means and variances, respectively, of the incremental changes, w_j for $j = 2, \ldots, r$.

Equation 7.13 clearly represents a factor analytic model. Thus, simplex developmental invariance over groups is essentially a special case of factorial invariance. Notice, however, that unlike the usual factor model, there are no specific factors.

The simplex model is more commonly represented by the equation

$$t_j = \beta_j t_{j-1} + w_j, \quad x_j = t_j = t_j + e_j, \tag{7.14}$$

in which t represents a true score and w_j represents the increment uncorrelated with t (Jöreskog, 1970). For our purposes the representation of Equation 7.12 is preferable because it clearly presents the simplex as a factor analytic model. The factor pattern matrix is $(\Delta \mathbf{L})$ and, again, there are no specific factors or arbitrary intercepts in this setup. Cross-sectional invariance requires then that Δ be invariant over groups. As a result, the β_j are invariant. (As an aside, longitudinal invariance of the β_j—i.e., β_j = constant—occurs when δ_j = a constant times δ_{j-1}.)

Now, to study cross-sectional invariance of simplex models, we can apply what we know about factorial invariance. Thus, we see that pattern invariance requires invariance of the diagonal matrix Δ. Also for a simplex to exist in each group, Φ_g must be diagonal in each subgroup—that is, the increments must be uncorrelated in each group. It can be further argued that a simplex in subgroups ought to imply simplex structure for $x_1, x_2, \ldots x_r$ in the population that is the union of subpopulations, inasmuch as there are no specific factors to carry differences. This would necessitate that Φ in the union be diagonal. Referring back to the discussion of means in connection with factorial invariance we see that the matrix Ξ, whose columns are the ξ_g expressed as deviations from the grand mean vector, must be such that $\Xi\Pi\Xi'$ be diagonal. Because the number of linearly independent columns of Ξ cannot exceed the number of groups minus 1, group differences in means can hold for no more than that number of the w_r. Notice that if two groups differed in mean on initial status, w_1, the group with the larger mean for w_1 would have larger means on the x_j, $j = 1, 2, \ldots, r$ despite the fact that there were no group differences in the means of the increments $w_2, \ldots, w_r$.

For latent curve analysis the basic equation is

$$x_j = \lambda_{j1}w_1 + \lambda_{j2}w_2 + \ldots + \lambda_{jq}w_q + \tau + e_j. \tag{7.15}$$

The coefficients λ_{jk} are the coordinates of $q(<p)$ curves at times (occasions) $j = 1, 2, \ldots, r$. There are no subscripts on the intercept term τ, for it is constant over occasions (and is not used in many models). No specific factors are invoked in latent curve models. The λ_{jk} may all be fixed as in polynomial (hierarchical linear) models, may be a mixture of free or fixed elements, or may be mostly free given minimal identification constraints. Note that if the first curve is constant representing initial status—that is, $\lambda_{11} = \lambda_{21} = \cdots = \lambda_{r1}$—the corresponding latent variable (individual differences in initial status) must either have a mean of zero, or τ must be eliminated. The $w_k k = 1, 2, \ldots, q$, are individual-difference terms in the model. For example, if the first curve is constant, and the second is linear in time, then w_1 captures individual differences in initial status, and w_2 is individual differences in slope (growth rate). (In polynomial models the correlation between latent attributes is strongly influenced by the choice of origin. In particular, one can always select numbers so that the correlation between initial status and linear growth rate is zero.) The mean vector and dispersion matrix become

$$\mu = \Lambda\xi + 1\tau \quad \text{and} \quad \Sigma = \Lambda\Phi\Lambda' + \Theta, \tag{7.16}$$

where 1 denotes a column of 1s. This, then, is obviously a factor analytic model and, like the simplex model, there is no provision for specific factors.

Developmental invariance relies on Λ being invariant over groups. Invariance is in a sense automatic when fitting polynomial curves, but note that in practice it can turn out that low-degree polynomials fit rather poorly. Again, one may encounter some problem with mean differences between groups that do not "pass through Λ." Because no specific factors are present, allowing intercept differences violates the fundamental invariance principle that the same developmental model holds in different subpopulations. We are definitely asserting here that the only reasonable explanation for intercept difference is that the differences reflect the operation of specific factors, which are, after all, an integral feature of the factor model in most applications. Because latent curve models do not involve specific factors, intercept differences between groups are inadmissible. Otherwise, invariance in latent curve analysis places no restrictions on either ξ_g or Φ_g over groups.

It is possible to combine latent curve ideas and simplex ideas into a single model with invariance. Consider the following:

$$x_1 = \lambda_1 w_1 + e_1, \quad x_2 = \lambda_2 w_1 + w_2 + e_2,$$

$$x_3 = \lambda_3 w_1 + \delta_3(w_2 + w_3) + e_3, \text{ etc.} \tag{7.17}$$

An example of this uses data on growth on a single intellectual factor taken from the archives of the Institute of Human Development at the University of California. The data consist of Stanford–Binet (Terman & Merrill, 1937) mental ages in months taken at ages 6, 7, 9, 10, 12, and 14 for 93 girls and 86 boys. In Table 7.2 a factor pattern matrix is presented that is invariant over sex. The first column is a fixed growth curve ($\lambda_1, \lambda_2, \ldots, \lambda_7$). The values in this curve are, except at age 14, the chronological ages in months (divided by 100) of the participants on the first occasion. At age 14 the number used is the divisor used by Terman and Merrill to calculate IQ at this age. This forces the first latent variable to be in IQ units. The remaining six columns introduce a simplex

TABLE 7.2
A Hybrid Model of Growth in Mental Age (MA)

VARIABLE	AGE (λ_i)	ΔL_2	ΔL_3	ΔL_4	ΔL_5	ΔL_6	ΔL_7
MA6	0.72	0.00	0.00	0.00	0.00	0.00	0.00
MA7	0.84	1.00	0.00	0.00	0.00	0.00	0.00
MA8	0.96	1.39	1.39	0.00	0.00	0.00	0.00
MA9	1.08	1.34	1.34	1.34	0.00	0.00	0.00
MA10	1.20	1.50	1.50	1.50	1.50	0.00	0.00
MA12	1.44	1.59	1.59	1.59	1.59	1.59	0.00
MA14	1.64	1.59	1.59	1.59	1.59	1.59	1.59
PHI	133.54	19.78	28.93	17.83	5.85	13.69	38.28
TSI	118.68	0.00	0.00	2.01	0.00	0.00	0.00

(ΔL) that provides for increments at each age to the basic growth curve. There are five free elements in ΔL. All latent variables are required to be uncorrelated because there is only one latent variable with a "curve." The second through seventh factors are simplex independent increments. Because Terman and Merrill made a serious, and largely successful, effort to eliminate sex differences it seemed reasonable to require that $\Phi_f = \Phi_m$ and $\xi_f = \xi_m = \xi$. The elements of ξ, other than the first, were all equated to zero on the grounds that the curve (the first column of Λ) should account for average growth and for a lot of individual differences in rate. It turned out that to obtain a satisfactory fit it was necessary to free the fourth element of ξ and to free the seventh element for females (= 2.59). Observe that ξ is not the intercept terms but in fact consists of the means of latent variables in the model.

The number of groups is two, and group differences between latent variable means are present for only one latent variable (w_7). As a result, the data meet the conditions described in the opening paragraphs of this section, leading to a diagonal-dispersion matrix in the union. The RMSEA for the model is .055 (CI = .000–.090).

Longitudinal Factor Analysis

Longitudinal factor analysis has been investigated by McArdle and Nesselroade (1993), Nesselroade (1983), and Tisak and Meredith (1989, 1990b). This is the case in which individuals are assessed with multiple measures, X, at several times, ages, or occasions indexed by j and k, j, $k = 1 \ldots r$. It is assumed that manifest time is discrete, which it must always be—days, weeks, years, and so on—even as it can be regarded theoretically as continuous. The successive measures in longitudinal studies may be the same measures obtained repeatedly, or they may be different measures but forms believed to be parallel, or they may be entirely different measures or any combination of these kinds of measurements. In any case, longitudinal invariance must involve the assumption that the factor pattern matrix is not a function of the "occasion" leading to

$$X_j = \Lambda W_j + S_j + E_j + T. \tag{7.18}$$

Additional assumptions that are somewhat stronger than actually needed but that succinctly characterize the nature of the longitudinal factor analytic model are as follows:

- *Assumption 1*: W_j is uncorrelated with S_j for all j.
- *Assumption 2*: The components of S_j are mutually uncorrelated for all j.
- *Assumption 3*: W_j is uncorrelated with S_k for all j, k.

- *Assumption 4*: The *h*th component of S_j is uncorrelated with the *i*th component of S_k for all pairs *h*, *i*, $h \neq i$.

The definition of E_j in terms of weak true score theory is operative within and across occasions. In particular, the assumption of experimental independence obtains across all occasions, which implies that E_j and E_k are (expected value) uncorrelated for all pairs of *j* and *k*.

What these assumptions assert is that the common factors, W, develop, grow, evolve, independently of specific factors, S, and the specifics of S develop independently of W and of each other. These assumptions, coupled with Equation 7.18, yield the following expressions for mean vectors and dispersion matrices.

$$\mu_j = \Lambda \xi_j + \eta_j + T, \tag{7.19}$$

$$\Sigma_{jj} = \Lambda \Phi_{jj} \Lambda' + \Omega_{jj} + \Theta_{jj} = \Lambda \Phi_{jj} \Lambda' + \Psi_{jj} \tag{7.20}$$

$$\Sigma_{jk} = \Lambda \Phi_{jk} \Lambda' + \Omega_{jk}. \tag{7.21}$$

For a two-occasion case, Equations 7.19, 7.20, and 7.21 can be written explicitly as follows

$$\begin{bmatrix} \mu_1 \\ \mu_2 \end{bmatrix} = \begin{bmatrix} \Lambda & 0 \\ 0 & \Lambda \end{bmatrix} \begin{bmatrix} \xi_1 \\ \xi_2 \end{bmatrix} + \begin{bmatrix} \eta_1 \\ \eta_2 \end{bmatrix} + \begin{bmatrix} T \\ T \end{bmatrix} \tag{7.22}$$

and

$$\begin{bmatrix} \Sigma_{11} & \Sigma_{12} \\ \Sigma_{21} & \Sigma_{22} \end{bmatrix} = \begin{bmatrix} \Lambda & 0 \\ 0 & \Lambda \end{bmatrix} \begin{bmatrix} \Phi_{11} & \Phi_{12} \\ \Phi_{21} & \Phi_{22} \end{bmatrix} \begin{bmatrix} \Lambda & 0 \\ 0 & \Lambda \end{bmatrix}' + \begin{bmatrix} \Psi_{11} & \Omega_{12} \\ \Omega_{21} & \Psi_{22} \end{bmatrix}, \tag{7.23}$$

which provide concrete specifications of the means and joint dispersion matrices that are the targets for analyses with standard SEM programs. Observe that change in the true score value of any x_i may be a complex function of change in W and s_i that militates against the likelihood that simple models of growth for individual x_i will apply.

Equations 7.19, 7.20, and 7.21 are usually taken as definitive of the longitudinal factor model. Notice here that Ω_{jk} is a diagonal matrix of covariances between homologous specific factors (not correlated error!). Because it is presumed that the specific factors may change over time there is no problem whatsoever with intercept differences over occasions. In fact, there is little point in including means when fitting a longitudinal factor model unless the investigator has specific hypotheses about common or specific factor means to be addressed.

If an invariant longitudinal model fits the data, the implication is that there exist common and unique factor scores that at least for the times of measurement used, satisfy Equation 7.18 for all occasions and satisfy Assumptions 1–4. There is an if-and-only-if theorem embedded in the relation of Equations

7.19, 7.20, and 7.21 to the assumptions. All that one can be confident about is that Assumptions 1–4 hold for the particular set of discrete times or ages chosen for study. It is tempting to assume that Assumptions 1–4 also hold for time or ages not included in fitting the model, but such generalization is not warranted by the results, as such, although theoretical considerations may suggest that the generalization is valid. As a rule, Equations 7.20 and 7.21 have been taken to characterize longitudinal factor analysis without a clear focus on the implications of the fact that they imply that Assumptions 1–4 hold. The most significant implications follow from the fact that the model and assumptions assert, in effect, that common and specific factors evolve, develop, or change in a quasi-independent (zero correlations) fashion.

There is a problem of identification that arises in connection with means. The usual procedures used in the implementation of standard SEM programs confounds change in common factor means with change in specific factor means. It is first necessary to choose a value for $\mathbf{T}$. A method that has much to recommend it is to set $\mathbf{T}$ equal to $\boldsymbol{\mu}_1$. This choice is simple to implement and requires setting $\boldsymbol{\xi}_1$ and $\boldsymbol{\eta}_1$ equal to zero. As a result, the other latent means are expressed as change from this baseline.

Alternately, one can require that the sum of the $\boldsymbol{\xi}_j$ be a null vector and let $(\boldsymbol{\eta}_j + \mathbf{T})$ be obtained from the intercept terms that occur. One could then define $\mathbf{T}$ as the average of the occasion-specific intercepts and compute $\boldsymbol{\eta}_j$ as deviations. Still another approach is to define $\mathbf{T}$ as the average of the $\boldsymbol{\mu}_j$ and compute $\boldsymbol{\xi}_j$ by use of Bartlett weights, as described previously in the Practical Aspects of Determining Means section. The specific factor means become $\boldsymbol{\eta}_j = \boldsymbol{\mu}_j - \Lambda\boldsymbol{\xi}_j - \mathbf{T}$ after $\mathbf{T}$ and the common factor means have been determined.

Previously, in considering invariance across cross-sectional samples or different groups, we discussed the fact that combining heterogeneous subpopulations may produce essentially artifactual correlations between common and specific factors and among specific factors. Does a similar problem arise in longitudinal analyses? The answer is yes.

It is fairly common in investigations of longitudinal factor invariance to group participants of different ages into sets regarded as equivalent for purposes of the analysis. Ages 22–28, for example, may be grouped and represented by a middle age of 25, as ages 29–35 are grouped and represented by age 32, and so on. As is seen clearly in Equation 7.23, if there are p manifest variables and m ages or times, fitting a longitudinal factor model uses a $pm \times pm$ manifest variable-dispersion matrix, which, if there are many variables and many ages, can be rather large. Despite the fact that the number of free parameters may be small (because of the structure of the problem), grouping of ages may be necessary to keep the size of the problem manageable in terms of the relationship between the number of parameters to be estimated and the sample size.

Unfortunately, the grouping of participants of different ages into equivalence sets poses a potential threat to the validity of the longitudinal factor model. Specifically, these grouping procedures can induce within-occasion correlations among the components of S_j and between the components of S_j and the components of W_j. Such grouping may also induce across-occasion relationships between the components of S_j and the components of W_k and between the components of S_j and the components of S_k. The mathematical demonstration of this is tedious (Meredith, 1997), but intuitively one can understand the correlation rather easily. For example, suppose n persons are observed at age 22 and again at 29, another n persons are observed at age 23 and again at 30, and so on, up through the case where yet another n persons are observed at age 28 and again at 35. Next, suppose these $7n$ individuals are combined into a single age cohort group measured on the first occasion—ages 22, 23, . . . , 28, and then measured on the second occasion—ages 29, 30, . . . , 35. Label the ages of measurement at the midpoints of 25 and 32. Now suppose, for example, that specifics s_1 and s_2 are both growing over the entire period from 22 to 35, and consider what the scatter plot of $s_{1,25}$ against $s_{2,32}$ would look like. In the age-25 group the older, age-28 individuals would tend to have higher s_1 scores than the younger, age-22 individuals because they would have had longer time in growth; these same older, age-35 individuals would also have relatively higher s_2 scores than the younger, age-29 individuals because, again, they would have had longer time in growth. Thus, s_1 at age 25 and s_2 at age 32 are constrained toward a positive relationship simply as a function of grouping people of different ages.

It is difficult, perhaps impossible, to escape this problem in principle. For if there is growth and people are classified as the "same" somewhere along in the period (however small) of growth, there are always some relatively older people and some relatively younger people in each such classification. To put it in terms of the example, only if the classification (grouping) is such that $\eta_{22} = \eta_{23} = \ldots = \eta_{28}$, and $\eta_{29} = \eta_{30} = \ldots = \eta_{35}$, and so on, would it be the case that the classification would not constrain toward producing a relationship. This would mean in the example that growth would have to come in jumps —no growth from age 22 to 28, then a jump in growth to the next classification, and no growth within that classification of age 29 to 35, and so on. Also, of course, what is said here applies to any systematic change, not simply growth —for example, decline. For S to be thus stationary in the mean is not very likely if the groupings are at all large and variables in question are indeed changing over developmental periods. It may be that in respect to some variables and some periods of development that change (growth) is very slow, in which case the stationary assumption $\eta_j = \eta_k = \ldots = \eta_m$ could be justified for relative narrow groupings, and the artifactual association produced by grouping would be largely avoided. Such conditions might obtain in middle adulthood with respect to some variables, but one would be especially unlikely to expect this in childhood or old age. Indeed, people who conduct longitudinal research —scientists who study development—mainly look for, and aim to demonstrate, substantial change. Hence, the problem is always there. The advice is to design studies with the aim of keeping groupings by age small relative to the amount of change to be expected.

Grouping also has some distorting effect on elements of the common factor dispersion matrix. The distortion in this case, however, does not threaten the validity of the model; that is, Equations 7.19, 7.20, and 7.21 hold.

The longitudinal factor model of Equation 7.23 can be expressed in another way that is useful for analyses and for illustrating principles. For two occasions this alternative expression is defined in the following equations, 7.24 and 7.25.

Defining

$$X_j = [\Lambda \quad I] \begin{bmatrix} W_j \\ S_j + E_j \end{bmatrix}, \tag{7.24}$$

then

$$\begin{bmatrix} \Sigma_{11} & \Sigma_{12} \\ \Sigma_{21} & \Sigma_{22} \end{bmatrix} = \begin{bmatrix} \Lambda & I & 0 & 0 \\ 0 & 0 & \Lambda & I \end{bmatrix} \begin{bmatrix} \Phi_{11} & 0 & \Phi_{12} & 0 \\ 0 & \Psi_{11} & 0 & \Theta_{12} \\ \Phi_{21} & 0 & \Phi_{22} & 0 \\ 0 & \Theta_{21} & 0 & \Psi_{22} \end{bmatrix} \begin{bmatrix} \Lambda & I & 0 & 0 \\ 0 & 0 & \Lambda & I \end{bmatrix}' \tag{7.25}$$

In expressing the model for the dispersion matrix in this fashion the null blocks of the center matrix of Equation 7.25, which is the dispersion matrix of all the latent variables, both common and specific, reflect the assumptions. Freeing elements in the null blocks permits the investigator to introduce terms indicating relationships between common factors on Occasion 1 and specific factors on Occasion 2, or between specific factors at Time 1 and common factors at Time 2. For example, the covariances between common factors at Time 1 and specifics at Time 2 would be found in the 1,4 and 4,1 positions of the matrix. The introduction of such relations should rely on theoretical considerations. Thoughtlessly freeing up arbitrary elements simply to achieve a better fit is not likely to promote good science. On the other hand, the conditions implied by Assumptions 1–4 may be so unreasonable that allowing relations to exist as suggested in this formulation may help clarify what is going on in a set of data.

Longitudinal Factor Models of Change

In this section we briefly introduce some ways of formulating factor models explicitly aimed at the evaluation of change. The need for factorial invariance should be clear from the presentation. The developments are presented for the case of two occasions of measurement. Extensions to more times are generally fairly easy to see. We begin with a recapitulation and re-expression of the longitudinal factor model in which Λ is the longitudinally invariant factor pattern matrix:

$$X_1 = \Lambda W_1 + S_1 + E_1 + T,$$

$$X_2 = \Lambda W_1 + \Lambda(W_2 - W_1) + S_2 + E_2 + T. \tag{7.26}$$

We now set $\xi_1 = 0$ and $\eta_1 = 0$ and may write

$$\mu_2 = \Lambda\xi_2 + \eta_2 + \mu_1 \tag{7.27}$$

and

$$\begin{bmatrix} \Sigma_{11} & \Sigma_{12} \\ \Sigma_{21} & \Sigma_{22} \end{bmatrix} = \begin{bmatrix} \Lambda & 0 \\ \Lambda & \Lambda \end{bmatrix} \begin{bmatrix} \Phi_{11} & P_{12} \\ P_{21} & P_{22} \end{bmatrix} \begin{bmatrix} \Lambda' & \Lambda' \\ 0 & \Lambda' \end{bmatrix} + \begin{bmatrix} \Psi_{11} & \Omega_{12} \\ \Omega_{21} & \Psi_{22} \end{bmatrix}. \tag{7.28}$$

In Equation 7.28 P_{12} is a matrix of covariances between initial status on the common factors, W_1, and change $(W_2 - W_1)$ in those factors; P_{22} is the dispersion matrix of differences. In essence, the approach described in Equations 7.26, 7.27, and 7.28 is the equivalent of that in Equations 7.19, 7.20, 7.21, 7.22, and 7.23. It is a simple reparameterization.

Now consider the following extension of the foregoing.

$$X_1 = \Lambda W_1 + S_1 + E_1 + T, \quad X_2 = \Lambda W_1 + \Gamma Z + S_2 + E_2 + T. \tag{7.29}$$

Set $\xi_1 = 0$ and $\eta_1 = 0$ as before, and it follows that

$$\mu_2 = \Gamma\zeta + \eta_2 + \mu_1 \tag{7.30}$$

and

$$\begin{bmatrix} \Sigma_{11} & \Sigma_{12} \\ \Sigma_{21} & \Sigma_{22} \end{bmatrix} = \begin{bmatrix} \Lambda & 0 \\ \Lambda & \Gamma \end{bmatrix} \begin{bmatrix} \Phi_{11} & P \\ P' & Q \end{bmatrix} \begin{bmatrix} \Lambda' & \Lambda' \\ 0 & \Gamma' \end{bmatrix} + \begin{bmatrix} \Psi_{11} & \Omega_{12} \\ \Omega_{21} & \Psi_{22} \end{bmatrix}. \tag{7.31}$$

In this formulation a new latent variable of dimension, $r < p$, perhaps $r < q$, is introduced to account for change in X from Occasion 1 to Occasion 2. For example, in research on cognitive aging a common finding is that termed *cognitive slowing*. If the manifest variables are a cognitive test battery it would not be unreasonable if a single latent variable, Z, representing this phenomenon, accounted for changes in X over and above the contribution of the common factor part, ΛW_1, of X_2. The matrix P consists of the covariances of W_1 with Z, and Q is the dispersion matrix of Z. One might set P to be a null matrix and η_2 to be a null vector, which would imply that Z "independently" accounts for change in X (at least as far as its mean and dispersion matrix are concerned). In a version of Equations 7.28, 7.29, and 7.30 developed by Meredith (1991), termed *latent change analysis*, Λ taken to be an identity matrix is the central feature. In that approach no latent variable model is proposed for X; the only latent variables introduced are those responsible for change.

Combining Longitudinal and Cross-Sectional Approaches

It is fairly obvious that longitudinal factor models can be considered in conjunction with cross-sectional or group differences (McArdle & Epstein, 1987; McArdle, Hamagami, Elias, & Robbins, 1991; Tisak & Meredith, 1989, 1990a). All that is required is that we apply all we know about cross-sectional invariance to the longitudinal model. Essentially we would assume that for m groups or subpopulations model Equation 7.18 in the form $\mathbf{X}_{j,g} = \Lambda\mathbf{W}_{j,g} + \mathbf{S}_{j,g} + \mathbf{E}_{j,g} + \mathbf{T}$ holds in each with the evident pattern invariance. Coupled with the appropriate assumptions, we would obtain

$$\mu_{j,g} = \Lambda\xi_{j,g} + \eta_{j,g} + \mathbf{T}, \tag{7.32}$$

$$\Sigma_{jj,g} = \Lambda\Phi_{jj,g}\Lambda' + \Omega_{jj,g} + \Theta_{jj,g} = \Lambda\Phi_{jj,g}\Lambda' + \Psi_{jj,g}, \tag{7.33}$$

and

$$\Sigma_{jk,g} = \Lambda\Phi_{jk,g}\Lambda' + \Omega_{jk,g} \tag{7.34}$$

for all $j, k = 1, \ldots, r$ and $g = 1, \ldots, m$. This setup can be modified to allow some nonzero covariances between $\mathbf{W}_j$ and $\mathbf{S}_k$, as indicated in the previous section.

Cohort Sequential Designs

A special case of multiple groups is the cohort sequential design (Schaie, 1965). It turns out that consideration of invariance is fundamental in modeling growth in conjunction with such designs. In the prototypic form one group of individuals is measured at ages $A_1, A_2, \ldots A_r$; a second group is observed at ages $A_2, A_3, \ldots, A_{r+1}$; a third group at ages $A_3, A_4, \ldots, A_{r+2}$; and so on. The central feature of this design is the planned overlap in independent groups of the ages at which measurements are taken. If one intends to evaluate an independent-increments (simplex) or latent curve developmental model of the sorts we have dealt with in conjunction with a cohort sequential design it is obvious that consideration of invariance is fundamental. Specifically, those portions of the factor pattern matrix that correspond to the common ages at which groups are assessed ought to be invariant. For example, in latent curve analyses if Groups 1 and 2 have ages $A_2, A_3, \ldots, A_r$ in common the submatrix composed of the last $r - 1$ rows of Group 1's pattern must equal the submatrix composed of the first $r - 1$ rows of Group 2's pattern matrix, and so on. For an invariant simplex it is essential that δ_1 in Group 2 equal δ_2 in Group 1, that δ_2 in Group 2 equal δ_3 in Group 1, and so on. Only if such invariance holds can it be argued that one is in fact fitting a growth process model that characterizes development over the age span encompassed in the design.

Some other considerations arise. Essentially a cohort sequential design is a substitute for measuring a single group at all ages of interest, so ideally successive pairs of subgroups should be homogeneous with respect to mean and dispersion parameters. Consider two cohorts. For the simplex the lagged factor means, except the first, ought to be equal: the third in Cohort 1 equal to the second in Cohort 2; the fourth in Cohort 1 equal to the third in Cohort 2, and so on. However, note carefully that the mean of the first latent variable in Cohort 2 should equal the sum of the means of the first and second factors in Cohort 1. In other words, we expect the mean of x at age A_2 to be the same in both cohorts. Furthermore, it is necessary that the dispersion matrix of latent variables be diagonal in each group and that φ_{22} in Cohort 2 be equal to φ_{11} + φ_{22} in Cohort 1, φ_{33} in Cohort 2 be equal to φ_{22} in Cohort 1, and so on. The last mean and variance in Cohort 2, at age A_{r+1}, is free, because it has no counterpart in Cohort 1. For a latent curve model one ought to have ξ and Φ invariant over cohorts. The curves themselves are supposed to explain growth in a latent curve model.

Note that such restrictions do not imply homogeneity over time of the means and dispersion matrices of the manifest variables. On the contrary, the central feature of growth modeling with cohort sequential approaches is that the chosen developmental model should account for change over time and for change over the cohorts only because cohorts provide information about different age sequences. Cohort differences ought not to occur in the latent variable parameters unless cohort effects on them have been specifically anticipated. On the other hand, cohort differences can be expressed by differences in cohort means and variances. This is fairly straightforward for latent curve models, but because of the relatively large number of latent means and variances per cohort in simplex models caution must be advised in simplex cases. Some simple linear models applied to latent variables could model cohort effects in conjunction with simplex models. It would be incumbent on the researcher to make a compelling case for cohort differences, in either case. It can also be argued that the lagged elements of Θ should be equated over cohorts, that is, that θ_{22} in Cohort 1 be equal to θ_{11} in Cohort 2, and so on, in both types of models.

When longitudinal factor analysis is applied to a cohort sequential design the pattern matrix Λ should be invariant over both cohorts and ages. Unlike the (essentially univariate) growth models, in this case the latent variables must carry growth and change directly, so the common factor means and specific factor means should show growth and change both within and between cohorts. The following conditions on means should be met: $\xi_{2,1} = \xi_{1,2}$, $\xi_{3,1} = \xi_{2,2} = \xi_{1,3}$, and so on; analogous constraints should hold for the $\eta_{j,g}$. For the various dispersion matrices $\Phi_{jj,g}$, $\Omega_{jj,g}$, and $\Theta_{jj,g}$ the same sort of constraints ought to apply, for example, $\Phi_{33,1} = \Phi_{22,2} = \Phi_{11,3}$, and so on. Basically one expects that in the absence of cohort effects (or sampling bias possibly due to differential dropout or mortality) the mean vector of $\mathbf{X}_{2,1}$, at age A_2 in Cohort 1 should equal the mean of $\mathbf{X}_{1,2}$ also at age A_2 but in Cohort 2 and that the dispersion matrix of $\mathbf{X}_{2,1}$, at age A_2 in Cohort 1 should equal that of $\mathbf{X}_{1,2}$ also at age A_2 but in Cohort 2. If there are more than two ages per cohort we would want $\Phi_{23,1} = \Phi_{12,1}$, and so on, and similarly for the $\Omega_{jk,g}$.

Now cohort effects could appear as the failure to hold of the constraints given in the previous paragraph. Again, we assert that it is essential that the researcher make a reasonable case for cohort effects with some anticipation of their form. Some linear modeling is possible (Tisak & Meredith, 1989).

Anyone who studies developmental change by repeated administration of the same (or parallel) measures to the same individuals needs to be aware of the possibility that repeated exposure to the same device has consequences, which can be regarded in some situations as practice effects, as period effects in others, and as fatigue in still other situations (Meredith & Tisak, 1990; Tisak & Meredith, 1989). The design of any study of development that involves longitudinal observations should ideally make a provision for a series of control groups: one for each age, time, or occasion on which repeated observations are taken. These control groups would be assessed once only, and their results could be incorporated into the modeling process. This ideal may be nearly unattainable in practice because it surely requires large numbers of participants. Also, it may be hard to get representative control samples.

Fortunately, the cohort sequential design offers a very attractive approach that permits linear modeling of the effects of repeated exposure. We first consider the univariate simplex and latent curve models. Imagine, as before, that in Cohort 1 individuals are measured at ages $A_1, A_2 \ldots, A_r$; in Cohort 2 at ages $A_2, A_3 \ldots, A_{r+1}$; and so on. Express the true score ($t = x - e$) for $x_{j,g}$ in Cohort g as $t_{j,g} = \beta_j f_{j,g}(\mathbf{W}) + \alpha_j$, where $f_{i,g}(\mathbf{W})$ denotes the expected value of the jth element of x in the gth cohort as function of the developmental model used. There is one linear function for each level of repeated exposure; β_1 must equal 1, and α_1 must equal 0. Then in Cohort 1 $t_{2,1}$, which underlies $x_{2,1}$, observed at A_2, is $\beta_2 f_{2,g}(\mathbf{W}) + \alpha_2$, whereas in Cohort 2 $t_{2,1}$, which underlies $x_{2,1}$, observed at A_3, is $\beta_2 f_{3,g}(\mathbf{W}) + \alpha_2$. Here $f_{2,g}(\mathbf{W})$ and $f_{3,g}(\mathbf{W})$ differ to represent the lagged terms that apply at ages A_2 and A_3, respectively, whereas β_2 and α_2 are used at the different ages because within each cohort the second measure is involved. Let $\mathbf{B}$ denote a diagonal matrix formed from the $\beta_1, \beta_2, \ldots, \beta_r$, and let $\mathbf{A}$ denote a vector of $\alpha_1, \alpha_2 \ldots, \alpha_r$. In addition, let $\mathbf{F}_g$ denote the partially invariant factor pattern, either lagged simplex structure or lagged latent curve elements, and so on, that is appropriate for the gth cohort. The linear "practice effects" model becomes the second-order factor model

$$\mu_g = \mathbf{BF}_g\xi_g + \mathbf{A} + \mathbf{1}\tau \quad \text{and} \quad \Sigma_g = \mathbf{BF}_g\Phi_g(\mathbf{BF}_g)' + \Theta_g. \qquad (7.35)$$

Note that for simple simplex models τ is zero.

We suggest that in the absence of period or practice effects it is possible to use a linear model for cohort effects. This would be accomplished by expressing $x_{j,g}$ in Cohort g as $t_{j,g} = \beta_g f_{j,g}(\mathbf{W}) + \alpha_g$. The subscript change on β and α from j to g indicates the change from a measurement occasion effect to cohort effect. The matrix $\mathbf{B}$ becomes $\beta_g\mathbf{I}$, and $\mathbf{A}$ becomes $\alpha_g\mathbf{1}$.

In the context of longitudinal factor analysis a cohort sequential design is not a prerequisite; neither are control groups essential. Further period or practice effects can be modeled with a single group of participants studied longitudinally. A slightly altered approach is needed as a different set of linear parameters would be essential for each manifest variable. Let $\mathbf{B}_j$ and $\mathbf{A}_j$ now denote a diagonal matrix and vector, and rewrite Equation 7.18 as

$$\mathbf{X}_j = \mathbf{B}_j(\Lambda\mathbf{W}_j + \mathbf{S}_j + \mathbf{T}) + \mathbf{A}_j + \mathbf{E}_j = \mathbf{B}_j\Lambda\mathbf{W}_j + (\mathbf{B}_j\mathbf{S}_j) + \mathbf{B}_j\mathbf{T} + \mathbf{A}_j + \mathbf{E}_j. \quad (7.36)$$

This results in modifying Equations 7.32, 7.33, and 7.34 as

$$\mu_j = \mathbf{B}_j\Lambda\xi_j + \eta_j + \mathbf{T}_j, \quad (7.37)$$

$$\Sigma_{jj} = \mathbf{B}_j\Lambda\Phi_{jj}\Lambda'\mathbf{B}_j' + (\Omega_{jj} + \Theta_{jj}), \quad (7.38)$$

and

$$\Sigma_{jk} = \mathbf{B}_j\Lambda\Phi_{jk}\Lambda'\mathbf{B}_j' + \Omega_{jk}, \quad (7.39)$$

in which $\mathbf{B}_j$ has been absorbed into η and Ω and $\mathbf{T}_j$ is $\mathbf{B}_j\mathbf{T} + \mathbf{A}_j$. These equations are those of second-order factor analysis. For identification one must set $\mathbf{B}_1 = \mathbf{I}$ and set $\mathbf{A}_1$ to a null vector. For the two-occasion case, then,

$$\begin{bmatrix} \mu_1 \\ \mu_2 \end{bmatrix} = \begin{bmatrix} \mathbf{I} & \mathbf{0} \\ \mathbf{0} & \mathbf{B}_2 \end{bmatrix} \begin{bmatrix} \Lambda & \mathbf{0} \\ \mathbf{0} & \Lambda \end{bmatrix} \begin{bmatrix} \xi_1 \\ \xi_2 \end{bmatrix} + \begin{bmatrix} \eta_1 \\ \eta_2 \end{bmatrix} + \begin{bmatrix} \mathbf{T} \\ \mathbf{T}_2 \end{bmatrix}, \quad (7.40)$$

and

$$\begin{bmatrix} \Sigma_{11} & \Sigma_{12} \\ \Sigma_{21} & \Sigma_{22} \end{bmatrix} = \begin{bmatrix} \mathbf{I} & \mathbf{0} \\ \mathbf{0} & \mathbf{B}_2 \end{bmatrix} \begin{bmatrix} \Lambda & \mathbf{0} \\ \mathbf{0} & \Lambda \end{bmatrix} \begin{bmatrix} \Phi_{11} & \Phi_{12} \\ \Phi_{21} & \Phi_{22} \end{bmatrix} \begin{bmatrix} \Lambda & \mathbf{0} \\ \mathbf{0} & \Lambda \end{bmatrix}' \begin{bmatrix} \mathbf{I} & \mathbf{0} \\ \mathbf{0} & \mathbf{B}_2 \end{bmatrix}$$
$$+ \begin{bmatrix} \Psi_{11} & \Omega_{12} \\ \Omega_{21} & \Psi_{22} \end{bmatrix}. \quad (7.41)$$

When a cohort sequential design is used in conjunction with longitudinal factor analysis even more interesting schemes can be articulated to model both period or practice effects and cohort effects.

Equations 7.36, 7.37, 7.38, and 7.39 can be applied to solve another sort of problem, in which repeated exposure effects may be confounded. Consider the problem that arises when participants are assessed with different, but linearly equivalent (so-called *congeneric*) tests on different occasions. For example, in a life span study of cognitive development it might occur that a group of participants were examined with the Wechsler–Bellevue Intelligence Test at age 20, with the Wechsler Adult Intelligence Scale (WAIS) at age 40, and with the WAIS–Revised at age 60. It is a reasonable supposition that the subtests are linearly equivalent, which is to say that Equation 7.36 applies but with a different interpretation than that of simple practice effects. Equations 7.37 and 7.38 can be adapted to a similar setup involving different forms of a test battery given to different groups of individuals.

Methods for Studying Multivariate Development

There are a number of approaches to using latent curve models in connection with multivariate rather than univariate growth. We have found no instances in psychology of the use of simplex models in modeling multivariate growth, but it is clearly possible to develop such. It is not our intention to go into multivariate growth models in this chapter. The interested reader is directed to a growing literature (e.g., Duncan et al., 1997, 1999; McArdle, 1986, 1988, 1989, 1991; McArdle & Aber, 1990; McArdle & Anderson, 1990; McArdle & Hamagami, 1992, 1996; Sayer & Willett, 1998; Willett & Sayer, 1994). We do observe that multivariate growth modeling by way of latent curve models inevitably becomes a form of longitudinal factor analysis. We also observe that no one seems to have paid serious attention to the role of specific factors as a source of growth in multivariate modeling. This is a rapidly developing field, however, and this oversight is soon rectified. At any rate, once it is recognized that special cases of the factor analytic model (basically higher order models) are at the heart of multivariate developmental models it is obvious that what we have had to say about factorial invariance is relevant. The precise details would require consideration on a case-by-case basis.

Discussion and Recommendations

It is our view that attaining factorial invariance is in large part a matter of good design and planning. Pilot studies appear to be sadly neglected in current psychological research endeavors. We suggest that more and better pilot work be done. Good design requires careful selection of measuring instruments, thoughtful regard for demographic variables, and reasonable attempts to acquire participants other than samples of convenience. Good research design should include approaches that allow the investigator to evaluate the effects of repeatedly measuring the same individuals in longitudinal research.

The developments in this presentation make it clear that an impediment to factorial invariance is the presence of specific factors in the factor analytic model. We have seen that this is true for cross-sectional invariance when viewed either through selection theory or from the point of view of the empirical approach and that it also is true for longitudinal invariance. One must take specific factors seriously; they cannot be ignored. Good study design should minimize the role of specifics. In this one should remember that a specific factor depends on the company it keeps. Masters of the art of theory-driven development of measures (e.g., Cattell, Guilford, and Thurstone) have attested to the difficulty inherent in creating univocal measures of a single latent attribute that are not influenced by their companions in a study. Spearman argued that the problem of "swollen specifics" essentially invalidated work presented as threatening his two-factor theory of intelligence (Spearman & Jones, 1950).

Recall again the case of spatial visualization "contaminated" by spatial orientation. This kind of situation is very common. In a test battery with other visualization tests, each visualization test is likely to have a large specific factor associated with it. If the battery also has spatial orientation tests, the associated specific is less prominent, provided the factorial complexity of the test is recognized.

However, be careful in taking such advice. It is possible to eliminate specific factors by choosing linear equivalent measures to mark a factor. This builds specifics into the common factor, which reduces the factor's generality in the domain-sampling sense. Factors, which is to say the concepts, of substantive theory generally should be latent to a broad selection of measures indicating different aspects of the attribute. If the set of measures marking a factor of verbal ability, for example, are all simply multiple-choice vocabulary tests, one should be hesitant to regard it as indicative of the verbal-comprehension concept indicated in Thurstone's early work.

We now come to our first recommendation, which devolves from the way that specific factor mean differences may induce apparent common factors.

Recommendation 1

Demographic factors such as sex, age, ethnicity, SES, and school enrolled in should be used to their utmost to partition the total population into subpopulations. The only effective limits should be imposed by sample size, although in some cases there may be software constraints. In particular, one should not combine sexes even in cases where it is supposed that no sex differences exist. Similarly, one should not combine across major differences in age, perhaps especially in childhood and old age. Too much is going on developmentally. We have indicated the reasoning behind this recommendation: The presence of such groups (subpopulations) can induce relationships between common and specific factors, and among specific factors, that are inconsistent with the assumptions of factor models, which means that the models do not fit in the form anticipated. This is true for longitudinal factor models and ordinary factor models. Putting this recommendation into practice means that research should be based on multiple-group invariance analysis.

Because the essentially univariate growth models do not entail specific factors, this suggestion is not as important for these cases, but we would still encourage partition on the grounds that one needs to establish pattern invariance as a matter of routine.

Recommendation 2

Remain alert to the fact that specific factors are not "errors" and that correlated specifics can, and probably should be expected to, crop up. However, the recognition of correlated specifics should not be used to gain good fit at the cost of interpretability. Anticipate correlation between homologous specifics in longitudinal factor models. Many correlated specifics may be indicative of factors whose inclusion in the analysis can be enlightening.

Recommendation 3

The implementation of fitting procedures for developmental models requires fitting mean vectors and dispersion matrices. This is true despite the fact that usually in the evaluation of simplex models means have been ignored. In cross-sectional factor analysis, means should always be modeled along with the modeling of dispersion matrices. Here, means should be modeled such that differences between manifest mean vectors "pass through" the common factor means to a maximized extent, as pointed out in the Practical Aspects of Determining Means section. If means are included in longitudinal factor analysis, one should remain especially alert to the fact that as the correlation between variables across occasions increases, more correlation of specifics is likely, and the analysis rests to an increasing degree on crossproducts of the means. It is desirable that group mean differences and mean longitudinal change be interpretable, first in terms of differences and change in the common factors, and second in terms of residualized differences and change in specific factors, as these are required.

Recommendation 4

Design studies so that period or practice effects can be effectively dealt with and not simply swept under the rug. In particular, consider using a cohort sequential design. This design is potentially powerful, can describe long-term development with a relatively brief investment of time, and can facilitate understanding of period or practice effects. It is often fundamentally important to disentangle practice effects from growth or from the effects of experimental intervention. See the work of Raykov (1995) for an example of dealing with practice effects in an intervention study.

Recommendation 5

Let invariance take precedence over meta-theory, such as that of simple structure. This has at least two aspects: an aspect that appears in connection with latent curve models and a somewhat different aspect that arises in connection with ordinary factor analysis, either cross-sectional or longitudinal. Both are aspects of pattern invariance.

First, as concerns latent curve analyses, investigators mainly seem to work off an assumption that development is linear, or at most quadratic. This means that they accept a particular form of specification of an invariant factor pattern matrix. Now, experience indicates that simple models with few latent variables can be found if many curve coordinates are free and determined by the data. Straight lines work over the short term, but they are unlikely to characterize long-term development. Quadratics also oversimplify and are not the solution. Ideally one would have theoretically driven nonlinear curves, very possibly developed using differential equations. Although the young science of psychology may not be fully ready for sophisticated mathematical derivation of growth processes, the mathematical tools are surely there, and applications are beginning to appear (Boker, 1997; Boker & Graham, 1998).

Second, considering the usual applications of factor analysis, slavish commitment to a meta-theoretical structure, such as strict simple structure, should not drive analyses. It is very difficult to construct factor-pure measures, and it is relatively easy to slip into putting together swollen specifics. The fact that it is difficult to attain factor-pure measures suggests that a degree of factorial complexity is, perhaps unexpectedly, encountered in practice. Minor adjustments that do not jeopardize the basic theory are certainly reasonable under such conditions. Unfortunately, much of the SEM work appearing in the literature seems to be premised on the belief that the only acceptable so-called "measurement model" (an unfortunate term representing what is really a common-factor model) is a cluster structure in which each of a very few indicators of a common factor is thought to regress onto one and only one factor.

A Remark

Take simple autoregressive (simplex) models with a grain of salt (Raykov, 1998; Rogosa & Willett, 1985). These are independent (uncorrelated, actually) increment models and imply that past history is unimportant. For example, imagine two persons measured at ages 8, 9, 10, and 11 with a reading comprehension test, and suppose that for one individual the scores are 35, 40, 43, and 46, and for the other they are 31, 36, 41, and 46. Any Markov model of independent increments can predict the same outcome at age 12 for both children even though, clearly, this does not represent well what has gone before, and is likely to determine, the outcome.

References

Ahmavaara, Y. (1954). The mathematical theory of factorial invariance under selection. *Psychometrika, 19,* 27–38.

Bloxom, B. (1972). Alternative approaches to factorial invariance. *Psychometrika, 37,* 425–440.

Boker, S. M. (1997). *Linear and nonlinear dynamical systems data analytic techniques and an application to developmental data.* Unpublished doctoral dissertation, University of Virginia, Charlottesville.

Boker, S. M., & Graham, J. (1998). A dynamical systems analysis of adolescent substance abuse. *Multivariate Behavioral Research, 33,* 479–507.

Browne, M. W. (1993). Structured latent curve models. In C. M. Cuadras & C. R. Rao (Eds.), *Future directions 2: Multivariate analysis* (pp. 171–197). New York: Elsevier.

Byrne, B. M., Shavelson, R. J., & Muthén, B. (1989). Testing for the equivalence of factor covariance and mean structures: The issue of partial measurement invariance. *Psychological Bulletin, 105,* 456–466.

Cunningham, W. R. (1982). Factorial invariance: A methodological issue in the study of psychological development. *Experimental Aging Research, 8*(1), 61–65.

Cunningham, W. R. (1991). Issues in factorial invariance. In L. M. Collins & J. L. Horn (Eds.), *Best methods for the analysis of change: Recent advances, unanswered questions, future directions* (pp. 106–113). Washington, DC: American Psychological Association.

Duncan, T. E., Duncan, S. C., Alpert, A., Hops, H., Stoolmiller, M., & Muthén, B. O. (1997). Latent variable modeling of longitudinal and multilevel substance use data. *Multivariate Behavioral Research, 32,* 275–318.

Duncan, T. E., Duncan, S. C., Strycker, L. A., Li, F., & Alpert, A. (1999). *An introduction to latent variable growth curve modeling: Concepts, issues, and applications.* Mahwah, NJ: Erlbaum.

Gibson, W. A. (1959). Three multivariate models: Factor analysis, latent structure analysis and latent profile analysis. *Psychometrika, 24,* 119–135.

Holzinger, K. J., & Swineford, F. (1939). *A study in factor analysis: The stability of a bi-factor solution.* Chicago, IL: University of Chicago.

Horn, J. L., & Engstrom, R. O. (1979). Cattell's scree test in relation to Bartlett's chi-square test and other observations on the number of factors problem. *Multivariate Behavioral Research, 14,* 283–300.

Horn, J. L., & McArdle, J. J. (1980). Perspectives on mathematical and statistical model building (MASMOB) in research on aging. In L. Poon (Ed.), *Aging in the 1980's: Psychological issues* (pp. 503–541). Washington, DC: American Psychological Association.

Horn, J. L., & McArdle, J. J. (1992). A practical guide to measurement invariance in research on aging. *Experimental Aging Research, 18,* 117–144.

Horn, J. L., McArdle, J. J., & Mason, R. (1983). When is invariance not invariant: A practical scientist's view of the ethereal concept of factorial invariance. *The Southern Psychologist, 1,* 179–188.

Jöreskog, K. G. (1970). Estimation and testing of simplex models. *British Journal of Mathematical and Statistical Psychology, 23,* 121–145.

Jöreskog, K. G., & Sörbom, D. (1979). *Advances in factor analysis and structural equation models* (J. Magidson, Ed.). Cambridge, MA: Abt Books.

Lord, F. M., & Novick, M. R. (1968). *Statistical theories of mental test scores.* Reading, MA: Addison-Wesley.

MacCallum, R. C., Kim, C., Malarkey, W. B., & Kiecolt-Glaser, J. K. (1997). Studying multivariate change using multilevel models and latent curve models. *Multivariate Behavioral Research, 32,* 215–253.

MacCallum, R. C., & Tucker, L. R. (1991). Representing sources of error in the common-factor model: Implications for theory and practice. *Psychological Bulletin, 109,* 502–511.

McArdle, J. J. (1986). Latent variable growth within behavior genetic models. *Behavior Genetics, 16,* 163–200.

McArdle, J. J. (1988). Dynamic but structural equation modeling of repeated measures data. In J. R. Nesselroade & R. B. Cattell (Eds.), *The handbook of multivariate experimental psychology* (Vol. 2, pp. 561–614). New York: Plenum.

McArdle, J. J. (1989). Structural modeling experiments using multiple growth functions. In P. Ackerman, R. Kanfer, & R. Cudeck (Eds.), *Learning and individual differences: Abilities, motivation, and methodology* (pp. 71–117). Hillsdale, NJ: Erlbaum.

McArdle, J. J. (1991). Comments on "Latent variable models for studying differences and change" by William Meredith. In L. Collins & J. L. Horn (Eds.), *Best methods for the analysis of change: Recent advances, unanswered questions, future directions* (pp. 164–169). Washington, DC: American Psychological Association.

McArdle, J. J., & Aber, M. S. (1990). Patterns of change within latent variable structural equation modeling. In A. von Eye (Ed.), *New statistical methods in developmental research* (pp. 151–224). New York: Academic Press.

McArdle, J. J., & Anderson, E. (1990). Latent variable growth models for research on aging. In J. E. Birren & K. W. Schaie (Eds.), *The handbook of the psychology of aging* (pp. 21–43). New York: Plenum.

McArdle, J. J., & Cattell, R. B. (1994). Structural equation models of factorial invariance in parallel proportional profiles and oblique confactor problems. *Multivariate Behavioral Research, 29,* 63–113.

McArdle, J. J., & Epstein, D. B. (1987). Latent growth curves within developmental structural equation models. *Child Development, 58,* 110–133.

McArdle, J. J., & Hamagami, F. (1992). Modeling incomplete longitudinal and cross-sectional data using latent growth structural models. *Experimental Aging Research, 18,* 145–166.

McArdle, J. J., & Hamagami, F. (1996). Multilevel models from a multiple group structural equation perspective. In G. Marcoulides & R. Schumacker (Eds.), *Advanced structural equation modeling techniques* (pp. 89–124). Mahwah, NJ: Erlbaum.

McArdle, J. J., Hamagami, F., Elias, M. F., & Robbins, M. A. (1991). Structural modeling of mixed longitudinal and cross-sectional data. *Experimental Aging Research, 17,* 29–52.

McArdle, J. J., & Nesselroade, J. R. (1993). Structuring data to study development and change. In S. H. Cohen & H. W. Reese (Eds.), *Life-span developmental psychology: Methodological innovations* (pp. 223–267). Hillsdale, NJ: Erlbaum.

Meredith, W. (1964). Notes on factorial invariance. *Psychometrika, 29,* 177–185.

Meredith, W. (1984, June). *On tuckerizing curves.* Symposium paper presented at the annual meeting of the Psychometric Society, Santa Barbara, CA.

Meredith, W. (1991). Latent variable models for studying differences and change. In L. M. Collins & J. L. Horn (Eds.), *Best methods for the analysis of change: Recent advances, unanswered questions, future directions* (pp. 149–169). Washington, DC: American Psychological Association.

Meredith, W. (1993). Measurement invariance, factor analysis and factorial invariance. *Psychometrika, 58,* 525–543.

Meredith, W. (1997, October). *Factorial invariance revisited.* Saul B. Sells address to the annual meeting of the Society for Multivariate Experimental Psychology, Mahwah, NJ.

Meredith, W., & Tisak, J. (1990). Latent curve analysis. *Psychometrika, 55,* 107–122.

Mussen, P., Eichorn, D. H., Honzick, M. P., Beiber, S. L., & Meredith, W. (1980). Continuity and change in women's characteristics over four decades. *International Journal of Behavioral Development, 3,* 118–133.

Muthén, B. O. (1989a). Factor structure in groups selected on observed scores. *British Journal of Mathematical and Statistical Psychology, 42,* 81–90.

Muthén, B. O. (1989b). Latent variable modeling in heterogeneous populations. *Psychometrika, 54,* 557–585.

Nesselroade, J. R. (1983). Temporal selection and factor invariance in the study of development and change. In P. B. Baltes & O. G. Brim, Jr. (Eds.), *Life-span development and behavior* (Vol. 5, pp. 59–87). New York: Academic Press.

Novick, M. R. (1966). The axioms and principal results of classical test theory. *Journal of Mathematical Psychology, 3,* 1–18.

Nunnally, J. C. (1967). *Psychometric theory.* New York: McGraw-Hill.

Raykov, T. (1995). Multivariate structural modeling of plasticity in fluid intelligence of aged adults. *Multivariate Behavioral Research, 30,* 255–287.

Raykov, T. (1998). Satisfying a simplex structure is simpler than it should be: A latent curve analysis revisited. *Multivariate Behavioral Research, 33,* 343–363.

Rogosa, D., & Willett, J. B. (1985). Satisfying a simplex structure is simpler than it should be. *Journal of Educational Statistics, 10,* 99–107.

Sayer, A. G., & Willett, J. B. (1998). A cross-domain model for growth in adolescent alcohol expectancies. *Multivariate Behavioral Research, 33,* 509–543.

Schaie, K. W. (1965). A general model for the study of developmental problems. *Psychological Bulletin, 64,* 92–107.

Spearman, C., & Jones, L. W. (1950). *Human ability.* London: Macmillan.

Terman, L. M., & Merrill, M. A. (1937). *Measuring intelligence: A guide to the administration of the new revised Stanford–Binet tests of intelligence.* New York: Houghton Mifflin.

Thomson, G. H. (1951). *The factorial analysis of human ability* (5th rev. ed.). New York: Houghton-Mifflin.

Thurstone, L. L. (1947). *Multiple-factor analysis; a development and expansion of the vectors of mind.* Chicago: University of Chicago Press.

Tisak, J., & Meredith, W. (1989). Exploratory longitudinal factor analysis in multiple populations. *Psychometrika, 54,* 261–281.

Tisak, J., & Meredith, W. (1990a). Descriptive and associative developmental models. In A. von Eye (Ed.), *Statistical methods in longitudinal research* (Vol. 2). San Diego, CA: Academic Press.

Tisak, J., & Meredith, W. (1990b). Longitudinal factor analysis. In A. von Eye (Ed.), *Statistical methods in longitudinal research* (Vol. 1). San Diego, CA: Academic Press.

Willett, J. B., & Sayer, A. G. (1994). Using covariance structure analysis to detect correlates and predictors of individual change over time. *Psychological Bulletin, 116,* 363–381.

Editors' Introduction

I s a particular phenomenon a *trait*—that is, a more or less immutable feature of an individual—or is it a transient *state*? This question, one of the most intriguing and often-posed questions in an analysis of change, can be addressed with longitudinal data. However, it is not always a simple matter to decide how to divide variance into the relevant partitions to identify that which changes over time and that which remains stable. David Kenny and Alex Zautra present several approaches for testing state–trait models. They discuss several models, including the multitrait–multimethod models, and explain the advantages and disadvantages of each. This chapter goes a long way toward clarifying what has been a confusing body of literature. In his commentary, Adam Davey talks about the past underuse and future potential of state–trait analyses. Readers may be interested in comparing Kenny and Zautra's approach to disentangling stability and change with those of Curran and Bollen (chapter 4) and McArdle and Hamagami (chapter 5). Also relevant are the factorial invariance issues explored by Meredith and Horn (chapter 7).

Trait–State Models for Longitudinal Data

David A. Kenny
Alex Zautra

S tability is a fundamental aspect of longitudinal data in need of careful es- timation. By *stability*, we mean invariance of relative standing or rank or- dering of people and not the lack of change in the scores themselves. To use the field's jargon, stability is "the consistency of interindividual differences in intraindividual change" (Rudinger, Andres, & Rietz, 1991, p. 275; also Nes- selroade, 1991). Examination of the correlation or covariance structure among variables measured over time is a key way of estimating this type of stability for constructs. Within psychology, stability of this kind is often referred to as evidence of a *trait*, and a theoretical distinction is drawn between a trait and a state. A trait implies that the rank orderings on the construct being measured do not change much (i.e., are stable), whereas a state implies that the construct varies considerably (i.e., the rank orderings are unstable). A common misper- ception implies that traits are necessarily biological. Trait variance may be due to stable environments, and genetics might even create changes and stability. Another common misperception is that variables measure either traits or states, as if a dichotomy exists in nature between these forms. In truth, most psycho- logical constructs vary along a continuum of stability or what we call *traitness*. The problem for social scientists is to cast the key components of this quality of traitness within an analytic structure. In a series of theoretical and method- ological articles, John Nesselroade (1987; Nesselroade & Bartsch, 1977) has elaborated these themes, making distinctions between traits that change, albeit slowly over time, and traits that are temporally invariant.

In the past 10 years or so, teams of investigators have attempted to decom-

We thank Rolf Steyer for his careful reading of a prior draft of this chapter. We also thank Herb Marsh, who provided earlier assistance in the estimation of the multipli- cative multitrait–multimethod matrix model. This research was supported in part by grants from the National Science Foundation (DBS-9307949) and the National Institute of Mental Health (RO1-MH51964).

pose variance in measures simultaneously into trait and state variance. There are currently two major approaches. They are the latent state–trait (LST) model, suggested by Steyer and his colleagues (Schmitt & Steyer, 1993; Steyer, Ferring, & Schmitt, 1992; Steyer, Majcen, Schwenkmezger, & Buchner, 1989) and our stable trait (ST), autoregressive trait (ART or AR), and state (S), or STARTS, model (previously called the "trait–state–error model"; Kenny & Zautra, 1995). Both of these models partition variance in longitudinal data into trait and state components. In this chapter we focus on these two models.

In addition, we show that the multitrait–multimethod matrix (Campbell & Fiske, 1959) is relevant for the analysis of longitudinal data. We discuss the traditional additive models for the multitrait–multimethod matrix (MTMM) and the multiplicative model of the matrix suggested by Kenny and Campbell (1989). We show that a preliminary MTMM analysis is helpful in determining how to proceed in the analysis of stability.

In this chapter we evaluate these different models in terms of the following criteria: design requirements (number of waves and variables), conceptualization of the model, plausibility of the model's assumptions, and estimation methods and difficulties. We then illustrate each model's strengths and weakness through analyses of a secondary data set. These data were collected by Dumenci and Windle (1996) and were collected from 433 female adolescents measured at four times in 6-month intervals on the Center for Epidemiological Studies —Depression Scale (CES–D), which contains four subscales: Depressive Affect, Positive Affect, Somatic, and Interpersonal. We used the covariance matrix presented by Dumenci and Windle in Table 1 of their article. When we estimate the fit of a model, we use the Tucker–Lewis (TLI) or non-normed index. A value of .95 or better is generally considered a good fit.

Latent State–Trait Model

Steyer and his colleagues (Schmitt & Steyer, 1993; Steyer et al., 1992; Steyer et al., 1989) have suggested an orthogonal decomposition of variance of each measure into four components. Although there are different versions of the model, we present its most general form, a model that Steyer called the *single-trait, multistate model*. The variance of a measure is partitioned into four different sources:

- trait: all measures at all times loading on the factor
- state: all measures at one time loading on the factor
- method: all measures of the same variable loading on the factor
- error: each measure at each time loading on the factor.

This model requires having at least three variables measured at three times.

However, if stationarity assumptions are plausible (temporally invariant loadings), fewer time points and variables are needed. Within each time, the variables are assumed to measure the same construct (i.e., to be unidimensional).

The model can also be understood in terms of generalizability theory (Crocker & Algina, 1986). Each participant produces a two-way data structure: measure × time. The trait factor is analogous to the person's grand mean, the state factor to the main effect of time, the method factor to the main effect of measure, and error to the Time × Measure interaction.

Estimation

The estimation of the LST model, shown in Figure 8.1, can be accomplished by a confirmatory factor analysis. Each measure loads on a time factor (the open circles in Figure 8.1) and a method factor (the circles with Ms inside). The trait factor (the circle with a T inside) is a second-order factor that causes each of the time factors. All of the covariation between the time factors is assumed to be explained by the trait factor. The remaining unexplained variance in the time factors is attributed to state or what Steyer et al. (1992) referred to as *residual state factors*. Variance that is unexplained by trait, state, or method is error variance. Each measure then loads on two factors: one time factor and one method factor. The method factors are all uncorrelated with each other as well as with the trait and state factors.

FIGURE 8.1
The latent state–trait model with trait (T), state (S), and method (M) factors.
PA = positive affect; DA = depressive affect.

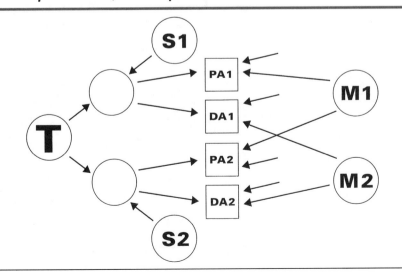

There are several possibilities for forcing equal factor loadings and variances. If any equality constraints are made, the covariance matrix, not the correlation matrix, should be analyzed (Cudeck, 1989). One possibility is a model of temporal invariance, which would imply the equality of the following:

- the loadings of the time factors on the trait factor
- the loadings of the same measures on the different time factors
- the variances of the state factors (the unexplained variance of the time factors) over time
- the error variances of the same measures at different times.

In addition, if the units of measurement of the measures are equivalent, consideration might be given to forcing the loadings and error variances of the different measures within times to be equal. Appendix 8A presents the setup for this model.

Latent State–Trait Example

Dumenci and Windle (1996) fitted the LST model. We found, as they did, that the Method factor for the depressive-affect variable is weak. In fact, in the models that we estimated, its variance is negative. The negative variance is a signal that the model may be misspecified. Later, we discuss the likely source of that misspecification. Nonetheless, we still estimated the model including this factor with a negative variance. The model fits well, $\chi^2(84, N^1 = 433) = 131.206$, TLI = .968. To increase comparability across the different models, we did not force any equality constraints on the factor loadings or variances. In terms of the partitioning variance, Dumenci and Windle (1996) found that 38% was due to trait, 31% was due to state, 10% was due to method, and 11% was due to error.

The STARTS Model

We (Kenny & Zautra, 1995) proposed a different general model of change for multiwave longitudinal data. The model postulates that a score is composed of three different components similar to the classification given by Nesselroade (1991):

- stable trait: a component that does not change over time.
- autoregressive trait: a component that changes over time in that the

---

[1]N = 433 for all chi-square equations.

current state depends partly on the previous state and a random component (first-order autoregressive model).

- state: component that is random over time; some of, but not the entire component, is measurement error.

The STARTS model contains all three of these components.

The path diagram for the STARTS model is shown in Figure 8.2. There is one stable trait (T) that causes each measure at each time. There is an autoregressive trait (S) for each measure, but there is a path between adjacent factors (e.g., S1 and S2). Finally, there are states (E) for each measure.

It helps to consider the overtime correlational structure of the three components of the model. The correlations of the stable trait factor over time are all 1. As its name suggests, the stable trait factor is assumed to be a relatively unchanging component. The correlational structure for the autoregressive factor is assumed to be a simplex (Humphreys, 1960). Correlations over longer periods of time are lower than correlations over shorter time periods. Finally, the state factor has no stability over time. In terms of autoregressive parameters, the stable trait has a coefficient of 1, the autoregressive trait a coefficient of some value between zero and 1, and the state has a value of zero.

FIGURE 8.2

The STARTS (stable trait, autoregressive trait, and state) model with a stable trait (T), autoregressive trait (S), and error (E). U = state disturbance; PA = positive affect.

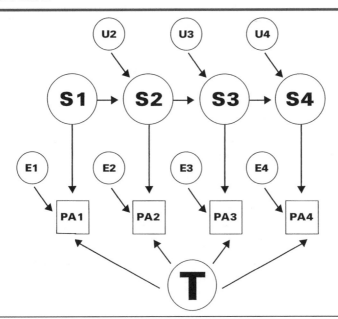

There are some important differences between the STARTS model and the LST model. First, there are two types of traits in the STARTS model—stable and somewhat stable—whereas in the LST model there is only one type of trait, an invariant one. Second, state in the STARTS model contains error variance, whereas most of state variance in LST is true state. Third, the LST model requires three measures of the construct at two or more times, whereas STARTS requires a single measure but at least four times.

In addition, some form of stationarity or equality of parameters over time must be assumed for the STARTS model to be identified, whereas no assumption of stationarity is required for the LST model. In STARTS, variance due to stable trait, autoregressive trait, and state is assumed to be the same at all times. Furthermore, the rate of change for the autoregressive trait factor is the same between all pairs of adjacent waves (assuming that the waves are equally spaced). We denote the stable trait variance as Φ^2_{ST}, the autoregressive trait variance as Φ^2_{AR}, and the state variance as Φ^2_S. The wave-to-wave stability parameter for the autoregressive trait variable is denoted as ρ, and its autocorrelation is ρ^k, where k is the lag length.

There is another important feature that sets apart the STARTS model from the other models featured in this chapter. For all of the other models, if one reordered the time points one would estimate the same model. Thus, the other models do not really integrate the temporal nature of the data in the model. The estimates of STARTS depend on the ordering of the data points. In our view, this feature of STARTS provides a more realistic portrayal of the data than do other models. We concur with Rudinger et al. (1991), who stated that "it is a drawback of every [confirmatory factor analysis] model that the essential feature of a *longitudinal* design is getting lost. The sequential *time order* of the assessments is no longer part of the model" (p. 293, emphasis in original). The estimation details of the STARTS model were presented by us (Kenny & Zautra, 1995). We also include some technical information about estimation and identification in Appendix 8B of this chapter.

Except for an article by Zautra et al. (1995) and an analysis of the stability of physical attractiveness across the life span by Campbell and Kenny (1999), there have been no other published uses of the model. We suspect that investigators have attempted to estimate the model and have encountered problems in the estimation. In fact, small changes in the covariances can produce large changes in parameter estimates.

For example, consider the illustration in Table 8.1. In the first column of numbers we present the population values. In the next two columns, we present two samples, the covariances differing from the population values by at most .02. Note that there are large changes in the parameter estimates, especially the variances. Small changes in the covariances can produce large changes in the estimates. The STARTS model, although general, can be difficult to fit.

TABLE 8.1

Sensitivity of STARTS Estimates to Small Changes in Correlations

LAG	POPULATION	SAMPLE 1	SAMPLE 2
	Covariances		
0	1.000	1.000	1.000
1	.750	.770	.730
2	.670	.670	.670
3	.630	.650	.620
	Estimates[a]		
ρ	.500	.200	.833
σ^2_{ST}	.590	.645	.370
σ^2_{AR}	.320	.625	.432
σ^2_S	.090	−.270	.198

Note. Data are hypothetical. STARTS = stable trait (ST), autoregressive trait (AR), and state (S) model; ρ = autoregressive parameter.
[a]The first set of estimates is the set of population values.

A STARTS Example

We summed the four measures of depression to create an overall measure of depression, something that is commonly done with the CES–D. We first tested the assumption of stationarity by setting the four variances equal, the three Lag–1 covariances equal and the two Lag–2 covariances equal. We found marginally significant evidence of nonstationarity, $\chi^2(6) = 11.965$, $p < .10$. The variances and covariances decline over time. For simplicity, we fitted a model that assumed stationarity.

We had difficulty fitting a full STARTS model. (The LISREL 8 setup is provided in Appendix A.) The value of the autoregressive trait factor was much greater than 1 (3.35!), an impossible value. In the STARTS model, r_{13}/r_{12} should tend to be less than r_{14}/r_{13}, but just the opposite happens in Dumenci and Windle's (1996) data set. We believe that this anomaly is due in part to seasonal effects in depression. If there were a yearly cycle in depression (some people get more depressed in the winter than do others, and some are more elated in the summer) then, given a 6-month measurement interval, the Lag 2 autocorrelations should be "too large," and the Lag 1 and 3 correlations would be "too small." If we had more than four waves we might be able to estimate a STARTS model with cyclicity.

We dropped the stable trait factor and estimated a model with just the autoregressive trait and state factors, forcing the disturbance variance in the autoregressive trait factor to be equal across Times 2, 3, and 4. This model fit reasonably well, $\chi^2(2) = 5.558$, TLI $= .982$, and fit better than a model with stable trait variance and no autoregressive trait variance, $\chi^2(2) = 9.552$, TLI $= .962$. About 65% of the total variance is autoregressive trait variance; the remaining 35% is state. These findings highlight the differences between the models in their estimates of traitness in the measures. Our AR trait incorporates some change in the rank orderings among people over time, which leads to a doubling of the estimated trait variance of depression over the LST model. Of interest is the size of the autoregressive parameter. In STARTS, this value was .88 for depressive symptoms. To many researchers, this value is certainly high enough to constitute a traitlike behavior. Once the stability of the situation is allowed to be included in our definition of AR traits, it is possible to entertain even relatively low autoregressive parameters as evidence of trait-like stability. We liken this AR trait as akin to Dewey's (1922) concept of *habit*: a pattern of behavior or thinking whose endurance depends on the degree of stability in the person's interactions with his or her social world.

The Multitrait–Multimethod Matrix

Several authors (Dumenci & Windle, 1996; Kenny & Campbell, 1989) have commented that trait–state models bear a strong resemblance to models that have been developed for the analysis of the multitrait–multimethod matrix (MTMM; Campbell & Fiske, 1959). In this and the next section, we explicitly consider these models. In this section, we consider traditional, additive models; in the next, we consider the more complicated multiplicative models.

The Multitrait–Multimethod Model

Traditionally, in MTMM analysis, there are two sets of factors: traits and methods. In this model there are three sources of variance:

- occasion: each measure at a given time loading on the factor
- method: each measure of a given variable loading on the factor
- error: each measure having its own factor.

Notice that for this application what is usually "method" and what is usually "trait" are reversed in this analysis. Normally in MTMM analyses of longitudinal data, the measures are the traits, and times are the methods. It is the opposite in this analysis. The MTMM model for longitudinal data is presented in Figure 8.3.

The LST is a special case of this model. The difference is that the LST model imposes a constraint that the correlational structure of the occasion or time factors is unidimensional. Steyer et al. (1992) referred to the multidimensional model as the *multistate model*.

FIGURE 8.3

The multitrait–multimethod model with trait (T) and orthogonal method (M) factors. PA = positive affect, DA = depressive affect.

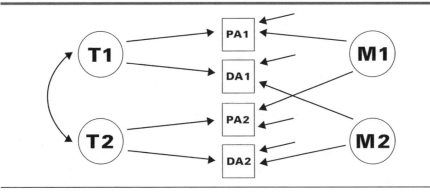

Following a suggestion by Kenny (1979), Marsh (1989) urged a revision of the MTMM model. In his *correlated uniqueness* formulation, there are no method factors; rather, measures that share the same method have correlated errors. The path model for the correlated uniqueness MTMM model is presented in Figure 8.4. Notice that two measures of the same variable at different times have correlated uniquenesses. This correlated uniqueness model always fits as well as the model with method factors, so it is the more general model.

In terms of identification, the MTMM model with method factors requires at least three times and three measures. The MTMM model with correlated uniquenesses requires three measures but just two times. If equality constraints were imposed, either fewer measures or times might be needed.

FIGURE 8.4

The correlated uniqueness multitrait–multimethod model. PA = positive affect; DA = depressive affect.

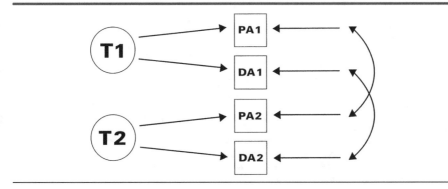

We should note that a model with correlated method factors or method factors correlated with occasion factors is empirically underidentified (Kenny & Kashy, 1992). Thus, these models are not practical and generally should not be estimated.

A Multitrait–Multimethod Example

We estimated the MTMM model with four method factors, $\chi^2(82) = 122.576$, TLI = .985, and the model with correlated uniqueness, $\chi^2(74) = 107.718$, TLI = .986. The correlated uniqueness model fits marginally significantly better, $\chi^2(8) = 14.858$, $p < .10$. As with the LST model, there was some difficulty in estimating the method factor for the depressive-affect variable. The estimates of the correlations of the factor across time were essentially the same for both models, and they showed a simplex pattern of decreasing correlations for longer lags. We present the over-time correlations of both MTMM models and the LST model in Table 8.2.

As we stated earlier, the LST model is a constrained version of the MTMM model with method factors. The constraints imposed by this second-order factor of LST result in significantly worsened fit, $\chi^2(2) = 8.630$, and so the assumption of those constraints for this data set is implausible.

Of the 24 correlated uniqueness parameters, 5 were not significant, and 1 was a significant negative covariance. We believe that it is generally ill advised to trim from the model insignificant correlated errors in the model. Moreover, we think it especially ill advised to specify correlated errors between only adjacent waves, as is sometimes done. Most of the correlated errors between nonadjacent waves (e.g., Waves 1 and 3) in the example are statistically significant.

TABLE 8.2
Estimated Correlations Across Time for Dumenci and Windle's (1996) Data Set Using the Different Models

MODEL	LAG 1			LAG 2		LAG 3:
	r_{12}	r_{23}	r_{34}	r_{13}	r_{24}	r_{14}
LST	.578	.644	.501	.560	.517	.449
MTMM[a]	.608	.626	.534	.578	.535	.386
MTMM[b]	.608	.623	.533	.574	.538	.384
MMTMM	.596	.607	.561	.567	.554	.431

Note. The STARTS (stable trait, autoregressive trait, and state) model is not included because it uses a single variable. LST = latent state trait, MTMM = multitrait–multimethod; MMTMM = multiplicative MTMM.
[a]Method factors. [b]Correlated uniqueness model.

This requirement leads to a higher number of parameters to estimate and thus demands a greater number of participants for precise estimation.

The Multiplicative MTMM Model

Campbell and O'Connell (1967) doubted that the traditional additive model of methods was adequate at capturing methods effects in the MTMM. In the past few years, elaborate multiplicative MTMM models have been developed, and specialized computer programs have been written (Browne, 1992). In regard to longitudinal data, Kenny and Campbell (1989) discussed the multiplicative model.

Unlike the traditional MTMM models, it is unnecessary to assume that the measures are single factored within each time. For this model to be identified there must be at least three measures and three time points.

The multiplicative model can be represented in the following way. The correlation between two measures (D and F) at two different times (1 and 2) equals:

$$r_{D1,F2} = c_{D1}c_{F2}r_{DF}r_{12}. \qquad (8.1)$$

The r_{DF} is the correlation between measures D and F. The terms c_{D1} and c_{F2} are factor loadings (more technically, the square root of the communalities) that refer to the measure at a specific time. Finally, the term r_{12} represents the overall similarity between Methods 1 and 2 or the over-time correlation. In summary, a multiplicative model has the following parameters: factor loadings, trait correlations, and method correlations.

Estimation

The details of how to fit these models are complex and elaborate. However, Kenny and Campbell (1989) presented a relatively simple way to fit them (see their description of their "two-wave multiple factor" model). One might consult Millsap's (1995) chapter for a description of how to fit the multiplicative MTMM models. Fortunately, despite these difficulties, identification problems are rare. Unlike the MTMM model with method factors, one normally does not encounter estimation difficulties. Appendix A presents the setup for this model.

A Multiplicative MTMM Example

The fit of the model is good, $\chi^2(92) = 125.71$, TLI = .989. (The LISREL 8 setup for this model appears in Appendix 8A.) It is the best-fitting model of all the models that we have estimated, although its fit is only trivially better than the correlated uniqueness model.

The estimated correlations among the measures indicate that the correlation between depressive affect and somatic complaints is high relative to other correlations, and so a single factor cannot account well for the correlations between measures. This is likely why there are problems with the method factor of depressive affect for LST and MTMM.

General Discussion of the Results

We present a summary of the results of our analyses of Dumenci and Windle's (1996) data set. First, the over-time correlations, presented in Table 8.2, between time points are similar to that of the MTMM analyses and are somewhat simplex-like. One can see that LST, in trying to fit a single factor to the correlations, overestimates the correlation between the middle two waves (r_{23}) and between the first and last wave (r_{14}), something that typically happens when a single factor is estimated with simplex data (Humphreys, 1960). We believe that the difficulty in estimating the method factor for depressive affect in the LST model and MTMM model with method factors is likely due to this specification error.

As mentioned earlier, the over-time correlations point to cyclicity. When the lag is 6 (r_{12}, r_{23}, and r_{23}) or 18 months (r_{14}), the correlations are "too large" but "too small" for 12-month lags (r_{13} and r_{24}) for a quasisimplex pattern. There might be a yearly cycle in depression.

In terms of components, there is considerable state variance, that is, variance that is time specific and unstable. We do not know if this source of variance reflects transitory levels of depression or just some method factor or temporary response set. The source of variance is nontrivial and represents 30%–40% of the total variance. We suspect that much of this variance is due to processes that have a much shorter half-life than 6 months. Variations in small stressors and daily biochemical shifts in brain norepinephrine and serotonin levels are examples of such processes that can affect levels of depressive affect.

The other component of variance is an autoregressive trait factor that is a relatively slow-changing component. Its stability is on the order of .88. It is not a perfectly stable trait in that it does change. Our failure to find stable trait variance in depression surprised us. However, the result of a fairly, but not perfectly stable autoregressive factor with a year-to-year stability of about .80 is supported by the analyses of Cole, Peeke, Martin, Truglio, and Seroczynski (1998).

General Recommendations

We first considered the two major models of trait–state processes, LST and STARTS. We saw that there were difficulties with each model. We urge the initial estimation of an MTMM model. If the additive model is to be estimated, we feel that the correlated uniqueness model is preferable.

An MTMM analysis produces an over-time correlation matrix. The researcher should study that matrix and pick an appropriate model to be subsequently fitted. In essence, our recommendation is to fit a second-order model within the MTMM analysis. Recall that the LST model is second order, but we urge consideration of other models besides one with trait and state. Exhibit 8.1 presents the seven possible models of correlational structure that might result from the MTMM analysis.

The simplest model is a pure state model (Nesselroade, 1987). In this model, all of the over-time correlations are zero. The correlational structure of an autoregressive trait model is a simplex whose structure was discussed by Humphreys (1960), among others. All too often, models of longitudinal data assume this structure without testing any other variants. Perhaps one reason this model is assumed is that it can be estimated with just two waves of data if there are multiple indicators. In the stable trait component of the STARTS model, there is no discriminant validity between the time factors, and all the factor correlations are 1.

Also possible are mixtures of two types of factors. One candidate model is the LST model, which contains stable traits and states (see also Kraemer, Gullion, Rush, Frank, & Kupfer, 1994). The data set examined by Rovine and Molenaar (chapter 3, this volume) appears to be of this type. A second possibility is a model that contains an autoregressive trait and state whose correlational structure is called a *quasisimplex*. This appears to be the best model for Dumenci and Windle's (1996) data. The final model with two factors was previously discussed by Ormel and Schaufeli (1991). This model contains a stable trait and an autoregressive trait.

The most complex model is STARTS, which we have discussed in this

EXHIBIT 8.1

Possible Combinations of Stable Trait (ST), Autoregressive Trait (AR), and State (S) Factors

COMBINATION	MODEL
ST	Nesselroade's (1987) pure trait
AR	Guttman's simplex (Humphreys, 1960)
S	Nesselroade's (1987) pure state
ST + AR	Ormel and Schaufeli (1991) model
ST + S	Steyer et al.'s (1992) latent state–trait model
AR + S	Quasisimplex (Humphreys, 1960)
ST + AR + S	Kenny and Zautra's (1995) STARTS model

chapter. This second-order model may not have the empirical identification problems that the first-order model sometimes has. All too often researchers with multiwave data estimate only one particular model (e.g., LST) without considering alternatives. We believe that the general framework outlined here can assist researchers in the selection of the most reasonable model to estimate for their data.

Concluding Comments

The two of us, having now labored for over 50 years combined in the study of longitudinal data analysis techniques, wish to offer a few observations. Whether these are "words of wisdom" or "dated reflections" is for the reader to decide.

Overcomplexity

For many years, researchers did not fully exploit the advantages of longitudinal data. For instance, they conducted simple analyses of variance on their data. In some cases, analyses were limited to tests of changes in means over time. However, today, as this volume superbly illustrates, we have available elaborate models for longitudinal data and several extraordinarily sophisticated computer programs for their analysis. Whereas researchers previously underexploited their data, today they can estimate elaborate models for their data. Researchers are reaching the point now where some models for longitudinal data are not really practical for the data that they typically collect. Given the sample sizes that one usually has, and the degree of measurement error in one's measures, sometimes one's models are just too complex. This complexity results in models that are intractable, unfeasible, or unreplicable. Researchers, editors, and grant reviewers need to learn that models that are "best" in terms of statistical complexity are not necessarily "best" for empirical analysis of the actual data.

We are not advocating that researchers use inefficient and old-fashioned techniques for their longitudinal analyses. We recognize that most researchers still do not fully exploit the methods that could uncover the insights lurking in their data. However, we worry that methodologists are now developing methods that are just too powerful, leading to errors in estimation. Even an answer to a relatively simple question, such as the degree of stability over time in a set of measures, can be made opaque by a self-absorbed data analyst who has forsaken the question to champion application of a new technique—effectively, and unwisely, exchanging old lamps for new.

Growth Curve Versus Autoregressive Models

In recent years, stochastic models, like the autoregressive model, have fallen out of favor (Hertzog & Nesselroade, 1987; Rogosa & Willett, 1985). Instead, the fashion has been growth curve models (see Curran & Bollen, chapter 4, this volume). Autoregressive models typically subtract the grand means, which are retained in growth curve modeling.

Although a complete model ideally should explain the change in the sample means and the change of people within groups, being students of Campbell and Stanley (1963), we worry that the mean changes reflect not just maturation but also history; instrumentation; and, of course, that old nemesis, regression to the mean (Campbell & Kenny, 1999). So removing the grand mean from the data may often be a reasonable practice.

Several of the chapters in this volume attempt to blend autoregressive and growth curve models (e.g., chapter 4, by Curran & Bollen, and chapter 5, by McArdle & Hamagami). The stable trait within the STARTS model can be viewed as a restricted growth model, one in which individuals have different origins but the rate of growth (or decline) is the same for all people. Thus, STARTS can be viewed as a mixture of the two types of models.

Summary

This volume, as well as the previous one, shows that models for the analysis of change have made great progress. However, one should not lose sight of some of the insights of the past. In this chapter we have illustrated that the MTMM (codeveloped by one of the presenters at the first Measurement of Change Conference in Madison, WI, 1962) is still a useful technique in the analysis of stability.

References

Browne, M. W. (1992). *MUTMUM user's guide*. Columbus: Ohio State University, Department of Psychology.

Campbell, D. T., & Fiske, D. W. (1959). Convergent and discriminant validation by the multitrait–multimethod matrix. *Psychological Bulletin, 56*, 81–105.

Campbell, D. T., & Kenny, D. A. (1999). *Primer on regression artifacts*. New York: Guilford Press.

Campbell, D. T., & O'Connell, E. J. (1967). Method factors in multitrait–multimethod matrices: Multiplicative rather than additive? *Multivariate Behavioral Research, 2*, 409–426.

Campbell, D. T., & Stanley, J. C. (1963). Experimental and quasi-experimental designs for research on teaching. In N. L. Gage (Ed.), *Handbook of research on teaching* (pp. 171–246). Chicago: Rand McNally.

Cole, D. A., Peeke, L. G., Martin, J. M., Truglio, R., & Seroczynski, A. D. (1998). A longitudinal look at the relation between depression and anxiety in children and adolescents. *Journal of Consulting and Clinical Psychology, 66*, 451–460.

Crocker, L., & Algina, J. (1986). *Introduction to classical and modern test theory.* New York: Harcourt, Brace & Jovanovich.

Cudeck, R. (1989). Analysis of correlation matrices using covariance structure models. *Psychological Bulletin, 105,* 317–327.

Dewey, J. (1922). *Human nature and conduct: An introduction to social psychology.* New York: Carlton House.

Dumenci, L., & Windle, M. (1996). A latent trait–state model of adolescent depression using the Center for Epidemiologic Studies—Depression Scale. *Multivariate Behavioral Research, 31,* 313–330.

Hertzog, C., & Nesselroade, J. R. (1987). Beyond autoregressive models: Some implications of the trait–state distinction for the structural modeling of developmental change. *Child Development, 58,* 93–109.

Humphreys, L. G. (1960). Investigations of the simplex. *Psychometrika, 25,* 313–323.

Jöreskog, K., & Sörbom, D. (1993). *LISREL 8.* Chicago: Scientific Software.

Kenny, D. A. (1979). *Correlation and causality.* New York: Wiley-Interscience.

Kenny, D. A., & Campbell, D. T. (1989). On the measurement of stability in over-time data. *Journal of Personality, 57,* 445–481.

Kenny, D. A., & Kashy, D. A. (1992). Analysis of multitrait–multimethod matrix by confirmatory factor analysis. *Psychological Bulletin, 112,* 165–172.

Kenny, D. A., & Zautra, A. (1995). The trait–state–error model for multiwave data. *Journal of Consulting and Clinical Psychology, 63,* 52–59.

Kraemer, H. C., Gullion, C. M., Rush, A. J., Frank, E., & Kupfer, D. (1994). Can state and trait variables be disentangled? A methodological framework for psychiatric disorders. *Psychiatry Research, 52,* 55–69.

Marsh, H. W. (1989). Confirmatory factor analyses of multitrait–multimethod data: Many problems and a few solutions. *Applied Psychological Measurement, 13,* 335–361.

Millsap, R. E. (1995). The statistical analysis of method effects in multitrait–multimethod data: A review. In P. E. Shrout & S. T. Fiske (Eds.), *Personality research, methods, and theory: A festschrift honoring Donald W. Fiske* (pp. 93–110). Hillsdale, NJ: Erlbaum.

Nesselroade, J. R. (1987). Some implications of the trait–state distinction for the study of development across the life-span: The case of personality research. In P. B. Baltes, D. L. Featherman, & R. M. Lerner (Eds.), *Life-span development* (Vol. 8, pp. 163–189). Hillsdale, NJ: Erlbaum.

Nesselroade, J. R. (1991). Interindividual differences in intraindividual change. In L. M. Collins & J. L. Horn (Eds.), *Best methods for the analysis of change* (pp. 92–105). Washington, DC: American Psychological Association.

Nesselroade, J. R., & Bartsch, T. W. (1977). Multivariate perspectives on the construct validity of the trait–state distinction. In R. B. Cattell & R. M. Dreger (Eds.), *Hand-*

book of modern personality theory (pp. 221–238). Washington, DC: Hemisphere/ Halstead.

Ormel, J., & Schaufeli, W. B. (1991). Stability and change in psychological distress and their relationship with self-esteem and locus of control: A dynamic equilibrium model. *Journal of Personality and Social Psychology, 60*, 288–299.

Rogosa, D. R., & Willett, J. B. (1985). Satisfying a simplex structure is simpler than it should be. *Journal of Educational Statistics, 10*, 99–107.

Rudinger, G., Andres, J., & Rietz, C. (1991). Structural equation models for studying intellectual development. In D. Magnusson, L. R. Bergman, G. Rudinger, & B. Torestad (Eds.), *Problems and methods in longitudinal research: Stability and change* (pp. 274–307). New York: Cambridge University Press.

Schmitt, M. J., & Steyer, R. (1993). A latent trait–state model (not only) for social desirability. *Personality and Individual Differences, 14*, 519–529.

Steyer, R., Ferring, D., & Schmitt, M. J. (1992). States and traits in psychological assessment. *European Journal of Psychological Assessment, 8*, 79–98.

Steyer, R., Majcen, A.-M., Schwenkmezger, P., & Buchner, A. (1989). A latent state–trait anxiety model and its application to determine consistency and specificity coefficients. *Anxiety Research, 1*, 281–299.

Zautra, A. J., Marbach, J. J., Raphael, K. G., Dohrenwend, B. P., Lennon, M. C., & Kenny, D. A. (1995). The examination of myofascial face pain and its relationship to psychological distress. *Health Psychology, 3*, 223–231.

Appendix 8A
Program Setups

The setup below is for the computer program LISREL 8 (Jöreskog & Sörbom, 1993).

Dumenci and Windle (1996; sum of the four measures): Full STARTS Model
```
DA NI=4 NOBS=433 MA=CM
LA
T1 T2 T3 T4
CM FI=A:WINDSUM.COV SY
MO NY=4 NE=5 LY=FU,FI PS=DI,FR TE=DI,FR BE=FU,FI
VA 1.0 LY 1 1 LY 2 1 LY 3 1 LY 4 1 LY 1 2 LY 2 3 LY 3 4 LY 4 5
FR TE 1 BE 3 2
EQ PS 3 3 PS 4 4 PS 5 5
EQ BE 3 2 BE 4 3 BE 5 4
EQ TE 1 TE 2 TE 3 TE 4
CO PS(3,3) = PS(2,2) - PS(2,2)*BE(3,2)*BE(3,2)
ST .5 BE 3 2
ST 10 PS 1 1
ST 5 PS 2 2
ST 5 PS 3 3
ST 10 TE 1
OU AD=OFF SC RS NS
```

The basic format for this run was provided to us by Herb Marsh.

Dumenci and Windle (1996) Multiplicative Multitrait Multimethod Matrix
```
DA NI=16 MA=CM NOBS=433
LA
DA1 PA1 SO1 IN1 DA2 PA2 SO2 IN2 DA3 PA3 SO3 IN3 DA4 PA4 SO4 IN4
CM FI=WINDLE.COV SY
SE
1 5 9 13 2 6 10 14 3 7 11 15 4 8 12 16/
MO NY=16 NE=16 NK=16 LY=DI,FR GA=FU,FI PH=SY,FI PS=DI,FR BE=ZE
TE=ZE
ST .8 LY 1-LY 16
EQ LY 1 LY 5 LY 9 LY 13
ST 1. GA 1 1 GA 2 2 GA 3 3 GA 4 4
FR GA 5 1 GA 9 1 GA 13 1 GA 9 5 GA 13 5 GA 13 9
FR GA 5 5 GA 9 9 GA 13 13
ST 1.0 GA 5 1 GA 9 1 GA 13 1 GA 9 5 GA 13 5 GA 13 9
```

ST 1.0 GA 5 5 GA 9 9 GA 13 13
EQ GA 5 1 GA 6 2 GA 7 3 GA 8 4
EQ GA 5 5 GA 6 6 GA 7 7 GA 8 8
EQ GA 9 1 GA 10 2 GA 11 3 GA 12 4
EQ GA 9 5 GA 10 6 GA 11 7 GA 12 8
EQ GA 13 1 GA 14 2 GA 15 3 GA 16 4
EQ GA 13 5 GA 14 6 GA 15 7 GA 16 8
EQ GA 13 9 GA 14 10 GA 15 11 GA 16 12
EQ GA 9 9 GA 10 10 GA 11 11 GA 12 12
EQ GA 13 13 GA 14 14 GA 15 15 GA 16 16
FR PH 2 1 PH 3 1 PH 3 2 PH 4 1 PH 4 2 PH 4 3
EQ PH 2 1 PH 6 5 PH 10 9 PH 14 13
EQ PH 3 1 PH 7 5 PH 11 9 PH 15 13
EQ PH 3 2 PH 7 6 PH 11 10 PH 15 14
EQ PH 4 1 PH 8 5 PH 12 9 PH 16 13
EQ PH 4 2 PH 8 6 PH 12 10 PH 16 14
EQ PH 4 3 PH 8 7 PH 12 11 PH 16 15
ST .4 PH 2 1 PH 3 1 PH 3 2 PH 4 1 PH 4 2 PH 4 3
ST 1 PH 1 1 PH 2 2 PH 3 3 PH 4 4 PH 5 5 PH 6 6 PH 7 7 PH 8 8 PH 9 9
ST 1 PH 10 10 PH 11 11 PH 12 12 PH 13 13 PH 14 14 PH 15 15 PH 16 16
OU NS SO TV RS SC AD=OFF

Appendix 8B
Specification and Identification of the STARTS Model

The STARTS (stable trait, autoregressive trait, and state) model can be understood by its covariance structure. We denote c_i as the covariance of different lags. Using this notation, c_0 would refer to the variance of observations.

$$\text{Lag 0: } c_0 = \sigma^2_{ST} + \sigma^2_{AR} + \sigma^2_S$$

$$\text{Lag 1: } c_1 = \sigma^2_{ST} + \rho\sigma^2_{AR}$$

$$\text{Lag 2: } c_2 = \sigma^2_{ST} + \rho^2\sigma^2_{AR}$$

$$\text{Lag 3: } c_3 = \sigma^2_{ST} + \rho^3\sigma^2_{AR}.$$

The STARTS model would usually be estimated by a structural equation modeling computer program using the procedure discussed by Kenny and Zautra (1995). It is instructive to consider the formulas for the estimates of the parameters:

$$\rho = \frac{c_2 - c_3}{c_1 - c_2}$$

$$\sigma^2_{ST} = \frac{c_1 c_3 - c_2^2}{c_1 + c_3 - 2c_2}$$

$$\sigma^2_{AR} = \frac{(c_1 - c_2)^3}{(c_2 - c_3)(c_1 + c_3 - 2c_2)}$$

$$\sigma^2_S = c_0 - \frac{c_1^2 + c_2^2 - c_1(c_2 + c_3)}{c_2 - c_3}.$$

If there are more than four waves, it can be shown that $(c_{i+1} - c_{i+2})/(c_i - c_{i+1})$ provides an estimate of ρ as long as i is greater than zero.

Besides this univariate model, we (Kenny & Zautra, 1995) proposed a bivariate model. We discuss this model only briefly in this chapter. In that model, each variable is assumed to have the three components of the STARTS model. Also assumed are lagged cause effects between the autoregressive trait factors and synchronous correlations between the three factors. In some cases, it might be reasonable to consider a model in which for the synchronous trait factors the two measures' correlation equal 1 for the synchronous trait factors, and the state factor's correlation could be used to partition true state variance from error variance.

It is instructive to examine the denominators of all of the estimators and consider what would happen to them if there were no autoregressive trait variance in the model. In such a case, $c_1 = c_2 = c_3$, and all of the estimates would have denominators of zero. Thus, if there is a great deal of stable trait variance, or if the autoregressive parameter is fairly large, STARTS estimators are unstable.

We have conducted some small-scale simulations of the STARTS model and have found that the precision of estimates depends as much on the number of waves of data as the sample size. We think it is understandable that the published applications of the model all have many waves of data (e.g., 10). It seems advisable to use this technique only with many waves of data.

Another method for improving the precision of estimation of STARTS is to use a priori information. In general, researchers have strong hunches about how much of the variance is due to traits and how much is due to states. A Bayesian type of analysis might be used to incorporate this a priori information so as to improve the precision of the estimates. We strongly encourage the exploration of this approach.

COMMENT:

The Trait–State Distinction and Its Dialectic Balance

Adam Davey

The trait–state distinction has long captivated the attention of developmental social scientists (cf. Nesselroade, 1988) and cuts to the very core of issues regarding stability and change. Only recently, however, have tools begun to emerge for researchers to move beyond the "trait or state" distinction to consider the dialectic balance between trait and state. The models that David Kenny and Alex Zautra review so thoroughly in their chapter provide an integrated framework from which developmental researchers may add to their repertoire of techniques suitable for the analysis of longitudinal data. There is enormous value in including these models in a volume on "new methods for the analysis of change," because they have only occasionally been applied to longitudinal data (e.g., Davey, Sayer, & Flaherty, 1997; Dumenci & Windle, 1996; Duncan-Jones, Fergusson, Ormel, & Horwood, 1990; Hertzog & Nesselroade, 1987; Kenny & Zautra, 1995; Schmitt & Steyer, 1993; Steyer, Schwenkmezger, & Auer, 1990), even when theory suggests that both traitlike and situationally specific variability is to be expected. This underuse of methods for partitioning trait and state variance has likely occurred for several reasons, and I hope to continue Kenny and Zautra's exploration of several of these.

Reconciling Theory and Methods

At the heart of a volume such as this one is a desire to more adequately reconcile theory and methods that are available for studying developmental phenomena. "Developmental" theories generally lag well behind developmental methods: In reality, there are relatively few areas of development that include an explicit model of how and why things change over time. Instead, what is typically discussed is how and why things differ, but not how or why they change or unfold over time. Without an explicit model of change, and of how and why it occurs, there may be a tendency to apply whatever model seems most current

265

or most preferred. Examples of such models include autoregressive models, repeated-measures analysis of variance, and growth curve models.

However, if one is truly interested in understanding time-dependent processes, then one needs a repertoire of methods that is as comprehensive as possible. Trait–state models are certainly a potentially powerful addition to one's toolkit of methodologies to develop, test, and further refine theoretical propositions regarding longitudinal stability and change. This is particularly true in areas such as adult personality development, which has a well developed (and well defended) trait theory of development.

Trait–State Models as Longitudinal Measurement Models

Given all of this potential, what can explain the relative paucity of examples where trait–state models have been applied in the social sciences? As noted in Collins's chapter (chapter 9) in this volume, classical test theory assumes that an observed value, X, consists of a true score, T, and measurement error, E. Classical test theory, however, was designed around an assumption of independent observations, not repeated observations of the same individuals over time. Thus, researchers desire an extension of this measurement model to longitudinal data, and I argue that this is the goal of all trait–state methods: to further partition the true score variability into its situationally dependent and situationally independent components. In addition, as Kenny and Zautra illustrate, consideration of the temporal sequencing of observations may (or may not; cf. Davey, Halverson, McCrae, Zonderman, & Costa, 1999) prove important in a given trait–state model and needs to be explicitly considered because it structures the relationships among states over time. This leads to a consideration of the meaning of traits and states within each of the frameworks Kenny and Zautra outline.

Traits refer to stable, enduring, situationally independent interindividual differences. Thus, although levels of traits may change over time, they must change in a similar fashion for all individuals. If this assumption does not seem sensible, then trait–state models are likely not the appropriate choice. When considering states, several considerations are evident, and I suggest that at least three potential sources of variability need to be considered by the researcher interested in applying trait–state models to developmental data. Specifically, researchers need to: (a) consider the role of autocorrelated uniquenesses in estimates of statelike variability (and the plausibility of methods being uncorrelated); (b) test, rather than assume, that statelike variance is (or is not) correlated over time; and (c) more fully consider the reciprocal relations between people and their environment. I briefly discuss each of these topics below.

In essence, the objective in applying trait–state models is the same as with any other longitudinal model. The model being tested implies a certain covariance (and perhaps mean) structure among observations over time. Under all trait–state models, the traitlike variability is attributed to the variance observations share in common over time. Statelike variability is assumed to be independent of traitlike components, a sensible assumption under most practical circumstances. However, there are at least three reasons why observations may be still correlated over time, even once traitlike variability is partitioned out. First, almost all social science measures contain at least some residual variability, part of which is likely to be due to systematic sources (hence the preference for terms such as *item-specific variance* and *uniqueness* over *error*). Furthermore, the sources of this residual variability may be correlated over time. For this reason, a longitudinal factor model typically tests for the possibility that uniquenesses may be autocorrelated over time. It is only in the presence of multiple indicators that this source of variability may be distinguished from statelike variability. In situations where autocorrelated uniquenesses may be expected (perhaps the majority of social science applications), a multiple-indicator model such as those proposed by Steyer et al. (1990) or Dumenci and Windle (1996) may be preferred over what Kenny and Zautra refer to as the *trait–state–error model*. In the former model, the "error" component appears in the measurement model, leaving the traitlike and statelike components to be modeled as all of the reliable variance in the constructs of interest. In the latter model, autocorrelated residual variance cannot be separated from the trait and state components.

Whereas the ability to consider the structure of residual covariances over time represents an important step forward (such extensions to other longitudinal models, such as growth curve modeling, are presented elsewhere in this volume, for example, in chapter 3, by Rovine and Molenaar), there still remain "artefactual" reasons why estimates of the traitlike and statelike components of true score variability may be incorrect. Consider the analogy Kenny and Zautra draw to multitrait–multimethod (MTMM) models. For proper model estimation, methods should be selected as independent as possible or at least conditionally independent once previous state levels are controlled. If one is truly interested in separating out traitlike variability that is stable across situations then one should select situations that reflect the full variability of contexts across which one wishes to generalize, or across periods of time.

Thus, the application Dumenci and Windle (1996) considered, in which item-specific variability must be assumed to be independent, seems less plausible than one in which no attempt is made to partition systematic—but usually nuisance—"methods" variance from other types of residual variance that are not due either to traitlike variance or to statelike variance. Depending on how Dumenci and Windle's model is scaled, it is possible to conclude that more than one source of methods variance is nonsignificant, consistent with the conclusion that their model is empirically underidentified. As with the MTMM models discussed by Kenny and Kashy (1992), the correlated uniquenesses model appears to work better, being easier to estimate in most situations and typically leading to similar substantive conclusions regarding traitlike and state-like variability.

A second consideration has to do with whether an autoregressive (or other time-dependent) process ought or needs to be modeled. If situations are selected so as to be as independent as possible, then the occasions should be inter-changeable in the statistical sense. No time-dependent process should need to be modeled. In fact, this can be assured under experimental assignment to situations of interest and often can be tested empirically by modeling an au-toregressive process and assessing the significance of stability coefficients across occasions. The trait–state model presented by Dumenci and Windle (1996) and a trait–error model with an autoregressive component, as tested by Kenny and Zautra, substantively imply different mechanisms of development, at least over the short term. In Dumenci and Windle's model, all residual effects of the previous "state" have already diminished to zero by the time of the subsequent measurement occasions. As Kenny and Zautra note so insightfully, previous effects involving seasonal trends may not operate simply according to a first-order autoregressive model. In Kenny and Zautra's model, however, there may be some enduring (over the short term) residual effects of the accretion of experiences over time. Situationally specific effects from one or more previous occasions may still be exerting a measurable influence on behavior at subse-quent measurement occasions. Only by considering and comparing across a range of theoretically and empirically meaningful models can the researcher gain full insight into the dynamic processes at work in his or her data. For this reason, I believe that the MTMM framework that Kenny and Zautra suggest is an exceptionally sound and insightful strategy that should be fully exploited.

All of the discussion to this point neglects some of the most basic principles of current developmental thought. Specifically, consider the reciprocal relation-ship between individual and environment. We know that context is important in shaping individual development. We know as well that individuals select their environments to some extent and that individuals also exert an influence on their own environments. Thus we also need to consider how the various trait–state models Kenny and Zautra present may partition variance differently depending on the degree of stability in the unmeasured components of the individual's environment and typically result in an overestimate of the propor-tion of variance that is traitlike. In this sense, greater application of trait–state models in developmental research requires an emphasis on measurement of contextual features that are important for individual development. As well, these models open the door for a greater understanding of the role of experience in shaping individual differences and the complex interdependence between individual and environment.

References

Davey, A., Halverson, C. F., Jr., McCrae, R. R., Zonderman, A. B., & Costa, P. T., Jr. (1999, November). *Stability and change in depressive symptoms over time: Evidence from the Baltimore Longitudinal Study of Aging.* Paper presented at the annual meeting of the Gerontological Society of America, San Francisco, CA.

Davey, A., Sayer, A. G., & Flaherty, B. F. (1997, August). *Models for examining latent trait, state, and method variance: An application to children's problem behaviors.* Paper presented at the 107th Annual Convention of the American Psychological Association, Boston.

Dumenci, L., & Windle, M. (1996). A latent trait–state model of adolescent depression using the Center for Epidemiologic Studies—Depression scale. *Multivariate Behavioral Research, 31*, 313–330.

Duncan-Jones, P., Fergusson, D. M., Ormel, J., & Horwood, L. J. (1990). A model of stability and change in minor psychiatric symptoms: Results from three longitudinal studies. In *Psychological medicine monograph* (Suppl. 18, pp. iii–28). New York: Cambridge University Press.

Hertzog, C., & Nesselroade, J. R. (1987). Beyond autoregressive models: Some implications of the trait–state distinction for the structural modeling of developmental change. *Child Development, 58*, 93–109.

Kenny, D. A., & Kashy, D. A. (1992). Analysis of the multitrait–multimethod matrix by confirmatory factor analysis. *Psychological Bulletin, 112*, 165–172.

Kenny, D. A., & Zautra, A. (1995). The trait–state–error model for multiwave data. *Journal of Consulting and Clinical Psychology, 63*, 52–59.

Nesselroade, J. R. (1988). Some implications of the trait–state distinction for the study of development over the life-span: The case of personality. In P. B. Baltes, D. L. Featherman, & R. M. Lerner (Eds.), *Life-span development and behavior* (Vol. 8, pp. 163–189). Hillsdale, NJ: Erlbaum.

Schmitt, M. J., & Steyer, R. (1993). A latent state–trait model (not only) for social desirability. *Personality and Individual Differences, 14*, 519–529.

Steyer, R., Schwenkmezger, P., & Auer, A. (1990). The emotional and cognitive components of trait anxiety: A latent state–trait model. *Personality and Individual Differences, 11*, 125–134.

Editors' Introduction

Latent class theory is a latent variable model for categorical latent variables, similar conceptually, but not in implementation, to factor analysis. Linda Collins uses the latent class model as a starting point for a flexible approach to developing and evaluating instruments to measure change. Collins's approach is based on an extension of latent class models to longitudinal data known as "latent transition analysis." Using this approach, it is possible first to specify a change process and then to set about developing an instrument tailor made for this process. In his comments on this chapter and on chapter 10, David Rindskopf places this work in the context of previous literature. Readers may wish to compare Collins's perspective on latent variables with that of Meredith and Horn (chapter 7) and Kenny and Zautra (chapter 8). Latent class theory, briefly described in this chapter, is one of the underpinnings of the general approach to analysis of change described in Muthén's chapter 10.

Reliability for Static and Dynamic Categorical Latent Variables

Developing Measurement Instruments Based on a Model of the Growth Process

Linda M. Collins

Measures in the social sciences are never perfect. Researchers are usually in a position of trying to distinguish the signal, or latent variable, from the noise, or error, in these imperfect instruments. Reliability is a standard by which researchers judge whether an instrument is an acceptably accurate detector of the signal and a basis on which researchers work toward developing better instruments. This cornerstone of measurement theory has been elegantly and extensively developed for measurement of continuous latent variables that are static, that is, not expected to change over time (see Lord & Novick, 1968). It is much less developed for measurement of categorical latent variables and for dynamic latent variables, that is, latent variables that are expected to change over time (but see, e.g., Clogg & Manning, 1996; Collins & Cliff, 1990; DeShon, Ployhart, & Sacco, 1998; Embretson, 1991a, 1991b; and Fischer & Ponocny, 1994; Willett, 1989).

The lack of a mathematical definition of reliability for static and, in particular, dynamic categorical latent variables has left researchers who wish to measure these quantities without a basis for evaluating or improving their instruments. The purpose of this chapter is to suggest a definition of *reliability* specifically for categorical latent variables, based on latent class models (Clogg & Goodman, 1984; Goodman, 1974; Lazarsfeld & Henry, 1968). The definition presented here is a direct analogue of the traditional definition of reliability. As I show later, this definition is easily extended to situations in which stage-sequential change over time is being measured, that is, to latent transition

---

This work was supported by National Institute on Drug Abuse Grant 1 P50 DA10075.

models (Collins, Graham, Rousculp, & Hansen, 1997; Collins & Wugalter, 1992; Graham, Collins, Wugalter, Chung, & Hansen, 1991; Hyatt & Collins, 2000). On the basis of this approach, it is possible to develop instruments to be highly accurate measures of specific types of change processes.

In this chapter I first briefly introduce latent class models and review the concept of reliability. Then I show an analogue of the classical definition of reliability, derived from latent class model quantities. Next, I introduce latent transition models. I show how the new definition of reliability can be extended to latent transition models and how this provides a vehicle for using a model of the change process as a starting point for a measure of the change process. Finally, I demonstrate some properties of the new definition of reliability.

A Brief Introduction to Latent Class Models

Latent class models are a hybrid of contingency table models and factor analysis, with many conceptual similarities to factor analysis. In both latent class and factor analysis models, manifest responses are determined by a shared latent variable plus error that is individual to each manifest indicator. Whereas in factor analysis there is a continuous latent variable measured by continuous (usually) manifest indicators, in latent class models there is a categorical latent variable measured by categorical manifest indicators. For example, suppose a researcher is interested in estimating the proportion of individuals in a population who have a drinking problem, based on responses to three yes–no questions about problems associated with alcohol use. In this case, the categorical latent variable might have two latent classes, say, "drinking problem" and "no drinking problem," and the manifest indicators are the three yes–no questions.

In much the same way that factor analysis models attempt to reproduce a correlation or covariance matrix, latent class models attempt to reproduce the contingency table formed by crosstabulating all of the manifest indicators. Each cell is associated with a response pattern, which is the set of item responses corresponding to the cell. In the example involving three yes–no questions, one response pattern is a response of "no" to every question ("no, no, no"), another a response of "yes" to the first question and "no" to the remaining two ("yes, no, no"), and so on. The observed frequencies of each of these response patterns—in other words, the observed cell frequencies—are the data analyzed by latent class models.

Suppose there are C latent classes and, for purposes of this example, three manifest items. There is an array of response patterns Y of length NP. Then the latent class mathematical model is as follows:

$$P(Y = y) = \sum_{c=1}^{C} \gamma_c \Pi \rho, \qquad (9.1)$$

where if response pattern y is made up of responses (i, j, k), and response i corresponds to Question 1, response j corresponds to Question 2, and response k corresponds to Question 3:

$$\Pi\rho = \rho_{i|c}\,\rho_{j|c}\,\rho_{k|c}, \qquad\qquad (9.2)$$

and γ_c = the probability of membership in latent class c. In this example, one γ parameter would be the probability of membership in the drinking problem latent class. Also, $\rho_{i|c}$ = the probability of response i to Question 1, conditional on membership in latent class c. In this example one ρ parameter would be the probability of a response of "yes" to the question "Has alcohol use ever interfered with your work?" conditional on membership in the drinking problem latent class.

From a measurement perspective, the role played by the ρ parameters in latent class models, that of expressing the relation between the latent variable and the manifest variables, is very similar conceptually to the role played by factor loadings in factor analysis. However, there is an important difference. Whereas factor loadings are standardized regression weights and therefore are more or less in a correlation metric, ρ parameters are probabilities and must be interpreted differently. A ρ parameter of either 1 or zero means that the response to that item is completely determined by latent class membership. (Contrast this with a factor loading of zero, which indicates no relation between the indicator and the factor.) Thus, in general the relation between the latent variable and the manifest variables is stronger the closer the ρ parameters are to zero and 1. The relation between the latent variable and the manifest variables is weakest (analogous to a factor loading of zero) when the ρ parameter is equal to 1/(number of response categories) or, in the case of dichotomous data, .5. In this case, the information contained in the latent class is no more helpful for predicting the item response than a coin toss would be. (From a strictly measurement point of view, ρ parameters near 1/[number of response categories] are often seen as undesirable, in much the same way that small factor loadings may be seen as undesirable. However, if a latent class analysis is aimed primarily at modeling categorical data, it may be of great substantive interest that one or more ρ parameters are in this range.)

Classical Reliability

Classical test theory for continuous variables starts with the idea that each observed score x is a composite of a true score, which can be thought of as the signal, and a random error score, which can be thought of as the noise. The true score is usually designated τ, but in this chapter it is denoted τ^* to avoid confusion with the τ parameter in latent transition models, which are discussed in the next section:

$$x = \tau^* + e. \tag{9.3}$$

An individual's true score is defined as the expectation of the observed score across the propensity distribution, which is a hypothetical distribution over an infinite number of test administrations, with no carryover effects, fatigue, and so on:

$$\tau^* = E(x). \tag{9.4}$$

Because

$$E(e) = 0, \tag{9.5}$$

the true score is the observed score an individual would receive if random measurement error were zero.

Let X represent the distribution of xs obtained in a standard measurement situation involving a population of individuals, and let T^* and E represent the distributions of τ^* and e, respectively. Because according to classical test theory the true score and the error score are uncorrelated, it follows that the observed score variance is made up of true score variance and error variance:

$$\sigma_X^2 = \sigma_{T^*}^2 + \sigma_E^2. \tag{9.6}$$

The classical definition of reliability is then the proportion of observed score variance attributable to true score variance:

$$reliability = \frac{\sigma_{T^*}^2}{\sigma_{T^*}^2 + \sigma_E^2}. \tag{9.7}$$

A few properties of reliability that are important for subsequent discussion are noted here:

1. Reliability ranges from zero to 1, with zero representing observed score variance completely attributable to random error and 1 representing observed score variance completely attributable to true score variance.

2. Reliability is a property not solely of a measure but of a measure in relation to a population in which it is to be applied. Examination of the definition of reliability shows that, given a fixed amount of error variance, a measure will have a larger reliability in a population with a large amount of true score variance as compared to a population with a smaller amount of true score variance.

3. Reliability increases as items are added to a measure (assuming they are of at least equal quality to those already in the measure, Lord & Novick, 1968).

Although the classical definition of reliability is highly useful for continuous latent variables, it is not nearly as useful when there is a categorical latent variable being measured by an instrument made up of categorical items. Often the items making up a measure of a categorical latent variable have nominal response categories, thus the idea of an observed composite score formed by summing items is meaningless, as a single composite score can be produced by several different profiles of item responses, which may have very different meanings and implications. This also renders irrelevant the classical test theory idea of true score as an expectation across a distribution of observed composite scores. Furthermore, the categorical latent variable itself may involve nominal, unordered categories, rendering the concept of true score variance meaningless.

Nevertheless, the essential idea of reliability—that of an operational definition of the amount of detectable signal embedded in a background of noise when an instrument is used in a particular population—can be applied here. To be useful to researchers who already have a background in classical test theory, such a definition should be as close an analogue as is reasonable to the classical definition of reliability.

Reliability of Categorical Latent Variables

In the definition of reliability proposed here, in place of the true score there is an array of binary scores, representing the classification an individual would receive if the ρ parameters were all zero or all 1. Each individual has a true score for each latent class, with a 1 corresponding to the true classification and a zero corresponding to the others. (It is important that this classification may or may not be the "correct" or valid one, just as in classical test theory a true score may or may not be valid.) The γ parameters are the expectation of each of these true scores:

$$\gamma_c = E(\xi_c), \tag{9.8}$$

where the expectation is taken over individuals and ξ_c = true score for latent class c.

Suppose a measure of a categorical latent variable is to be used to categorize individuals. Associated with each response pattern is an array of probabilities, representing probability of membership in each latent class. The response pattern contains information about this array of probabilities, but it does not definitively place individuals in latent classes. Thus, a reasonable way to classify individuals would be to use the probabilities associated with an individual's response pattern vector to make random assignments to categories. The probability of latent class membership based on response pattern is

$$P(C = c|Y = y) = \frac{\gamma_c \Pi \rho}{P(Y = y)}, \tag{9.9}$$

where, as before, $\Pi \rho$ represents the product of all relevant ρ parameters.

If there is a high degree of signal in relation to noise in this instrument as applied to this population, then the response pattern contains a great deal of information about latent class membership. If there is no error in the data—that is, all ρ parameters are zero or 1—then each response pattern points to one and only one latent class membership. If there is error in the data, then there is some uncertainty about latent class membership. One way to express the degree of certainty or uncertainty is to determine the probability of making the same categorization twice, in two independent random categorizations. For a single response pattern y, this probability is computed as follows:

$$\sum_{c=1}^{C} P(C = c|Y = y)^2. \tag{9.10}$$

To aggregate this across all the response patterns it is necessary to weight this expression by the number of individuals in each response pattern.

Furthermore, the interpretation of this probability is facilitated by transforming it to a normed index. This can be done by referring to the idea of a *quality index* (Cliff, 1979). In general, the quantities going into a quality index are (a) the *best* value that could be obtained; (b) the *worst* reasonable value that could be expected, usually under the assumption of some kind of random process; and (c) the *observed* quantity. The quality index is then a way of expressing where the observed quantity falls between the best and the worst—in other words, whether it is closer to the best possible value or the worst expected value:

$$\text{quality index} = \frac{\text{observed} - \text{worst}}{\text{best} - \text{worst}}. \tag{9.11}$$

The "best" in this case is probability 1 of identical categorization at both occasions. There are two clear alternatives for "worst." The "worst" proposed here is categorization with no information, simply using probability equal to 1/(number of latent classes), for example, a coin toss in the case of two latent classes. The alternative possibility uses the information contained in the γ parameters to arrive at a baseline. For example, if there are two latent classes, and the γ parameters are .7 and .3, a random classification using these marginal probabilities results in agreement 58% of the time.

The reason for choosing the former possibility for worst rather than the latter is that of the two alternative definitions, the former creates a quality index that is closer conceptually to the classical test theory definition of reliability: The signal detection ability of an instrument rests not only in the instrument itself but also on the strength of the signal as it is emitted by the population of interest. In other words, as mentioned above, an instrument with a fixed error variance is more reliable when applied to a population with a larger true score variance than it is when applied to a population with a smaller true score variance. The former definition of worst creates an index with an analogous characteristic: All else being equal, the strong signal created when the γ parameters are very different results in a quality index closer to 1. Using the latter approach, in which the information in the gamma parameters is included in computing the worst classification agreement, is saying that the signal detection ability of the instrument rests entirely in the ρs and has nothing to do with the strength of the signal as it exists in the population to be measured.

Aggregating across response patterns and turning the index into a quality index results in the following expression for reliability for categorical data, which from now on will be referred to as RC:

$$
RC = \frac{\displaystyle\sum_{y=1}^{NP} \sum_{c=1}^{C} f(y)P(C = c|Y = y)^2 - 1/C}{N(1 - 1/C)},
\tag{9.12}
$$

where NP represents the number of response patterns.

This is a suggested definition of reliability for measures of categorical latent variables. It can be interpreted as percentage improvement over chance classification provided by the observed response patterns. If RC = 1, the measure perfectly determines classification. If RC = 0, the measure provides no information that improves over a completely random classification.

A Model-Based Definition of Reliability for Measures of Change

The above definition of reliability applies to static categorical latent variables, but what about situations in which a researcher wishes to measure change in a categorical latent variable over time? Collins and Cliff (1990) argued that "measurement of growth cannot proceed without an explicit a priori model of growth" (p. 133), suggesting that a definition of reliability for a measure of growth must include a way to incorporate a model of growth. This allows the evaluation of an instrument based on how well it measures a particular change process. Latent transition analysis (LTA), described next, provides a method for incorporating any of a number of models of the change process into a definition of reliability.

Latent Transition Analysis

An extension of the latent class model to include dynamic categorical variables, called *LTA* (Collins et al., 1997; Collins & Wugalter, 1992; Graham et al., 1991; Hyatt & Collins, 2000), provides a means for estimating and testing stage-sequential models of change in longitudinal data. In LTA the stages or categories that individuals move into and out of over time are called *latent statuses*. For example, a researcher might be interested in whether individuals move into and out of the latent status "drinking problem" between two times. In LTA models the response pattern is essentially the same as in latent class models, but it tends to be longer because it now contains responses from two (or more) times. In this example, assuming the same three manifest indicators are used at each time, a response pattern might be $y = \{no, no, no, yes', no', yes'\}$, where a prime denotes responses at the second time.

Suppose, as in this example, there are two times and three items. The number of latent statuses is denoted S, with a representing the latent status at Time 1 and b representing the latent status at Time 2. The LTA mathematical model is

$$P(Y = y) = \sum_{a=1}^{S} \sum_{b=1}^{S} \delta_a \tau_{b|a} \Pi \rho, \tag{9.13}$$

where if response pattern y is made up of responses $\{i, j, k, i'j', k'\}$, and responses i, i' correspond to Question 1, responses j, j' correspond to Question 2, and responses k, k' correspond to Question 3, then

$$\Pi \rho = \rho_{i|a} \rho_{j|a} \rho_{k|a} \rho_{i'|b} \rho_{j'|b} \rho_{k'|b}. \tag{9.14}$$

The interpretation of the ρ parameters in LTA is exactly the same as the interpretation discussed previously for latent class models. The other parameters are defined as follows:

1. δ_a = the probability of membership in latent status a at Time 1. In this example, one δ parameter would be the probability of membership in the drinking problem latent status at Time 1.

2. $\tau_{b|b}$ = the probability of membership in latent status b at Time 2, conditional on membership in latent status a at Time 1.

In this example, one τ parameter would be the probability of membership in the drinking problem latent status at Time 2, conditional on membership in the no drinking problem latent status at Time 1. Typically the τ parameters are arranged in a transition probability matrix, in which the rows correspond to latent status membership at time t and the columns correspond to latent status membership at time $t + 1$.

LTA makes it possible to define various models of stage-sequential change by restricting parameters, particularly τ parameters. If the model of interest is one in which movement from a particular latent status to another is not allowed, the corresponding τ parameter can be fixed to zero. For example, if a model specifies that no backward development is permitted, the entire lower triangle of the transition probability matrix can be fixed to zero. It is also possible to constrain certain τs to be equal to each other, or to designate a latent status as an absorbing state out of which movement is not permitted. Any of these restrictions can be used to specify details of a model of change.

Extending the Definition of Reliability to Measurement of Stage-Sequential Change

The definition of reliability presented above can easily be extended to apply to measurement of transitions. When transitions are measured, the goal is to classify the individual at two successive times. The true score array in this case includes the classification at the two successive times, and

$$\delta_a = E(\xi_a), \tag{9.15}$$

where a refers to latent status at Time 1. Also,

$$\tau_{b|a} = \frac{E(\xi_a, \xi_b)}{E(\xi_a)}, \tag{9.16}$$

where b refers to latent status at Time 2. Essentially the same procedure as was followed above can be used to compute the probability of membership in latent status a at Time 1 and latent status b at Time 2, conditional on response pattern

$$P(A = a, B = b|Y = y) = \frac{\delta_a \tau_{b|a} \pi \rho}{P(Y = y)}. \tag{9.17}$$

Note that the agreement is based on latent status membership at Time 1 and latent status membership at Time 2. In other words, the classification must agree at both times to be counted as an agreement. Then RC becomes

$$RC = \frac{\sum\limits_{y=1}^{NP} \sum\limits_{a=1}^{S} \sum\limits_{b=1}^{S} f(y)P(A = a, B = b|Y = y)^2 - 1/S^2}{N(1 - 1/S^2)}. \tag{9.18}$$

In the longitudinal case the adjustment for chance agreement is based on S^2 rather than S because, as described above, agreement is based on Time 1 and Time 2. For example, in a two-latent-status problem, an individual could be classified as in Latent Status 1 at both times, Latent Status 1 at Time 1 and Latent Status 2 at Time 2, and so on, up to $S^2 = 4$ possibilities. This is equivalent to a latent class model with four latent statuses and twice as many manifest items.

Reliability for categorical data as a function of rho parameters and number of items, for a two-latent-class model with gamma = .5, .5.

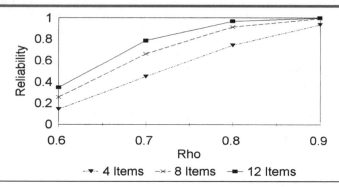

Some Properties of Reliability for Categorical Data

The upper limit of RC is 1, representing a probability of 1 of identical classification. Although the expectation of RC is zero when classification agreement is about equal to chance, the index can become negative when agreement is worse than chance levels.

RC shares some characteristics with classical reliability. Figures 9.1–9.4 illustrate these characteristics, using as examples data generated using a model with two latent classes. In Figures 9.1 and 9.3 the latent class probabilities are .5; in Figures 9.2 and 9.4 they are .9 and .1. Data were generated using dichotomous manifest indicators with ρ parameters equal to .6/.4 (the ρ param-

Reliability for categorical data as a function of rho parameters and number of items, for a two-latent-class model with gamma = .9, .1.

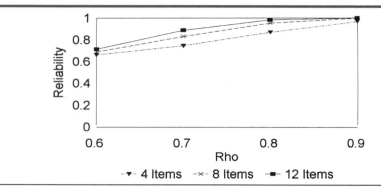

FIGURE 9.3

Reliability for categorical data as a function of number of items and rho parameters, for a two-latent-class model with gamma = .5, .5.

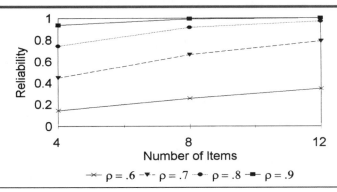

eters sum to 1 across response alternatives for a single item–latent class combination), .7/.3, .8/.2, or .9/.1. In addition, data were generated with 4, 8, and 12 manifest items. First, as Figures 9.1 and 9.2 show, RC approaches 1 as the values of the rho parameters approach zero and 1, asymptoting at 1. Second, as Figures 9.3 and 9.4 show, RC increases as a function of the number of items [assuming items of equal or better ρ value are added, and except for the degenerate case in which all ρs = 1/(number of response categories)]. Third, a comparison of Figures 9.1 and 9.3 versus 9.2 and 9.4 shows that the spread of individuals across latent classes has an effect on the value of RC. A large disparity in γ parameters produces a stronger "signal" and, given the same amount of random error, a stronger signal-to-noise ratio. As discussed in the

FIGURE 9.4

Reliability for categorical data as a function of number of items and rho parameters, for a two-latent-class model with gamma = .9, .1.

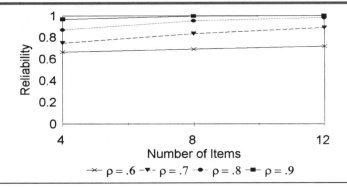

FIGURE 9.5

Reliability for categorical data as a function of rho parameters and number of items, for a latent transition model with two latent statuses and

$$\delta = \begin{bmatrix} .5 \\ .5 \end{bmatrix}, \quad \tau = \begin{bmatrix} .5 & .5 \\ .5 & .5 \end{bmatrix}.$$

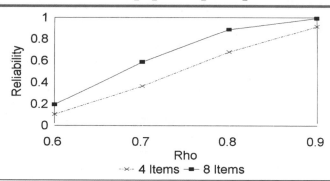

previous section, this is conceptually similar to the effect that a large true score variance has on classical reliability.

Figures 9.5–9.7 illustrate some properties of RC as it is applied to the dynamic-variable case. These figures are based on data generated as described in the preceding paragraph, except using an LTA model with two latent statuses and a full (i.e., no elements zero) transition probability matrix. This corresponds to a model of change that allows all possible transitions between latent statuses.

FIGURE 9.6

Reliability for categorical data as a function of rho parameters and number of items, for a latent transition model with two latent statuses and

$$\delta = \begin{bmatrix} .5 \\ .5 \end{bmatrix}, \quad \tau = \begin{bmatrix} .9 & .1 \\ .1 & .9 \end{bmatrix}.$$

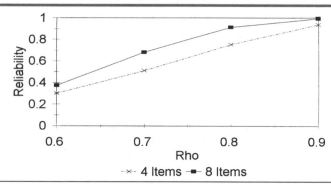

FIGURE 9.7

Reliability for categorical data as a function of rho parameters and number of items, for a latent transition model with two latent statuses and

$$\delta = \begin{bmatrix} .9 \\ .1 \end{bmatrix}, \quad \tau = \begin{bmatrix} .9 & .9 \\ .1 & .1 \end{bmatrix}.$$

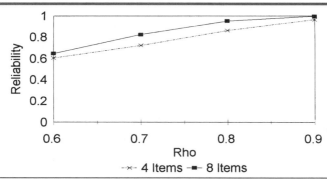

Data were generated using three combinations of values of δ and τ parameters. For Figure 9.5,

$$\delta = \begin{bmatrix} .5 \\ .5 \end{bmatrix}, \quad \tau = \begin{bmatrix} .5 & .5 \\ .5 & .5 \end{bmatrix}, \quad (9.19)$$

representing a situation in which individuals are evenly spread across latent statuses at the outset, and the change process maintains this even spread. For Figure 9.6,

$$\delta = \begin{bmatrix} .5 \\ .5 \end{bmatrix}, \quad \tau = \begin{bmatrix} .9 & .1 \\ .1 & .9 \end{bmatrix}, \quad (9.20)$$

representing a situation in which individuals are evenly spread across latent statuses at the outset, but the change process operates to increase the disparity in membership across latent statuses. For Figure 9.7,

$$\delta = \begin{bmatrix} .9 \\ .1 \end{bmatrix}, \quad \tau = \begin{bmatrix} .9 & .1 \\ .1 & .9 \end{bmatrix}, \quad (9.21)$$

representing a situation where there is a large disparity in membership across the two latent statuses at the outset, and the change process increases this disparity further. Only the 4-item and 8-item conditions were used here because 12 items at two times produces a response pattern vector of length 2^{24} = 16,777,216.

Several observations emerge from studying Figures 9.5–9.7. First, the relation between RC and strength of the ρ parameters is essentially the same in the application of RC to dynamic latent variables as it was in the static case:

RC increases as a function of increasing ρ strength. Second, RC is larger in the 8-item case as compared to the 4-item case. Third, as observed above, the disparity in latent status membership has an effect on RC. The greater the disparity in latent status membership as produced by the combination of δ and τ parameters, the larger is RC, all else being equal. A comparison of Figures 9.1–9.4 on the one hand and Figures 9.5–9.7 on the other shows that for the dynamic variables measured longitudinally, reliability is a little lower overall, reflecting the requirement that the classification agree at not one time, but two.

Discussion

Researchers rely heavily on the guidelines and support offered by measurement theory and practice in order to develop high-quality instruments. However, researchers wishing to develop instruments to measure categorical latent variables, particularly dynamic categorical latent variables, have had little to go on, because the standard classical test theory approach does not apply to this situation. In this chapter, I have presented a method for assessing reliability when the construct of interest is a categorical latent variable. RC, the reliability index presented here, is a direct analogue of classical test theory reliability for the categorical-variable domain. Thus, it is in a metric familiar to researchers and behaves in familiar ways.

Often a developmental or longitudinal researcher is interested in developing an instrument to measure a dynamic latent variable exhibiting a particular type of stage-sequential development. Using RC, a researcher who wishes to develop a measure of a dynamic categorical latent variable can start by identifying a model of this development. RC is suitable for any a priori model of development that can be expressed in terms of LTA. This includes a variety of stage-sequential processes, including models with various kinds of restricted development and absorbing states. Once empirical data have been collected on the measure, the LTA model can be estimated (using software such as WinLTA[1]), and RC can in turn be estimated using the results of the LTA analysis and the empirical data. This provides the researcher with an idea of the overall quality of the measure. The ultimate goal of this procedure is to develop an instrument tailor made to be sensitive to a particular, theoretically interesting kind of change.

With the approach suggested in this chapter, it is possible to identify weaker items in a measure. The LTA analysis necessary to compute RC yields estimates of all parameters, including ρs. The ρ parameters reflect how closely individual items are related to the latent variable. Items that appear only weakly related to the latent variable might be candidates for elimination. Of course, it is always

---

[1]WinLTA is a freeware program that estimates latent class and latent transition models.

possible that there will be a tradeoff between eliminating a poor item and maintaining the content validity of the measure. Such tradeoffs have been faced by many researchers developing measures of continuous latent variables.

The quantities computed for the figures in this chapter were all based on population values. A researcher who wishes to estimate RC in practice needs to base the computations on a latent class or LTA solution obtained on empirical data but of course does not know the true model underlying the data. The effects of model misspecification on the estimation of RC is unknown at this writing. It seems reasonable to speculate that a poorly specified model will produce a lot of uncertainty in classification and, therefore, a poor RC. However, this has not been proven analytically or demonstrated with a simulation.

It is important to note that like the classical definition of reliability, this definition says nothing about validity. Even if each response pattern definitively determines latent class or latent status membership, the classification may be meaningless. Validity must be established in the usual ways. For example, construct validity would be established by making a priori theoretical predictions and showing that data collected using the instrument bear them out. For further discussion of this and other issues, see Rindskopf's comment on chapter 10 of this volume.

Conclusion

In this chapter, I have suggested an index of reliability, RC, for use with static and dynamic categorical latent variables. This index is interpreted as the percentage of improvement over chance classification provided by the observed response patterns. Like classical reliability, RC increases as the number of items increases. It is partially a function of characteristics of the population in which the instrument is to be applied. RC approaches 1 as the ρ parameters approach their boundary and becomes larger as items are added to the instrument. An important advantage of RC is that it provides a way of incorporating a model of the change process into the development and evaluation of a measure of change.

References

Cliff, N. (1979). Test theory without true scores? *Psychometrika, 44*, 373–393.

Clogg, C. C., & Goodman, L. A. (1984). Latent structure analysis of a set of multidimensional contingency tables. *Journal of the American Statistical Association, 79*, 762–771.

Clogg, C. C., & Manning, W. D. (1996). Assessing reliability of categorical measurements using latent class models. In A. von Eye & C. C. Clogg (Eds.), *Categorical variables in developmental research* (pp. 169–182). San Diego, CA: Academic Press.

Collins, L. M., & Cliff, N. (1990). Using the longitudinal Guttman simplex as a basis for measuring growth. *Psychological Bulletin, 108*, 128–134.

Collins, L. M., Graham, J. W., Rousculp, S. S., & Hansen, W. B. (1997). Heavy caffeine and the beginning of the substance use onset process: An illustration of latent transition analysis. In K. Bryant, M. Windle, & S. West (Eds.), *The science of prevention: Methodological advances from alcohol and substance abuse research* (pp. 79–99). Washington, DC: American Psychological Association.

Collins, L. M., & Wugalter, S. E. (1992). Latent class models for stage-sequential dynamic latent variables. *Multivariate Behavioral Research, 27*, 131–157.

DeShon, R. P., Ployhart, R. E., & Sacco, J. M. (1998). The estimation of reliability in longitudinal models. *International Journal of Behavioral Development, 22*, 493–515.

Embretson, S. E. (1991a). Implications of a multidimensional latent trait model for measuring change. In L. M. Collins & J. L. Horn (Eds.), *Best methods for the analysis of change: Recent advances, unanswered questions, future directions* (pp. 184–197). Washington, DC: American Psychological Association.

Embretson, S. E. (1991b). A multidimensional latent trait model for measuring learning and change. *Psychometrika, 56*, 495–515.

Fischer, G. H., & Ponocny, I. (1994). An extension of the partial credit model with an application to the measurement of change. *Psychometrika, 59*, 177–192.

Goodman, L. A. (1974). Exploratory latent structure analysis using both identifiable and unidentifiable models. *Biometrika, 61*, 215–231.

Graham, J. W., Collins, L. M., Wugalter, S. E., Chung, N. K., & Hansen, W. B. (1991). Modeling transitions in latent stage-sequential processes: A substance use prevention example. *Journal of Consulting and Clinical Psychology, 59*, 48–57.

Hyatt, S. L., & Collins, L. M. (2000). Using latent transition analysis to examine the relationship between parental permissiveness and the onset of substance use. In J. Rose, L. Chassin, C. Presson, & S. Sherman (Eds.), *Multivariate applications in substance use research* (pp. 259–288). Mahwah, NJ: Erlbaum.

Lazarsfeld, P. F., & Henry, N. W. (1968). *Latent structure analysis*. Boston: Houghton Mifflin.

Lord, F. M., & Novick, M. R. (1968). *Statistical theories of mental test scores*. Reading, MA: Addison-Wesley.

Willett, J. B. (1989). Some results on reliability for the longitudinal measurement of change: Implications for the design of studies of individual growth. *Educational and Psychological Measurement, 49*, 587–601.

Editors' Introduction

For some time, it has been possible to model individual growth using growth curve modeling. It has also been possible to test models specifying subgroups of individuals using latent class analysis. Bengt Muthén has integrated latent class analysis and growth curve analysis into a single elegant model, the general growth mixture model. The result is an exciting new and general procedure for addressing an issue that is at the forefront of much longitudinal work: Is it possible to identify subgroups of individuals who undergo similar patterns of growth? In his commentary, David Rindskopf makes several interesting observations and brings in other relevant literature. Readers unfamiliar with latent class models may wish to read chapter 9, by Collins, before reading this one. Readers may also wish to compare Muthén's approach with those of Curran and Bollen (chapter 4), McArdle and Hamagami (chapter 5), Raudenbush (chapter 2), Rovine and Molenaar (chapter 3), and Sayer and Cumsille (chapter 6).

Second-Generation Structural Equation Modeling With a Combination of Categorical and Continuous Latent Variables

New Opportunities for Latent Class–Latent Growth Modeling

Bengt Muthén

This chapter focuses on the interplay between growth curve modeling and structural equation modeling (SEM). Growth curve modeling is concerned with the study of individual differences in development over time, typically captured by random effects, that is, growth parameters that vary across individuals. SEM is concerned with relationships among observed and latent variables. The two areas connect because random coefficients may be viewed as continuous latent variables (see, e.g., Meredith & Tisak, 1990). Growth modeling in a latent variable SEM framework thereby benefits from the full generality of such a framework. For example, in the SEM framework it is convenient to study regressions among the random effects; to do growth analysis in multiple populations; to analyze growth in latent variable constructs measured by multiple indicators; to analyze both parallel and sequential growth processes simultaneously; and to include other model parts that relate to the growth

This research was supported by Grant K02 AA 00230 from the National Institute on Alcohol Abuse and Alcoholism (NIAAA), by Grant R21 AA10948 from NIAAA, and by Grant 40859 from the National Institute of Mental Health. The work benefited from discussions in Hendricks Brown's Prevention Science Methodology group and Muthén's Methods Mentoring Meeting. I thank Tom Harford for suggestions regarding the National Longitudinal Survey of Youth application; Hendricks Brown and Jason Liao for discussion related to intervention studies; Linda Muthén for useful comments; and Siek-Toon Khoo, Booil Jo, Noah Yang, Christy Kim Boscardin, and Ching Yu for helpful research assistance.

model, such as mediators and distal outcomes. For an overview of examples of this kind, see B. Muthén and Curran (1997).

The realization that growth curve modeling is possible using a latent variable conceptualization has enriched SEM research in recent years. By its general modeling framework, however, SEM has also enriched growth modeling. SEM is not about to take a radical leap forward in terms of modeling capabilities, and this will further benefit growth curve modeling. As I describe in this chapter, conventional SEM models using continuous latent variables are for the first time integrated with models using categorical latent variables. Although categorical latent variable modeling has long traditions in the form of latent class analysis (LCA), latent profile analysis (LPA), and latent transition analysis (LTA), these traditions have been completely separated from SEM. Categorical latent variable modeling also encompasses finite mixture modeling in general and goes well beyond LCA, LPA, or LTA. New research reviewed here provides an integration of categorical and continuous latent variable models. Given its generality, it is fitting to describe the emerging methodology as second-generation SEM, where the focus is on the generality of latent variable modeling (LVM). This LVM development promises to be extremely beneficial to growth modeling. The aim of this chapter is to briefly introduce new LVM analyses in the form of general growth mixture modeling (GGMM) and to show examples of the new analysis opportunities for growth modeling that are opened up. In this chapter, I discuss several different types of GGMM applications and analyze two different examples. My presentation is as nontechnical as possible to reach applied researchers. The analyses of the examples were carried out by the new computer program Mplus (L. K. Muthén and Muthén, 1998). Input specifications are available from the website http://www.statmodel.com.

Conventional Latent Growth Modeling

Conventional growth modeling with random coefficients is a useful starting point for introducing the new modeling ideas. The basic ideas, scope, and limitations of conventional growth modeling are discussed here.

Figure 10.1 shows three ways of representing growth modeling: (a) using a graph of individual trajectories, (b) using a two-level model, and (c) using a latent variable model. The top panel of Figure 10.1 shows trajectories for 4 individuals. The mean trajectory is also given as a solid line. One can see that there is variation in the initial status as well as the growth rate. Individuals who start higher grow faster.

The middle panel of Figure 10.1 translates the individual-differences idea into a random-effect model expressed as a multilevel model. The Level 1 equation describes variation as a function of the time score x_t at time point t. For

FIGURE 10.1

Three representations of individual differences in growth.

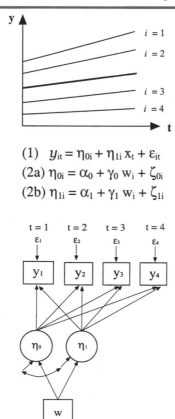

$$(1) \quad y_{it} = \eta_{0i} + \eta_{1i} x_t + \varepsilon_{it}$$
$$(2a) \quad \eta_{0i} = \alpha_0 + \gamma_0 w_i + \zeta_{0i}$$
$$(2b) \quad \eta_{1i} = \alpha_1 + \gamma_1 w_i + \zeta_{1i}$$

example, in an educational study t can be Grade 7, Grade 8, and Grade 9, and the x_ts can be scores representing linear growth—for example, 0, 1, 2—or nonlinear growth—for example, 0, 1, 2.5. Here, η_0 and η_1 represent intercept and slope coefficients in the regression of y on x. The individual differences are captured by letting the intercept and slope vary across individuals, so that the η coefficients have subscript i. These coefficients are referred to as *random coefficients* or *random effects*. Although this allows for across-individual heterogeneity, all individuals are assumed to come from one and the same population so that the analysis benefits from estimating all individuals together. The two Level 2 equations describe variation across individuals for the intercepts and slopes and relate this variation to a background variable w, referred to as a *time-invariant covariate* (time-varying covariates can be included in the Level 1 equation). The fact that the individuals come from a single population is reflected by the absence of a subscript i for the Level 2 parameters of α and γ. Further single population parameters appear in the covariance matrix for the residuals ζ and for the residuals ε. Inserting the intercept and slope of the Level 2 equations into the Level 1 equation gives the model in a form referred to as the *mixed linear model*.

The bottom panel of Figure 10.1 translates the two-level model into a latent variable framework in which the random effects are reconceptualized as latent variables. The Level 1 equation and the Level 2 equations correspond to a measurement and a structural part of a latent variable model, respectively. An advantage of growth modeling in a latent variable framework is that the framework opens up possibilities for general structural equation modeling, including regressions among random coefficients; multiple population analysis with flexible across-group differences in covariance matrix structures; growth modeling of latent variable constructs with multiple indicators; analysis of multiple processes; and the inclusion of other model parts, such as mediational modeling and the analysis of distal outcomes.

A Simple Conventional Growth Model and Its Limitations

Consider a simple linear growth model with an outcome y_{it} for individual i observed at time point t,

$$y_{it} = \eta_{0i} + \eta_{1i}x_t + \varepsilon_{it}, \tag{10.1}$$

where η_{0i} is the intercept factor, η_{1i} is the growth rate factor, x_t is a time score, and ε_{it} is the time-specific residual assumed to be normally distributed. A given individual i has the values η_{0i} and η_{1i} on the two growth factors. The growth process for this individual develops over time as t changes as

$$\eta_{0i} + \eta_{1i}x_t. \tag{10.2}$$

This is individual i's trajectory, describing the systematic part of the variation of the outcome at different time points. The individual's outcome at a certain time point t, y_{it}, is equal to the sum of the systematic part of the variation plus the time-specific residual ε_{it}.

As mentioned above, Equation 10.1 is often referred to as the *Level 1 equation*, describing the repeated measures over time. The Level 2 equation describes the variation in the η_{0i} and η_{1i} factors as a function of covariates x,

$$\eta_{0i} = \alpha_0 + \sum_r \gamma_{0r}w_{ri} + \zeta_{0i}, \tag{10.3}$$

$$\eta_{1i} = \alpha_1 + \sum_r \gamma_{1r}w_{ri} + \zeta_{1i}, \tag{10.4}$$

where α coefficients are intercept parameters, γ coefficients are regression weights for the covariates w_r, and the ζs represent residuals assumed to be bivariate normally distributed.

The parameters of Equations 10.1, 10.3, and 10.4 can be estimated by maximum likelihood. Given such estimates, individual estimates of the growth factor values η_{0i} and η_{1i} can be obtained by the Bayesian approach of maximizing the posterior distribution of the factors given the individual's observed data. In statistics this is referred to as *empirical Bayes estimation*, whereas in psychometrics it is referred to as *factor score estimation using the regression method*.

The five trajectories shown in Figure 10.1 follow the random coefficient growth model of Equations 10.1, 10.3, and 10.4. The bold line is the average trajectory, which is evaluated at the means of the two growth factors η_{0i} and η_{1i}; that is, these factor means are inserted into Equation 10.2. In addition, trajectories are shown for intercept growth factor values of 1 and 2 *SD* below and above the mean, with corresponding slope factor values derived from the bivariate normal distribution. The variation across these five trajectories is due to the individual-specific influence of the covariate x_{ri} and the residuals ζ_{0i} and ζ_{1i}.

Some of the trajectories in Figure 10.1 represent quite different development over time. For example, if the outcome represents reading skills in Grade 1, the two bottom lines labeled $i = 3$ and $i = 4$ may correspond to somewhat problematic or very problematic reading development, whereas the two top lines labeled $i = 2$ and $i = 1$ may correspond to good or excellent reading development. An assumption of the conventional growth model is that all individuals belong to one and the same population. In particular, it is assumed that the w covariates have the same influence on the growth factors for all trajectories; that is, the γ covariate slopes of Equations 10.3 and 10.4 are the same for all individuals. Using the example of the two types of good reading development versus the two types of poor reading development, this assumption of a homogeneous population may not be realistic. For example, the variation in reading development among poor readers may be influenced more by the school environment, whereas the variation in reading development for good readers may be influenced more by the home environment or vice versa. In addition, the variances of the residuals may differ for these two types of development, violating a second assumption in the conventional growth model. Although the conventional growth model captures individual differences in trajectories, it is not always realistic to assume that a single-population model can account for all types of individual differences.

In general, the two types of development just discussed may have not only different antecedents but also different growth shapes, different concurrent processes, and different consequences. For example, problematic first-grade reading development may have a nonlinear shape, may co-occur with the development of aggressive classroom behavior, and may increase the probability of subsequent deficits in achievement development or school dropout. This type of developmental heterogeneity is presumably quite common. In mental health, drug, and alcohol research the recognition of heterogeneity has led to theories of multiple developmental pathways (see, e.g., Moffitt, 1993; on adolescent-limited vs. life-course-persistent antisocial behavior), subtypes (see, e.g., Zucker, 1994, and Schulenberg, O'Malley, Bachman, Wadsworth, & Johnston, 1996, on alcoholism; and Nagin, Farrington, & Moffitt, 1995, on criminal offenders), and different disease processes (see, e.g., Pearson, Morrell, Landis, Carter, & Brant, 1994, on prostate cancer development). Pearson et al.'s (1994) study illustrates some key modeling ideas. It examined the development of prostate-specific antigen (PSA) and related this to later occurrence of tumors and cancers. Whereas the normative development of PSA over age can be described by a linear growth model with variation in intercept and slope, development leading to tumors and cancers is characterized by a change from linear to exponential PSA growth in which the severity of the outcome corresponds to different forms of the growth curves.

In summary, the conventional growth model allows heterogeneity corresponding to different growth trajectories across individuals and captures that by variation in the continuous growth factors. However, the conventional growth model cannot capture heterogeneity that corresponds to qualitatively different development. Although multiple-group SEM growth modeling is a flexible tool for studying qualitatively different development across individuals belonging to known groups, the problem here is that the group membership is typically not known but needs to be inferred from the data. In the next section, I discuss new methodology that introduces categorical latent variable modeling to greatly add to the capability of capturing heterogeneity in development.

Second-Generation Structural Equation Modeling

Second-generation SEM uses a combination of categorical and continuous latent variables. The ideas can be described with the help of the prototypical model structure of Figure 10.2. The figure shows four different modeling frameworks, labeled A, B, C, and D. After describing the statistical techniques, I discuss each framework in turn, with an emphasis on C and D, which provide the new growth modeling opportunities studied in the remainder of this chapter.

What follows is a brief technical description of the model in Framework D, its estimation, and testing. A nontechnical reader can skip this section because the understanding of later sections does not depend on it. The full specifications of the general LVM are given in the Mplus User's Guide (L. K. Muthén & Muthén, 1998), which generalizes the approach of B. Muthén and Shedden

FIGURE 10.2
A general framework for latent variable modeling.

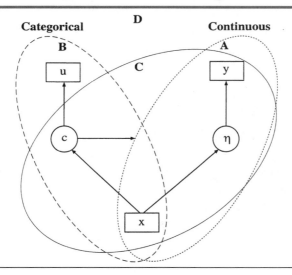

(1999). The formulas below are for a simple example. With linear growth in latent class k ($k = 1, 2, \ldots, K$) the Level 1 growth part of the model is the *measurement model*,

$$y_{itk} = \eta_{0ik} + \eta_{1ik}x_t + \kappa_{tk}w_{itk} + \varepsilon_{itk}, \tag{10.5}$$

whereas the Level 2 part of the model is the *structural model*,

$$\eta_{0ik} = \alpha_{0k} + \gamma_{0k}w_{ik} + \zeta_{0ik}, \tag{10.6}$$

$$\eta_{1ik} = \alpha_{1k} + \gamma_{1k}w_{ik} + \zeta_{1ik}, \tag{10.7}$$

where w_{itk} is a time-varying covariate and w_{ik} is a time-invariant covariate.

A second part of the model includes predictors of the latent class membership variable vector c_i of length K, where $c_{ik} = 1$ if individual i belongs to class k and 0 otherwise. For example, with a single predictor z_{ik},

$$P(c_{ik} = 1 \mid z_{ik}) = \frac{e^{\alpha_{ck} + \gamma_{ck}z_{ik}}}{\sum_{k=1}^{K} e^{\alpha_{ck} + \gamma_{ck}z_{ik}}}, \tag{10.8}$$

a multinomial logistic regression that uses the standardization of zero coefficients for the last class, $\alpha_{cK} = 0$, $\gamma_{cK} = 0$ (see also Agresti, 1990). This gives the logit for the odds of class k relative to class K,

$$logit \; c = \log[P(c_{ik} = 1 \mid z_{ik})/(P(c_{iK} = 1 \mid z_{ik})] = \alpha_{ck} + \gamma_{ck}z_{ik}, \tag{10.9}$$

which is a regular logistic regression in the case of two latent classes.

A third part of the model includes categorical indicators of the latent class variable, u say. The full model can, however, be identified without such latent class indicators. In line with latent class modeling conditional independence is specified for the us given latent class and the background variables of $x_i' = (z_i, w_i, w_{i1}, w_{i2}, \ldots, w_{iT})$. Assuming binary us, a logit regression is specified for each u_j, $(j = 1, 2, \ldots, p)$, for example,

$$logit[P(u_{ij} = 1 | c_{ik} = 1, z_i)] = \lambda_{ujk} + \kappa_{uj} z_{ik}. \tag{10.10}$$

This translates into a probability for u_j,

$$P(u_{ij} = 1 | c_{ik} = 1, z_i) = \frac{1}{1 + e^{-\lambda_{ujk} + \kappa_{uj} z_{ik}}}, \tag{10.11}$$

which, when there is no covariate z, gives the usual conditional probability of latent class analysis. If κ_{uj} is different from zero there is a direct effect from the covariate to the latent class indicator, indicating within-class heterogeneity.

Estimation of model parameters uses maximum likelihood and the EM algorithm. Here, c is considered the missing data in the EM algorithm. EM maximizes the expected complete-data log likelihood log L_c for the vector of outcomes at the T time points $y_i' = (y_{i1}, y_{i2}, \ldots, y_{iT})$ and the vector of c indicators $u_i' = (u_{i1}, u_{i2}, \ldots, u_{ip})$, conditional on the vector $x_i' = (z_i, w_i, w_{i1}, w_{i2}, \ldots, w_{iT})$,

$$E(\log L_c) = E\left\{ \sum_{i=1}^{n} [\log(c_i | x_i) + \log(u_i | c_i, x_i) + \log(y_i | c_i, x_i)] \right\}, \tag{10.12}$$

where $(c_i | x_i)$ denotes the probabilities corresponding to Equation 10.8, $(u_i | x_i)$ denotes the probabilities of the latent class indicators, and

$$(y_i | c_i, x_i) = [N(\mu_{ik}, \Sigma_k)]^{c_{ik}} \tag{10.13}$$

denotes a mixture of normal distributions. The EM iterations consist of E steps followed by M steps, followed by new E and M steps until convergence. The E step computes the expectation of log L_c, which centers on the posterior probability of individual i belonging to class k,

$$p_{ik} = P(c_{ik} = 1 | y_i, u_i, x_i) = P(c_{ik} = 1 | z_{ik}) N(\mu_{ik}, \Sigma_k)(u_i | c_{ik} = 1)/(y_i, u_i | x_i). \tag{10.14}$$

In this way, the E step computation of p_{ik} draws on information from three observed data sources, y_i, u_i, and x_i. The maximization of Equation 10.12 in the M step involves three separate maximizations using the posterior probabilities: a multinomial regression optimization for c on x, a latent class optimization for the u indicators, and an optimization of

$$E\left[\sum_{i=1}^{n} \log(y_i | c_i, x_i) \right] = \sum_{i=1}^{n} \sum_{k=1}^{K} p_{ik} \log N(\mu_{ik}, \Sigma_k). \tag{10.15}$$

The expression in Equation 10.15 corresponds to a simultaneous optimization for the K classes with sampling weights p_{ik}. Using SEM language, the growth mixture modeling with respect to the y part of the model can therefore be seen as a multiple-group analysis but with unobserved group membership. Here, any parameter in μ_{ik}, Σ_k may vary across the K classes. Parameters may be fixed or constrained to be equal in all three parts of the model. Equalities are not permitted between parameters in the different model parts.

Model testing is somewhat more complex with mixture models. For comparison of fit of models that have the same number of classes and are nested, the usual likelihood-ratio chi-square difference test can be used. Comparison of models with different numbers of classes, however, cannot be made using the likelihood-ratio chi-square test common in SEM. It may instead be accomplished by standard information criteria such as Akakike's and Bayesian (BIC). The measures are based on the negative of the log likelihood of the model, with a penalty for the number of parameters. In this way, smaller values indicate better models. In this chapter, I use BIC. The BIC penalty is the number of parameters r multiplied by $ln\ n$, where n is the sample size (Schwartz, 1978),

$$\text{BIC} = -2 \log L + r \ln n. \tag{10.16}$$

Further technical aspects of LVM and its estimation by maximum likelihood were described by B. Muthén, Shedden, and Spisic (1998). The analyses of all examples presented here were carried out by this method as implemented in the computer program Mplus (L. K. Muthén & Muthén, 1998). Mplus is a program that replaces my LISCOMP program. Despite its ability to carry out such general types of models as indicated by Framework D, Mplus has a simple model specification language without matrices or equations that is suitable for applied researchers.

Framework A: Conventional Latent Variable Growth Modeling

The modeling framework labeled A in Figure 10.2 has observed continuous outcomes or latent variable indicators y, latent continuous variables η, and observed background variables x. This encompasses conventional SEM as it has been practiced in the past 25 years (see, e.g., Bollen, 1989). When the observed outcomes represent repeated measures over time, the latent variables are the growth factors, and the background variables are the covariates as in Equations 10.1, 10.3, and 10.4. Framework A was used by B. Muthén and Curran (1997) in their discussion of extensions of conventional growth modeling, particularly for randomized treatment-control studies.

Framework B: Latent Class Modeling

The modeling framework labeled B in Figure 10.2 has categorical latent class indicators u, a categorical latent class variable c, and observed background variables x. This includes conventional latent class analysis (see, e.g., Clogg, 1995) and more recent extensions that add covariates (see Bandeen-Roche, Miglioretti, Zeger, & Rathouz, 1997; Dayton & Macready, 1988; Formann, 1992; and van der Heijden, Dessens, & Böckenholt, 1996). When the latent class indicators represent repeated measures over time, LTA (see, e.g., Collins & Wugalter, 1992) specifies a latent class variable for each time point and analyzes the transition probabilities between classes.

Framework C: Finite Mixture Modeling

The modeling framework labeled C in Figure 10.2 extends Framework A by the categorical latent class variable. The arrow from the latent class variable c to model framework A indicates that the parameters of A can be different for different latent classes. The analogy to conventional SEM is that the latent classes represent multiple populations or groups, but in contrast to multiple-group SEM, group membership is unobserved. This analogy makes it clear that Framework C provides very flexible modeling given that multiple-group SEM allows group differences in any of the parameters. Model C analysis also produces a counterpart to factor scores for continuous latent variables. Given that the latent class variable is categorical, the factor score notion is generalized to posterior probabilities of membership in the different latent classes. A person may be classified into the class that has the highest probability.

Mixture Models for Clustering

In statistics, the latent classes are viewed as mixture components or missing data. A key reference for mixture analysis is Titterington, Smith, and Makov (1985). Most of the statistical research using Framework C does not include latent continuous variables. A typical application is a multivariate model for the outcomes in which the mixture components have the same covariance matrix and different mean vectors. This is a form of cluster analysis given that posterior probabilities of class membership are produced (see, e.g., McLachlan & Basford, 1988). An example is the classic three-component analysis of the Fisher Iris data (see, e.g., Everitt & Hand, 1981). In psychometrics, related classic work considers latent profile analysis (see, e.g., Bartholomew, 1987; Gibson, 1959), assuming a diagonal covariance matrix for each component.

Complier Average Causal Effect Modeling

Little and Yau (1998) gave a novel example of a latent class variable viewed as missing data. This introduces the concept of complier average causal effect (CACE) estimation. In intervention studies, not all individuals invited for treatment actually choose to participate. Those who do choose to participate are typically not a random subset of those invited. Because of the randomization, the control group has the same subgroup of individuals who potentially would participate had they been invited. Here, latent classes corresponding to those who participate versus those who do not participate are used to give an assessment of treatment effects comparing participants in the treatment group with potential participants in the control group. For those randomized into the treatment group, the latent class membership is observed. For individuals in the control group, however, information on category membership is missing, that is, class membership is a latent categorical variable. This is a promising new technique that can also be used in growth modeling contexts.

Mixture Structural Equation Modeling

Framework C has been considered in an SEM context. For example, Blåfield (1980); Jedidi, Ramaswamy, DeSarbo, and Wedel (1996); Arminger and Stein (1997); Yung (1997); Jedidi, Jagpal, and DeSarbo (1997); and Arminger, Stein, and Wittenberg (1999) have studied mixture confirmatory factor analysis and SEM. The models studied by these authors, however, are more limited than what is shown as Framework C in Figure 10.2. This is because the models do not allow for the regression of the latent class variable on the background variables. This limitation is shared by most mixture modeling, two recent exceptions being those by Little and Yau (1998) and by Nagin (1999). Not including the regression of the latent class variable on the background variables has two drawbacks. First, the probabilities of latent class membership are taken to be the same for individuals with different values on the background variables, which may be unrealistic in many settings. Second, a two-stage estimation is necessary when exploring the characteristics of the latent classes. Instead of a joint maximum-likelihood analysis of the full model for the latent variable indicators, the latent continuous variables, the latent class variable, and the background variables, a second-stage analysis is needed in which estimated posterior probabilities for the latent classes are related to the background variables.

Growth Mixture Modeling

The primary focus for Framework C in this chapter is growth mixture modeling. Verbeke and Lesaffre (1996) discussed a mixed linear model approach to random coefficient growth modeling with a mixture that allows for different means of the random coefficients. Extending the work of Nagin and Land (1993), Nagin (1999); and Roeder, Lynch, and Nagin (1999) have discussed modeling of different trajectory classes with normal and non-normal outcomes. Nagin also recognized the importance of estimating the effects of class membership on covariates. His modeling considers fixed-effect growth within class so that all individuals are assumed to have the same within-class trajectory. His approach is termed *latent class growth mixture analysis.*

In this chapter, I consider a flexible random coefficient growth mixture model that allows within-class variation in individual trajectories. Allowing for within-class variability appears to be important in practice. Analyses of several data sets have shown that a clear-cut choice of the number of classes is not provided by BIC when requiring no within-class variability, whereas a clear-cut choice is provided when allowing within-class variability. The growth mixture model is based on Framework C. Framework C may be viewed as providing Model Framework A for each latent class category and therefore allows for considerable modeling generality. It can also be extended to Framework D, discussed next.

Framework D: General Latent Variable Modeling

The modeling framework labeled D in Figure 10.2 is a combination of the other frameworks and is referred to as *general latent variable modeling* (LVM). This may be seen as second-generation SEM, given that the modeling capabilities are vastly enhanced relative to conventional SEM. Because the generality is gained by the introduction of both categorical and continuous latent variables, it seems appropriate to focus on the concept of latent variables and use LVM. LVM expands latent class modeling, finite mixture modeling, and SEM. On the one hand, LVM recognizes the usefulness of expanding the latent class framework. LCA concerns a particular mixture model of independence among a set of categorical latent class indicators. In contrast, LVM lets the latent classes also influence more general mixture models for the other model parts of Framework A. On the other hand, LVM recognizes the usefulness of expanding finite mixture modeling to include direct indicators of the mixture components. Finite mixture modeling infers mixture component membership from the distribution of the latent variable indicators and the background variables. In contrast, LVM can let the latent class and latent class indicator part of the model be a specific measurement model from which class membership can be inferred beyond the information from the observed variables in Framework A.

From a growth modeling perspective, the new growth modeling opportunities made available in LVM may be labeled general growth mixture modeling, as was done by B. Muthén, Brown, Khoo, Yang, & Jo (1998). In summary, GGMM goes beyond conventional random coefficient growth modeling by using latent trajectory classes that allow for heterogeneity with respect to the influence of antecedents, growth shapes, concurrent outcomes, and later consequences. Two additional features of the analysis are particularly noteworthy: confirmatory analysis and estimation of class membership probabilities.

Confirmatory analysis is a key element in conventional SEM. A priori hypotheses can be captured by parameter restrictions. For instance, factor loadings may be fixed at zero to reflect the belief that a certain factor is not measured by a certain indicator. GGMM in Framework D offers not only the same kind of confirmatory analysis but also a second type of confirmatory analysis that concerns not hypotheses about parameters but about individuals' class membership.

Confirmatory analysis with respect to parameters is very useful in growth settings. For example, there may be quadratic growth for one class, but the growth shape of a second class is hypothesized to be linear. Here, the quadratic growth factor mean and variance are fixed to zero for the second class. Or one class may have the mean of one of its growth factors constrained to be larger than that of another class. The mixture analysis benefits greatly from these types of confirmatory restrictions. In contrast, conventional finite mixture analysis is typically exploratory. Finite mixture analysis is known to sometimes give rise to numerical analysis problems, such as nonconvergence and multiple maxima of the likelihood. Confirmatory mixture analysis limits the occurrence of such problems. Recent experiences show that growth mixture analysis is a relatively well-behaved form of mixture analysis, given the multivariate trend information in the data and the possibilities for formulating confirmatory hypotheses.

Confirmatory analysis with respect to the class membership of the individuals is a feature not found in SEM. With a latent class variable, however, a researcher may want to incorporate the hypothesis that certain individuals are known to represent typical trajectories corresponding to a certain class. This knowledge may be due to auxiliary information or because the individual displays such a typical growth pattern. For example, students who are known to have been diagnosed as having reading disability in second grade may have a characteristic reading skills trajectory in the first grade. Individuals with known class membership are sometimes referred to as *training data*. As is the case of using parameter restrictions, the numerical performance of the mixture analysis benefits greatly from incorporating training data. It may be noted that multiple-group SEM corresponds to the case of all sample units contributing training data so that the latent class variable is in effect an observed categorical variable.

GGMM is a promising tool for the analysis of randomized trials. A discussion of GGMM in preventive intervention settings was given by Muthén, Brown, et al. (1998). Interventions often show an interaction between treatment and characteristics of the individual. Important individual characteristics can be captured by developmental trajectory classes. Differences between classes may refer not only to baseline characteristics, such as the initial status of a growth model (B. Muthén & Curran, 1997), but also to growth rate and, more generally, growth shape. GGMM analysis allows the effect of treatment to vary across trajectory class and is therefore able to give a more detailed assessment of treatment effects. It is also useful to add the notion of partial compliance and use CACE estimation based on latent compliance classes. The use of GGMM in conjunction with CACE gives a flexible analysis framework for randomized trials; for some initial work see Jo and Muthén (in press).

GGMM solves a problem with piecewise growth modeling used to represent different stages of development. A weakness of piecewise growth modeling is that the point of transition from one stage to the next needs to be both known and the same for all individuals in the sample. GGMM allows more flexible piecewise growth modeling in which different unknown classes of individuals make the transition at different time points. The model would seem to be of particular interest in intervention studies in which a certain treatment may take effect after different amounts of time for different classes of individuals.

A final general comment on GGMM concerns the benefit of estimating an individual's posterior probabilities of class membership. This is the counterpart of factor scores in conventional SEM. Given an estimated model, each individual obtains a posterior probability estimate for each class computed as a function of the model parameter estimates and the individual's values on his or her observed variables. The class to which the individual most likely belongs can therefore be determined.

Estimation of class membership probabilities is of particular interest with longitudinal data. Consider as an example a model for development of reading skills through first and second grades. A GGMM analysis estimates the parameters for this development. The class membership probabilities can then be estimated for a new student before the student reaches the end of second grade using only the subset of the repeated measures available at that point in time. It is of interest to study the precision with which such probabilities can be estimated at different points in time. As an example, B. Muthén, Khoo, Francis, and Kim Boscardin (1998) conducted a study in which first-grade development was related to kindergarten precursors. This allows for a mechanism for early prediction of problematic development. The analysis approach may be particularly useful in diagnostic or preventive intervention settings. Not only may individuals who belong to different classes benefit differently from a treatment program, but also the analysis could possibly guide in the choice of treatment variation.

Examples

1. Analysis of Math Achievement Development

Example 1 uses a subset of data from the Longitudinal Study of American Youth. The analyses consider females in the younger cohort measured at four time points, Grade 7–Grade 10, beginning in 1987. Math achievement items and background information from parents on mother's education and home resources are used. Conventional random coefficient growth analysis of both girls and boys indicates that mother's education and home resources play important roles in predicting math achievement development.

In Example 1, a growth mixture model is explored for 984 girls with complete data on the variables. Figure 10.3 shows the general GGMM framework applied to this example. The latent categorical variable is represented by the circle labeled c. The intercept factor is labeled I, and the slope factor is labeled S. The analysis is first carried out without the two covariates mother's education and home resources (unconditional analysis) and then including these covariates (conditional analysis). The prediction of latent class membership from the covariates will be introduced as the last step of the analysis.

Unconditional Analysis

Growth mixture modeling encompasses many different model variations, and it is therefore helpful to have a good model-fitting strategy. As an initial step, one can explore the data by plotting individual observed or fitted curves. For example, with the four time points available here, a line can be estimated and plotted for each person. It may be difficult, however, to see clusters in such a set of individual curves. Two initial modeling approaches are recommended. One is to perform a conventional (one-class) growth model to get a notion of the extent of growth factor variation. Estimated individual curves can be plotted. Another approach is to search for typical classes of growth curves using latent class growth mixture analysis (LCGA), referred to in Growth Mixture Modeling. LCGA is a special case of the GGMM framework in which the growth factor covariance matrix has been fixed at zero so that there is no within-class trajectory variation. LCGA can be carried out for several different numbers of classes, producing a plot of BIC against a number of classes. The LCGA solution for the number of classes above in which no important drop in BIC occurs can be used to plot estimated mean curves. This curve plot gives an idea of how many qualitatively different numbers of classes there are; say, m. Choosing the m-class LCGA solution as a starting point, a GGMM analysis can be carried out to explore within-class variability, letting the growth factor covariance matrix be freely estimated. This model-fitting strategy will now be used. As mentioned earlier, comparison of models with different numbers of classes can be accomplished by using an information criterion such as BIC. For models that have the same number of classes and are nested, the usual likelihood-ratio chi-square difference test can be used.

The conventional one-class growth model has a BIC value of 25,534.45. The model fits well as tested against an unrestricted mean- and covariance-

FIGURE 10.3

Math achievement modeling. Mothed = mother's education; Homeres = home resources.

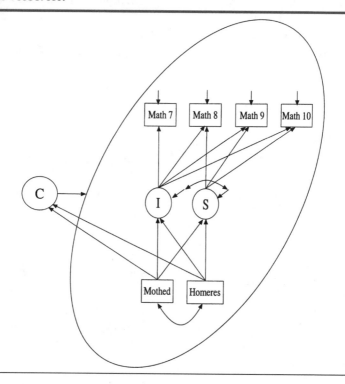

structure model: $\chi^2(3, N = 984) = 4.22$, $p = .237$, root mean square error of approximation (RMSEA) = .020 (confidence interval [CI]: .000, .061). The intercept mean, which is equal to the initial status at Grade 7, is 52.78, and the growth rate mean is 2.59. Nonlinear growth is accommodated by estimated time score values x_t at the last two grades. The growth is accelerated between Grade 8 and Grade 9, with the time score value for Grade 9 estimated as 2.45 instead of the linear growth value of 2.0. The estimated time score value for Grade 10 is 3.50. The growth factor variances are 64.50 and 1.29, respectively. Both are significantly different from zero. The growth factor correlation is .34. The residual variances for the outcomes are estimated at 14.55, 13.20, 14.13, and 26.53.

For the series of LCGA, starting values for the growth curves can be based on the conventional one-class growth model estimates, using values in the range of the growth factor means and ±2 growth factor standard deviations. The corresponding BIC values are shown in Figure 10.4. The LCGA BIC curve levels off smoothly as the number of classes increases and does not point to a definite

FIGURE 10.4

Longitudinal Study of American Youth Bayesian information criteria (BIC) values for latent class growth mixture analysis (LCGA) and general growth mixture modeling (GGMM).

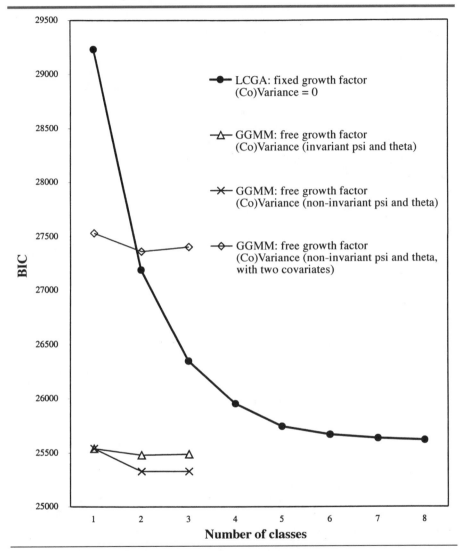

number of classes as the best model. In fact, the figure shows that not even with eight classes is the LCGA BIC better than for the conventional one-class growth model. The estimated mean curves for the eight-class LCGA are shown in Figure 10.5. The more frequent the curve, the thicker the curve. Typical curves have high initial status with high growth rate and low initial status with

FIGURE 10.5

Longitudinal Study of American Youth mean curves for eight classes with zero factor variance.

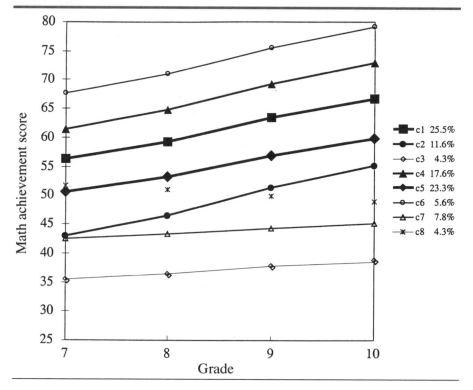

low growth rate. It is unclear if there are several major types of classes of curves or if there is only one class with individual variation. Figure 10.6 shows the LCGA mean curves using two and three classes. These solutions are used as starting values for GGMM analyses.

A first GGMM uses two latent classes and lets the growth factor means for the intercept factor and the slope factor vary across the classes while all other parameters are held invariant across the classes. This results in a BIC value of 25,478.22, which should be compared with the conventional single-class growth model BIC of 25,534.45 with three fewer parameters (two growth factor mean parameters and one class probability parameter). This means that the two-class model is preferable on the basis of BIC. A corresponding three-class model has a worse BIC value of 25,488.68. GGMM with two and three classes are also fitted with class-varying growth factor covariance matrix and residual variances, resulting in BIC values of 25,330.92 and 25,331.80, slightly favoring the two-class model. The BIC curves are included in Figure 10.4; see bottom left of the figure. Figure 10.4 also includes the corresponding GGMM curve with class-varying (co)variances when adding the two covariates; see top left of the figure. The two-class model is also favored when including the covariates.

The first two-class model imposes class invariance of the covariance matrix for the two growth factors as well as class invariance of the variances for the residuals of the outcomes. Letting the variances for the residuals of the outcomes vary across the two classes gives a log likelihood value of $-12,597.91$. Because the two-class model with invariant residual variances has a log likelihood value of $-12,690.87$, the test of invariance is given by a likelihood-ratio chi-square difference test value with 4 df equal to 185.92. This indicates that the residual variances need to be different across classes.

Also letting the factor covariance matrix differ across the two classes gives a log likelihood value of $-12,593.10$ and $\chi^2(3, N = 984) = 9.62$, $p = .025$, providing a weak indication that these parameters need to be different across the classes. For this model there are 42% in Class 1 which, compared with Class 2, is characterized by low starters who grow slowly. The mean curves are shown in Figure 10.6. For Class 1 the outcome residual variances are estimated as 16.42, 16.33, 22.97, and 49.06, whereas for Class 2 they are estimated as 12.52, 11.28, 8.34, and 7.80. The largest difference is for Grade 10, showing a larger degree of time-specific variance for the low-performing class. For Class 1 the intercept variance is 53,88, whereas for Class 2 it is 40.49. For Class 1 the slope variance is 1.81, whereas for Class 2 it is 0.20. All of these variances are significant except the last one mentioned. Although the growth rate variation for Class 1 is significant, the insignificant slope variance for Class 2 indicates that students in this well-performing class develop equally fast. In summary, the two classes show quite different development.

Conditional Analysis

In the conditional analysis the growth factors are predicted using the two covariates mother's education and home resources. The sample size is now reduced to 935. A conventional one-class growth model indicates that mother's education and home resources are both significant predictors of the intercept growth factor, whereas only home resources is significant for the slope factor. The BIC value is 27,534.74. The model fits well as judged by conventional means—the chi-square test of model fit is 15.85 with 7 degrees of freedom ($p = .027$), RMSEA = .037 (CI: .012, .061). The Figure 10.4 BIC plot for the GGMM with covariates suggests a two-class model when using a class-varying factor covariance matrix and residual variances. The two-class model has a BIC value of 27,364.85. The percentage of individuals in Class 1 is estimated as 42%, the same value as for the unconditional analysis indicating a stable classification. For Class 1, mother's education is a significant predictor of the in-

FIGURE 10.6

Longitudinal Study of American Youth mean curves for two and three classes. BIC = Bayesian information criteria.

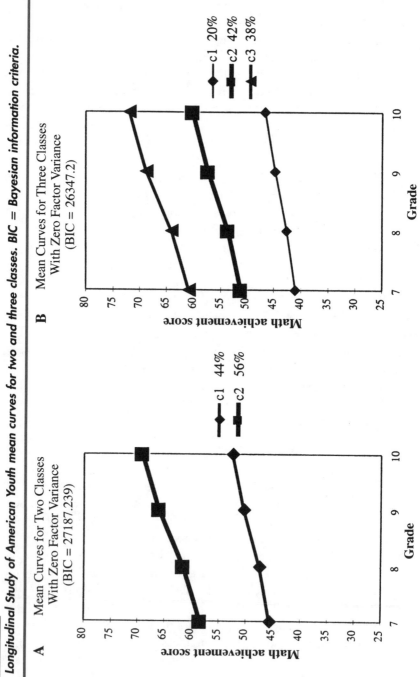

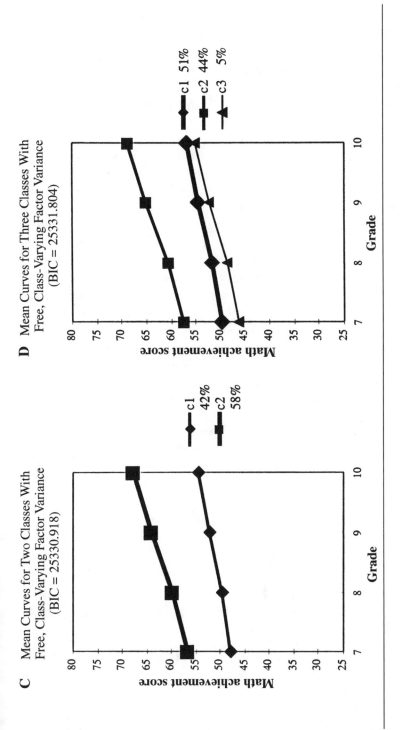

D Mean Curves for Three Classes With Free, Class-Varying Factor Variance (BIC = 25331.804)

c1 51%
c2 44%
c3 5%

C Mean Curves for Two Classes With Free, Class-Varying Factor Variance (BIC = 25330.918)

c1 42%
c2 58%

tercept factor but not the slope factor, whereas home resources is a significant predictor of the slope factor but not the intercept factor. For Class 2, mother's education and home resources are both significant for the intercept but not for the slope. The two-class analysis shows that the home-resource variable plays different roles in the two classes. Home resources is an important factor for the Grade 7 math achievement initial status only for students who are developing well (Class 2) and is important for the math growth rate only for those who are not developing well (Class 1).

The estimated model is given in Table 10.1. The estimated time scores are held equal across class. When allowed to vary across class, a worse BIC value is obtained: 27,375.63. The two-class results can be contrasted with the conventional one-class analysis. The conventional analysis mistakenly concludes that home resources are important for initial status and for growth for all individuals. Conventional tests of model fit indicate no misfit of the one-class model. In contrast, GGMM BIC testing suggests a mixture of two subpopulations. The two-class analysis is of educational importance in that it unmixes these two different subpopulations and carefully delineates the impact of home resources on math achievement development. An ad hoc alternative is to divide the sample into subsets of low- and high-scoring individuals in Grade 7 before the analysis. Such subsetting, however, is not recommended for three reasons. First, the subsetting would be made with respect to the observed score, which is a fallible measure of the initial status growth factor. Second, the subsetting would be made with respect to a dependent variable in the growth model, which distorts the underlying population relationships. Third, the subsetting would be made in a subjective fashion. GGMM avoids all of these problems.

As shown in the GGMM Framework C in Figure 10.3, the latent class membership may also be related to the two covariates. As part of the GGMM analysis, the logit regression of c on mother's education and home resources for the final two-class model showed no significant influence on the probability of membership in Class 1, although the logit coefficients were negative, as expected. Other, more powerful covariates may be brought in to predict class membership. Finally, posterior probabilities of class membership can be computed for each individual for further study.

2. Analysis of Normative and Non-Normative Development in Heavy Drinking

Example 2 uses a subset of data from the National Longitudinal Survey of Youth (NLSY). The outcome variable is frequency of heavy drinking (six or more drinks on one occasion) during the past 30 days. Covariates are gender, ethnicity, family history of alcohol problems, early start of regular drinking (age 14 or younger), dropping out of high school, and college attendance. For this

TABLE 10.1

Estimates for Final LSAY Two-Class Model

PARAMETER	CLASS 1 (42%)			CLASS 2 (58%)		
	ESTIMATE	SE	z	ESTIMATE	SE	z
Intercept factor regression						
Intercept	42.73	1.65	25.92	45.37	1.46	31.05
Mothed	1.66	0.63	2.65	2.09	0.38	5.55
Homeres	0.72	0.38	1.91	1.81	0.29	6.33
Residual variance	54.30	6.09	8.91	32.43	4.65	6.97
Slope factor regression						
Intercept	0.82	0.37	2.23	2.85	0.32	9.02
Mothed	0.15	0.15	0.95	0.03	0.08	0.36
Homeres	0.23	0.09	2.63	0.05	0.06	0.94
Residual variance	1.64	0.63	2.62	0.19	0.26	0.72
Residual covariance, intercept–slope	0.73	1.64	0.44	0.48	0.58	0.83
Residual variance						
Grade 7	17.20	2.84	6.06	12.25	1.59	7.72
Grade 8	15.26	2.08	7.35	11.38	1.24	9.14
Grade 9	24.17	3.29	7.34	8.01	1.42	5.64
Grade 10	49.11	10.04	4.89	7.35	1.31	5.60

PARAMETER	ESTIMATE	SE	z
Time score			
Grade 9	2.42	0.13	18.16
Grade 10	3.50	0.20	17.57
Latent class logit	−0.33	0.31	−1.06

Note. Bayesian information criteria = 27,364.85. Number of parameters = 29. LSAY = Longitudinal Study of American Youth.

FIGURE 10.7
Modeling of heavy drinking.

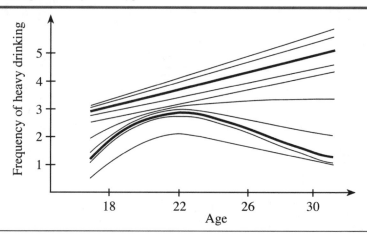

illustration heavy drinking is considered for one of eight NLSY cohorts covering ages 18, 19, 20, 24, 25, and 30. The sample size is 922.

A quadratic growth model has been found suitable for the development of heavy drinking over ages 18–37 (B. Muthén & Muthén, 2000). The growth curve shape at the average of the three growth factors is given as the bottom solid curve in Figure 10.7, showing an increase from 18 to 21 with a subsequent decrease. This normative growth curve shape has also been found for delinquent behavior and illicit drug sampling. One may ask if there are also other, non-normative, growth curve shapes represented in this population. For example, some individuals may show an increase from 18 to 21 but no downturn as illustrated by the solid line. Given that the conventional, single-class, quadratic random coefficient model allows for individual variation in all three growth factors, the solid line trajectory shape is actually included as a special case in the conventional model. The question is whether a better fit to the data can be obtained by a two-class growth model in which the classes differ in their means on the three growth factors. In line with the GGMM model Framework C, such a two-class model can be used to estimate the influence of covariates on the probability of class membership. The model can also be used to estimate each individual's most likely trajectory class membership.

Growth Curve Shapes

B. Muthén and Shedden (1999) performed GGMM analyses on the NLSY data. The same model search strategy as in Example 1 can be carried out. The BIC plot for LCGA with 1–8 classes is shown in Figure 10.8 together with BIC

FIGURE 10.8

National Longitudinal Survey of Youth Bayesian information criteria (BIC) values for latent class growth mixture analysis (LCGA) and general growth mixture modeling (GGMM).

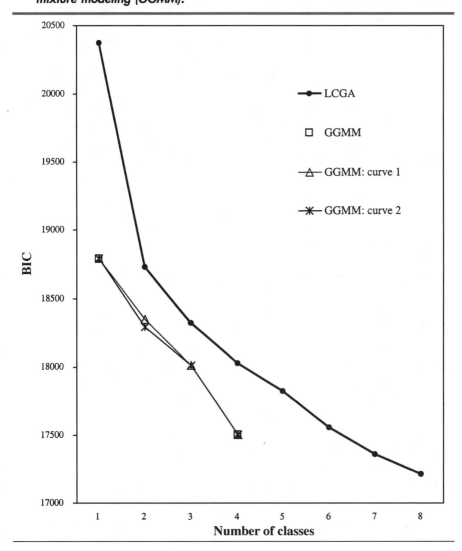

values for GGMM with 1–4 classes. The two-class GGMM resulted in two different solutions; the two solutions shared the normative curve for the majority but had different non-normative curves. A three-class solution showed all three kinds of curve shapes and was also found to fit the data better in terms of BIC value. A three-class solution in line with Muthén and Shedden is shown in Figure 10.9. The normative class probability was estimated as 77%, whereas the two non-normative class probabilities were estimated as 14% and 9%, respectively. The four-class solution has an even better BIC value, with two classes starting high at age 18, but does not alter the general conclusions and is not presented here.

As part of the GGMM analysis, membership in the three classes is also related to the set of covariates. Table 10.2 shows the estimates of the corresponding multinomial logistic regression. In the table, *High* refers to the class in Figure 10.9 that is high already at age 18, *Increase* refers to the class that increases over age, and *Norm* refers to the normative class. In the column labeled *High vs. norm* the coefficients show how the odds of belonging to the high class compared to the normative class is significantly increased for individuals who are male and have early onset and is significantly decreased for individuals who are Black and did not go to college. In the column labeled *Increase vs. norm*, the coefficients show how the odds of belonging to the increasing class compared to the normative class is significantly increased for individuals who are male, have a family history of alcohol problems, and dropped out of high school.

Growth Curve Shapes as Predictors of Distal Outcomes

The three-class model is now embedded in a larger model shown in Figure 10.10. The model will now be used to predict a binary variable of alcohol dependence at age 30. The latent trajectory class variable in Figure 10.10 is seen to influence the growth curve shape of heavy drinking development by means of the growth factor means, and the latent trajectory class variable is predicted by covariates. The additional feature in Figure 10.10 is the prediction of alcohol dependence by trajectory class. This is a logistic regression relationship, although the predictor variable is latent. In Figure 10.2 terms, alcohol dependence is an example of a latent class indicator variable, and the model is an example of Model Framework D.

The use of a latent trajectory class variable as a predictor solves a dilemma that occurs when one tries to use the continuous growth factors as predictors. Consider as an example the two trajectory classes of Figure 10.7. Here the growth factor representing linear growth rate concerns the rate of increase right after age 18. This linear growth rate factor is not, however, a suitable predictor of later problematic alcohol use outcomes, because both classes have a high positive slope value. Likewise, if there is a third class that is high already at age 18, a nonpositive slope may be predictive of problematic outcomes. The key issue is that the growth factor values interact in determining the growth shape, and it is the shape that is predictive.

Table 10.3 shows the resulting estimates of the relation between trajectory

FIGURE 10.9

Estimated heavy-drinking curves.

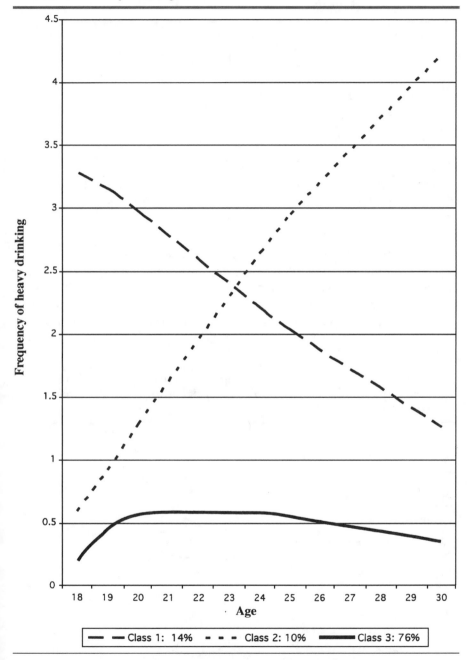

Class 1: 14%   Class 2: 10%   Class 3: 76%

TABLE 10.2

Predicting Trajectory Class Membership in the NLSY:
Estimated Logit Coefficients

COVARIATE	HIGH VS. NORM	INCREASE VS. NORM
Male	1.45*	1.50*
Black	−1.94*	−0.14
Hispanic	−0.49	−0.10
Early onset	1.49*	0.78*
FH123	0.45	1.07*
Dropout	0.37	0.77*
College	−0.63*	−0.92*

Note. NLSY = National Longitudinal Survey of Youth; FH123 = Family history of alcohol problems among first- and second- or third-degree relatives.
*$p < .05$.

class and alcohol dependence. Although the normative class ($c = 3$) has an estimated probability of .05 of developing alcohol dependence by age 30, the two non-normative classes have elevated probabilities of .59 ($c = 2$) and .20 ($c = 1$), respectively. Table 10.3 also gives the odds of developing alcohol dependence in each class and the corresponding odds ratios when comparing a class with

FIGURE 10.10

Modeling of heavy drinking: Predicting a distal outcome. FH = family history of alcohol problems; ASB = antisocial behavior; HSDrp = high school dropout.

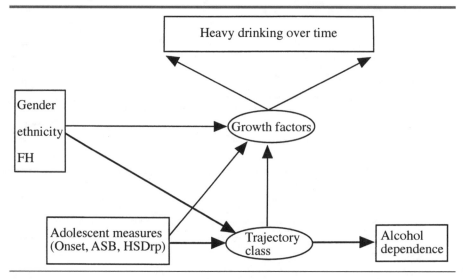

TABLE 10.3
Probability of Dependence Given Class

PROBABILITY FUNCTION	ODDS	ODDS RATIO
$P(\text{Dep}|c = 1) = .20$	0.26	5.19
$P(\text{Dep}|c = 2) = .59$	1.43	29.07
$P(\text{Dep}|c = 3) = .05$	0.05	1.00

the normative class. Given that the probabilities vary so strongly as a function of the latent trajectory class membership, it is of great importance to be able to predict the class membership as early as possible using both covariate information and early information on heavy-drinking development.

Conclusion

It is clear from the examples that GGMM is an important new development for the study of change. The new modeling opportunities will enrich growth modeling and allow more complex ideas of development based on substantive theories in various fields. GGMM is strengthened by the fact that it is part of a general latent variable framework. In this way, it is likely that growth modeling and latent-variable modeling will each continue to benefit from developments in the other's area.

References

Agresti, A. (1990). *Categorical data analysis*. New York: Wiley.

Arminger, G., & Stein, P. (1997). Finite mixtures of covariance structure models with regressors. *Sociological Methods and Research, 26,* 148–182.

Arminger, G., Stein, P., & Wittenberg, J. (1999). Mixtures of conditional mean- and covariance-structure models. *Psychometrika, 64,* 475–494.

Bandeen-Roche, K., Miglioretti, D. L., Zeger, S. L., & Rathouz, P. J. (1997). Latent variable regression for multiple discrete outcomes. *Journal of the American Statistical Association, 92,* 1375–1386.

Bartholomew, D. J. (1987). *Latent variable models and factor analysis*. New York: Oxford University Press.

Blåfield, E. (1980). *Clustering of observations from finite mixtures with structural information*. Unpublished doctoral dissertation, Jyväskyla Studies in Computer Science, Economics, and Statistics, Jyväskyla, Finland.

Bollen, K. A. (1989). *Structural equations with latent variables*. New York: Wiley.

Clogg, C. C. (1995). Latent class models. In G. Arminger, C. C. Clogg, & M. E. Sobel (Eds.), *Handbook of statistical modeling for the social and behavioral sciences* (pp. 311–359). New York: Plenum Press.

Collins, L. M., & Wugalter, S. E. (1992). Latent class models for stage-sequential dynamic latent variables. *Multivariate Behavioral Research, 27,* 131–157.

Dayton, C. M., & Macready, G. B. (1988). Concomitant variable latent class models. *Journal of the American Statistical Association, 83,* 173–178.

Everitt, B. S., & Hand, D. J. (1981). *Finite mixture distributions.* London: Chapman & Hall.

Formann, A. K. (1992). Linear logistic latent class analysis for polytomous data. *Journal of the American Statistical Association, 87,* 476–486.

Gibson, W. A. (1959). Three multivariate models: Factor analysis, latent structure analysis, and latent profile analysis. *Psychometrika, 24,* 229–252.

Jedidi, K., Jagpal, H. S., & DeSarbo, W. S. (1997). Finite-mixture structural equation models for response-based segmentation and unobserved heterogeneity. *Marketing Science, 16,* 39–59.

Jedidi, K., Ramaswamy, V., DeSarbo, W. S., & Wedel, M. (1996). On estimating finite mixtures of multivariate regression and simultaneous equation models. *Structural Equation Modeling, 3,* 266–289.

Jo, B., & Muthén, B. (in press). Intervention studies with noncompliance: Complier average causal effect estimation in growth mixture modeling. In N. Duan & S. Reise (Eds.), *Multilevel modeling: Methodological advances, issues, and applications.* Mahwah, NJ: Erlbaum.

Little, R. J., & Yau, L. H. Y. (1998). Statistical techniques for analyzing data from prevention trials: Treatment of no-shows using Rubin's causal model. *Psychological Methods, 3,* 147–159.

McLachlan, G. J., & Basford, K. E. (1988). *Mixture models: Inference and applications to clustering.* New York: Marcel Dekker.

Meredith, W., & Tisak, J. (1990). Latent curve analysis. *Psychometrika, 55,* 107–122.

Moffitt, T. E. (1993). Adolescence-limited and life-course persistent antisocial behavior. *Psychological Review, 100,* 674–701.

Muthén, B., Brown, C. H., Khoo, S., Yang, C., & Jo, B. (1998, June). *General growth mixture modeling of latent trajectory classes: Perspectives and prospects.* Paper presented at the annual meeting of the Prevention Science and Methodology Group, Tempe, AZ.

Muthén, B., & Curran, P. (1997). General longitudinal modeling of individual differences in experimental designs: A latent variable framework for analysis and power estimation. *Psychological Methods, 2,* 371–402.

Muthén, B., Khoo, S. T., Francis, D., & Kim Boscardin, C. (1998). *Analysis of reading skills development from kindergarten through first grade: An application of growth mixture modeling to sequential processes.* Unpublished manuscript, University of California, Los Angeles.

Muthén, B., & Muthén, L. (2000). The development of heavy drinking and alcohol-related problems from ages 18 to 37 in a U.S. national sample. *Journal of Studies on Alcohol, 61*, 290–300.

Muthén, B., & Shedden, K. (1999). Finite mixture modeling with mixture outcomes using the EM algorithm. *Biometrics, 55*, 463–469.

Muthén, B., Shedden, K., & Spisic, D. (1998). *General latent variable mixture modeling.* Unpublished manuscript, University of California, Los Angeles.

Muthén, L. K., & Muthén, B. (1998). *Mplus user's guide.* Los Angeles, CA: Muthén & Muthén.

Nagin, D. S. (1999). Analyzing developmental trajectories: A semi-parametric, group-based approach. *Psychological Methods, 4*, 139–157.

Nagin, D., Farrington, D., & Moffitt, T. (1995). Life-course trajectories of different types of offenders. *Criminology, 33*, 111–139.

Nagin, D. S., & Land, K. C. (1993). Age, criminal careers, and population heterogeneity: Specification and estimation of a nonparametric, mixed Poisson model. *Criminology, 31*, 327–362.

Pearson, J. D., Morrell, C. H., Landis, P. K., Carter, H. B., & Brant, L. J. (1994). Mixed-effect regression models for studying the natural history of prostate disease. *Statistics in Medicine, 13*, 587–601.

Roeder, K., Lynch, K. G., & Nagin, D. S. (1999). Modeling uncertainty in latent class membership: A case study in criminology. *Journal of the American Statistical Association, 94*, 766–776.

Schulenberg, J., O'Malley, P. M., Bachman, J. G., Wadsworth, K. N., & Johnston, L. D. (1996). Getting drunk and growing up: Trajectories of frequent binge drinking during the transition to young adulthood. *Journal of Studies on Alcohol, 57*, 289–304.

Schwartz, G. (1978). Estimating the dimension of a model. *Annals of Statistics, 6*, 461–464.

Titterington, D. M., Smith, A. F. M., & Makov, U. E. (1985). *Statistical analysis of finite mixture distributions.* Chichester, UK: Wiley.

van der Heijden, P. G. M., Dessens, J., & Böckenholt, U. (1996). Estimating the concomitant-variable latent-class model with the EM algorithm. *Journal of Educational and Behavioral Statistics, 21*, 215–229.

Verbeke, G., & Lesaffre, E. (1996). A linear mixed-effects model with heterogeneity in the random-effects population. *Journal of the American Statistical Association, 91*, 217–221.

Yung, Y. F. (1997). Finite mixtures in confirmatory factor-analysis models. *Psychometrika, 62*, 297–330.

Zucker, R. A. (1994). Pathways to alcohol problems and alcoholism: A developmental account of the evidence for multiple alcoholisms and for contextual contributions to risk. In R. A. Zucker, J. Howard, & G. M. Boyd (Eds.), *The development of alcohol problems: Exploring the biopsychosocial matrix of risk* (NIAAA Research Monograph No. 26, pp. 255–289). Rockville, MD: U.S. Department of Health and Human Services.

The Next Steps in Latent Variable Models for Change

David Rindskopf

I am delighted to provide commentary on the thoughtful chapters of Bengt Muthén and Linda Collins. Each chapter breaks new ground in latent variable analysis. In addition, each chapter stimulated a number of ideas and led me to consider some general points about data analysis and about possible future steps; these ideas form the basis for my comments.

Should a Latent Variable Be Continuous or Categorical?

If a latent variable is really discrete and is modeled as continuous, then the distribution should be multimodal, or at least distinctly non-normal. Estimates of such a latent variable, when used in a mixture analysis, should form a distinct number of components. In between the extremes of believing in continuity without checking and doing a formal mixture analysis is the possibility of using exploratory graphical methods to examine the distribution of estimates of latent variables.

The other side of this issue is when latent variables that are "really" continuous are modeled as discrete in a latent class or similar analysis. For example, people may be classified as drug or alcohol dependent, when drug and alcohol usage could actually be measured on a quantitative scale. Similarly, the diagnosis of people on psychiatric conditions implies a categorical nature of such conditions that may not be warranted. Sometimes such categorization is done not because the researcher believes in categories for the variable but because the consequences are discrete; for example, one either gives someone treatment for drug or alcohol problems or one does not, and one treats someone with drugs, psychotherapy, both, or neither. Even if such categorization is inevitable at the stage of consequences, there is scientific interest in whether the behaviors appear to be closer to being on a continuum or to being discrete categories. This is always an empirical issue, and it deserves to be examined closely in each instance.

In the case of multilevel models, graphical techniques are sometimes useful for making this determination at Level 2 and above. For example, in growth curve modeling one is interested in whether individuals vary continuously or whether the growth curves can be put into discrete categories. One should also be interested in detecting outliers, which sometimes indicate a discrete, but rare, category. One can either plot the observed or estimated growth curves, or plot the parameter estimates from fitting the curves. The same techniques can be applied in any multilevel model, not just in growth modeling. As the famous exploratory statistical expert Yogi Berra said, "You can observe a lot by just watching." These plots will sometimes reveal interesting patterns that might not be discovered by merely fitting models. These principles are well accepted, and often practiced, in the usual regression framework, but they seem to be less common in multilevel modeling.

As an example that illustrates both the potentials and pitfalls of such graphical methods, consider a simple multilevel model in which Level 2 units (e.g., schools, or individuals in a repeated-measures context) are characterized by a slope, b1, and an intercept, b0. A plot for some hypothetical data is depicted in Figure 10C.1. One can discern two groups: one in the lower left of the figure, and the other in the upper right, but they are not as distinct as one might expect. The data were generated from two bivariate normal distributions in which the means on each variable differ by 4 SD in the two groups; this would be considered a large difference between two groups, and yet one might miss it. A standard cluster analysis will correctly assign all of the points to the correct clusters and is to be advised unless groups are so widely separated that visual inspection will suffice. (The difficulty of distinguishing clusters by visual inspection was noted by Waller & Meehl, 1998, who gave some nice illustrations of this problem.)

Consider Time-Independent Change Models

Another important principle for repeated-measures data is that change models should not be restricted to functions of time; sometimes time-independent models are more sensible. For example, consider the relationship between hormone level and mood. Although it is important to know that hormone levels vary with time in a fairly regular way, time is of little interest to the question of the relationship between hormones and mood. Instead, one wants to look at mood as a function of hormone level within each person and see how the relationship varies across people. Multilevel models offer a great deal of promise for examining models for change, and models for within-person relationships deserve to be more widely used.

FIGURE 10C.1

Plot of intercept versus slope for 50 Level 2 units. The data were generated as two groups: one with independent N(3, 1) distributions for b0 and b1, the other with independent N(7, 1) distributions for b0 and b1. The two groups can be discerned in the plot but are not as distinct as one might expect, given the large difference in means relative to standard deviations.

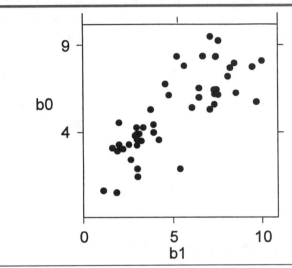

Expressing and Modeling Functions

One of the many new ideas in Muthén's chapter is the prediction of one growth curve from another. He shows how the growth pattern of prereading skills in kindergarten can predict the growth pattern of reading skills in the first grade. This opens the door for new methods in the area of functional data analysis (Ramsay & Silverman, 1997), which is concerned with situations in which the data one wishes to model are functions.

The idea of modeling functions naturally leads to the issue of how such functions are expressed. Some functional forms may be better than others, even when they are mathematically equivalent, either because one form has fewer parameters and is thus simpler or because one form has parameters that have simple interpretations in terms of the subject matter. As an example, consider a case from obesity research in which the typical relationship between mortality and body mass index (BMI, an index of "fatness") is U shaped—that is, people who are either too thin or too fat die at a higher rate than those who are at intermediate BMI levels. Such a curve is typically fit by a quadratic equation. But what do the parameters mean? Only one parameter is related in a simple way to anything of interest: The quadratic term is related to the spread of the

U. Another parameterization would be better, so that the three parameters indicate (a) the BMI at which mortality is lowest, (b) the mortality rate at the low point, and (c) the spread of the curve (which indicates the sensitivity of mortality to BMI). Stephen Raudenbush (chapter 2) gives an excellent example of changing the parameterization in a similar fashion.

This is only one example of a more general principle: Models should be expressed so that the parameters are meaningful. In multilevel models in particular, and regression in general, this principle is ignored in favor of other rules; the most common example is the current concern with "centering" predictors. In my view this concern is too narrow. Because the parameters in the Level 1 equation are being modeled in the Level 2 equations the primary concern is choosing a scale for the Level 1 predictors so that the parameters make substantive sense; only in this way will the Level 2 equations be modeling a quantity of substantive interest. Muthén's chapter illustrates the judicious choice of scales: The time variable for kindergarten achievement was scaled so that the intercept represented performance at the end of kindergarten rather than at the beginning (if time were scaled so that zero was the start of the school year) or the middle (if centering were used).

Reliability in Latent Class Analysis

Collins's chapter represents one of only two chapters of which I am aware that have addressed the topic of reliability in latent class analysis (the other was authored by Clogg & Manning, 1996). Clogg and Manning's (1996) chapter deals less with reliability of a whole scale, although that is part of their work; they place more emphasis on what psychometricians would call "item analysis." Collins's chapter develops the idea of reliability for latent class analysis in a way that parallels traditional psychometric methods.

Because this idea is so new, I place it into context for readers. First, note that it deals with the idea of reliability of a scale. This step presumably follows an analysis of the utility of each item, analogous to the computation of item–total correlations in classical test theory. Some possibilities especially suited for latent class analysis are discussed by Clogg and Manning (1996). In turn, investigation of reliability is presumably followed by studies of the validity of the scale for particular uses.

Hazards of One-Number Summaries

A second important point about reliability measures is that all one-number summaries represent a tradeoff. They are simple, which is good, but they may oversimplify. In every context one must investigate the degree to which a one-number summary is appropriate and when it is misleading. Often, a good one-number summary is useful, even when one knows it oversimplifies.

In classical test theory, one often presents a standard error of measurement for a test as if it applies to everyone. In fact, the usual standard error is an average over the population, and in truth one measures people at the extremes less well than in the middle. In latent class analysis one runs into problems even at the item level. An item can have, in medical terminology, good sensitivity but poor specificity, or vice versa. (Equivalently, in a different context, one can say that dichotomous items can differ both in their false-negative and false-positive rates.) In these cases, a one-number summary does not do the job. Similarly, at the scale level, one could have some observed response patterns that can be accurately classified into latent classes, whereas others are not so accurately classified; this is analogous to having different standard errors at different points on a scale. One commonly used summary statistic in latent class analysis, the percentage of cases correctly classified, represents another attempt to capture how well the classification procedure works and has the same potential pitfalls.

Summarizing the accuracy of classification has some subtle problems, some of which are not so well recognized. Of course, the most common problem, that of correcting for chance agreement, has a long history. Cohen's kappa is one example of the recognition of this problem. Furthermore, most people recognize that it is more difficult to obtain agreement when a variable has many categories.

What is not generally recognized is that if categories are structured in a hierarchy, so that each level at the highest is divided into finer categories at a lower level, then odd results can occur. For example, suppose that people are divided into two major diagnostic categories: neurosis and psychosis. Suppose further that neurotics are subclassified as Type A or Type B, and psychotics are subclassified as Type C or Type D. Although unlikely, it is possible that raters could agree completely on whether patients are neurotic or psychotic but disagree completely on whether neurotic individuals are Type A or B and about whether psychotic individuals are Type C or Type D. If this occurred, then reliability is perfect (by any reasonable measure) at the higher level but zero at the lower level. The conclusion is that if such hierarchies exist, it is worthwhile to measure reliability at each level of the hierarchy.

A Scheme for Classifying Reliability Indices for Latent Class Models

Now let me place Collins's contribution into a broader context of possible measures of reliability. The first step in developing a general procedure is to choose one or more measures of information or certainty in classification. One measure is then applied conditionally, given an observed response pattern, and is compared with a measure made unconditionally (ignoring response pattern). Reliability is measured by how much more information (less uncertainty) there is in classifying on the basis of the response pattern rather than ignoring the response pattern. If this seems similar to the procedure for constructing a wide variety of measures of association in crossclassified tables, it is for good reason. Agresti (1990) pointed out that a large number of such measures are calculated using the general form $[V(y) - V(y|x)]/V(y)$, in which $V(y)$ is an unconditional measure of variability, and $V(y|x)$ is a conditional measure of variability. These measures can be applied to latent class analysis because such models can be viewed as a crossclassification of the observed response pattern by the latent classification.

Three measures of information or uncertainty are commonly used in categorical data analysis. The *repeat rate*, which is the sum of squared proportions in each category, is used in Collins's measure and in Goodman and Kruskal's tau. It is used in information theory (as an approximation for entropy) and is the chance agreement factor in Cohen's kappa. It is also closely related to the variance of a categorical variable. A second common measure is the amount of *entropy* or negative of the information. This is calculated as minus the sum, over categories of the variable, of $p \ln(p)$. In special cases this is related to the logarithm of the likelihood function for certain models. The third common measure is the *modal* (most frequent) *value* of p. The rationale for this measure is that to minimize classification errors, one would guess that everyone is in the most likely category. This measure is used by Goodman, and by Clogg, in the evaluation of latent class models and in certain proportional reduction of error measures. Table 10C.1 shows these quantities computed for three possible distributions over three categories of a variable.

In constructing an index of reliability one must also choose which baseline to use for comparison. A *baseline* is a measure of the information in the unconditional distribution of the latent variable. Ignoring the baseline issue is the

TABLE 10C.1

Information Measures for Three Distributions of a Categorical Variable

DISTRIBUTION	MODAL p: MAX (p_i)	REPEAT RATE: Σp_i^2	ENTROPY: $-\Sigma p \ln(p_i)$
1, 0, 0	1.0	1.00	0.00
0.7, 0.2, 0.1	0.7	0.54	0.80
0.3, 0.4, 0.3	0.4	0.34	1.09

Note. For the first distribution, the entropy of 0 is the limit, as the proportions in two categories approach 0.

same as assuming that one will incorrectly classify everyone; this is seldom a defensible position, although it is implicit in the measure reported by Clogg's (1977) MLLSA computer program, percentage of correct classification. Collins uses the inverse of the number of categories. As for the information measures discussed above, in the conditional case, other choices include the repeat rate of the marginal (unconditional) distribution of the variable (as is done in Cohen's kappa), the entropy, and the modal category (as in Goodman and Clogg's latent class measures and in Goodman and Kruskal's proportional reduction in error measures).

The combination of various measures of information in the conditional classification (averaged over the observed response patterns), with various measures of information in unconditional classification (including no adjustment), give rise to various possible measures of reliability. The general form for such measures is the one given by Collins in her general "consistency index" and relates the improvement in prediction due to the use of the conditional probabilities (based on response patterns) over the prediction made using the unconditional probabilities (i.e., ignoring response pattern).

Some of these measures will be symmetric; that is, they will use the same information measure for both the conditional and unconditional measures. Collins's index is asymmetric; it combines one measure for the conditional classification (sum of squared proportions) with a different measure for unconditional classification (1/number of categories). Although there is nothing inherently wrong with asymmetric measures, they do have potential drawbacks. One possible concern is that they sometimes can be greater than zero even if the conditional classification is no better than the unconditional classification. For example, suppose the unconditional-classification probabilities for a two-class model are .7 and .3. The base rate for the Collins measure is $1/2 = .5$. The repeat rate is $.7**2 + .3**2 = .49 + .09 = .58$, where $**$ indicates exponentiation. The Collins reliability index, ignoring the observed response pattern, is $(.58 - .50)/(1 - .50) = .08/.50 = .16$. This explains why the graphs in Collins's chapter show higher reliabilities for more extreme class splits, even when the item characteristics are the same.

As an example of a (symmetric) reliability index using the proportional reduction in error (PRE) measure, suppose that there are three latent classes. If the (unconditional) distribution into the three classes is .4, .3, and .3, then I would classify everyone as being in Category 1. Doing so is correct for .40 of the population, and the error rate is therefore $1 - .40 = .60$. This is the baseline error rate. If using the information in the observed variables to categorize people leads me to correctly classify .70 of the population, then my error rate is decreased to .30, and my proportional reduction in error is the decrease $(.60 - .30 = .30)$ divided by the baseline error rate, or $.30/.60 = .50$; that is, using information in the responses will reduce the errors by half.

PRE measures sound reasonable, and they work well when the unconditional probabilities of being in each latent class are approximately equal. When those probabilities are extreme, however, the PRE can be zero even when the items are good. In another context, this is called the *base rate problem*, as originally described by Meehl and Rosen (1955). A simple example is trying to evaluate a diagnostic test that is 90% accurate, for a disease that is rare (e.g., present in only 1% of the population). One cannot hope to have much improvement in error rate over the strategy of ignoring the test result and diagnosing everyone as not having the disease. One would be right 99% of the time using this strategy, whereas making use of the test result will achieve a correct result only 90% of the time. What is ignored, however, is the relative costs of the two different types of errors (false positives and false negatives).

One conclusion that can be drawn after considering this problem is that all measures of the type one is considering combine (either directly or indirectly) both the marginal (unconditional) distribution across latent classes and the conditional probabilities of response given latent class membership. In some statistical areas, measures are recomputed after the base rates (and sometimes additional characteristics) are adjusted. For example, the binomial effect size display of Rosenthal and Rubin (1982) adjusts both margins of 2 × 2 tables to have equal proportions in each category. This strategy maximizes the effect size and eliminates the base-rate problem. A similar strategy might be appropriate in latent class models. Another possibility is to base reliability coefficients on accepted population distributions for a variable, if such knowledge exists.

One must weigh the drawbacks against the advantages of each potential reliability index. Each possible index constructed from the above scheme of combining one unconditional and one conditional measure has drawbacks. All, of course, are one-number summaries, with all of the potential drawbacks of one-number summaries. All ignore the distinction among possible kinds of classification errors. In many situations, one can assign differential costs to different kinds of errors, so that generalizations of reliability measures to include these costs would be advantageous. As illustrated above, many measures, including generalizations of the widely used PRE, are sensitive to extreme distributions of the latent variable.

Reliability, Validity, or Both?

So far my discussion of Collins's chapter has focused on reliability, but validity also is an issue. When measuring people over time, one concern is whether the person is stable in regard to the characteristic being measured. *Traits* are generally characteristics that are relatively stable over relatively long periods of time; *states* are characteristics that are relatively changeable over shorter periods of time. With latent variable models one can separate changes over time into those that are due to unreliability and those that are due to true changes in the characteristic being measured. These true changes are related to one form of validity. Another form of validity would be assessed if the observed measures at Time 2 were different than those used at Time 1.

In either case, Collins's latent transition approach can help separate reliability from validity and stability. One could estimate the reliability at each time point and the validity (or stability, depending on context) of the connection between the two times. Note that this can be done even in cases where the reliability at each time could not be estimated separately because of insufficient numbers of items at each time point, that is, cases in which the model may not be identified if fitted separately at each time.

A related issue is whether one should use the data from more than one time point to estimate reliability. If the time periods were close enough to each other or if one wanted to classify people into patterns that they follow over time, then a case could be made for doing so. In other cases, one would not want to use data from a later time point to classify people at an earlier time point. To borrow an example from Muthén's chapter, it would not make sense to use data from both kindergarten and first grade to diagnose readiness to learn to read in first grade. Empirical results, theoretical results, and practical considerations must all be weighed in deciding on appropriate procedures in a specific case.

Conclusion

I congratulate both Muthén and Collins for their pioneering contributions to the methodology for measuring change. Their work not only breaks new ground but also shows researchers how to further develop their approaches to modeling with latent variables. I thank them for the work they have completed and for showing what lies in the future for latent variable modeling.

References

Agresti, A. (1990). *Categorical data analysis.* New York: Wiley.

Clogg, C. C. (1977). *Unrestricted and restricted maximum likelihood latent structure analysis: A manual for users* (Working paper 1977-09). University Park, PA: Population Issues Research Office.

Clogg, C. C., & Manning, W. D. (1996). Assessing reliability of categorical measurements using latent class analysis. In A. von Eye & C. C. Clogg (Eds.), *Categorical variables in developmental research* (pp. 169–182). San Diego, CA: Academic Press.

Meehl, P. E., & Rosen, A. (1955). Antecedent probability and the efficiency of psychometric signs, patterns or cutting scores. *Psychological Bulletin, 52,* 194–216.

Ramsay, J. O., & Silverman, B. W. (1997). *Functional data analysis.* New York: Springer.

Rosenthal, R., & Rubin, D. B. (1982). A simple, general purpose display of magnitude of experimental effect. *Journal of Educational Psychology, 74,* 166–169.

Waller, N. G., & Meehl, P. E. (1998). *Multivariate taxometric procedures: Distinguishing types from continua.* Thousand Oaks, CA: Sage.

Editors' Introduction

In this chapter, John Graham, Bonnie Taylor, and Patricio Cumsille make a suggestion that appears radical on the surface: Why not build planned missingness into a longitudinal study? Although deliberately opting not to collect certain data in a longitudinal study may seem highly inadvisable, even insane, Graham et al. argue persuasively that there are times when a researcher should do just that. In fact, by planning missingness, a researcher can save money and lighten respondent burden. The key—and this is important—is having the missing-data mechanism under the control of the researcher. Under these conditions, a judiciously chosen missing-data design can be superior in many ways to a traditional complete-data design, particularly for longitudinal research. Readers may want to read chapter 12, by Schafer, first; Schafer introduces multiple-imputation procedures for longitudinal data and discusses several important general missing data issues. In his commentary on the Schafer chapter and the Graham et al. chapter, Adam Davey points out some benefits of this approach and offers some sensible cautionary words.

Planned Missing-Data Designs in Analysis of Change

John W. Graham

Bonnie J. Taylor

Patricio E. Cumsille

Statistical procedures for handling missing data are becoming increasingly common in a wide range of social research. Schafer's (1997) NORM software for multiple imputation has been available for some time as a stand-alone Microsoft Windows application, and several articles and chapters have been written describing its use (Schafer & Olsen, 1998; also see Graham & Hofer, 2000; Graham, Hofer, Donaldson, MacKinnon, & Schafer, 1997; Graham & Schafer, 1999). In addition, Arbuckle's (Arbuckle & Wothke, 1999) Amos program and Neale's (Neale, Boker, Xie, & Maes, 1999) Mx program for performing structural equation modeling (SEM) with data sets containing missingness are both well developed, and the user base is increasing. The multiple-group SEM procedure (Allison, 1987; Muthén, Kaplan, & Hollis, 1987), although supplanted for mainstream missing data analysis by NORM, Amos, and Mx, remains a highly useful option for certain special applications (e.g., see Duncan, Duncan, & Li, 1998).

It is important to understand that these missing-data procedures do not give the researcher something for nothing. One of the primary criticisms of these approaches in previous years was that users were somehow thought to be "helping" themselves, for example, by increasing the chances that hypotheses would be supported. Fortunately, unfounded criticisms such as these are finally becoming less common as the methods are better understood, and attention is now more properly focused on how the details of these procedures can be worked out in order to serve analysis needs better. In fact, the main reason for using missing-data procedures such as NORM, Amos, or Mx is to make use of all the data available, that is, to avoid throwing data away as a means of achieving a missing-data pattern that is convenient for traditional statistical procedures. The main goal of acceptable missing-data procedures is to preserve

This research was supported by National Institute on Drug Abuse Grant P50 DA 10075.

important characteristics of the data. In particular, one would like parameter estimates to be unbiased and the assessment of the variability around those parameter estimates (i.e., standard errors or confidence intervals) to be reasonable. Sound missing-data procedures enable the user to preserve these important characteristics and are easy to implement.

Kinds of Missingness

Three types of missing data have been described (e.g., by Little & Rubin, 1987): (a) missing completely at random (MCAR), (b) accessible missingness (Graham & Donaldson, 1993; also described by Little & Rubin as "missing at random" (MAR) or "ignorable missingness," and (c) inaccessible missingness (Graham & Donaldson, 1993; also described by Little & Rubin as "nonignorable missingness").

MCAR occurs when the cause of missingness is a completely random process—for example, a random number generator, flip of a coin, and so on. This type of missingness can also occur when the cause of missingness is systematic but uncorrelated with the variable containing the missing data. In light of this latter fact, MCAR may be common in many research situations. This type of missingness is easily handled by the recommended analysis procedures.

Accessible missingness is different from MCAR in that the cause of missingness is systematic and correlated with the variable containing the missing data. An important characteristic of accessible missingness is that the cause of missingness has been measured and is available for inclusion in the missing-data analysis. All biases associated with this type of missingness are eliminated by the recommended missing-data analysis procedures, as long as the cause of missingness is included in the missing-data model.

Like accessible missingness, with inaccessible missingness the cause of missingness is systematic and correlated with the variable containing the missingness. However, unlike accessible missingness, with inaccessible missingness the cause of missingness has not been measured or is otherwise not available for inclusion in the missing-data model. Because this cause of missingness is not available for inclusion in the missing-data model the biases associated with this type of missingness cannot be eliminated.

It has been argued, however, that inaccessible missingness may represent a small and often trivial part of the overall missingness in many research studies (Graham et al., 1997). First, whenever a missing value is suspected of having an inaccessible cause, in virtually all cases the missing value will have all three causes of missingness—that is, when inaccessible missingness exists, it is usually the case that the variable is more likely to be missing when the value is high, for example, than when it is low. The phrase *more likely* in the previous sentence implies that another process (either random or accessible) is also at work in this same situation to cause the missing value. In short, it may virtually never be correct to say that the cause of missingness is inaccessible. Although one can never know the relative contribution of the three causes of missingness, especially the contribution of inaccessible causes, one can make plausible guesses about the relative contributions (e.g., see Graham et al., 1997), and examine the probable effect of inaccessible missingness given a range of plausible assumptions (Rubin, 1987). Graham et al. (1997) recommended that researchers conduct this sort of sensitivity analysis to determine the likely effects of inaccessible missingness in their particular study. In the final analysis, however, use of one of the recommended procedures (e.g., NORM, Amos, or Mx) may often be the best one can do and produces excellent results in most applications.

"Old" Procedures

Several procedures have been used over the years for handling missing data. We mention them here mainly to be explicit about what methods are not advisable.

Complete Cases

Use of complete cases—that is, discarding whole cases containing any missing data—is the most common of the old procedures. Analyzing complete cases is not generally advisable because it may produce bias in the estimates (although this is not always the case). Perhaps the more important drawback to analyzing complete cases is that statistical power is always lower than with better procedures.

With some increasingly common missing data patterns, use of complete cases may be associated with bias in the parameter estimates and huge loss of power. For example, consider the following example involving four variables (V1–V4). Suppose 20% of the sample has each of the following patterns of missing data (1 indicates data present, 0 indicates data missing):

V1	V2	V3	V4	Percent of cases with pattern
1	1	1	1	20
1	1	1	0	20
1	1	0	1	20
1	0	1	1	20
0	1	1	1	20

In this case, only 20% of the cases have complete data, but 80% of the total number of data points are actually present. This type of pattern arises with the planned missing-data designs discussed in this chapter, but it also arises naturally when a small amount of missingness occurs for a larger number of variables.

One valuable aspect of analyzing complete cases is that the standard errors from the analysis are meaningful. This leads us to recommend that when no more than about 5% of the cases are lost to missing data, analyzing complete cases may be an acceptable alternative. If only 5% of the cases are lost to missing data, the amount of bias that could be present will likely be extremely small, and the loss of power will be minimal. In this situation, critics would be hard pressed to mount a strong argument against the use of complete cases.

Pairwise Deletion (Inclusion)

With the pairwise deletion procedure one estimates each covariance in the matrix using observations that have data for both variables. Thus, the different elements of the covariance matrix are estimated using different subsets of participants. This procedure produces bias in parameter estimates unless the missing data are MCAR. In addition, even if the data are MCAR, there is no guarantee that the covariance matrix produced in this way will be "positive definite." Finally, there is no simple direct way to calculate standard errors with this procedure. This procedure is not recommended.

Mean Substitution

With this procedure, when a data point is missing one substitutes on this variable the mean for all nonmissing values. This procedure yields highly biased parameter estimates (Graham et al., 1997; Graham, Hofer, & MacKinnon, 1996; Graham, Hofer, & Piccinin, 1994). Also there is no basis for estimating standard errors. This procedure should not be used.

Section Summary

Missing-data procedures are now readily available, easy to use, and inexpensive or free. It is gradually becoming standard practice to make use of one of these new procedures. When missing data occur in one's research these procedures can prove to be immensely useful.

The presence of these new procedures also opens up the possibility that researchers might make use of measurement strategies that contain missing data by design. We devote the remainder of this chapter to the topic of planned missing-data designs in the analysis of change.

Planned Missing-Data Designs

An often-asked question is, Why would anyone ever want to plan to have missing data? Is it not always better to limit the amount of missing data one has? In the remainder of this chapter we address this question.

Planned missing-data designs are not new. Designs such as the Latin square (e.g., Neter, Kutner, Nachtsheim, & Wasserman, 1990) have been around for a long time. Such designs can be thought of as variations of other kinds of sampling designs, which are not only common in social research but also often a requirement if the research is to be feasible. Other designs—for example, the cohort sequential design—have become common in longitudinal research (e.g., Duncan et al., 1998; McArdle & Hamagami, 1991; Nesselroade & Baltes, 1979).

The Three-Form Design

Recently, a measurement design (the *three-form design*) has been suggested that reduces the work load for research participants in situations where there are time constraints (Hansen, Johnson, Flay, Graham, & Sobel, 1988; Hansen & Graham, 1991; Graham et al., 1994, 1996, 1997). The idea behind the three-form design is to ask a manageable number of questions of each participant— for example, 100 questions—but to vary which questions are presented to participants to collect data on a larger number of items—for example, 133 items—all of which are then available for analysis. With this planned missing-data design, items are divided into four item sets: *X*, *A*, *B*, and *C*. Questions are then presented (or not) to participants as follows.

Questions in _____ Item Set asked?

	X	A	B	C
Form 1	yes	yes	yes	no
Form 2	yes	yes	no	yes
Form 3	yes	no	yes	yes

With this version of the three-form design, items in Set *X*, which are essential to the hypotheses under study, are asked of everyone. Because of their importance, the items in Set *X* may actually be asked first, although this is certainly not a requirement. It is typically the case that item sets in the three forms are rotated so that different item sets appear last in each form. For example, in the Adolescent Alcohol Prevention Trial (AAPT; Hansen & Graham, 1991), items were presented as follows: Form 1, *XAB*; Form 2, *XCA*; Form 3, *XBC*.

The advantages of the three-form design are that (a) participant fatigue is minimized, and (b) the logistics of producing and implementing the three-form design are manageable. Also, given the availability of missing-data analyses, such as NORM, Amos, and Mx, the data produced by this planned missing-data design are easily analyzed.

Planned Missing-Data Designs To Use With Growth Modeling

The implementation of longitudinal designs is particularly taxing for researchers and participants. Planned missing-data designs can be successfully used to reduce the number of measurement waves at which any particular participant needs to be measured, thereby minimizing participant "saturation" with the project, and attrition, over time. To exemplify the utility of planned missing-data designs for longitudinal research, we now examine such designs for use with one of the primary tools for analysis of change: growth modeling. The artificial data to be used for our example are similar to data we have collected from adolescents taking part in a drug use prevention project (the AAPT study). For our illustration, we have a hypothetical program versus control dummy variable (program = 1, control = 0) and artificial alcohol use data for each of 5 years from 7th to 11th grades. The seventh-grade data collection took place just prior to program implementation, and the 8th, 9th, 10th- and 11th-grade measures took place after the program implementation. For the purposes of this example, we use a model described by Willett and Sayer (1994), that is, a one-group growth model with program represented by the dummy variable.

In this example, the hypothesis is that alcohol use in the program group will increase at a rate slower than alcohol use in the control group. This differential rate of growth is expressed in the regression coefficient linking our program dummy variable to the rate of change in alcohol use. Thus this regression coefficient constitutes the parameter of primary interest in our analyses, and the power to detect the program effect represented by this regression coefficient becomes of central interest for the design of the study.

Results from analysis of this program effect with our artificial data show the statistical power that can be achieved with different patterns of missingness. The value of performing a full simulation in this situation—that is, using hundreds or thousands of randomly generated data sets—is that we could estimate the degree of random variability (e.g., standard errors) around the parameter estimates for a given set of population parameter values (variances, covariances, and means). However, a much simpler way to do this involves the use of any of the standard SEM programs (e.g., LISREL, Jöreskog & Sörbom, 1993). One simply analyzes the population covariance matrix as if it were real data. If one sets sample size $N = 1,000$, for example, the standard error obtained for any parameter estimate is a reasonable estimate of that standard error.

This provides us with a useful way of obtaining standard errors in the complete-data case, but the situation is more complicated when there are missing data. Fortunately, there is a missing-data analog of this procedure. By using the multiple-group SEM procedure outlined by Allison (1987) and Muthén et al. (1987), we can easily determine the effects each planned missing-data design has on estimated standard errors. Furthermore, with these procedures, it is an easy matter to explore the sample size needed in a one-group analysis (no missing data) that yields the same standard error for any selected parameter estimate as that obtained from a particular planned missing-data design.

As described by Muthén and Curran (1997; Curran & Muthén, 1999) and following Satorra and Saris (1985), one can easily test the statistical power for the program effect on the factor representing the slope, or rate of growth. First one estimates the model of choice, writing out the covariance matrix and vector of means implied by the model. One then reads those covariances and means back into the model as if they were the real data. Of course, this model fits perfectly. Next, one constrains a single, previously estimated parameter to be zero. In this case, we constrain the regression weight of the program predicting the slope factor (the parameter estimate of primary interest in all our analyses) to be zero. This model does not fit perfectly and has 1 df more. The chi-square from this model is an estimate of the noncentrality parameter (NCP) for testing the significance of this one parameter (with 1 df). Given this NCP, one can easily estimate the power for testing this parameter using the PROBCHI function in SAS (SAS Institute, 1990):

$$\text{power} = 1 - \text{probchi}(3.842, 1, ncp)$$

where 3.842 is the critical value of the chi-square for the usual central chi-square test, and ncp is the estimate of the NCP obtained from the previous analysis.

We consider seven planned missing-data designs, all of which are based on five measurement times. For each design, a small number of cases are designed to have no missing data across the five measurement times. Although this is not a requirement with these designs, it does help with estimation of higher order partial correlations. For all designs, we assumed $N = 1,000$ (500 per condition). Thus, for all of the following designs, with $k = 5$ variables, we have a total of $N \times k$ (1,000 $\times$ 5) = 5,000 data points overall.

Design 1 involves all combinations of one time missing. As shown in Table 11.1, there are six different groups for this design, including the group with no missing data. To obtain the total sample size, 167 participants are assigned randomly to each planned measurement pattern shown in Table 11.1 ($N = 166$ for the last two patterns).

TABLE 11.1

Planned Missing-Data Design 1

RANDOM GROUP	OCCASION OF MEASUREMENT					N
	1	2	3	4	5	
1	1	1	1	1	1	167
2	1	1	1	1	0	167
3	1	1	1	0	1	167
4	1	1	0	1	1	167
5	1	0	1	1	1	166
6	0	1	1	1	1	166
Total						1,000

Note. Within each wave, 1 = data present, and 0 = data missing.

With Design 1, 833 [(3 × 167) + (2 × 166)] cases have data missing for one time. Thus, for this design 833/5,000 = 16.67% of the data points are missing by design.

Design 2 involves all possible combinations of one or two times missing, as shown in Table 11.2. With Design 2, 315 (63 × 5) participants have data missing from one time point, and 622 [(63 × 2) + (62 × 8)] participants have data missing from two time points. Thus, in this case, 315 + (2 × 622) = 1,559 data points (31.18%) are missing by design.

Design 3 involves all possible combinations of two times missing. The sample sizes for this design are shown in the N_A column of Table 11.3. With Design 3, 909 [(91 × 9) + (90 × 1)] participants have data missing from two time points. Thus, in this case, 909 × 2 = 1,818 data points (36.36%) are missing by design.

Two variants of Design 3 are also shown in Table 11.3. With both of these variants, the overall percentage of missing data points is exactly the same as for Design 3 (36.36%). Also, for each variant the number of cases with no missing data remains at 91.

The first variant (sample sizes shown in the N_B column of Table 11.3) weights more heavily those patterns in which the participant is measured at Times 1 and 5 (N = 160), nearly eliminates the pattern in which participants are measured at neither Time 1 nor Time 5 (N = 9), and weights the remaining patterns an intermediate amount (N = 70). Because this pattern emphasizes the first and last times, the regression weight for program predicting the slope should have greater statistical power.[1]

---

[1] We thank Joe Schafer for suggesting this design.

TABLE 11.2
Planned Missing-Data Design 2

OCCASION OF MEASUREMENT					
1	**2**	**3**	**4**	**5**	**N**
1	1	1	1	1	63
1	1	1	1	0	63
1	1	1	0	1	63
1	1	0	1	1	63
1	0	1	1	1	63
0	1	1	1	1	63
1	1	1	0	0	63
1	1	0	1	0	63
1	0	1	1	0	62
0	1	1	1	0	62
1	1	0	0	1	62
1	0	1	0	1	62
0	1	1	0	1	62
1	0	0	1	1	62
0	1	0	1	1	62
0	0	1	1	1	62

Note. Within each wave, 1 = data present, and 0 = data missing.

Sample sizes for the second variant of Design 3 are shown in the N_C column of Table 11.3. With this design, all participants are measured at Time 1. We examined this design for a very practical reason: When participants are recruited to take part in the study, they are more likely to acquiesce if they are asked to take part right away. With this design, patterns with data collected at Time 5 are weighted more heavily ($N = 202$), whereas patterns with no measurement at the last time are weighted less ($N = 101$).

Design 4 involves all possible combinations of two and three times missing. With Design 4, 2,376 (10 patterns with 48 participants, each with two times missing; plus 2 patterns with 48 participants, each with three times missing; plus 8 patterns with 47 participants, each with three times missing) data points (47.52%) are missing by design.

Design 5 involves all possible combinations of three times missing. With Design 5, 2,727 (9 patterns with 91 participants, each with three times missing, plus 1 pattern with 90 participants, each with three times missing) data points (54.54%) are missing by design.

TABLE 11.3

Planned Missing-Data Design 3: Three Variations

OCCASION OF MEASUREMENT					SAMPLE SIZE FOR DESIGN (N)		
1	2	3	4	5	3_A	3_B	3_C
1	1	1	1	1	91	91	91
1	1	1	0	0	91	70	101
1	1	0	1	0	91	70	101
1	0	1	1	0	91	70	101
0	1	1	1	0	91	9	0
1	1	0	0	1	91	160	202
1	0	1	0	1	91	160	202
0	1	1	0	1	91	70	0
1	0	0	1	1	91	160	202
0	1	0	1	1	91	70	0
0	0	1	1	1	90	70	0
Total *N*					1,000	1,000	1,000

Note. Within each wave, 1 = data present, and 0 = data missing.

The Artificial-Data Study

The empirical data used as a model for the artificial data used in this study came from Panel 4 of the AAPT (Hansen & Graham, 1991), a school-based alcohol prevention program that was implemented in southern California in the late 1980s.

For the artificial-data study, we posited an overall growth model containing both linear and quadratic growth such that there was a positive overall linear growth (e.g., positive mean slope). In addition, the population model posited slight (overall) negative quadratic growth, which is common in growth models. In the population, the mean for the linear growth differed by .14 in treatment and control groups (.14 steeper slope in control). The covariance structure for the data was taken directly from five waves of data from the AAPT study.

Preparation of the Population Covariance Matrices

A different version of the population covariance matrix and vector of means was created as follows for each pattern of a planned missing-data design. For example, if the design had 16 different missing-data patterns (as with Design 3), we created 16 different versions of the population covariance matrix, 1 for each pattern. If a covariance or mean element was estimable for that particular pattern, it was set to the population value. If it was not estimable for that pattern because of a missing value, it was set to 0.00. If a variance element was estimable for that particular pattern, it was set to the population value. Otherwise it was set to 1.00.

We then estimated the growth model using the multiple-group missing-data procedure outlined by Allison (1987) and Muthén et al. (1987). With this procedure, each different missing-data pattern forms a different group in the multiple-group SEM analysis. With this procedure, all factor-level parameter estimates (factor variances and covariances, factor regressions, factor means) are constrained to be equal across groups. All item-level parameters are estimated (factor loadings, residual variances, and covariances) and are also constrained to be equal across groups, provided that the pattern has data bearing on the parameter estimate. Otherwise the parameter estimate is fixed at 0.00 (residual variances are fixed at 1.00). The covariance matrix and vector of means that result from use of this procedure are identical to the results based on the EM algorithm for covariance matrices (Graham et al., 1994).

The initial setup of this multiple-group model is somewhat tedious and error prone. As a general solution to analyzing data with missingness, other methods (e.g., raw data maximum likelihood with Amos or Mx, or multiple imputation with NORM) are preferable in most respects. However, in this particular context, these usually better methods are not as good as the multiple-group SEM procedure (Allison, 1987; Muthén et al., 1987). After the initial setup, each planned missing-data design can be evaluated by conducting a single, multiple-group SEM analysis. The standard errors obtained from this analysis were highly similar to those from a more computation-intensive Monte Carlo simulation procedure involving 10,000 simulation replications and were much easier to obtain.

We analyzed each missing-data design as described above using LISREL 8 (Jöreskog & Sörbom, 1993). In addition, for each missing-data design, we estimated a corresponding model with no missing data, trying several different sample sizes (ranging from $N = 1,000$ to $N = 329$) until we found the one that yielded the same power (e.g., the same standard error) as the missing-data design.

Statistical Power Calculations

Although power is easily calculated with the Satorra–Saris (1985) procedure when no data are missing, calculating power in the missing-data case is generally much more complicated. However, another advantage of the multiple-group missing-data procedure is that calculation of power is as straightforward as it is when there are no missing data.

Results of the Artificial-Data Study

The results of the artificial-data study appear in Table 11.4. The first column of Table 11.4 gives the design labels (1–5) given previously. The second column presents the proportion of total data points present for that design (i.e., the proportion of the $N \times k = 5,000$ total data points that are not missing for that design). The third column of Table 11.4 shows the standard errors for the parameter estimate (program predicting slope) for the different planned missing-data designs. The fourth column shows the statistical power for each design. The fifth column of Table 11.4 shows the proportion of power for the design in this row, relative to the power for the complete-data design (i.e., column 4 divided by the power when $N = 1,000$ with no missing data). The rightmost column of Table 11.4 shows the sample size for the complete-cases model that yielded the same standard error and statistical power as the planned missing-data design in that row.

As expected, missing-data designs with more data points missing yield higher standard errors. Of course, this is also true of complete-cases designs (for these designs, we are thinking of the number of cases fewer than 1,000 as missing data). What was unexpected, however, is that the rate of standard error increase is different for complete-cases and planned missing-data designs. In fact, as illustrated in Figure 11.1, the rate of increase in standard errors is steeper for the complete-cases designs than for the planned missing-data designs. The top curve in Figure 11.1 shows the rate of standard error increase given changes in the total percentage of missing values. The second curve shows the rate of change for the planned missing-data designs. For all of the designs, the planned missing-data design has a lower standard error than the complete-cases design costing the same, that is, the design with the same number of total data points.

The two variants of Design 3_A, Designs 3_B and 3_C, are shown in the bottom two curves of the figure. These two variants performed even better than Design 3_A and were more clearly superior to the complete-cases option costing the same. The bottom curve is for Design 3_C, in which all participants are measured at Time 1, and patterns are weighted relatively more heavily, in which participants also were measured at Time 5. The other variant, Design 3_B, performed nearly as well.

Column 4 in Table 11.4 shows the fall-off of power when the different missing-data designs are used. For this discussion we give the label *Design 0* to the model with $N = 1,000$ and no missing data. In some sense, this is the basis for considering power of planned missing-data designs. The power for Design 0 was a modest .82, and power for all planned missing-data designs in our particular example fell below .80. However, by examining the power for a particular design divided by the power for Design 0, we get a sense of the

TABLE 11.4

Standard Error for Testing Program Effect on Slope

PLANNED MISSING-DATA DESIGN	PROPORTION OF DATA POINTS AVAILABLE WITH PLANNED MISSING-DATA DESIGNS (%)	SE FOR PROGRAM PREDICTING SLOPE	POWER	% OF POWER (N = 1,000) WITH NO MISSING DATA	N NEEDED TO ACHIEVE SAME POWER WITH DESIGN INVOLVING NO MISSING DATA
0	100.0	.0481	.822	—	1,000
1	83.3	.0512	.773	.94	883
2	68.8	.0556	.703	.86	749
3_A	63.6	.0573	.677	.82	705
3_B	63.6	.0536	.735	.89	806
3_C	63.6	.0528	.747	.91	830
4	52.5	.0637	.585	.71	570
5	45.5	.0691	.519	.63	485

Note. Standard errors were calculated with the multiple-group structural equation modeling procedure (Allison, 1987). Power was calculated with the Satorra–Saris method (Satorra & Saris, 1985).

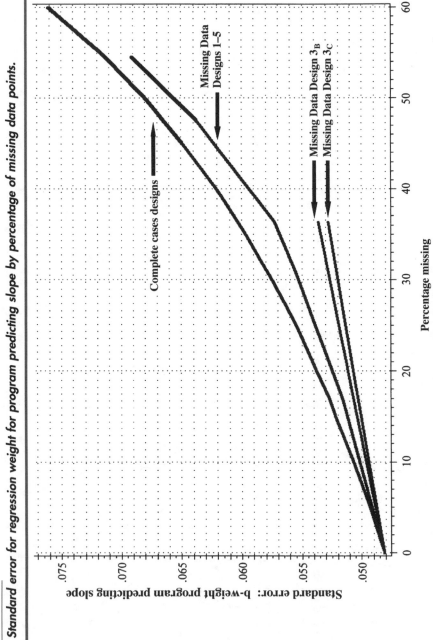

FIGURE 11.1

Standard error for regression weight for program predicting slope by percentage of missing data points.

practical fall-off in power for the various missing-data designs, relative to the design with $N = 1,000$ and no missing data.

As shown in Table 11.4, the power for Design 1 was 94% of the power for Design 0. Power then drops off to 86% and 82% for Designs 2 and 3, respectively. After that, power dropped off more dramatically: 71% for Design 4 and 63% for Design 5. Power for the two variants of Design 3_A was good by comparison. Power for Design 3_B was 89% of that obtained in Design 0, and power for Design 3_C was 91% of that obtained in Design 0.

The differences between planned missing-data designs and complete-cases designs can also be cast in terms of the cost of collecting data with a particular level of power. Table 11.5 shows the cost for each missing-data design and the cost for the complete-cases design with the same power. It is clear that the missing-data design is less expensive in every case, sometimes substantially less expensive. The largest difference for the standard designs was obtained for Design 3. For this design, the complete-cases design would cost an additional $3,430, or nearly 11% more.

The two hybrid designs (Design 3_B and Design 3_C) were substantially less expensive than the corresponding complete-cases design. The complete-cases design with the same power would cost $8,480 more than Design 3_B and $9,680 more than Design 3_C. These two values represent 26.6% and 30.4% increases in cost, respectively, over the planned missing-data design.

In fact, if we examine the complete-cases design with a full $N = 1,000$, we find that the overall cost is $50,000. This design yielded power = .82 in this context. However, this design costs $18,180 (57%) more than missing-data Design 3_C, which had 36% missing data. The gain in statistical power (.82 vs. .75) does not seem cost effective in this case.

Discussion

When we look at our results we must conclude that planned missing-data designs are better than various complete-cases designs for testing hypotheses about the difference in the rate of change between program and control groups. The missing-data designs have greater statistical power than complete-cases designs that cost exactly the same, and the missing-data designs cost less than complete-cases designs having only slightly greater statistical power.

In analyzing the effects of a program on linear change over five times, our conclusion seems warranted. For the two variations of Design 3_A (i.e., 3_B and 3_C), in which the first and last time points were more heavily weighted, the results show even more promising advantages. The best design (i.e., 3_C) yielded a standard error that was the same as a complete-cases design with over 30% more data. The cost savings using this design, compared to the complete-cases design with the same power, are substantial.

TABLE 11.5

Data Collection Costs for Missing-Data Designs and Corresponding Complete-Cases Design: Hypotheses Relating to Slopes

DESIGN	PLANNED MISSING-DATA DESIGNS		COMPLETE-CASES DESIGN WITH SAME SE			
	PROPORTION OF DATA POINTS (%)	COST ($)	N	COST ($)	ADDITIONAL COST ($)	PERCENTAGE INCREASE
0	100.0	50,000	1,000	50,000	—	—
1	83.3	41,665	883	44,150	2,485	6.0
2	68.8	34,410	749	37,450	3,040	8.8
3_A	63.6	31,820	705	35,250	3,430	10.8
3_B	63.6	31,820	806	40,300	8,480	26.6
3_C	63.6	31,820	830	41,500	9,680	30.4
4	52.5	26,250	570	28,500	2,250	8.6
5	45.5	22,750	485	24,250	1,500	6.6

Note. Figures given here assume $10/participant. 100% data points (Design 0) was based on total N = 1,000 for five waves of measurement.

In general, planned missing-data procedures may be especially valuable with longitudinal measurement designs. It is often the case with these designs that there is considerable redundancy in the longitudinal measures, and fewer measures, up to a point, will generally provide hypothesis tests that are nearly as powerful as tests involving all possible cases.

There may also be some hidden cost savings in such designs. For example, participants who are asked to take part in a study multiple times in a relatively short period (e.g., five times over a 1-year period) may begin to complain after a few waves of measurement. Thus, with many measurement waves, especially waves that are close together in time, there may be more attrition than would be expected. Another problem with several measurement waves that are close together in time is that there may be carryover effects. That is, at one point in time participants may recall their responses from the previous wave of measurement. To the extent that this occurs participants may bias their later responses to be consistent with the previous responses. A planned missing-data design may reduce the level of attrition because the burden to individual participants is lessened. Also, because in a planned missing-data design the time between measures would be longer for most participants, the problem of carryover effects will be lessened.

On the other hand, there is a limit to the value of these planned missing-data designs. For example, Designs 4 and 5, although apparently better than the corresponding complete-cases designs, did not show as much of an advantage as did Design 3 (even version 3_A). This suggests that there is a point of diminishing returns in choosing these designs—that is, Design 3 appears to have the best combination of low cost and reasonable statistical power. If one opts for a design that calls for more missing data, it may be that the cost savings do not offset the loss of statistical power. Still, if cost were of paramount importance then a researcher might, in some circumstances, reasonably consider one of the planned missing-data designs with more missing data points.

An important second issue relates to the fact that the calculations in this chapter involved analysis of linear growth models. There is no guarantee that these missing-data models will perform equally well with other models. For example, if one wanted to test a traditional analysis of covariance model using these data—for example, with Time 5 and the dependent variable and Time 1 as a covariate—the model would be tested with greatly reduced statistical power. Similarly, these designs could be limited if one were interested in growth models involving higher order polynomials. For example, it seems likely that Design 5, which calls for all combinations of three times missing, would be very weak in testing quadratic functions or higher order polynomials.

In this chapter, we have described several measurement designs involving planned missing data. Although such procedures are not suited for every circumstance, it is likely that these designs will be an enormous benefit to researchers in a variety of research settings. We have shown that the benefit of the three-form design extends nicely to the analysis of change in the context of growth modeling.

Perhaps it is time to reconsider the question Why would anyone ever want to plan to have missing data? A better question might be Why would anyone not want to consider a planned missing-data design?

References

Allison, P. D. (1987). Estimation of linear models with incomplete data. In C. Clogg (Ed.), *Sociological methodology* (pp. 71–103). San Francisco: Jossey Bass.

Arbuckle, J. L., & Wothke, W. (1999). *Amos users' guide*. Chicago: Smallwaters.

Curran, P. J., & Muthén, B. O. (1999). The application of latent curve analysis to testing developmental theories in intervention research. *American Journal of Community Psychology, 27,* 567–595.

Duncan, T. E., Duncan, S. C., & Li, F. (1998). A comparison of model- and multiple imputation-based approaches to longitudinal analysis with partial missingness. *Structural Equation Modeling, 5,* 1–21.

Graham, J. W., & Donaldson, S. I. (1993). Evaluating interventions with differential attrition: The importance of nonresponse mechanisms and use of follow-up data. *Journal of Applied Psychology, 78,* 119–128.

Graham, J. W., & Hofer, S. M. (2000). Multiple imputation in multivariate research. In T. D. Little, K. U. Schnabel, & J. Baumert (Eds.), *Modeling longitudinal and multiple-group data: Practical issues, applied approaches, and specific examples* (pp. 201–218). Hillsdale, NJ: Erlbaum.

Graham, J. W., Hofer, S. M., Donaldson, S. I., MacKinnon, D. P., & Schafer, J. L. (1997). Analysis with missing data in prevention research. In K. Bryant, M. Windle, & S. West (Eds.), *The science of prevention: Methodological advances from alcohol and substance abuse research* (pp. 325–366). Washington, DC: American Psychological Association.

Graham, J. W., Hofer, S. M., & MacKinnon, D. P. (1996). Maximizing the usefulness of data obtained with planned missing value patterns: An application of maximum likelihood procedures. *Multivariate Behavioral Research, 31,* 197–218.

Graham, J. W., Hofer, S. M., & Piccinin, A. M. (1994). Analysis with missing data in drug prevention research. In L. M. Collins & L. Seitz (Eds.), *Advances in data analysis for prevention intervention research.* (National Institute on Drug Abuse Research Monograph Series, No. 142, pp. 13–63). Washington, DC: National Institute on Drug Abuse.

Graham, J. W., & Schafer, J. L. (1999). On the performance of multiple imputation for multivariate data with small sample size. In R. Hoyle (Ed.), *Statistical strategies for small sample research* (pp. 1–29). Thousand Oaks, CA: Sage.

Hansen, W. B., & Graham, J. W. (1991). Preventing alcohol, marijuana, and cigarette use among adolescents: Peer pressure resistance training versus establishing conservative norms. *Preventive Medicine, 20*, 414–430.

Hansen, W. B., Johnson, C. A., Flay, B. R., Graham, J. W., & Sobel, J. L. (1988). Affective and social influences approaches to the prevention of multiple substance abuse among seventh grade students: Results from Project SMART. *Preventive Medicine, 17*, 135–154.

Jöreskog, K. G., & Sörbom, D. (1993). *LISREL 8 user's reference guide.* Moorseville, IN: Scientific Software.

Little, R. J. A., & Rubin, D. B. (1987). *Statistical analysis with missing data.* New York: Wiley.

McArdle, J. J., & Hamagami, F. (1991). Modeling incomplete longitudinal and cross-sectional data using latent growth structural models. In L. M. Collins & J. C. Horn (Eds.), *Best methods for the analysis of change* (pp. 276–304). Washington, DC: American Psychological Association.

Muthén, B. O., & Curran, P. J. (1997). General longitudinal modeling of individual differences in experimental designs: A latent variable framework for analysis and power estimation. *Psychological Methods, 2*, 371–402.

Muthén, B., Kaplan, D., & Hollis, M. (1987). On structural equation modeling with data that are not missing completely at random. *Psychometrika, 52*, 431–462.

Neale, M. C., Boker, S. M., Xie, G., & Maes, H. H. (1999). *Mx: Statistical Modeling* (5th ed.). (Available from M. C. Neale, Box 126 MCV, Department of Psychiatry, Virginia Commonwealth University, Richmond, VA 23298)

Nesselroade, J. R., & Baltes, P. B. (1979). *Longitudinal research in the study of behavior and development.* New York: Academic Press.

Neter, J., Kutner, M. H., Nachtsheim, C. J., & Wasserman, W. (1990). *Applied statistical models* (4th ed.). Chicago: Irwin.

Rubin, D. B. (1987). *Multiple imputation for nonresponse in surveys.* New York: Wiley.

SAS Institute. (1990). *SAS language: Reference, version 6, first edition.* Cary, NC: Author.

Satorra, A., & Saris, W. (1985). Power of the likelihood ratio test in covariance structure analysis. *Psychometrika, 51*, 83–90.

Schafer, J. L. (1997). *Analysis of incomplete multivariate data.* New York: Chapman & Hall.

Schafer, J. L., & Olsen, M. K. (1998). Multiple imputation for multivariate missing data problems: A data analyst's perspective. *Multivariate Behavioral Research, 33*, 545–571.

Willett, J. B., & Sayer, A. G. (1994). Using covariance structure analysis to detect correlates and predictors of individual change over time. *Psychological Bulletin, 116*, 363–381.

Editors' Introduction

I t is difficult to imagine any large-scale, field-based research study, particularly a longitudinal study, without any missing data. The best researchers take heroic measures to minimize the amount of missing data; despite these efforts, the problem can never be completely eliminated. For years, researchers routinely threw out of every analysis data from any individual who did not provide data on all the variables included in a particular analysis. The costs of this approach were great. At best, statistical power was greatly undermined; at worst, internal and external validity were compromised. Today, modern missing-data procedures allow researchers to make use of all the data they have, complete or not, on all individuals. These procedures completely eliminate bias caused by missingness when the assumptions of ignorability are met and, in most cases, improve the situation even when the ignorability assumption is partially violated. Joseph Schafer offers an accessible introduction to missing-data procedures and presents multiple imputation based missing-data procedures, especially for longitudinal data. These procedures do not replace prevention of missing data—it is still better to minimize accidental participant nonresponse and attrition. However, thanks to Schafer's work, the longitudinal researcher faced with uncontrolled missingness now has a powerful tool for making the most of available data. In his commentary on the Schafer chapter and on the Graham, Taylor, and Cumsille chapter, Adam Davey points out some benefits of this approach and offers some sensible cautionary words. In chapter 11, Graham, Taylor, and Cumsille take Schafer's ideas in a slightly different direction and discuss why, when, and how a researcher might actively impose missingness on a research design. Readers may wish to contrast Schafer's approach to dealing with missing data with the approach presented by McArdle and Hamagami (chapter 5).

Multiple Imputation With PAN

Joseph L. Schafer

M issing values are a nuisance in many research efforts but especially so in the collection and analysis of longitudinal data. Multiple occasions bring greater opportunities for missed measurements. Fortunately, missing data is one area where statisticians have made substantial progress in recent years. In this chapter, I present a strategy for analyzing incomplete longitudinal data by multiple imputation (Rubin, 1987; Schafer, 1997a).

Missing data pose a difficulty because the overwhelming majority of paradigms and software for statistical analysis assume that the input data are complete. For this reason, the quickest and most convenient method for handling incomplete observations is case deletion, that is, ignoring participants with missing information. Case deletion suffers from a number of serious drawbacks, which have been well documented (e.g., Little & Rubin, 1987). For multivariate analyses involving a large number of items case deletion can be very inefficient, discarding an unacceptably high proportion of participants; even if the per-item rates of missingness are low, few participants may have complete data for all items. Moreover, case deletion leads to valid inferences in general only when missing data are missing completely at random (MCAR), in the sense that the discarded cases are like a random subsample of all cases. If the discarded cases differ systematically from the rest, then the resulting estimates may have potentially serious bias.

A natural alternative to case deletion is *imputation*, the practice of replacing missing data with plausible values. Various forms of imputation have been applied in federal surveys and censuses for decades (Madow, Nisselson, & Olkin, 1983). Imputation has been the survey statistician's method of choice for handling *item nonresponse*, situations in which a participant provides some infor-

This research was supported by Grant 1-P50-DA10075 from the National Institute on Drug Abuse and by Grant 2R44CA65147-02 from the National Cancer Institute. I extend special thanks to John Graham for providing data from the Adolescent Alcohol Prevention Trial and advice on their analysis.

mation but fails to respond to one or more individual items on a questionnaire. Imputation is attractive because it apparently solves the missing-data problem at the outset; once the missing values have been imputed, the data set can be summarized and analyzed by familiar complete-data methods. Another attractive feature of imputation is its efficiency: Unlike case deletion, imputation allows one to make full use of the data at hand.

Methods of imputation range from simple procedures, such as mean substitution—replacing each missing value with the observed mean for that variable—to elaborate hot-deck algorithms that jointly replace missing items with data obtained from donor cases chosen to match the original on selected items (e.g., Bailey, Chapman, & Kasprzyk, 1985). In longitudinal data sets with substantial participant-to-participant variation, analysts have sometimes filled in missed measurements by linear interpolation, extrapolation, or "last value carried forward." Unless great care is taken, these ad hoc imputation procedures may seriously distort important aspects of the distribution of a variable or its relationships with other variables. In general, it is desirable for the distribution of imputed values to resemble the distribution of the observed values, particularly with respect to intervariable relationships.

Even if an imputation method successfully preserves important aspects of the data distributions, a potentially serious problem remains: Imputation adds fictitious information to a data set. If imputed values are treated the same way as observed values in subsequent analyses, then the resulting inferences will be artificially precise, because the imputed values are imperfect proxies for the data they represent. With single imputation, there is no simple way to reflect uncertainty in the imputed values. In response, Rubin (1987, 1996) proposed the method of multiple imputation, by which each missing value is represented by a set of $m > 1$ simulated values. Let $Y = (Y_{obs}, Y_{mis})$ denote a generic data set, in which Y_{obs} is the observed part and Y_{mis} is the missing part. Multiple imputation replaces Y_{mis} with a set of simulated draws $Y_{mis}^{(1)}, Y_{mis}^{(2)}, \ldots, Y_{mis}^{(m)}$ from a predictive probability distribution $P(Y_{mis} | Y_{obs})$ arising from a model. After multiple imputation, one has m simulated complete data sets, $Y^{(j)} = (Y_{obs}, Y_{mis}^{(j)})$, $j = 1, 2, \ldots, m$, which are analyzed with standard complete-data methods. The results are then combined, using simple arithmetic rules, to produce overall estimates and standard errors that account for missing-data uncertainty. I reviewed these rules (Schafer, 1997a) and demonstrate them in the example near the end of this chapter.

The key idea of multiple imputation is that it treats missing data as an explicit source of random variability over which to be averaged. The process of creating imputations, analyzing the imputed data sets, and combining the results is a Monte Carlo version of averaging the statistical results over the predictive distribution $P(Y_{mis} | Y_{obs})$. In practice, a large number of multiple imputations are not required; sufficiently accurate results can often be obtained with $m \leq 10$.

Carrying out multiple imputation requires two sets of assumptions. First, one must propose a model for the distribution of Y. This data model should be plausible and should bear some relation to the type of analysis to be performed. For example, one could assume that the variables in the data set are jointly normally distributed. In the case of longitudinal analyses the model should be capable of preserving the correlation structure and time trends within individuals. The second set of assumptions pertains to the manner in which the missing values became missing. It is most common to assume that the missing data are missing at random (MAR) in the technical sense defined by Rubin (1976), which means that the probabilities of missingness may depend on the observed values Y_{obs} but not on the missing data Y_{mis}. The MAR assumption is primarily a mathematical convenience that allows one to perform imputation without explicitly modeling the missing-data mechanism. In practice, MAR is essentially untestable; it cannot be verified or contradicted by examination of the observed data. If the assumption seems *prima facie* implausible, then alternative procedures can be developed by modeling the probabilities of missingness. General techniques and software for creating multiple imputations under non-MAR models have not yet been developed; this is an important area for future research. Further discussion on the plausibility and ramifications of MAR was given by Little and Rubin (1987); Graham, Hofer, and Piccinin (1994); and Schafer (1997a).

Multiple imputation is not the only principled method for handling missing data. For parametric models, a main competitor is the technique of direct maximum likelihood, sometimes called *raw* or *full-information* maximum likelihood, which maximizes a likelihood function on the basis of the observed data Y_{obs} alone. This likelihood function may be written as

$$L(\theta \,|\, Y_{obs}) = \int L(\theta \,|\, Y_{obs}, Y_{mis}) \, dY_{mis}, \qquad (12.1)$$

where θ represents the unknown parameters of the data model, and $L(\theta \,|\, Y_{obs}, Y_{mis})$ denotes the likelihood function that one would use if no data were missing. The integration in Equation 12.1 eliminates the dependence on Y_{mis}, broadening the likelihood function to reflect the additional uncertainty due to the fact that Y_{mis} is unknown. In effect, this integration is nearly the same as the averaging over $P(Y_{mis} \,|\, Y_{obs})$ that takes place in multiple imputation. Except in very simple problems, the likelihood function Equation 12.1 tends to be complicated, often requiring complicated numerical techniques or approximations. When carried out properly, direct maximum likelihood can be statistically more efficient than multiple imputation because it is a deterministic procedure; no simulation is involved, so no extra variability is introduced into summary statistics. (In most cases, this extra randomness introduced by multiple imputation is quite minor.) In large samples, estimates and standard errors obtained by direct maximum likelihood and by multiple imputation tend to be very similar.

Applications of direct maximum likelihood are now common in longitudinal analyses. Modern algorithms for growth modeling as implemented in hierarchical linear modeling (HLM; Bryk, Raudenbush, & Congdon, 1996), Proc Mixed in SAS (Littell, Milliken, Stroup, & Wolfinger, 1996), and similar packages are designed for unbalanced data, where measurements on each participant may be taken at a different set of time points. Responses that are missing, either unintentionally or by design, are removed from the likelihood by integration as in Equation 12.1. An important limitation of these packages is that the missing values must be confined to the response variable; missing values on predictors are not allowed. If the individuals in the study have been assessed at a common set of occasions, models equivalent to those fit by HLM and Proc Mixed can be formulated using latent growth curves (McArdle, 1988; Meredith & Tisak, 1990; Willett & Sayer, 1994) and structural equations software. Two recent programs for structural equations, Mx (Neale, 1994) and Amos (Arbuckle, 1995), perform direct maximum likelihood from a raw data set with missing values. Missing data can be accommodated in other structural equations software by using the technique of multiple groups (Allison, 1987; Duncan & Duncan, 1994; Muthén, Kaplan, & Hollis, 1987). An advantage of the latent growth curve approach is that missing values may occur on predictors as well as the response; however, the measurements must be taken at a relatively small number of common time points.

When a direct maximum-likelihood procedure is available for a particular analysis, it may indeed be the most convenient and attractive method. Despite the increasing popularity of direct maximum likelihood, however, multiple imputation still offers some unique advantages for data analysts. First, it allows them to use their favorite models and software; an imputed data set may be analyzed by virtually any method that would be appropriate if the data were complete. As computing environments and statistical models grow increasingly complex, the value of using familiar methods and software should not be underestimated. Second, there are still many classes of problems for which no direct maximum-likelihood procedure is available. For example, in longitudinal analyses there is no direct maximum-likelihood method for incomplete covariates when occasions of measurement vary by individual.

A third reason why multiple imputation can be more attractive than direct maximum likelihood is that the separation of the imputation phase from the analysis phase lends a greater flexibility to the entire process. With multiple imputation the imputer is free to use additional variables that may be helpful for imputation but that are not of direct interest for the analysis. For example, consider a covariate that helps to explain reasons for nonresponse. Using this variable in the imputation procedure tends to reduce bias in subsequent analyses, even in analyses that do not involve that variable.

Finally, an important advantage of multiple imputation over direct maximum likelihood is that it singles out missing data as a source of random variation distinct from ordinary sampling variability. The likelihood function Equation 12.1 lumps these two types of variability together; summary statistics (e.g., standard errors) derived from direct maximum likelihood do not reveal two sources. With multiple imputation, however, the overall uncertainty is formally partitioned into sampling variability and missing-data uncertainty. This partition immediately yields an estimated rate of missing information, which can be quite helpful for assessing the impact of missing data on inferences for any parameter of interest.

The purpose of this chapter is not to criticize direct maximum likelihood in favor of multiple imputation; rather, it is my hope that more analysts will recognize the important advantages offered by both of these modern missing-data methods and begin to use them instead of case deletion or other ad hoc procedures. In most real-life applications, missing data are not the main focus of scientific inquiry but an unpleasant nuisance. Missing data should be handled quickly and effectively but without compromising the integrity of the analytic results. Multiple imputation might not be the optimal choice for every analysis, but it is a handy statistical tool and a valuable addition to a researcher's methodological toolkit.

In the remainder of this chapter, I describe a method for creating multiple imputations in longitudinal databases. Previous algorithms and software for multiple imputation, as described in Schafer (1997a), have focused on missing data in general multivariate settings. In response to the specific need for longitudinal analyses, a library of algorithms called *PAN* has been developed for imputing multivariate panel data, where a group of variables is measured for individuals at multiple time points. Alternatively, PAN may be applied to clustered data where variables are measured at a single point for participants nested within some larger unit (e.g., students within classrooms). Future versions of the software will be able to handle repeated measures and clustering simultaneously.

PAN is at present available as a library of functions for the statistical programming language S-PLUS (MathSoft, Inc., 1997).[1] Current efforts are focused on developing a version of PAN that operates as a stand-alone program in the Windows 95/98/NT environment.

---

[1] This can be downloaded free of charge from http://www.stat.psu.edu/~jls/misoftwa.html.

The PAN Model

Suppose that a group of time-varying continuous variables $Y_1, Y_2, \ldots, Y_r$ is measured for individuals $i = 1, 2, \ldots, N$ at multiple occasions. The responses for participant i may be arranged as a matrix with one column for each variable and one row for each occasion,

$$y_i = \begin{bmatrix} y_{i11} & y_{i12} & \cdots & y_{i1r} \\ y_{i21} & y_{i22} & \cdots & y_{i2r} \\ \vdots & \vdots & \ddots & \vdots \\ y_{in_i1} & y_{in_i2} & \cdots & y_{in_ir} \end{bmatrix}, \tag{12.2}$$

where y_{ijk} denotes the value of variable Y_k at occasion j. The number of occasions n_i and their temporal spacing may vary by participant. I assume that missing values occur throughout the matrices $y_1, y_2, \ldots, y_m$ and that these missing values are MAR. The immediate goal is to multiply impute the missing values so that the data can be analyzed in a straightforward manner. Ultimately, the analyst may choose to regard one column of Equation 12.2 as a response and the other columns as potential predictors in a conventional growth model. For the moment, however, I regard all r columns of y_i as random responses and model them jointly for the purpose of imputation. I construct a multivariate growth model to describe the joint distribution of the variables $Y_1, Y_2, \ldots, Y_r$, possibly given other time-varying or static covariates that are fully observed and require no imputation.

The model used by PAN was designed to preserve the following relationships: (a) relationships among the variables $Y_1, Y_2, \ldots, Y_r$ within an individual at each time point. These are reflected by the covariances among the elements of any row of y_i. (b) Growth or change in any variable Y_j within an individual across time points. This growth is reflected by trends within the columns of y_i. (c) Relationships between the response variables $Y_1, Y_2, \ldots, Y_r$ and any additional participant-level (non-time-varying) covariates included in the model. The participant-level covariates may be continuous or categorical, but they must be fully observed; missing values on these non-time-varying variables are allowed in the current version. Missing values in time-varying covariates are allowed and will be imputed, provided that they are included among $Y_1, Y_2, \ldots, Y_r$.

PAN relies on a multivariate extension of a linear mixed-effects model that has been popular for nearly 20 years. The model is

$$y_i = X_i\beta + Z_ib_i + \varepsilon_i, \tag{12.3}$$

where $X_i(\eta_i \times p)$ and $Z_i(\eta_i \times q)$ are known covariate matrices, β contains regression coefficients common to all units, and b_i contains coefficients specific to unit i. Note that Equation 12.3 is a multivariate regression; β and b_i are matrices with r columns, one column for predicting each of the variables Y_1, $Y_2, \ldots, Y_r$, and ε_i is also a matrix with the same dimensions as $y_i (\eta_i \times r)$. The univariate ($r = 1$) version, which was proposed by Hartley and Rao (1967) and later popularized by Laird and Ware (1982), Jennrich and Schluchter (1986), Bryk and Raudenbush (1992), and others, is the basis for many of the linear growth models in use today. The coefficients β and b_i are often called "fixed effects" and "random effects," respectively.

With univariate versions of this model, it is common to assume that the random effects and residuals are independently drawn from normal populations, $b_i \sim N(0, \psi)$ and $\varepsilon_i \sim N(0, \sigma^2 I)$, $i = 1, 2, \ldots, N$, where ψ is a $q \times q$ covariance matrix and I is the identity matrix ($n_i \times n_i$). For the multivariate case, one generalizes these assumptions to

$$\text{vec}(b_i) \sim N(0, \mathbf{\Psi}) \tag{12.4}$$

$$\text{vec}(\varepsilon_i) \sim N[0, (\mathbf{\Sigma} \otimes I)], \tag{12.5}$$

where vec denotes the vectorization of a matrix by stacking its columns. The covariance matrix $\mathbf{\Psi}$ in Equation 12.4 has dimension $qr \times qr$, and the Kronecker product notation in Equation 12.5 indicates that the rows of ε_i are independently distributed as $N(0, \mathbf{\Sigma})$, where $\mathbf{\Sigma}$ is $r \times r$.

In typical applications, the times of measurement are incorporated into X_i, and perhaps Z_i, as linear, quadratic, or higher order polynomials, and Z_i is a subset of the columns of X_i. For example, suppose that the first two columns of X_i are $(1, 1, \ldots, 1)^T$ and $(t_1, t_2, \ldots, t_{n_i})^T$, respectively, where $t_1, t_2, \ldots, t_{n_i}$ are the times of measurement for participant i; beyond these, X_i may have additional columns containing static or time-varying covariates for participant i. Setting Z_i equal to the first column of X_i produces a model of linear growth with intercepts randomly varying by individuals; setting Z_i equal to the first two columns of X_i produces random intercepts and slopes. Centering the distribution of b_i at zero causes β to become the population-averaged regression coefficients and the random effects $b_1, \ldots, b_m$ become perturbations due to interparticipant variation.

Note that in this multivariate model all of the covariates in X_i and Z_i appear as predictors for each of the columns of y_i. As a result, the same group of predictors and the same type of trend over time (e.g., linear mean growth with varying slopes and intercepts) are used to describe each of the response variables $Y_1, Y_2, \ldots, Y_r$. The actual coefficients for the response variables, as contained in the r columns of β and b_i, vary, but the same group of predictors is applied to each response. At first glance, this may appear to be a serious limitation of the model; in many scientific contexts there is no reason to believe that $Y_1, Y_2, \ldots, Y_r$ should depend on precisely the same set of covariates. One must remember, however, that the purpose of PAN is not to construct a theoretically meaningful model but to impute missing responses in such a way that important relations are preserved. If a covariate appears in subsequent analyses as a potential predictor of one or more of the response variables $Y_1, Y_2, \ldots, Y_r$, then that covariate should be included in the imputation model, even though its effects on some of the responses may be irrelevant or null. No biases incur by using an imputation model that is larger or more general than necessary for any given analysis. For more discussion on the purpose of imputation modeling and the interplay between the imputer's and analyst's assumptions, see Meng (1994), Rubin (1996), and Schafer (1997a, chapter 4).

The current version of PAN allows two types of assumptions about Ψ, the covariance matrix for the participant-level random effects $b_1, b_2, \ldots, b_N$. One allows the Ψ matrix to be either (a) an unstructured or arbitrary covariance matrix or (b) a block diagonal covariance matrix of the form

$$\Psi = \begin{bmatrix} \Psi_1 & 0 & \cdots & 0 \\ 0 & \Psi_2 & \cdots & 0 \\ \vdots & \vdots & \ddots & \vdots \\ 0 & 0 & \cdots & \Psi_r \end{bmatrix}, \tag{12.6}$$

where the nonzero blocks $\Psi_j, j = 1, \ldots, r$ are covariance matrices of size $q \times q$. The unstructured Ψ allows the random effects for any two responses Y_j and Y_k to be correlated, whereas the block-diagonal form assumes that the random effects for each response are independent of those for any other response.

The choice between these two depends on both theoretical and practical considerations. Suppose that $Y_1, Y_2 \ldots, Y_r$ represent achievement scores (mathematics, reading comprehension, etc.) recorded for schoolchildren over time, and one applies a model of linear growth with intercepts and slopes that vary by individual. If there is reason to believe that growth patterns for the various achievement scores are related—for example, that participants with high rates of increase for mathematics may also tend to have high rates of increase for reading comprehension—then it would be wise to use an unstructured Ψ. As the number of response variables grows, however, it often becomes impractical to estimate covariances among all of their random effects unless the number of participants is very large; to obtain a stable estimate for Ψ one may need to specify a block-diagonal structure. Unless the correlations among the random effects for some pairs of responses are unusually strong, the potential biases incurred by using a block-diagonal Ψ rather than an unstructured Ψ tend to be minor.

The basic strategy for specifying a PAN model can be summarized as follows. First, any time-varying covariates with missing values should be placed in the columns of y_i, regardless of whether they are treated as "responses" or "predictors" in later analyses. If a variable is to be imputed, then it must be included among the variables $Y_1, Y_2, \ldots, Y_r$. Second, other covariates of interest should be included in the columns of X_i and, possibly, Z_i. These include (a) variables that may be related to $Y_1, Y_2, \ldots, Y_r$ and (b) variables that may explain missingness on $Y_1, Y_2, \ldots, Y_r$. Placing a covariate in X_i allows it to influence the distribution of any or all of the variables $Y_1, Y_2, \ldots, Y_r$ in the population. Placing a time-varying covariate in both X_i and Z_i allows its degree of influence on $Y_1, Y_2, \ldots, Y_r$ to vary across individuals. Note that static or non-time-varying covariates (e.g., gender or pretest measures) should not be included in Z_i because it is impossible to estimate participant-specific effects for such variables. Finally, polynomial terms such as $1, time, time^2$, and so on, may be appended to X_i and Z_i as desired, to allow the mean levels of $Y_1, Y_2, \ldots, Y_r$ and the trends in these variables over time to vary across individuals. The choice of which terms to include will depend on what types of effects are believed to exist and what effects will be investigated in subsequent analyses.

Computational Algorithms

The computational engine of PAN is a Markov chain Monte Carlo (MCMC) algorithm called a *Gibbs sampler*. MCMC is a relatively new class of simulation techniques that are especially useful in Bayesian statistical analyses. A review of MCMC is beyond the scope of this chapter, but a gentle introduction is given by Casella and George (1992) and Schafer (1997a, chapters 3–4); more comprehensive references are the volume edited by Gilks, Richardson, and Spiegelhalter (1996) and the article by Gelfand and Smith (1990). Specific details and formulas for the computations used in PAN have been provided by me (Schafer, 1997b; Yucel & Schafer, 1998).

The MCMC algorithm in PAN is based on the observation that the model specified by Equations 12.3–12.5 has the following unknown components: the missing values in $y_1, y_2, \ldots, y_N$, the random effects $b_1, b_2, \ldots, b_N$, the fixed effects β, and the covariance matrices Σ and Ψ. For the purpose of imputation, I am interested only in simulating the missing data in $y_1, y_2, \ldots, y_N$; the other unknown quantities are merely a nuisance. To simulate the missing data properly, however, one must take into account the uncertainty in these other quantities and how it contributes to missing-data uncertainty. Expressing this uncertainty through mathematical formulas is difficult, so one accounts for the interdependence among the unknown quantities through a process of iterative simulation.

PAN simulates the unknown quantities in a three-step cycle.

1. Draw random values of $b_1, b_2, \ldots, b_N$ on the basis of some plausible assumed values for the missing data and the parameters β, Σ, and Ψ.

2. Draw new random values of the unknown parameters β, Σ, and

Ψ on the basis of the assumed values for the missing data and the values of $b_1, b_2, \ldots, b_N$ obtained in Step 1.

3. Draw new random values for the missing data given the values of $b_1, b_2, \ldots, b_N$ obtained in Step 1 and the parameters obtained in Step 2.

At the end of this cycle the parameters and missing data from Steps 2 and 3 become the values assumed in Step 1 at the start of the next cycle. Repeating Steps 1, 2, and 3 in turn defines a Markov chain, a sequence in which the distribution of the unknown quantities at any cycle depends on their simulated values at the previous cycle. The state of the process at Cycle 2 may be strongly correlated with its state at Cycle 1, but at subsequent Cycles 3, 4, 5, and so on, the relationship to the original state weakens. When a sufficient number of cycles has been taken to make the resulting state essentially independent of the original state, then the process is said to have *converged* or *achieved stationarity*. On convergence, the final simulated values for the missing data have in fact come from the distribution from which multiple imputations should be drawn.

This algorithm may be used to create m multiple imputations in the following way. Starting with some plausible initial values, run the Gibbs sampler for k cycles where k is large enough to ensure convergence, and take the final simulated version of the missing data as the first imputation; then return to the original starting values, run the Gibbs sampler for another k cycles, and take the final simulated version of the missing data as the second imputation; and so on. This method requires m runs of length k cycles each. Another and perhaps more convenient way is to perform one long run of mk cycles, saving the simulated values of the missing data after cycle $k, 2k, \ldots, mk$ as the m imputations. The latter method differs from the former only in that the final values from each subchain of length k become the starting values for the next subchain of length k.

It is important to note that convergence of an MCMC procedure means convergence to a probability distribution rather than convergence to a set of fixed values. To say that the algorithm has converged by k cycles actually means that the random state of the process at cycle $t + k$ is statistically independent of its state at cycle t for $t = 1, 2, \ldots$. After running the Gibbs sampler, one can examine the output stream over many cycles to see how many are needed to achieve this independence. Suppose that one collects and stores the simulated values for one parameter θ (a particular element of β, Ψ, or Σ) over a large number C of consecutive cycles. These values $\theta^{(1)}, \theta^{(2)}, \ldots, \theta^{(C)}$ can be regarded as a time series. The lag-k autocorrelation, which is the correlation between pairs $\theta^{(t)}$ and $\theta^{(t+k)}$ ($t = 1, 2, \ldots, C - k$), can be calculated for various values of k to determine how large k must be for the correlations to die down. In principle, one should examine autocorrelations for each parameter in the model and identify a value of k large enough to guarantee that the lag-k autocorrelations for all parameters are effectively zero. In my experiences with real data, however, I have found that the greatest levels of serial dependence are almost always seen in variance and covariance parameters, and in particular within the elements of Ψ. It is usually sufficient to monitor the behavior of the elements of Ψ because it is with respect to these parameters that the algorithm tends to converge the most slowly. For more discussion on monitoring the convergence of MCMC algorithms, see Schafer (1997a, chapter 4).

The rate of convergence of this Gibbs sampler is influenced by a combination of factors pertaining to the data and the model. First, it is affected by the amounts and patterns of missing data in the matrices $y_1, y_2, \ldots, y_N$; greater rates of missing information lead to slower convergence. It is also affected by one's ability to estimate the individual random effects $b_1, b_2, \ldots, b_N$; if estimates of random effects are highly variable, then convergence is slowed. Finally, convergence behavior is also influenced by the number of participants (N). As the sample size grows, the distribution of the random Ψ matrix at each cycle becomes more tightly concentrated around the sample covariance matrix of b_1, $b_2, \ldots, b_N$ from the previous cycle. As this distribution becomes tighter, the elements of Ψ are less free to wander away from their values at the previous cycle, producing higher correlations from one cycle to the next. It is somewhat ironic that the algorithm converges more slowly as one's ability to estimate the parameters increases. With a large number of participants and a small number of occasions per participant, it is not uncommon for the Gibbs sampler to require several hundred or even 1,000 cycles to converge. Slow convergence is not necessarily a problem, however, because in most cases only a few imputations are necessary. If $k = 1,000$ cycles are needed to achieve stationarity, then five imputations can be produced in 5,000 cycles, which even for a large data set requires no more than a few hours on a personal computer.

In addition to deciding how many cycles are needed, the user must also specify Bayesian prior distributions for the covariance matrices Ψ and Σ. Bayesian procedures, which are becoming increasingly popular in many areas of statistical analyses, treat unknown parameters as random variables and assign prior probability distributions to them to reflect one's knowledge of or belief about the parameters before the data are seen. An excellent introduction to the Bayesian statistical paradigm was given by Novick and Jackson (1974); for a modern overview of Bayesian modeling and computation, see Gelman, Rubin, Carlin, and Stern (1995). Some statisticians tend to prefer Bayesian procedures on principle, whereas others avoid them on principle. I hold a pragmatic view, accepting the prior distribution simply as a mathematical device that allows one to generate the imputations in a principled fashion. In applications, I like to use prior distributions that are weak or highly dispersed, reflecting a state of relative ignorance about model parameters. Weak priors tend to minimize the subjective influence of the prior, allowing the observed data to speak for themselves.

The prior distribution most commonly applied to a covariance matrix is the inverted Wishart distribution. The Wishart, a natural generalization of the chi-square to random matrices, is discussed in standard texts on multivariate analysis (e.g., Anderson, 1984; Johnson & Wichern, 1992). The prior distribution for Σ is

$$\Sigma^{-1} \sim W(a, B), \tag{12.7}$$

where $W(a, B)$ denotes a Wishart with a degrees of freedom and scale B. The scale is a symmetric, positive definite matrix with the same dimensions ($r \times r$) as Σ. The degrees of freedom, which should be greater than or equal to r, govern the spread or variability; lower values of a make the distribution more dispersed. The user of PAN must provide numeric values for a and B^{-1}. Our usual practice is to set $a = r$ to make the prior as dispersed as possible and then to set $B^{-1} = a\hat{\Sigma}$, where $\hat{\Sigma}$ is a reasonable prior guess or estimate of Σ. If a guess for Σ is unavailable, the data themselves may be used to obtain one. Yucel and Schafer (1998) recently developed a new expectation–maximization algorithm for calculating maximum-likelihood estimates of the parameters β, Ψ, and Σ from the incomplete data. Running this EM algorithm before the Gibbs sampler is an excellent way to obtain a reasonable guess for Σ.

In a similar fashion, I also use inverted Wishart prior distributions for the between-subjects covariance matrix Ψ. If Ψ is unstructured, one assumes $\Psi^{-1} \sim W(c, D)$ where D is a $qr \times qr$ matrix and $c > qr$. My usual practice is to set $c = qr$ and $D^{-1} = c\hat{\Psi}$, where $\hat{\Psi}$ is a prior guess or estimate of Ψ. If Ψ is taken to be block diagonal as in Equation 12.6, then independent inverted Wishart prior distributions are applied to the nonzero blocks, $\Psi_j^{-1} \sim W(c_j, D_j)$, $j = 1$, ..., r, where $c_j \geq q$. To make the priors weak, one sets $c_j = q$ and $D_j^{-1} = c_j\hat{\Psi}_j$ where $\hat{\Psi}_j$ is an estimate or guess for ψ_j. The EM algorithm described by Yucel and Schafer (1998) provides a maximum-likelihood estimate for an unstructured ψ or estimates of the submatrices Ψ, ..., Ψ_r when Ψ is block diagonal.

An Example: Expectancies and Alcohol Use in the Adolescent Alcohol Prevention Trial

The Adolescent Alcohol Prevention Trial (AAPT) was a longitudinal school-based intervention study of substance use carried out in the Los Angeles area (Hansen & Graham, 1991). In one panel of AAPT, attitudes and behaviors pertaining to the use of alcohol, tobacco, and marijuana were measured by self-report questionnaires administered yearly in Grades 5–10. The data exhibit typical rates of uncontrolled nonresponse due to absenteeism, attrition, and so on, which I assume to be MAR. This assumption has been given careful consideration by the researchers and appears to be plausible; for example, much of the attrition is due to students moving to other schools or districts, which is at most only weakly associated with substance use patterns (Graham et al., 1994).

In addition to this uncontrolled nonresponse, large amounts of truly MAR missing data (MCAR, in fact) arose by design. The AAPT study made use of an innovative three-form design in which each student received only a subset of the items in any year, as described in chapter 11 of this volume, by Graham, Taylor, and Cumsille. In some years, certain items were omitted entirely. For the present analysis, I examine a cohort of $m = 3,574$ children and focus attention on three variables: "drinking," a composite measure of self-reported alcohol use; POSCON, a measure of the degree to which the student perceives that alcohol use has positive consequences; and NEGCON, a measure of the perceived negative consequences of use. Drinking appeared on the questionnaire every year, where POSCON was omitted in Grade 8 and NEGCON was omitted in Grades 8–10. Missingness rates for the three variables by grade are shown in Table 12.1; observed means and standard deviations appear in Table 12.2.

My analysis will focus on the possible influences of POSCON and NEGCON on drinking. Without missing data, it would be straightforward to build a growth model for drinking that includes the expectancy measures POSCON and NEGCON as time-varying covariates. Current software for multilevel models cannot accommodate missing values on covariates, however, so I first use PAN to jointly impute the missing values for drinking, POSCON, and NEGCON.

Notice in Table 12.2 that both the average level of drinking and its variation increase dramatically over time. This is somewhat problematic, because standard growth models—and the multivariate model used by PAN—assume constant variance in a response over time. To make the assumption of constant

TABLE 12.1

Missingness Rates (%) for Three Variables by Grade

| | GRADE | | | | | |
VARIABLE	5	6	7	8	9	10
Drinking	2	24	24	33	35	44
POSCON	47	55	62	100	66	63
NEGCON	48	56	62	100	100	100

Note. POSCON = positive consequences; NEGCON = negative consequences.

TABLE 12.2
Means and Standard Deviations of Observed Variables by Grade

	GRADE										
	5		6		7		8		9		10	
VARIABLE	M	SD	M	SD	M	SD	M	SD	M	SD	M	SD
Drinking	−1.43	1.33	−1.12	1.96	−0.57	2.73	0.09	3.47	1.29	4.40	1.97	4.78
POSCON	1.30	0.61	1.34	0.62	1.48	0.74			1.84	0.89	1.96	0.91
NEGCON	2.94	0.76	3.05	0.75	3.07	0.77						

Note. POSCON = positive consequences; NEGCON = negative consequences.

variance more plausible, I transformed drinking by taking its logarithm (after adding a small constant to ensure that all values were positive). After this transformation, the increase in variation became much less noticeable. The log-transformed version of drinking was used both in the imputation procedure and in subsequent analysis described below, because the transformed version more closely fit the assumptions of both the imputation procedure and the analysis. With multiple imputation, however, it is not necessary for variables to be imputed and analyzed on the same scale. Applying transformations at the imputation phase can be a highly effective tool for preserving important distributional features of nonnormal variables, regardless of how the variables are later analyzed (Schafer & Olsen, 1998).

To set up the data for PAN, one first arranges the responses for each individual in the form of a matrix y_i of dimension 6×3, with the rows corresponding to occasions (Grades 5, . . . , 10) and columns for drinking, POSCON, and NEGCON. In devising the imputation model the primary concern is to preserve growth in the variable drinking and its potential relationships to the expectancy measures. With only six time points, the model for growth must be rather simple, so let us posit a linear model with intercepts and slopes randomly varying across individuals. That is, we create a model in which drinking, POSCON, and NEGCON are each described by a linear trend with a random intercept and a random slope, for a total of six random effects in each b_i. Random intercepts and slopes are specified by placing $(1, 1, 1, 1, 1, 1)^T$ and $(1, 2, 3, 4, 5, 6)^T$ into the columns of X_i and Z_i. Finally, to incorporate potential gender differences, I allow the population average slopes and intercepts for boys and girls to vary by adding two additional columns to each X_i matrix: $\text{sex}_i \times (1, 1, 1, 1, 1, 1)^T$ and $\text{sex}_i \times (1, 2, 3, 4, 5, 6)^T$, where sex_i is a dummy indicator for participant i's gender (0 for girl, 1 for boy).

In defining a PAN model, there is no particular importance attached to the specific coding scheme used to create the design matrices X_i and Z_i. For example, the linear effect of time could have been expressed as $(-5, -3, -1, 1, 3, 5)^T$ or any other set of equally spaced scores, and the gender effect sex_i could have been coded as any two values (e.g., -1 and $+1$) rather than as 0 and 1. The particulars of the coding scheme affect the precise meaning of the parameters in β, Σ, and Ψ, but these parameters are not of inherent interest—the goal at this stage is not to interpret parameters but to impute the missing values in y_i. Changing the coding scheme in X_i and Z_i does not change the distribution of imputed values, provided that the linear space spanned by the columns of these design matrices does not change.

Table 12.1 indicates that NEGCON is entirely missing for the last 3 years of the study. It may seem unusual to impute a variable that is entirely missing. Under this model the likely values of NEGCON for Grades 8–10 are being inferred from two sources: extrapolation from Grades 5–7 on the basis of the assumption of linear growth, and the residual covariances among the three response variables in Σ, which are assumed to be constant across time. Neither of these assumptions can be effectively tested with the data at hand, so inferences pertaining to NEGCON are heavily model based. In retrospect, it would have been very helpful to collect NEGCON in the final year (Grade 10) to provide more stable estimates of this variable's growth.

Before running the Gibbs sampler, I first obtained initial estimates of the unknown parameters β, Σ, and Ψ by running the EM algorithm. This EM procedure, which assumed an unstructured form for Ψ, converged in 134 iterations and took less than 1 h on a 400 MHz Pentium II computer. The resulting maximum-likelihood estimates for Σ and Ψ were then used to formulate weak prior distributions as described in the Computational Algorithms section.

Because of the high rates of missing information, I anticipated that the Gibbs sampler would converge slowly. To assess convergence, I ran it for an initial 2,000 cycles and examined time series plots and sample autocorrelations for a variety of parameters. As anticipated, the elements of Ψ pertaining to the slopes and intercepts of NEGCON were among the slowest to converge because of the extreme sensitivity of these parameters to missing data. On the basis of this exploratory run, it appeared that several hundred cycles might be sufficient to achieve approximate stationarity. The Gibbs sampler was then run for an additional 9,000 cycles, with the simulated value of Y_{mis} stored at cycles 2,000, 3,000, . . . , 11,000. Autocorrelations estimated from cycles 1,001–11,000 verified that the dependence in all components of θ had indeed died down by lag 200, so the 10 stored imputations could be reasonably regarded as independent draws from $P(Y_{mis}|Y_{obs})$. The entire imputation procedure took less than 2 hr with a 400 MHz Pentium II.

After imputation, the data were analyzed by a conventional linear growth-curve model for the logarithmically transformed drinking. The model was similar to the one used for imputation, except that POSCON and NEGCON now appear as time-varying covariates rather than responses. The model included an intercept and fixed effects for gender, grade, gender $\times$ grade, POSCON, and NEGCON, plus random intercepts and slopes for grade. Time was coded as $(1, 2, 3, 4, 5, 6)^T$, and gender was expressed as a dummy indicator (0 for girls, 1 for boys). Parameter estimates were computed for each imputed data set using a procedure equivalent to that used by standard packages such as HLM.

Finally, the 10 sets of fixed-effects estimates and their standard errors were then combined using Rubin's (1987) rules for multiple-imputation inference for scalar estimands. These rules are summarized as follows. Let Q denote the quantity to be estimated, in this case a regression coefficient. Let $\hat{Q}^{(j)}$ denote the estimate of Q from the jth imputed data set, and U_j its squared standard error $(j = 1, 2, . . . , m)$. The overall estimate of Q is simply the average

$$\bar{Q} = m^{-1}\Sigma\hat{Q}^{(j)}. \tag{12.8}$$

To obtain a standard error for $\bar{Q}$, one calculates the between-imputation variance $B = (m - 1)^{-1}\Sigma(\hat{Q}^{(j)} - \bar{Q})^2$ and the within-imputation variance $\bar{U} = m^{-1}\Sigma U^{(j)}$. The estimated total variance is

$$T = (1 + m^{-1})B + \bar{U}, \tag{12.9}$$

and tests and confidence intervals are based on a Student's t approximation

$$(\bar{Q} - Q)/\sqrt{T} \sim t_\nu, \tag{12.10}$$

with degrees of freedom

$$\nu = (m - 1)\left[1 + \frac{\bar{U}}{(1 + m^{-1})B}\right]^2.$$

The ratio $r = (1 + m^{-1})B/\bar{U}$ measures the relative increase in variance due to missing data, and the rate of missing information in the system is approximately $\lambda = r/(1 + r)$. A more refined estimate of this rate is

$$\lambda = \frac{r + 2/(\nu + 3)}{1 + r}. \tag{12.11}$$

The results of this procedure are summarized in Table 12.3, which shows the overall estimates, standard errors, degrees of freedom for the t approximation, and estimated percentage rates of missing information. All coefficients are highly statistically significant. The high rates of missing information indicate that the inferences for all coefficients (except sex) may be highly dependent on the form of the imputation model and the MAR assumption. The latter assumption is not particularly troubling for these data because the majority of

TABLE 12.3

Estimated Coefficients (Est.), Standard Errors, Degrees of Freedom, and Percentage Missing Information From Multiply Imputed Growth-Curve Analysis

VARIABLE	EST.	SE	df	% MISSING
Intercept	−2.572	0.084	19	71
Grade (1 = 5th, . . . , 6 = 10th)	0.386	0.011	35	53
Sex (0 = female, 1 = male)	0.370	0.046	324	17
Sex × grade	−0.105	0.013	88	33
POSCON	0.549	0.023	17	76
NEGCON	−0.090	0.023	15	80

Note.   POSCON = positive consequences; NEGCON = negative consequences.

missing values are missing by design. Certain assumptions of the imputation model, however—in particular, the assumed linear growth for NEGCON and constancy of the residual covariances across time—are not really testable from the observed data, so results from this analysis should be interpreted with caution.

Despite these caveats, the estimates in Table 12.3 provide some intriguing and plausible interpretations about the behavior of this cohort. The positive coefficient for sex indicates that boys reported higher average rates of alcohol use than girls in the initial years of the study. The negative effect of sex $\times$ grade, however, shows that girls exhibit higher rates of increase than boys, so that the girls' average overtakes the boys' by Grade 8. The large positive effect of POSCON indicates that increasing perceptions about the positive consequences of alcohol use are highly associated with increasing levels of reported use. The negative coefficient for NEGCON suggests that increasing beliefs about negative consequences do tend to reduce level of use, but the effect is much smaller than that of POSCON. These results are consistent with those of previous studies (e.g., MacKinnon et al., 1991) that demonstrate that perceived positive consequences may be influential determinants of substance use behavior, but beliefs about negative consequences have little or no discernible effect.

Discussion

The multivariate mixed model (Equation 12.3) used by PAN is a natural extension of univariate growth models, which are popular in the analysis of longitudinal data. The imputation procedures described here are appropriate for longitudinal analyses with partially missing covariates. These methods are also appropriate for multivariate cross-sectional studies in which units are nested within naturally occurring groups (e.g., children within schools). The algorithm and software described in this chapter provide a principled solution to missing-data problems for this important and frequently occurring class of analyses.

The imputation model and Gibbs sampler can be extended in a number of important ways. One extension pertains to models with additional random effects due to higher levels of clustering; this would arise, for example, in multivariate studies in which individuals are grouped into larger units and multiple observations on individuals are taken over time. Another useful extension pertains to columns of y_i that are necessarily constant across the rows $1, \ldots, n_i$. In longitudinal studies, these columns would represent covariates that do not vary over time; in clustered applications, they would represent characteristics of the clusters rather than the units nested with them. If these covariates have no missing values, they can be handled under the current model by simply moving them to the matrix X_i. When missing values are present, however, they must be explicitly modeled for purposes of imputation. If one imposes a simple parametric distribution on these covariates (e.g., multivariate normal), then it is straightforward to extend the Gibbs sampling procedure to impute these as well.

Another useful extension involves interactions among the columns of y_i. The multivariate normal model allows only simple linear associations among the variables $Y_1, \ldots, Y_r$, but in many studies one would like to preserve and detect certain nonlinear associations and interactions. In the AAPT example, it may have been useful to see whether the strong effect of POSCON on drinking may have been increasing or decreasing over time; the imputation model, however, imputed the missing values under an assumption of a constant POSCON $\times$ drinking association. Extensions of the multivariate model to allow more elaborate fixed associations, such as POSCON $\times$ drinking $\times$ grade, or random associations, such as POSCON $\times$ drinking $\times$ participant, are an important topic for future research.

In the current PAN model, the rows of y_i are assumed to be conditionally independent given b_i with common covariance matrix Σ. This assumption has been relaxed by Jennrich and Schluchter (1986), Lindstrom and Bates (1988), and others in the univariate case to allow a residual covariance matrix of the form $\sigma^2 V_i$, where V_i has a simple (e.g., autoregressive or banded) pattern dependent on one or more unknown parameters. Extensions of these patterned covariance structures to a multivariate setting tend to produce models and algorithms that are complex even apart from missing data. For example, the obvious extension of $\text{vec}(\varepsilon_i) \sim N[0, (\Sigma \otimes I)]$ to $\text{vec}(\varepsilon_i) \sim N[0, (\Sigma \otimes V_i)]$ seems too restrictive for many longitudinal data sets, because the response variables $Y_1, \ldots, Y_r$ are then required to have identical autocorrelations. Accounting for autocorrelated residuals in a sensible manner may prove to be a daunting task in the multivariate case. In practice, nonzero correlations among the rows of ε_i may arise because of a misspecified model for the mean structure over time. The problem may sometimes be reduced or eliminated by including additional (e.g., higher order polynomial) terms for time in the covariate matrices X_i or Z_i.

References

Allison, P. D. (1987). Estimation of linear models with incomplete data. *Sociological Methodology, 17*, 71–103.

Anderson, T. W. (1984). *An introduction to multivariate statistical analysis* (2nd ed.). New York: Wiley.

Arbuckle, J. L. (1995). *Amos users' guide*. Chicago: Small Waters.

Bailey, L., Chapman, D., & Kasprzyk, D. (1985). Nonresponse adjustment procedures at the Census Bureau: A review. In *Proceedings of the annual research conference* (pp. 421–444). Washington, DC: U.S. Bureau of the Census.

Bryk, A., & Raudenbush, S. (1992). *Hierarchical linear models: Applications and data analysis methods.* Newbury Park, CA: Sage.

Bryk, A. S., Raudenbush, S. W., & Congdon, R. T. (1996). *Hierarchical linear and nonlinear modeling with the HLM/2L and HLM/3L programs.* Chicago: Scientific Software International.

Casella, G., & George, E. I. (1992). Explaining the Gibbs sampler. *American Statistician, 46,* 167–174.

Duncan, S. C., & Duncan, T. E. (1994). Modeling incomplete longitudinal substance use data using latent variable growth curve methodology. *Multivariate Behavioral Research, 29,* 313–338.

Gelfand, A. E., & Smith, A. F. M. (1990). Sampling based approaches to calculating marginal densities. *Journal of the American Statistical Association, 85,* 398–409.

Gelman, A., Rubin, D. B., Carlin, J., & Stern, H. (1995). *Bayesian data analysis.* London: Chapman & Hall.

Gilks, W. R., Richardson, S., & Spiegelhalter, D. J. (Eds.). (1996). *Markov chain Monte Carlo in practice.* London: Chapman & Hall.

Graham, J. W., Hofer, S. M., & Piccinin, A. M. (1994). Analysis with missing data in drug prevention research. In L. Collins & L. Seitz (Eds.), *National Institute on Drug Abuse research monograph series* (Vol. 142, pp. 13–62). Washington, DC: National Institute on Drug Abuse.

Hansen, W. B., & Graham, J. W. (1991). Preventing alcohol, marijuana, and cigarette use among adolescents: Peer pressure resistance training versus establishing consecutive norms. *Preventive Medicine, 20,* 414–430.

Hartley, H. O., & Rao, J. N. K. (1967). Maximum-likelihood estimation for the mixed analysis of variance model. *Biometrika, 54,* 93–108.

Jennrich, R. I., & Schluchter, M. D. (1986). Unbalanced repeated-measures models with structured covariance matrices. *Biometrics, 38,* 967–974.

Johnson, R. A., & Wichern, D. W. (1992). *Applied multivariate statistical analysis* (3rd ed.). Englewood Cliffs, NJ: Prentice Hall.

Laird, N. M., & Ware, J. H. (1982). Random-effects models for longitudinal data. *Biometrics, 38,* 963–974.

Lindstrom, M. J., & Bates, D. M. (1988). Newton–Raphson and EM algorithms for linear mixed-effects models for repeated-measures data. *Journal of the American Statistical Association, 83,* 1014–1022.

Littell, R. C., Milliken, G. A., Stroup, W. W., & Wolfinger, R. D. (1996). *SAS system for mixed models.* Cary, NC: SAS Institute.

Little, R. J. A., & Rubin, D. B. (1987). *Statistical analysis with missing data.* New York: Wiley.

MacKinnon, D. P., Johnson, C. A., Pentz, M. A., Dwyer, J. H., Hansen, W. B., Flay, B. R., & Wang, E. Y. (1991). Mediating mechanisms in a school-based drug prevention program: First-year effects of the Midwestern Prevention Project. *Health Psychology, 10*, 164–172.

Madow, W. G., Nisselson, H., & Olkin, I. (1983). *Incomplete data in sample surveys, Vol. 1: Report and case studies.* New York: Academic Press.

MathSoft, Inc. (1997). *S-PLUS user's guide.* Seattle, WA: Author.

McArdle, J. (1988). Dynamic but structural modeling of repeated measures data. In J. R. Nesselroade & R. B. Cattell (Eds.), *Handbook of multivariate experimental psychology* (pp. 561–614). New York: Plenum Press.

Meng, X. L. (1994). Multiple-imputation inferences with uncongenial sources of input (with discussion). *Statistical Science, 10*, 538–573.

Meredith, W., & Tisak, J. (1990). Latent curve analysis. *Psychometrika, 55*, 107–122.

Muthén, B., Kaplan, D., & Hollis, M. (1987). On structural equation modeling with data that are not missing completely at random. *Psychometrika, 52*, 431–462.

Neale, M. C. (1994). *Mx: Statistical modeling* (2nd ed.). Richmond: Medical College of Virginia, Department of Psychiatry.

Novick, M. R., & Jackson, P. H. (1974). *Statistical methods for educational and psychological research.* New York: McGraw-Hill.

Rubin, D. B. (1976). Inference and missing data. *Biometrika, 63*, 581–592.

Rubin, D. B. (1987). *Multiple imputation for nonresponse in surveys.* New York: Wiley.

Rubin, D. B. (1996). Multiple imputation after 18+ years (with discussion). *Journal of the American Statistical Association, 91*, 473–489.

Schafer, J. L. (1997a). *Analysis of incomplete multivariate data.* London: Chapman & Hall.

Schafer, J. L. (1997b). *Imputation of missing covariates under a multivariate linear mixed model* (Tech. Rep. 97-10). University Park: Pennsylvania State University, The Methodology Center.

Schafer, J. L., & Olsen, M. K. (1998). Multiple imputation for missing-data problems: A data analyst's perspective. *Multivariate Behavioral Research, 33*, 545–571.

Willett, J. B., & Sayer, A. G. (1994). Using covariance structure analysis to detect correlates and predictors of change. *Psychological Bulletin, 116*, 363–381.

Yucel, R., & Schafer, J. L. (1998). Fitting multivariate linear mixed models with incomplete data. In *Proceedings of the Statistical Computing Section of the American Statistical Association* (pp. 177–182). Alexandria, VA: American Statistical Association.

COMMENT (on Chapters 11 and 12):
An Analysis of Incomplete Data

Adam Davey

The chapters by Joseph Schafer and by John Graham, Bonnie Taylor, and Patricio Cumsille are a clear indication that problems of incomplete or missing data are receiving greater attention and consideration than they ever have previously. In fact, these chapters, in conjunction with the considerable amount of accessible work in this area that is now beginning to accumulate (e.g., Arbuckle, 1996; Little, 1995; Little & Rubin, 1989), convince me that what structural equation modeling was in the 1980s and what mixed models have been in the 1990s, analysis with missing or incomplete data will be in the coming decade. For this reason and numerous others that researchers are only now beginning to appreciate, analysis with incomplete data is well worth careful attention. In the sections that follow, I outline some of the potentials and pitfalls that I see in each of these two chapters on incomplete-data problems.

Multiple Imputation

It is clear to a methodologist that there may be considerable benefits to data-based strategies such as multiple imputation (MI) for dealing with incomplete-data problems over model-based strategies such as full information maximum likelihood (FIML). It is also apparent that there is still a considerable way to go before MI techniques become as routinely applied as I suspect FIML methods will be.

For this reason, Schafer has a more difficult task than simply developing important methods: strengthening the case for when and why MI should be preferred over FIML. For one thing, data-based methods such as MI provide a replicable foundation on the basis of which multiple users may apply exactly the same data, whatever their purposes. Specifically, consider the case of large, nationally representative data sets. These may be multiply imputed once at the source and then distributed as a set to end users, an approach that is just now beginning to be applied. This common set of resources can then be analyzed by anyone according to his or her own purposes. Incorporating MI into large data sets has the potential for a large impact, and as this continues to happen, MI can be expected to do considerably more for the analysis of incomplete data than any other techniques that are currently available.

A second and considerable advantage is the ease with which these multiple rectangular data sets may be analyzed with standard software using standard techniques. Thus, for the end user, only very limited and widely available computational resources are required. With FIML techniques, however, large models quickly become difficult to estimate and are generally limited in standard statistical software to continuous data. Relatedly, because the multiply imputed data sets are rectangular, they can be analyzed according to any statistical model of interest. Using FIML, one's available repertoire of statistical models in statistical packages is much more limited, typically to Gaussian models with continuous variables.

As currently implemented, there are also several potential impediments to the more widespread proliferation of MI techniques. None of these appear to be intractable. Below I outline several issues that need to be addressed if model-based techniques are to become as widely used as possible.

Model Fitting

Assessment of model fit and model comparison are currently difficult to do in the context of MI with structural equation models (e.g., Meng & Rubin, 1992). Results from several models may be combined easily to yield good parameter estimates and confidence intervals. But how well does the model fit the data? In a nested sequence of models, how can the resulting plethora of chi-square statistics be combined? There would seem to be considerable benefit to incorporating this feature as soon as possible. Similar issues arise with FIML. Although the model chi-square can easily be recovered for the model of interest and independence model, all fit indices were not created equal in the presence of incomplete data (cf. Davey, Charak, & Rovine, 1999).

Pitfalls and Perils

It is clear that there are potential perils and pitfalls of MI relative to its alternatives. For example, unlike the situation with FIML, for which only a few analytic models are available, MI faces the problem of needing a greater variety of imputation models; this is one of the most significant advances in Schafer's chapter. The addition of an MI model for use with mixed models is a useful complement to normal, categorical, and mixed-scale models that have been presented elsewhere (Schafer, 1997). I propose a further related consideration, however: The relative costs and benefits of selecting an incorrect or overly restrictive model for imputation should be weighed against the selection of a more general but less efficient model. It is clear that there are several situations in which important interactions could be washed out if not incorporated into the imputation model, for example. Although one cannot do it all, if computational resources are not an issue, then it is probably better to choose a more general model for imputation and perhaps perform a greater number of data augmentation steps. Again, theory is likely to remain the best guide in choosing one's complete approach to analysis with incomplete data.

General Points Regarding Incomplete-Data Problems

By way of a transition between these two chapters on incomplete data, a few general points are worth making. One of the greatest obstacles facing any analysis with incomplete data is overcoming a decided lack of knowledge about these techniques and an inaccurate belief that ignoring missing data, as through listwise deletion, somehow involves making fewer assumptions about one's data. It cannot be stressed enough: Precisely the opposite is true, as Graham, Taylor, and Cumsille point out. For example, many journal editors are still reluctant to accept papers that use these techniques, believing that "making up data" requires stronger assumptions than believing that one's data are missing completely at random. Indeed, many researchers still do not realize how these techniques can improve their own substantive conclusions in situations with considerable selective nonresponse, such as longitudinal studies. Elsewhere, it has been demonstrated how listwise deletion leads to the incorrect conclusion that more time spent in poverty has beneficial consequences for the psychosocial adjustment of African American children, for example. The MI results, however, correct for the selective nonresponse, leading to the more sensible conclusion that duration of poverty has detrimental effects on psychosocial adjustment for all children (Davey, Shanahan, & Schafer, 1998).

Designed Missingness

Jack McArdle (1994) once wrote, somewhat facetiously, that he liked incomplete data and wished there were more of them, a sentiment I share. The methods that Graham et al. are developing reflect the serious side of McArdle's statement: There is a real and valuable place for incomplete data in the social sciences and developmental research. Graham et al.'s chapter also highlights several things about which researchers need to learn more.

First, there needs to be a careful exploration of which factors are important in identifying the optimal patterning and amount of missing data. For example, it is best to have some measures completed by all participants; it is best to pattern missingness by scale rather than within scale (i.e., by item). In other words, what are the other important factors that need to be considered, and to what extent can these be known a priori?

A second consideration is really procedural. In these designs, is it most efficient to randomize individuals to a pattern of missingness at the beginning of a study (which is ideal in principle, provided that everyone would, in theory, complete all waves of data collection had they been assigned to that condition) or to randomize participants to observed or missing status at each wave of data collection (a pragmatist's compromise, perhaps?). The former is truly random. The second is randomly conditioned on other reasons for nonresponse and attrition. A related consideration is whether this kind of design in and of itself might have implications for subsequent nonresponse. This point needs elaboration. On the one hand, designed missingness reduces testing burden for all participants, which might promote participant retention. On the other hand, it adds a little bit of irregularity, and perhaps unpredictability, to the process of data collection. Would implementing such a design actually lead to lower overall response rates than a design in which all participants were included at each wave of data collection? In other words, are there elements of designed missingness that may inadvertently induce subsequent nonresponse that are not present in complete-data designs? Finally, designed missingness still leaves researchers with the difficulty of how to correct for nonresponse that is unrelated to the study design.

Incorporation of missingness as a design issue opens the door as well to its fuller consideration within social sciences research; I would like to suggest a few possibilities I see for the strategies Graham et al. suggest. First, reasons for nonresponse (both within wave and across waves) need to be explored more fully, more explicitly, and more routinely—particularly as researchers move toward identifying distinct groups with different patterns of development—specifically those that may also be related to the pattern of missing data.

Second, designs of longitudinal studies need to focus more on participant retention, not just on controlled missingness. Graham et al. mention a financial "bottom line" reason for designed missingness. Perhaps some of this "saved" money should routinely be directed toward enhanced tracking and retention efforts, something that can only result in better data quality. Finally, I would like to identify several ways in which these designs might fruitfully be applied to developmental research.

Testing Burden

As Graham et al. mention, any number of factors may place an upper limit on the amount of testing a study participant will undergo. These include time, money, and stamina. In many cases, the testing burden may also affect performance. This undesirable consequence can and should be reduced or avoided through designed missingness.

High Attrition Rates

When dealing with high attrition rates (e.g., the Georgia Centenarian Study participants or other high-risk populations), it may also be possible to include a shorter time between waves to enhance retention by incorporating missingness into the design, both within and between waves. Again, a special effort at retention is required if there is a long lag between waves of data collection for a particular group of participants.

Disentangling Testing and Development

Although the importance of the issue of testing effects has faded a little in recent years, it probably remains an important one in many domains. Designed missingness bears an uncanny resemblance to the Soloman four-group design extended across multiple data waves. Testing for differences on the basis of observed data patterns could find some interesting applications in the developmental sciences. I hope many more implications of designed missingness and multiple imputation will be discovered as these strategies gain even more widespread use.

References

Arbuckle, J. L. (1996). Full information estimation in the presence of incomplete data. In G. A. Marcoulides & R. E. Schumacker (Eds.), *Advanced structural equation modeling: Issues and techniques* (pp. 243–277). Mahwah, NJ: Erlbaum.

Davey, A., Charak, D., & Rovine, M. J. (1999). *Comparison of fit indices under different missing data conditions.* Unpublished manuscript, University of Georgia, Athens.

Davey, A., Shanahan, M. J., & Schafer, J. L. (1998, October). *Using multiple imputation to correct for selective attrition in the National Longitudinal Survey of Youth.* Paper presented at the Institute for Survey Research Conference on Data Quality in Longitudinal Surveys, Ann Arbor, MI.

Little, R. J. A. (1995). Modeling the drop-out mechanism in repeated-measures studies. *Journal of the American Statistical Association, 90,* 1112–1121.

Little, R. J. A., & Rubin, D. B. (1989). The analysis of social science data with missing values. *Sociological Methods and Research, 18,* 292–326.

McArdle, J. J. (1994). Structural factor analysis experiments with missing data. *Multivariate Behavioral Research, 29,* 409–454.

Meng, X. L., & Rubin, D. B. (1992). Performing likelihood ratio tests with multiply-imputed data sets. *Biometrika, 79,* 103–111.

Schafer, J. L. (1997). *Analysis of incomplete multivariate data.* London: Chapman & Hall.

Cluster Analysis of Developmental Profiles: Relations Between Trajectories of Aggression and Popularity Over Adolescence

Daniel J. Bauer and David B. Estell

Tremendous strides have been made in recent years in the development of growth models such as hierarchical linear modeling (Bryk & Raudenbush, 1992) and latent curve analysis (Willett & Sayer, 1994). Rather than focusing on raw scores at each time point, growth models estimate smooth trajectories of change for each individual. The resultant growth parameters are then correlated or used as predictor or criterion variables. A difficulty with this approach is that the components of the growth trajectory are examined in isolation, although each parameter only partially captures the overall pattern of change. An alternative approach would center on trajectories as wholes rather than as component parameters. Toward this end, cluster analysis was explored as a method for studying the relationships between the trajectories of two variables: aggression and popularity. Earlier research suggests that (a) multiple patterns of adolescent development can be found in the two variables within each gender and (b) a negative relationship between the development of aggression and popularity can be observed in girls but not in boys (Xie, 1995).

A sample of 230 male and 255 female adolescents, assessed by their teachers yearly from ages 13 to 18, was drawn from the Carolina Longitudinal Study (Cairns & Cairns, 1994) to test these hypotheses. For each individual, growth parameters for intercepts and for linear, quadratic, and cubic slopes were calculated with ordinary least squares regression. Separate clusters for aggression and popularity were then formed for each sex on the basis of similarities on growth parameters. Because clustering algorithms are very sensitive to the scale and variability within variables, a weighting procedure was used in the analysis. A modified version of the coefficient of variation (CV: $100 \times \{SD(X)/[E(X) -$

This research was supported by National Institutes of Health Grants MH45532, HD22014, and MH524298 in which Robert B. Cairns and Beverley D. Cairns were the coprincipal investigators.

$MIN(X)]\})$ was used as a measure of variation relative to scale for each growth parameter. Standard scores were then calculated, weighted by the CV, and submitted to hierarchical cluster analysis using Ward's agglomeration algorithm. The number of clusters to extract was determined by a combination of the change in error sums of squares from solution to solution (with a minimum criterion that the solution explain 60% of the variance), the dendrogram, and the appearance of the differentiated clusters in a substantive sense.

In boys, four clear developmental patterns were identified for aggression. The cluster with the highest density of observations was characterized by relative stability at low levels of aggression over adolescence. The second greatest number of cases were found to have high intercepts of aggression, with a negative linear trend to asymptotically low aggression at later adolescence. The remaining two clusters consisted of boys who, to varying degrees, increased in aggression between ages 14 and 17. As for boys, the most predominant pattern of development of aggression in girls was one of stability at low levels throughout adolescence. Two clusters evidenced this pattern, with differing degrees of stability. The second most likely developmental pattern in girls was defined by high intercepts with a negative linear trend toward low values. Again, two clusters were differentiated within this pattern, characterized by varying degrees of initial aggression and steepness of decline over adolescence. Unlike boys, no developmental patterns were defined by marked increases in aggression in late adolescence. However, a small cluster of girls showed an increase in aggression in early adolescence, from ages 13 to 15, which then declined over late adolescence, returning to low values by age 17. Much less variability was observed in clusters of popularity. Three patterns of change in popularity were differentiated in boys and girls. In both genders, the predominant pattern was one of stability at relatively high levels. Of the remaining patterns, the first was characterized by decreasing levels in early adolescence with a rise in later adolescence, whereas the second pattern was the inverse of this trend.

The relationships between aggression and popularity trajectories were examined by contingency analysis using Fisher's exact tests (Fisher, 1934). These tests indicated whether certain combinations of development of aggression and popularity occurred more or less often than chance. In boys, no significant relationships were observed between changes in popularity and aggression over adolescence. As predicted, negative relationships between popularity and aggression were observed in girls, who tended to show declines in popularity as aggression increased. These findings replicated those obtained with other methods (Xie, 1995), providing some indication of the validity of this technique for identifying relationships between developmental trajectories.

References

Bryk, A. S., & Raudenbush, S. W. (1992). *Hierarchical linear models: Applications and data analysis methods.* Newbury Park, CA: Sage.

Cairns, R. B., & Cairns, B. D. (1994). *Lifelines and risks: Pathways of youth in our time.* New York: Cambridge University Press.

Fisher, R. A. (1934). *Statistical methods for research workers* (5th ed.). Edinburgh, Scotland: Oliver & Boyd.

Willett, J. B., & Sayer, A. G. (1994). Using covariance structure analysis to detect correlates and predictors of individual change over time. *Psychological Bulletin, 116,* 363–381.

Xie, H. (1995). *Social networks of children and adolescents in inner-city schools.* Unpublished master's thesis, University of North Carolina, Chapel Hill.

Change in the Field of Study Among Science Majors: A Multilevel Longitudinal Analysis

Dale J. Brickley, Joanne M. Cawley, and Maria Pennock-Roman

In previous studies, the probability that students planning to major in the science and mathematical fields will change majors has been predicted as a function of individual student level variables, such as gender, test scores, and academic background (Astin & Astin, 1992; Grandy, 1995; Hilton, Hsia, Cheng, & Miller, 1994; Strenta, Elliott, Adair, Matier, & Scott, 1994). Institutional factors, such as the gender composition of a college, also have been examined (Tidball, 1985; Tidball & Kistiakowsky, 1976). However, the simultaneous effects of student and institutional variables on changes in major have rarely been examined using a large data set that included multiple colleges and universities.

This research comprises the largest number of students and institutions to date and applies a multilevel statistical technique that produces more accurate estimates of regression parameters and standard errors than other techniques used in previous research. Prior studies have ignored the clustering of observations into groups within the same college or university, whereas the present multilevel analyses take into account the lack of statistical independence among observations for students attending the same institution.

The data set contained the scores of individual students on the Scholastic Achievement Test (SAT), 1979–1982, that had been matched to their corresponding record in the Graduate Record Examination files, 1985–1990. Information on undergraduate institutions was obtained from the College Board 1984 Annual Survey of Colleges (College Entrance Examination Board, 1985). Analyses were restricted to White, non-Hispanic male and female students in computer, engineering, mathematical, and physical (CEMP) sciences. Two transition points were studied: Stage I analyses examined the transition from intended undergraduate major as high school seniors to actual undergraduate major (N = 18,918 CEMP majors), and Stage II analyses examined the transition from actual undergraduate major to intended graduate major (N = 19,872 CEMP majors).

Separate logistic regressions with random coefficients (multilevel analysis) were run within each specific CEMP field, where the outcome variable was persistence within the broad category of all CEMP fields combined. Three types of explanatory variables were included as predictors of persistence in the analyses: student-level, institutional, and random effect variables. The analyses were run using the EGRET program (Statistics and Epidemiology Research Corporation, 1993).

As found in previous research, high SAT–Math scores, number of math and physical science courses in high school, and grades in high school physical science and math courses were usually associated with field persistence. In contrast, being female and having high SAT–Verbal scores were associated with changing into such fields as the biological sciences, social sciences, humanities, or other nonscience fields.

Unlike prior studies, it was found that the overall selectivity of the institution and the percentage of women enrolled in the institution as a whole were usually associated with change in field for both men and women in the majority of CEMP sciences.

References

Astin, A. W., & Astin, H. S. (1992). *Undergraduate science education: The impact of different college environments on the educational pipeline in the sciences* (Final report to the National Science Foundation). Los Angeles: Higher Education Research Institute, University of California. (ERIC Document Reproduction Service No. ED 362 404 SE 053 680)

College Entrance Examination Board. (1985). *The college handbook, 1985–86* (23rd ed.). New York: Author.

Grandy, J. (1995). *Persistence in science of high-ability minority students, Phase V: Comprehensive data analysis* (National Science Foundation Report No. 9255374). Princeton, NJ: Educational Testing Service.

Hilton, T. L., Hsia, J., Cheng, M. T., & Miller, J. D. (1994). *Persistence in science of high-quality minority students: Phase IV. Final report to the National Science Foundation Grant No. MDR-8955092.* Princeton, NJ: Educational Testing Service.

Statistics and Epidemiology Research Corporation. (1993). *EGRET reference manual* [Computer software manual] (first draft, 4th rev.). Seattle, WA: Author.

Strenta, C. A., Elliott, R., Adair, R., Matier, M., & Scott, J. (1994). Choosing and leaving science in highly selective universities. *Research in Higher Education, 35,* 513–547.

Tidball, M. E. (1985). Baccalaureate origins of entrants into American medical schools. *Journal of Higher Education, 56,* 385–402.

Tidball, M. E., & Kistiakowsky, V. (1976, August 20). Baccalaureate origins of American scientists and scholars. *Science, 193,* 656–652.

A Latent Growth Modeling Approach to Mediation Analysis

JeeWon Cheong, David MacKinnon, and Siek Toon Khoo

We explored latent growth curve analysis to model and assess the effect of a mediating process on an outcome process. Mediation analysis is used to identify a variable that is intermediate in the causal relationship between two variables. When the relationship between the independent and the dependent variables is partially or totally accounted for by the hypothesized mediating variable, this variable may be considered a mediator. When both the mediator and the outcome variables are measured repeatedly over time, the growth in the outcome and the growth in the mediator can be viewed as concurrent parallel processes. The treatment program is hypothesized to influence the growth of the outcome directly and also indirectly through its effect on the growth of the mediator.

To illustrate this approach, we used the data from the Adolescents Training and Learning to Avoid Steroids (ATLAS) Project (Goldberg et al., 1996), a school-based drug-prevention study designed to reduce high school football players' anabolic steroid use and to increase alternative healthy behaviors. The treatment group received multiple treatments: a full program after the baseline measurement and a booster program 1 year later. We used four waves of data: a baseline measurement, a posttest immediately after the full program, a 1-year follow-up measurement, and a posttest immediately after the booster program. The control group was measured at the same time but did not receive treatment. There were 1,506 participants at baseline, of which 428 provided data for all four measurement occasions. Participants were missing at follow-ups because of graduation, getting cut from the team, and absence. We analyzed the data with complete cases only and with partially missing data assumed to be missing at random. Nutrition behavior (Nutrit) and peer as an information source (PerIn) were the outcome and the mediator, respectively, because the ATLAS

This project was supported by an ATLAS grant from the National Institute on Drug Abuse (No. PHS07356) and the Estimating Mediation Effects in Prevention Studies Grant (No. 5R01DA09757-03).

FIGURE C.1

Influence of mediating process on outcome process. Estimation with complete cases (N = 428). Estimation including cases with missing data (N = 1,506) in italics.

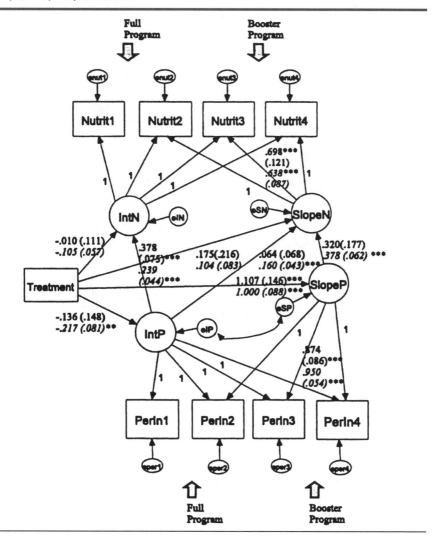

program was designed to increase the importance of peer teammates as information sources about sports nutrition, which was hypothesized to increase the players' nutrition behavior.

The analyses were conducted in two steps. In the first step, we modeled the treatment effects on the growth of the outcome and the growth of the mediator separately. To model the effects of the full program and the booster program, we used three linear segments. We hypothesized that there would be a linear increase after the full program, followed by a slight decline. After the booster program, there would be an increase to reach the same level as before the decline. For both processes, treatment was allowed to influence the initial status and the slope. In the second step, we analyzed these two separate growth processes simultaneously (see Figure C.1). In the model, the slope of the outcome (Nutrit) was influenced by the initial status and the slope of the mediator (PerIn), whereas the initial status of the outcome was influenced by the initial status of the mediator.

The model fit was acceptable, χ^2s(27) = 115.96, 154.44; RMSEA = .088, .056, in the analysis with complete cases and analysis with missing data, respectively. The treatment group's mean slopes on the outcome (Nutrit) were 0.501 in the analysis with complete cases and 0.477 in the analysis with missing data, whereas those of the mediator were 1.131 and 0.983. When analyzing the complete cases, the direct and indirect treatment effects on the growth of the outcome were not significant. When including cases with missing data, the direct treatment effect on the outcome process was not significant, whereas the mediated effect by means of the growth of the mediating process was significant (mediated effect size = .378, Z = 5.372, p < .001). This investigation indicates that parallel processes in longitudinal growth modeling can be used to model mediation.

Reference

Goldberg, L., Elliot, D., Clarke, G., MacKinnon, D. P., Moe, E., Zoref, L., Green, C., Wolf, S., Greffrath, E., Miller, D., & Lapin, A. (1996). The ATLAS (Adolescents Training and Learning to Avoid Steroids) Program: Effects of a multidimensional anabolic steroid prevention intervention. *Journal of the American Medical Association, 276,* 1555–1562.

A Comparison of First- and Second-Order Latent Growth Models of Alcohol Expectancies in Adolescence

Patricio E. Cumsille and Aline G. Sayer

Recent decades have seen an increase in the use of latent growth curve modeling to assess change over time. Most latent growth curve modeling studies use single indicators at each wave to estimate the growth parameters. Although multiple-indicators growth curve models (e.g., curve-of-factors models) have been discussed in the literature (McArdle, 1988), few researchers have used them (e.g., Duncan & Duncan, 1996).

In this study, we compared growth curve models of alcohol expectancies in adolescence using single versus multiple indicators (i.e., second-order models). In addition, second-order models were compared with and without equality constraints on loadings (invariance). Here, advantages and potential use of multiple indicators to analyze change over time are discussed.

The children (N = 3,584) participating in this study were recruited for the first panel of the Adolescent Alcohol Prevention Trial, a school-based alcohol prevention program that was implemented in southern California in the late 1980s. They responded to a questionnaire that included a number of alcohol- and drug-related items and were followed annually from fifth to tenth grades. The racial–ethnic distribution of the sample in fifth grade was 51.4% White (non-Hispanic), 28.4% Hispanic, 9.3% Asian, and 3.9% Black. Roughly speaking, boys and girls were represented about equally at each measurement period.

Expectancies were measured by three 4-point, Likert scale items that explored beliefs about alcohol as a social facilitator (e.g., "Does drinking alcohol make it easier to be part of a group?"). For the first-order model, a scale of alcohol expectancies was constructed at each grade by averaging the three items. For the second-order model, each item was used. In both models, the items ranged from low-positive expectancies (1) to high-positive expectancies (4).

This research was supported by National Institute on Drug Abuse Grant I-P50-DA 10075.

Covariance structure analyses (LISREL) were run on a logarithmic transformation of the items ($y = ln$[raw score $+$ 5]).

Initially, a piecewise model of alcohol expectancies was tested. This model had been identified in Cumsille and Sayer's (1998) study as appropriately describing growth in alcohol expectancies during early to middle adolescence. We then fit three different models.

1. A first-order (single-indicator) model was fit using the composite of the alcohol expectancy items

2. A curve-of-factors second-order model (multiple indicators) was fit using the individual items and imposing equality constraints on the loadings

3. A second-order model was fit without equality constraints to test for metric invariance of the factor loadings.

The results show that parameter estimates and the average growth trajectory of a second-order model with equality constraints were similar to estimates from the first-order model. However, the data did not support invariance over time, suggesting that the second-order model should be estimated without restricting the loadings. These results are particularly important considering that parameter estimates from a second-order model without constraints for the loadings are different from estimates from the first-order model.

References

Cumsille, P., & Sayer, A. (1998, June). *Predicting growth in positive alcohol expectancies from early to middle adolescence*. Poster presented at the annual meeting of the Society for Prevention Research, Park City, UT.

Duncan, S. C., & Duncan, T. E. (1996). A multivariate latent growth curve analysis of adolescent substance use. *Structural Equation Modeling, 3,* 323–347.

McArdle, J. J. (1988). Dynamic but structural equation modeling of repeated measures data. In J. R. Nesselroade & R. B. Cattell (Eds.), *Handbook of multivariate experimental psychology* (2nd ed., pp. 561–614). New York: Plenum Press.

A Latent Growth Curve Analysis of the Effects of Maternal Well-Being and Cocaine Use on the Home Environment and Infant Behavior From Birth to 24 Months

Evangeline R. Danseco and Paul R. Marques

A latent growth curve analysis was applied to determine the effects of maternal well-being and changes in maternal cocaine use on changes in home environment and infant behavior from birth to 24 months. The sample consisted of 162 women in their third trimester of pregnancy or women who had just given birth and were participating in a drug intervention program. Mothers' ages were 28 ± 3.9 years, with 11–12 years of education, and 2.9 ± 1.4 live children; 93% were African American, 85% had never married, and 96% were unemployed. Most women (89%) indicated cocaine as their primary drug of choice, with the other 11% indicating cocaine as a secondary drug of choice.

Maternal cocaine was measured through hair analysis for cocaine and cocaine metabolites through radioimmunoassay. Maternal well-being was measured using the Beck Depression Inventory, the Brief Symptom Checklist, and the Rosenberg Self-Esteem Scale. Home environment was assessed with the Caldwell Home Observation and Measurement of the Environment (HOME) Scales. Quality of infant behavioral interaction was measured through the Clarity of Cues and Responsiveness subscales of the Nursing Child Assessment Satellite Training Teaching Scales. All measures were administered four times, at 8-month intervals, beginning around birth.

The effect of maternal well-being and initial maternal cocaine levels on the home environment and infant behavior were estimated first separately and then altogether, using the maximum likelihood method. Models indicating a linear rate of change were found to have a better fit for changes in the home environment and infant behavioral interactions. Maternal well-being was related to

This research was supported by U.S. Department of Education Grant H324C980090 and by National Institute on Drug Abuse Grant R18 DA06379.

prenatal levels of maternal cocaine, but maternal cocaine was not significantly related to the home environment or to infant behavior. A model for a nonlinear rate of change in maternal cocaine levels and maternal well-being was predictive of initial HOME scores. Overall, however, there was little support for the hypotheses that the effects of changes in maternal cocaine use are detrimental to infant behavioral development and that the effects of changes in maternal cocaine are mediated by changes in the home environment.

Our previous reports on the same data also indicate that maternal cocaine levels were not significantly related to poor infant outcomes, with the exception of body length (Marques, Tippetts, & Branch, 1994). It is interesting that maternal cocaine levels were correlated to infant cocaine levels, which were also measured through hair analysis, at birth. Our results are consistent with a number of studies that show no differences in global cognitive functioning among prenatally exposed children from a control group. A follow-up study on the development of children in this sample is now underway. More sensitive and comprehensive child development measures will be administered to children who are now 8 or 9 years old. Examples of areas of development to measure include intelligence, academic achievement, attention, language, behavior problems, motor development, and physical anomalies. A comparison group of children who were not prenatally exposed to cocaine will also be included.

Reference

Marques, P. R., Tippetts, A. S., & Branch, D. G. (1994). Birth outcome not correlated with late-term cocaine exposure within an exposed sample. In L. Harris (Ed.), *Problems of drug dependence, 1994: Proceedings of the 56th annual scientific meeting* (National Institute on Drug Abuse Research Monograph No. 153, Vol. 2, p. 475). Washington, DC: National Institute on Drug Abuse.

Testing Mediational Effects of Competence on Drug Use Propensity in Childhood With Structural Equation Modeling

Zhihong Fan, Mary Ann Pentz, James Dwyer, and Gencie Turner

Although research shows relationships between drug use risk factors and drug use and between competence and problem behavior related to drug use in adolescents, little is known about the potential of competence to mediate the risk-of-drug-use relationship in childhood. This test—retest study attempted to link risk factors and drug use propensity, with academic and social competence as mediators, in children.

Data collection was conducted in January 1997 and again in April 1997, as a pilot study of a drug-use prevention intervention program in elementary school. Baseline (Time 1) and follow-up measurements (Time 2) were taken 3 months apart. The in-class 119-item survey included items representing demographic characteristics, hypothesized constructs of personal, social–situational, and environmental risk factors for problem behavior and drug use, hypothesized competence-related mediators, and behavioral outcomes. Participants were fourth graders from 48 elementary schools in Marion County, Indiana. The total sample was 53.8% female, 55.5% White, and 36.8% Black; 33% were from high-socioeconomic status families, 69% were from suburban schools, and the mean age was 9.5 years (range: 9–12). The complete data set included 1,110 participants at Time 1 and 1,047 at Time 2; 732 participants provided complete data at both waves.

Six constructs were identified: latchkey status, friend drug use, family drug use, academic competence, social competence, and drug use propensity. Each of the six constructs were measured by two to four indicators. Among the indicators, most were single items from the survey; the others were scales formed by the average of several items derived from the results of factor analyses. Items were recoded as necessary such that higher scores of the items for the same scale reflected the similar psychological meaning. Change factors were created from the corresponding factors at two waves. The academic competence construct was not reliable enough to create a change factor; thus, only social competence was considered for testing mediational effects.

The effect of latchkey status on drug use propensity was found to be mediated by social competence or by correlation with friend use and family use. Higher initial level and increase in latchkey status were linked with higher drug use propensity later on by impairing social competence. Increase in latchkey status was associated with increased drug use propensity and mediated by decreased social competence. Perceived friends' drug use was associated cross-sectionally with drug use propensity; change in friends' use was significantly related to change in drug use propensity. Perceived family drug use had a direct effect on change in drug use propensity; the time-lag effects of family drug use on drug use propensity were mediated through decreasing social competence.

Latchkey status and perceived family and friend drug use were strong predictors of drug use propensity in childhood, which suggests the need for designing drug use prevention programs for children. If the hypothesis that competence has a protective effect against drug use continues to be supported in future research, programs that focus on promoting competence-related coping strategies in children—such as support seeking, talking, and doing things with parents—should have effects on delaying or decreasing drug use in adolescence.

Future research needs to address (a) the impact of demographic characteristics, such as differences of gender, socioeconomic status, and ethnicity on the competence–drug use relationships in childhood and (b) whether competence has a mediating effect in longitudinal studies with longer periods of follow-up and preventive intervention trials in children and adolescents.

Modeling Transitions in Two-Stage Sequences Simultaneously

Brian P. Flaherty and Linda M. Collins

The current latent transition analysis model (LTA; Collins & Wugalter, 1992) is presented along with a reparameterized model that estimates two sequences simultaneously. The reparameterized model quantifies concurrent and longitudinal effects of a predictor sequence on a dependent sequence. This new model provides a better description of the impact of individuals' memberships in one-stage sequence on their memberships in another stage sequence. The single-sequence LTA model and the reparameterized model are both illustrated with an example examining the intraindividual effects of the level of tobacco use on the level of alcohol use for a sample of 9th- to 11th-grade students; that is, does an individual's level of tobacco use predict his or her concurrent level of alcohol use? Furthermore, does an individual's change in his or her level of tobacco use predict a change in alcohol use? Questions of this type are answered directly with the reparameterized LTA model. This type of analysis can also examine the reverse effect; for example, does an individual's level of alcohol use predict his or her level of tobacco use? Examining the effects of tobacco and alcohol on each other highlights the asymmetry of contingency table analysis. This is demonstrated by showing that relations observed when tobacco level is predictive of alcohol level do not necessarily hold when alcohol level predicts tobacco level. Tobacco level appears to be related to the concurrent level of alcohol use, and change in tobacco level is related to change in alcohol use level. However, alcohol is not predictive of tobacco in any of the examined cases. This paper develops and illustrates a useful method of modeling relations and changes among two-stage sequences.

Reference

Collins, L. M., & Wugalter, S. E. (1992). Latent class models for stage-sequential dynamic latent variables. *Multivariate Behavioral Research, 27,* 131–157.

This work was supported by National Institute on Drug Abuse Grant 1 P50 DA10075.

APPENDIX H

Stability and Change in Grip Strength During Adulthood: An Examination of Genetic and Environmental Influences

Julia D. Grant, Stig Berg, and Gerald E. McClearn

A number of variables, including grip strength, have been proposed as potential markers of aging (see Anstey, Lord, & Smith, 1996, and Arking, 1991, for reviews). Although researchers have indicated that genetic factors influence grip strength, no researchers have examined genetic and environmental contributions to stability and change in grip strength. The goals of these analyses were to examine genetic and environmental influences on stability in grip strength, the pattern of change in grip strength (through growth curve analyses), and genetic and environmental influences on change in grip strength.

The participants in these analyses took part in the in-person testing phase of the Swedish Adoption/Twin Study of Aging (see Pedersen et al., 1991, for details). In-person data were collected on three occasions, with 3 years between test sessions. Data from 215 like-sex twin pairs (monozygotic = 86, dizygotic = 129) with complete data from the first wave were included. Each participant's grip strength was tested for both hands with a hand dynamometer; the greater grip strength was used in the analyses.

Phenotypic stability was high (approximately .65 over 3 years and .55 over 6 years). Model-fitting analyses indicated that for each occasion, genetic and nonshared environmental influences each accounted for 40%–45% of the variance, age accounted for 10%–20% of the variance, and shared environmental influences were minimal. The genetic and shared environmental correlations approached 1.0, indicating that the influences were stable; nonshared environmental influences were less stable (correlations around .35 over 3 years and .15 over 6 years). Thus, 60%–65% of phenotypic stability was explained by genetic factors, 10%–25% was explained by nonshared environmental influences, and 15%–20% was explained by age effects.

This research was supported by Grants AG04563 and AG10175 from the MacArthur Foundation Research Network on Successful Aging and the Swedish Social Research Council.

An analysis of variance indicated that there was significant change in grip strength over the course of the study, $F(2, 622) = 98.82$, $p < .05$. Ordinary least squares regression was used to estimate individual growth curves, and a linear model was selected. Quantitative genetic analyses of the intercept (initial level) indicated that genetic influences accounted for 28% of the variance, nonshared environmental influences accounted for 68% of the variance, and age accounted for 3% of the variance. Nonshared environmental influences accounted for 98% of the variance in slope, with age accounting for the remaining 2% of the variance.

These analyses represent a preliminary attempt to extend the study of aging through the investigation of genetic and environmental influences on changes associated with the aging process. The analyses of stability corroborated previous research, which indicated that grip strength is influenced by genetic factors. The analyses of change indicated that change in grip strength is primarily influenced by nonshared environmental factors. Caution should be used in interpreting these analyses as they need to be confirmed with other samples.

References

Anstey, K. J., Lord, S. R., & Smith, G. A. (1996). Measuring human functional age: A review of empirical findings. *Experimental Aging Research, 22,* 245–266.

Arking, R. (1991). *Biology of aging: Observations and principles.* Englewood Cliffs, NJ: Prentice Hall.

Pedersen, N. L., McClearn, G. E., Plomin, R., Nesselroade, J. R., Berg, S., & deFaire, U. (1991). The Swedish Adoption/Twin Study of Aging: An update. *Acta Geneticae Medicae et Gemellologiae, 40,* 7–20.

Tapestry Over Time: A Way to Visualize the Dynamics of Multivariate Data

John C. Hanes, Jr.

A local agency with a group approach to therapy for parents at risk of losing their children engaged the Center for the Study of Social Issues for evaluation consulting. From several approaches to assessment, we developed a way to visualize client progress over time on a number of variables. Bound by the constraints of a very small sample size, the need to communicate identifiable change in client behavior in a rapid manner, and therapists with a limited statistical repertoire, we developed a simple, color-coded graphic device using the Microsoft Excel 97 spreadsheet and Microsoft Visual Basic for Applications. We called this device "Tapestry Over Time." On a single sheet of letter-size paper, we showed 32 behavioral constructs observed over 22 group therapy sessions for each client. We also calculated an average for each construct and each occasion; several of the therapy sessions included learning laboratory events that were coded in relation to changes in the constructs. Because two therapists observed each client, we used the same spreadsheet template to reveal patterns of rater agreement. The therapists distinguished five levels of behavior for the constructs, and these were represented by five distinct colors arranged in accordance with the visible spectrum (identified by a key at the bottom of the spreadsheet). Therapists could use the form each week to provide guidance both to individuals and the group.

In anticipation of further applications of this approach, we provided space for 40 constructs–items–participants and 36 occasions for 1,440 data points in the landscape orientation (66 × 24 in the portrait orientation for 1,584 data points; the larger, 11-in. × 17-in. format displays approximately 4,700 data points) and added the capacity for additional levels of behavior that take on additional colors. With some sacrifice of data points, the single sheet can present descriptive variables for individuals and groups.

Consistent with the idea of "interocular significance," Tapestry Over Time provides an intuitive, longitudinal, color-coded representation of dependent (and independent) variable dynamics with the capacity to sort, mobilize, and aggregate on construct-specific, occasion-specific, and categorical factors for exploratory purposes. This offers the simultaneous visualization of certain aspects of such methods as event history analysis, G theory, and repeated-measures multivariate analysis of variance.

Although color coding represents patterns based on clinical significance, Tapestry Over Time can reveal patterns of change in standardized and absolute effect size and statistical significance. We are currently exploring applications to experimental design using the orthogonal arrays (inner and outer) of Taguchi methods where sorting on various parameters of the dependent variable results in pattern changes among the independent and "noise" variables. We are also seeking to explicate graphically such aspects of generalizability as rater drift, fatigue, and bias.

Multivariate Survivorship Analysis Using Two Cross-Sectional Samples

Mark E. Hill

A major limitation of standard approaches to survival analysis is the need for prospective tracking of study participants to ascertain the occurrence of exit events. If the transitions of interest require many years to occur, the required follow-up period often becomes prohibitively expensive in terms of time and money. As an alternative to survival analysis with longitudinal data, this paper introduces a method that can be applied when one observes the same cohort in two cross-sectional samples collected at different points in time. The method allows for the estimation of a log-probability survivorship model that estimates the influence of multiple time-invariant factors on survival over the time interval separating the two samples:

$$\log \pi_i = \alpha + \beta' X_i,$$

where π_i represents the probability of surviving from Time t_1 to Time t_2 for individual i; X_i is a set of time-invariant covariates; α represents the log of the baseline probability (level), and β_k represents the log of the relative risk (differential) associated with covariate k adjusted for all other covariates in the model. The paper shows how this model can be estimated using standard logit regression software.

This unique method can be used whenever the survival process can be adequately conceptualized as an irreversible single-decrement process (e.g., the transition to first marriage among a cohort of never-married individuals). The multivariate method is illustrated through an investigation of the effects of race, parity, and educational attainment on the survival of older American women.

Gun Availability and Adolescent Substance Use: Using Multiple Imputation to Get Standard Errors

Stephanie L. Hyatt, Linda M. Collins, and Joseph L. Schafer

This study demonstrates the use of data augmentation to perform multiple imputation (Schafer, 1997), which now provides standard errors for the parameter estimates in latent transition analysis (LTA; Collins & Wugalter, 1992). LTA is a statistical procedure for examining stage-sequential models of individual development in longitudinal data. It was used here to examine the onset patterns of substance use for adolescents who do and do not have a gun available to them in their home.

In this study, the LTA model was made up of a dynamic stage sequence; adolescent substance use, measured at two times; and a static exogenous predictor, gun availability. LTA estimated the following parameters: the probability of having a gun available in the home; the probability of membership in each stage of substance use, given gun availability; the probability of transitioning to a different stage of substance use over time, given gun availability; and the amount of measurement error.

The expectation–maximization algorithm produces maximum-likelihood parameter estimates for latent transition models, but it does not provide standard errors for those estimates, which would be useful in making statistical comparisons across groups. LTA now uses a data augmentation algorithm to allow for the drawing of multiple imputations of missing data (Schafer, 1997). This simulation method treats the latent variables as missing data and generates a user-specified number of data sets with imputed latent variables. Complete-data techniques can then be used to analyze each data set, and results across imputations are combined to yield a point estimate and 95% confidence interval for each parameter. This allows parameter estimates to be compared for statistically significant differences.

The participants were drawn from the National Longitudinal Study of Ad-

This research was supported by National Institute on Drug Abuse Grant 1 P50 DA10075.

olescent Health, a study mandated by Congress to collect data to evaluate the effect of social context on the health and well-being of adolescents in the United States. The participants were 992 students who were measured in eighth grade during the 1994–1995 school year and again during the summer of 1996. The five measures of substance use asked if the adolescent has ever had alcohol more than two or three times, ever tried cigarettes, ever had five drinks or more in a row, ever been drunk, and ever tried marijuana. The measure of gun availability asked if a gun was easily available to the adolescent in his or her home. All items were coded 0 for missing, 1 for *no*, and 2 for *yes*. A latent transition model was specified to include eight stages of substance use.

Results show that 22.6% of eighth graders had a gun available to them. Several statistically significant group differences emerged. Eighth graders who had a gun available to them were less likely to be in the "no substance use" stage and more likely to be in the "alcohol, drunkenness, and cigarettes" stage. Prevalence rates indicate that adolescents who had a gun available to them were significantly more likely to have tried alcohol. No statistically significant group differences emerged in the transition probability matrix, although many of these parameters were based on very small sample sizes and therefore had large standard errors. Gun availability does appear to be related to substance use, especially to alcohol use. It will be important in the future to examine how and why this relationship exists and what differentiates adolescents who have guns available to them from those who do not.

References

Collins, L. M., & Wugalter, S. E. (1992). Latent class models for stage-sequential dynamic latent variables. *Multivariate Behavioral Research, 27,* 131–157.

Schafer, J. L. (1997). *Analysis of incomplete multivariate data.* London: Chapman & Hall.

APPENDIX L

Unraveling Alcohol–Tobacco Comorbidity Over Seven Years: A Latent Class Analysis

Kristina M. Jackson, Kenneth J. Sher, and Phillip K. Wood

The identification of distinct subtypes of abusers of alcohol is important for describing etiological pathways and optimal treatment matching. As alcohol use disorder (AUD) and tobacco dependence (TD) often co-occur, one approach to classifying alcohol involvement is to subtype individuals on the basis of comorbidity with tobacco use. Trajectories of alcohol and tobacco use disorder can be examined not only across individuals, as in a repeated-measures analysis of variance, but also within individuals, by identifying typologies that constitute discrete groups based on information about the joint sequencing of substance use disorders over time.

A mixed-gender high-risk sample of 450 young adults (baseline age = 18.2) was assessed five times over a 7-year period (Year 1, 2, 3, 4, and 7). Past year diagnoses of AUDs and TDs were made on the basis of criteria from the *Diagnostic and Statistical Manual of Mental Disorders* (3rd ed.; American Psychiatric Association, 1980). Response profiles derived from the endorsement of AUD and TD diagnoses over five waves were classified using latent class analysis, a categorical analog to factor analysis in which mutually exclusive discrete latent variables, or classes, are extracted from two or more discrete observed variables.

Five classes were identified and characterized by the following labels: persistent AUD (6%), developmentally limited AUD (16%), TD (11%), comorbid AUD and TD (7%), and nondiagnosers (60%). Figure L.1 presents latent class diagnosing probabilities, which reflect the likelihood of diagnosing a person with an AUD or TD and are analogous to factor loadings in factor analysis.

Next we determined the extent to which these latent class typologies differed with respect to five etiologically important third variables: sex, family history of alcoholism (FH+/FH−), retrospectively assessed childhood life stressors, behavioral undercontrol, and alcohol outcome expectancies. Latent class membership was assigned on the basis of the class most highly probable for an individual. Women were more likely to belong to the nondiagnoser class and the TD-only class and were less likely to belong to the persistent or de-

407

FIGURE L.1

Diagnosing probabilities by latent class.

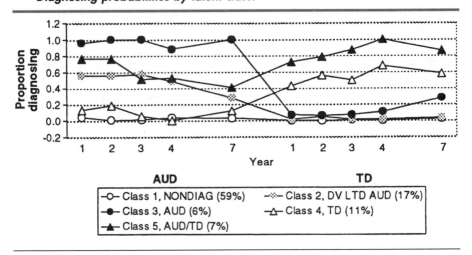

velopmentally limited AUD classes. FH− participants were substantially more likely to belong to the nondiagnoser class, whereas FH+ participants were more likely to belong to a diagnosing (persistent AUD, TD, or comorbid) class.

Behavioral undercontrol was highest among the persistent AUD and comorbid classes and lowest among the nondiagnoser class. A similar pattern was observed for alcohol expectancies: Although expectancies showed specificity for alcohol, there was evidence for predictive utility across substance. In contrast, life stressors were highest among the comorbid class and TD class, suggesting that a history of childhood life stressors puts individuals particularly at risk for tobacco dependence.

Reference

American Psychiatric Association. (1980). *Diagnostic and statistical manual of mental disorders* (3rd ed.). Washington, DC: Author.

Longitudinal Analysis of Complex Survey Data: Math and Reading Achievement From the National Longitudinal Survey of Youth, 1986–1994

Chi-Ming Kam and David A. Wagstaff

The impact of complex survey weights on standard errors and inference was assessed using mathematics and reading comprehension data from the National Longitudinal Survey of Youth. The weights were adjusted for unequal selection probabilities, the oversampling of minority and economically disadvantaged White youth, and unit and item nonresponse. Two regression-based approaches were compared: (a) a model-based approach, which includes in the substantive model the variables that determine sample selection, and (b) a design-based approach, which uses weights that reflect each participant's selection probability.

The data were obtained over an 8-year period from the children born to the mothers of the original survey cohort. The specific measures were the Peabody Individual Achievement Test (PIAT) Math test and the PIAT Reading Comprehension Test. The latter was administered to all children whose mental age was 5 years and older.

A linear mixed-effects model was used (Laird & Ware, 1982) to study the change in an individual's mathematics and reading comprehension. That is, Y_{it}, the ith individual's response at Time t, was modeled as a linear function of time, random participant effects, and individual-level error:

$$Y_{it} = B_o + B_1 \times \text{time}_{(\text{lin})} + B_2 \times \text{time}_{(\text{quad})} + u_i + e_{it}, i = 1, \ldots, N; t = 1, \ldots, 5,$$

where

$$e_{it} \sim N(0, R) \text{ and } u_i \sim N(0, D).$$

To implement the model-based approach, we added three variables to the basic model: gender, race–ethnicity, and the child's age at the time of the survey.

This research was supported by National Institute on Drug Abuse Grant 1 P50 DA10075.

To implement the design-based approach, we added the same three variables to the basic model, and we used the child's sampling weight.

We found that the regression estimates and standard errors obtained with the unweighted analysis were comparable with those obtained with the weighted analysis. Agreement was closer for the values obtained with the software package HLM (Bryk, Raudenbush, & Congdon, 1996) than for those obtained with STATA (StatCorp, 1997). We also found that the estimates and standard errors obtained with HLM were roughly comparable with those obtained with STATA. With both packages, the values of the regression coefficients and standard errors were consistent across various nested models that included effects for time, race–ethnicity, and gender. Finally, we found that the estimates of the time-invariant effects (gender, race–ethnicity) were more consistent across the various models than were the estimates of time (specifically, the linear and quadratic components). Further research is needed that considers the effect on point estimates, standard errors, and inference given the use of sampling weights (yes, no) and various combinations of design variables (completely specified, partially specified, partially misspecified, completely misspecified).

References

Bryk, A., Raudenbush, S., & Congdon, R. (1996). *HLM: Hierarchical linear and nonlinear modeling with the HLM/2L and HLM/3L programs.* Chicago: Scientific Software International.

Laird, N. M., Ware, J. H. (1982). Random-effects models for longitudinal data. *Biometrics, 38,* 963–974.

StatCorp. (1997). *Stata statistical software: Release 5.0.* College Station, TX: Stata.

Latent Ordinal Markov Models of Attitude Change

Jee-Seon Kim and Ulf Böckenholt

Because response scales with ordered categories are used frequently in the social and behavioral sciences, methods for the analysis of ordinal data have become increasingly important over the years. One method that has withstood the test of time is Samejima's (1969, 1997) graded response model. By allowing explicitly for individual differences in ordinal measurements of attitudes and abilities, this model has proved useful in a range of applications over the past 30 years. Similarly, latent Markov models for the analysis of categorical panel data have a long tradition of demonstrating their versatility for understanding time-dependent change processes. Recent applications involve the investigation of alcohol and tobacco consumption over time (Collins, Graham, Rousculp, & Hansen, 1997), learning processes of arithmetic word problems (Langeheine, Stern, & van de Pol, 1994), and factors influencing interest in physics and mathematics (Vermunt, Langeheine, & Böckenholt, 1999).

This paper presents a synthesis of latent Markov models and Samejima's graded response model because, in combination, these approaches provide a general framework for the investigation of stability and change in attitude measurements. The graded response model part facilitates the analysis of ordinal attitude measurements; the latent Markov model part provides a flexible representation of both individual attitude differences and attitude change over time. We refer to this modeling framework as the *latent ordinal Markov* (LOM) model. By using the LOM model, one can avoid the common practice of treating ordinal measurements as metric, which may lead to biased inferences. In addition, one does not have to make the strong assumption that attitude change is homogeneous but instead can allow for the possibility that individuals differ in the way their attitudes vary over time. These two features make LOM an attractive tool for understanding person-specific change over time.

Our work is based on previous methodological developments of time-

This research was partially supported by National Science Foundation Grant SBR-9409531.

411

dependent latent class models for nominal data, such as Collins and Wugalter (1992), Langeheine et al. (1994), and Vermunt et al. (1999). These authors developed latent Markov models for binary and nominal polytomous response variables. In contrast, we focused on ordinal responses and allow for both continuous and discrete covariates. We also note that implementations of the LOM approach are straightforward. The freely available program LEM (Vermunt, 1992) can be used to estimate the LOM model. An analysis of the National Youth Survey (Elliott, Huizinga, & Menard, 1989) about attitudes toward substance use illustrates the new modeling approach. In this study, 854 individuals, representing a random sample of the 11- to 21-year-old American youth population, were interviewed about their attitudes toward alcohol and marijuana consumption in five annual waves. Although, on average, respondents developed a more positive attitude toward alcohol and drug use over time, it is unclear whether this mean trend is representative for all members of the population. Using the LOM model, we found that this is not the case: A substantial percentage of the panel members (about 40%) did not change their attitudinal positions at all. Of the remaining panel members, 90% developed a more positive attitude, and the remaining 10% changed their attitudes in the opposite direction. More detailed investigations revealed that latent attitude change can be predicted by several variables, including gender and cohort membership of the respondents.

References

Collins, L. M., Graham, J. W., Rousculp, S. S., & Hansen, W. B. (1997). Heavy caffeine use and the beginning of the substance use onset process: An illustration of latent transition analysis. In K. J. Bryant, M. Windle, & S. G. West (Eds.), *The science of prevention: Methodological advances from alcohol and substance abuse research* (pp. 79–99). Washington, DC: American Psychological Association.

Collins, L. M., & Wugalter, S. E. (1992). Latent class models for stage-sequential dynamic latent variables. *Multivariate Behavioral Research, 27,* 131–157.

Elliott, D. S., Huizinga, D., & Menard, S. (1989). *Multiple problem youth: Delinquency, substance use, and mental health problems.* New York: Springer-Verlag.

Langeheine, R., Stern, E., & van de Pol, F. (1994). State mastery learning: Dynamic models for longitudinal data. *Applied Psychological Measurement, 18,* 277–291.

Samejima, F. (1969). Estimation of ability using a response pattern of graded scores. *Psychometrika Monograph* (No. 17).

Samejima, F. (1997). Graded response model. In W. J. van der Linden & R. K. Hambleton (Eds.), *Handbook of modern item response theory* (pp. 85–100). New York: Springer-Verlag.

Vermunt, J. K. (1992). *LEM: Log-linear and event history analysis with missing data. User's manual.* Department of Social Sciences, Tilburg University, Tilburg, The Netherlands.

Vermunt, J. K., Langeheine, R., & Böckenholt, U. (1999). Discrete-time discrete-state latent Markov models with time-constant and time-varying covariates. *Journal of Educational Statistics, 24,* 179–207.

Estimating Cognitive Growth Curves From Environmental Risk Factors: Mediating the Role of Parenting and Child Factors

Ambika Krishnakumar and Maureen Black

I n a longitudinal examination of the individual and environmental determinants of cognitive performance of low-income children, two successive models were tested. The first model included the role of environmental risk factors (perception of neighborhood quality, negative life events, and poverty). The second model built on the first one and contained parent (education, depression, quality of play materials, maternal warmth) and child characteristics (adaptability and gender) obtained through self-reports, home visits, and observation of parent–child interactions. These models were analyzed using hierarchical growth curves. Change was assessed at two levels: (a) individual patterns of cognitive development over time and (b) characteristics that differentiate patterns of change between children.

The sample included 281 children recruited from an urban pediatric clinic; they were followed annually from ages 3 to 6. Most were African American and lived in single-parent families that received public assistance. In the Level 1 model (within subject), cognitive growth curves were formulated for each child as a function of time-varying covariates (e.g., age). In the Level 2 model (between subjects), time-invariant covariates (e.g., perception of neighborhood quality, adaptability) were used to predict betas from Level 1.

Cognitive scores were estimated using standardized assessments administered at four time points between ages 3 and 6 years. Perception of neighborhood quality, negative life events, and maternal depression were assessed through self-reports. Poverty was operationalized as an index of household density. Maternal warmth and child adaptability (flexible and assertive behaviors) were assessed through observations of mother–child interactions. The results indicated that individual patterns of cognitive scores were associated with a linear change over time, $\chi^2(3, N = 281) = 498.85771$, $p < .001$. A negative correlation between the mean level of cognitive performance and the rate of change (intercept and the slope) signified that children had an average level of cognitive performance at age 3 and exhibited a gradual decline from ages 3 through 6.

From an examination of risk factors that predicted children's standardized scores at baseline, children who experienced higher levels of poverty were significantly more likely to have lower cognitive scores. No interactions among the risk factors were found. At baseline, boys had significantly higher cognitive scores than girls, and children who were less adaptable had significantly higher cognitive scores.

When we examined linear change (i.e., slope) in cognitive scores, we found that poverty alone predicted poor cognitive performance; this relationship was mediated through children's adaptability. Over time, boys experienced a significantly steeper decline in cognitive scores than did girls.

These findings suggest that in a low-income urban environment marked by single parenthood, (a) children experience a decline in cognitive scores over preschool years; (b) family poverty, rather than other environmental risk factors, plays a detrimental role in determining the level of children's cognitive performance; and (c) under conditions of poverty, cognitive performance over time may be improved by socialization practices that facilitate children's adaptable and assertive skills, which they can use to overcome environmental risks.

Modeling Prevention Program Effects on Growth in Substance Use

Bonnie Taylor, John W. Graham, and Patricio E. Cumsille

Evaluating the efficacy of a prevention program is an essential part of program development. Data for evaluation are frequently collected prior to implementation and at selected intervals for a follow-up period. These data could be analyzed in a pretest–posttest fashion, in which the posttest varies as one of the follow-up measures. However, with longitudinal data, program effects may be assessed with growth modeling. Growth curve modeling allows for an explicit expression of the expected shape of change and provides the advantage of analyzing several waves of data in a single analysis. In the basic latent growth curve model, data for each individual participant are used to estimate an intercept and slope in a simple regression model, with time as the predictor. If enough time points are available, one may represent the growth in terms of other, higher order polynomial functions (e.g., quadratic or cubic). If there is significant variability around the individual growth parameters (e.g., intercept and slope), this variability may be predicted by other variables of interest (e.g., program dummy variables). The authors used growth modeling to evaluate a drug use prevention program.

The sample (N = 3,027) consisted of Los Angeles-area school students in Grade 7 at the outset of the Adolescent Alcohol Prevention Trial (AAPT; Hansen & Graham, 1991). The AAPT program contained four treatment groups: (a) ICU—information only (control), (b) RT—resistance training plus information, (c) NORM—normative education plus information, and (d) COMB—combined RT and NORM plus information. The program was administered after the seventh-grade pretest measure. Participants responded to questions regarding recent and lifetime cigarette and alcohol use. Follow-up data were collected in Grades 8–11.

Several latent growth curve models were tested to determine the effect of

This research was supported by National Institute on Drug Abuse Grant P50 DA 10075.

the program on substance use over the 5 years. The first model tested showed the program effects on the rate of growth of drug use over the 5 years, but in doing so it did not control for pretest differences in drug use between groups. The second model controlled for pretest differences by using the pretest as a covariate. With this model, the rate of growth of drug use was modeled over the last four time points. This model was most suitable for assessing program effects on the overall level of use; however, this model ignored potentially important growth between seventh and eighth grades. Model 3 showed the program effects on the rate of growth of drug use over the 5 years with adjustment for pretest differences by using the intercept as a predictor of the slope. This model did not allow for the intercept to be tested as a dependent variable.

Missing data were handled by means of imputation using NORM (Schafer, 1997) software. Independent analyses were performed on the 20 imputed data sets. The parameter estimates were then combined to obtain an unbiased estimate of the population values.

The findings controlled for the effects of gender and ethnicity in all models. The program group receiving the normative education component of AAPT had a significantly lower level and growth rate of substance use over the 5 years of the study compared with the ICU (control) group. There were no significant effects for either RT or COMB for any of the models. The authors conclude that there is no single best model for the interpretation of the program effects; however, the three models collectively provide convincing evidence for the effectiveness of the programs.

References

Hansen, W. B., & Graham, J. W. (1991). Preventing alcohol, marijuana, and cigarette use among adolescents: Peer pressure resistance training versus establishing conservative norms. *Preventive Medicine, 20,* 414–430.

Schafer, J. (1997). *Analysis of incomplete multivariate data.* New York: Chapman & Hall.

Linking Children's Poverty History to Change in Behavior Problems and Self-Concept: Latent Growth Curve Versus Piecewise Models

Peter C. Tice and Steve Carlton-Ford

We present preliminary analyses from a study in which we investigated the link between children's poverty history and change in behavior problems and self-concept simultaneously. Using three waves of data from the National Longitudinal Survey of Youth (NLSY), we followed 735 children making the transition into adolescence. Prior research shows that behavior problems of persistently poor children increase at a faster rate than do those of children with shorter or no poverty histories (McLeod & Shanahan, 1996). In addition, persistently poor children have lower self-esteem than intermittently poor and never-poor children (Bolger, Patterson, Thompson, & Kupersmidt, 1995). Researchers have not previously examined the association between change in children's behavior problems and change in self-concept (e.g., self-esteem) as a function of poverty history.

Conducting a cross-domain analysis of change (see Willett & Sayer, 1996) in behavior problems and self-concept requires that the researcher specify the appropriate functional form for each dependent variable. We collapsed the data into three equal categories (i.e., low = 1, medium = 2, high = 3) for cross-tabular analyses to determine the appropriate functional form for modeling growth. On the basis of a 27-pattern matrix (i.e., $3 \times 3 \times 3$ crosstab), we condensed individual change patterns into five idealized growth trends. We labeled these five growth trends (a) *increase with time,* (b) *flat increase,* (c) *flat,* (d) *flat decrease,* and (e) *decrease with time.* The labels for these growth trends correspond to the intercept and slope (change) coefficients for a latent growth curve as determined in the equations below:

$$\text{intercept coefficient} = [(ti1 + ti2 + ti3)/3] - \text{slope coefficient}$$

and

$$\text{slope coefficient} = (ti3 - ti1)/2,$$

where $ti1$ is equal to an individual's score at Time 1, $ti2$ is an individual's score at Time 2, and $ti3$ is an individual's score at Time 3.

418

In brief, the meaning of these five growth trends is as follows. The increase-with-time growth trend includes individual change patterns characterized by a positive slope coefficient (e.g., $ti1 = 1$, $ti2 = 2$, $ti3 = 3$). The flat-increase growth trend includes individual change patterns characterized by a zero slope coefficient but with an increase between Time 1 and Time 2, followed by an approximately equal decrease between Time 2 and Time 3 (e.g., $ti1 = 2$, $ti2 = 3$, $ti3 = 2$). The flat growth trend includes individual change patterns characterized by a zero slope coefficient with stable scores across measurement periods (e.g., $ti1 = 1$, $ti2 = 1$, $ti3 = 1$). The flat-decrease growth trend includes individual change patterns also characterized by a zero slope coefficient but with a decrease between Time 1 and Time 2, followed by an equal increase between Time 2 and Time 3 (e.g., $ti1 = 2$, $ti2 = 1$, $ti3 = 2$). Finally, the decrease-with-time growth trend includes individual change patterns characterized by a negative slope coefficient (e.g., $ti1 = 3$, $ti2 = 2$, $ti3 = 1$).

The typical slope coefficient for a latent growth curve masks particular patterns of individual change. For example, when we compare the slope coefficients for the individual change patterns in the flat-increase, flat, and flat-decrease idealized growth trends, we see a common coefficient of zero. Despite having the same slope coefficient, one should not simply assume that the patterns of individual change within these growth trends are either empirically or substantively equivalent; using a simple latent growth curve model may mask theoretically and empirically significant differences in change.

To what extent does this masking process occur? With the present sample of 735 children, 53.1% fall within these three growth trends for behavior problems, and 40.5% do so for the self-concept measure. These large percentages indicate that this masking process is widespread, thus warranting caution in the conclusions drawn from latent growth curve models. Finally, it raises the possibility for conducting studies that permit comparisons of the results from a latent growth curve and piecewise model of change, especially if theory links change in the independent variable to change in the dependent variable.

References

Bolger, K. E., Patterson, C. J., Thompson, W. W., & Kupersmidt, J. B. (1995). Psychosocial adjustment among children experiencing persistent and intermittent family economic hardship. *Child Development, 66,* 1107–1129.

McLeod, J. D., & Shanahan, M. J. (1996). Trajectories of poverty and children's mental health. *Journal of Health and Social Behavior, 38,* 72–86.

Willett, J. B., & Sayer, A. G. (1996). Cross-domain analysis of change: Combining growth modeling and covariance structure analysis. In G. A. Marcoulides & R. E. Schumacker (Eds.), *Advanced structural equation modeling: Issues and techniques* (pp. 125–157). Mahwah, NJ: Erlbaum.

Understanding Caregiver Stress: Scalar and System Models

Virginia Moore Tomlinson and Patrick Doreian

Caregiving is a process that occurs over time. The process is one of stress and coping with stress. In this paper, caregiver stress is the outcome of the interrelation of components that change over time. The components are objective conditions conducive to stress, conditioning measures, social support, and characteristics of the caregiver. The process of caregiver stress is analyzed as a system of components or driving forces that change over time, influencing each other and determining the time path of the system.

The formal model of differential equations is built on existing theoretical considerations and includes the stated components. First, the scalar model is estimated as an integral equation with the single outcome of stress as measured by depression. The system model of differential equations is then estimated with all components as input and outcomes, except the disability level of the stroke survivor, which is an exogenous factor. The differential equations are estimated as integral equations within specific boundary conditions provided by the time periods. The process parameters are calculated on the basis of the parameter estimates of the integral equations.

Parameter estimates of the integral equation and the differential equation and their respective variance and covariance matrices are produced using maximum-likelihood methods. The authors used data from female caregivers to stroke survivors collected at three points during the first 12–16 months after the stroke. The analysis focuses on two time periods: the first 6–8 months poststroke and the second 6–8 months poststroke.

The findings of both models suggest that these caregivers experience a trajectory of gradual improvement, or decreases in depression, over time, which is driven by social support. On the basis of the scalar model, the reduction in depression experienced by this group of caregivers is due to the satisfaction with the amount of social contact and the size of the support network. This influence is negative, and it increases during the second 6–8 months under study.

The system model indicates that the system is stable and convergent during

420

the two periods under study. Measures of responsiveness in the system model indicate that the influence of the components on each other increases over time. This behavior indicates that the relationships within the system become more "systemlike." Increased connectedness is also observed in increases in the magnitude of the parameter estimates during the second 6–8 months. Additional findings suggest that depression is increased by poor physical health. Physical health is sustained by a satisfaction with social contact and the size of the social network. Satisfaction with amount of social contact is reduced consistently by depression. The size of the social support network is reduced by depression and increased by poor physical health. The disability of the stroke survivor has minimal influence during the first 6–8 months poststroke, yet improvements in functioning reduce caregiver depression during Months 12–16. This paper concludes with a comparison of the scalar and system models, including a discussion of the contributions, limitations, and methodological issues of each.

Measuring the Zone of Proximal Development: An Application of Individual Growth Analysis

Zheng Yan

he *zone of proximal development* (ZPD) is both an important concept in Vygotskian social–cultural theory (Vygotsky, 1978) and a well-documented developmental phenomenon (e.g., McNaughton & Leyland, 1990). It has significant implications for learning, education, and assessment (e.g., Lidz, 1987; Moll, 1990). However, little developmental research addresses how to empirically measure and analyze the ZPD (Hayward, 1995; Smagorinksy, 1995), and methodologists have not used this concept to analyze change over time (Collins & Horn, 1991; Gottman, 1995). Thus, the ZPD is merely a widely used theoretical metaphor for general developmental arguments but not yet a powerful quantitative construct for the analysis of change.

This presentation demonstrates how to measure and analyze changes of the ZPD over time by applying individual growth analysis (Willett, 1997; Willett & Sayer, 1994) to exemplary data from a multiple-condition cross-sectional study on adolescents' social development (Fischer & Kennedy, 1997). The basic procedure includes the following.

1. Empirical growth trajectories under two different conditions, providing and not providing scaffoldings, are used to establish the upper and lower boundaries of the ZPD, respectively.

2. The Level 1 and Level 2 models are combined to fit the growth trend lines of the lower and upper boundaries of the ZPD.

3. A variety of the ZPD profiles across individuals are formulated and compared on the basis of the two parameters of initial growth level and growth rate.

4. The results of individual growth modeling are further constructed into indexes of the ZPD, such as $index_{initial}$, $index_{end}$, $index_{rate}$, and $index_{area}$, so that the ZPD could become an empirical concept for the analysis of change over time.

Possible implications and existing methodological issues for the analysis of the ZPD are discussed.

References

Collins, L. M., & Horn, J. L. (Eds.). (1991). *Best methods for the analysis of change.* Washington, DC: American Psychological Association.

Fischer, K. W., & Kennedy, B. P. (1997). Tools for analyzing the many shapes of development: The case of self-in-relationships in Korea. In E. Amsel & K. A. Renninger (Eds.), *Change and development* (pp. 117–152). Mahwah, NJ: Erlbaum.

Gottman, J. M. (Ed.). (1995). *The analysis of change.* Mahwah, NJ: Erlbaum.

Hayward, P. A. (1995). *The use of Vygotsky's theory of the zone of proximal development in quantitative research: A critical review.* (ERIC Document Reproduction Service No. ED 389 609)

Lidz, C. S. (Ed.). (1987). *Dynamic assessment: An interactive approach to evaluating learning potential.* New York: Guilford Press.

McNaughton, S., & Leyland, J. (1990). The shifting focus on maternal tutoring across different difficulty levels on a problem-solving task. *British Journal of Developmental Psychology, 8,* 147–155.

Moll, L. C. (Ed.). (1990). *Vygotsky and education: Instructional implications and applications of the zone of proximal development.* New York: Cambridge University.

Smagorinksy, P. (1995). The social construction of data: Methodological problems of investigating learning in the zone of proximal development. *Review of Educational Research, 65,* 191–212.

Vygotsky, L. S. (1978). *Mind in society.* Cambridge, MA: Harvard University.

Willett, J. B. (1997). Measuring change: What individual growth modeling buys you. In E. Amsel & K. A. Renninger (Eds.), *Change and development* (pp. 213–243). Mahwah, NJ: Erlbaum.

Willett, J. B., & Sayer, A. G. (1994). Using covariance structural analysis to detect correlates and predictors of change. *Psychological Bulletin, 116,* 363–381.

Author Index

Numbers in italics refer to listings in reference sections.

Aber, M. S., 141, 155, *172*, 233, *238*
Acock, A. C., 167, *174*
Adair, R., 388, *389*
Agresti, A., 297, *319*, 328, *331*
Ahmavaara, Y., 212, *237*
Albert, P., 37, *64*
Algina, J., 245, *258*
Allison, P. D., 142, *169*, 335, 341, 345, 347n, *352*, 360, *375*
Alpert, A., *237*
American Guidance, 140, *169*
American Psychiatric Association, 407, *408*
Anderson, E., 141, *172*, 233, *238*
Anderson, T. W., 112, *132*, 368, *375*
Andres, J., 243, *259*
Anstey, K. J., 400, *401*
Arbuckle, J. L., 90, *91*, 110, *132*, 335, *352*, 360, *375*, 379, *383*
Arking, R., *401*
Arminger, G., 141, 142, 148, 154, *169*, *170*, 301, *319*
Astin, A. W., 388, *389*
Astin, H. S., 388, *389*
Auer, A., 265, *269*

Bachman, J. G., 296, *321*
Bai, D., 9, *25*
Bailey, L., 358, *375*
Baker, P. C., 140, 151, 152, *169*
Baltes, P. B., 139, 168, *169*, *173*, 339, *353*
Bandeen-Roche, K., 300, *319*
Bank, L., 141, 164, *174*
Barber, B., 183, *199*
Barr Taylor, C., *199*
Bartholomew, D. J., 300, *319*
Bartsch, T. W., 243, *258*
Basford, K. E., 300, *320*
Bast, J., 107, *132*
Bates, D. M., *375*, *376*

Bauer, M. S., 8, *26*
Bayley, N., 9, *25*, 139, *169*
Beiber, S. L., 205, *239*
Bell, R. Q., 139, 147, 152, 153, 166, *169*, *172*
Belsky, J., 71, 84, 86, 89, *92*
Bentler, P. M., 67, *92*, 114, *132*
Berg, S., *401*
Berk, R. A., 142, *169*
Berkovits, I., 197, *199*
Bertenthal, B., 9, 22, *25*
Blafield, E., 301, *319*
Bloxom, B., 214, *237*
Böckenholt, U., 300, *321*, 411, *413*
Bohrnstedt, G. W., 113, *132*
Boker, S. M., 8, 9, 13, 15, 16, 19, 22, *25–27*, 144, 148, 151, 165, 168, *169*, *172*, *174*, 236, *237*, 335, *353*
Bolger, K. E., 418, *419*
Bollen, K., 108, 119, 121, 130, 131, *132*, *133*, 141, 155, *170*, 192, 195n, *198*, 299, *319*
Bowman, S. R., 167, *174*
Branch, D. G., 396, *396*
Brandt, D., 99, *104*
Brant, L. J., 296, *321*
Brooks-Gunn, J., 151, *170*
Brown, C., 167, *170*
Brown, C. H., 302, 303, *320*
Browne, M., 30, 32, 121, *132*, 141, 148, 154, *170*, 220, *237*, 253, *257*
Bryk, A., 41, 59, 61, *62*, *63*, 67, 88, *92*, 98, 99, 103, *104*, 122, *132*, 142, 149, 167, *170*, 185, *198*, 360, 363, *376*, 385, 387, 410, *410*
Buchner, A., 244, *259*
Butterworth, G., 15, *26*
Byrne, B. M., 192, *198*, 212, *237*

Cairns, B. D., 385, *387*

Cairns, R. B., 385, *387*
Campbell, D. T., 107, 113, *132, 134,*
	164, *170,* 244, 248, 250, 253, 257,
	257, 258
Capaldi, D. M., 108, 109, *132*
Carlin, J., 367, *376*
Carter, H. B., 296, *321*
Casella, G., 365, *376*
Cattell, R. B., 167, *172,* 209, *238*
Chan, D., 180, *198*
Chan, W., 45, 49, 51, *63*
Chapman, D., 358, *375*
Charak, D., 380, *383*
Chase-Lansdale, P. L., 151, *170*
Chassin, L., 116, *133*
Cheng, M. T., 388, *389*
Christiansen, B., 183, *199*
Chung, N. K., 274, *288*
Clark, J. E., 9, 15, *26*
Clarke, G., *392*
Cleveland, W. S., 15, *26*
Cliff, N., 273, 278, 279, *287, 288*
Clogg, C. C., 273, *287,* 300, *320,* 326,
	329, *331*
Cohen, P., 31, 32, 152, *170*
Cole, D. A., 254, *257*
Coleman, J. S., 148, *170*
College Entrance Examination Board,
	388, *389*
Collins, L. M., 31, 32, 141, *170,* 273,
	274, 279, 280, *288,* 300, *320,* 399,
	399, 405, 406, 411, 412, *412,* 422,
	423
Congdon, R., 88, *92,* 360, *376,* 410, *410*
Cook, T. D., 164, *170*
Costa, P. T., Jr., 266, *269*
Critchlow, B., 183, *199*
Crocker, L., 245, *258*
Cudeck, R., 121, *132,* 246, *258*
Cumsille, P., *394*
Cunningham, W. R., 205, *237*
Curran, P., 107, 109, 116, 119, 125,
	130, 131, *132–134,* 167, *170,* 182,
	199, 292, 299, 303, *320,* 341, *352,*
	353

Davey, A., 265, 266, *269,* 380, 381, *383*

Dayton, C. M., 300, *320*
deFaire, U., *401*
Delaney, M., 152, *174*
Dempster, A., 37, *63*
de Pijper, W. M., 164, *174*
DeSarbo, W. S., 301, *320*
DeShon, R. P., 273, *288*
Dessens, J., 300, *321*
Devlin, S. J., 15, *26*
Dewey, J., 250, *258*
Diggle, P., 51, *63,* 141, *170*
Dohrenwend, B. P., *259*
Donaldson, S. I., 335, 336, *352*
Dumenci, L., 244, 246, 249, 250, 254,
	255, *258,* 260, 265, 267, 268, *269*
Duncan, G., 191, *199*
Duncan, O. D., 113, *133*
Duncan, S. C., 116, *133,* 142, *170,* 180,
	199, 237, 335, *352,* 360, *376,* 393,
	394
Duncan, T. E., 116, *133,* 142, *170,* 180,
	199, 220, 233, *237,* 335, 339, *352,*
	360, *376,* 393, *394*
Duncan-Jones, P., 265, *269*
Du Toit, S. H. C., 30, *32,* 141, 148, *170*
Dwyer, J. H., 141, *170, 377*

Eccles, J. S., 183, 184, *199*
Eichorn, D. H., 205, *239*
Elias, M. F., 229, *239*
Elliot, D., *392*
Elliott, D. S., 43, *63,* 412, *412*
Elliott, R., 388, *389*
Embretson, S. E., 273, *288*
Engstrom, R. O., 209, *237*
Epstein, D., 97, *104,* 114, *134,* 149, 167,
	172, 197, 198, *199,* 229, *238*
Escobar, M. D., 168, *174*
Everitt, B. S., 300, *320*

Farish Haydel, K., *199*
Farmer, M. M., 51, 53, 62, *63*
Farrington, D., 296, *321*
Featherman, D. L., 169, *170*

Feinleib, M., 141, *170*
Fergusson, D. M., 265, *269*
Ferring, D., 244, *259*
Fidell, L. S., 67, *93*
Fischer, K. W., 422, *423*
Fisher, G. H., 273, *288*
Fisher, R. A., 386, *387*
Fiske, D. W., 244, 250, *257*
Flaherty, B. F., 265, *269*
Flay, B. R., 339, *353, 377*
Fletcher, J. M., 168, *174*
Formann, A. K., 300, *320*
Francis, D., 304, *320*
Frank, E., 255, *258*

Geert, P. van, 15, *26*
Gelfand, A. E., 365, *376*
Gelman, A., 367, *376*
George, E. I., 365, *376*
Gibbons, R. D., 51, *63*
Gibson, W. A., 216n, *237*, 300, *320*
Gilks, W. R., 365, *376*
Glass, L., 8, *26*
Goldberg, L., 390, *392*
Goldberg, S., 142, *170*
Goldman, M., 183, *199, 200*
Goldstein, H., 44, 61, *63*, 67, 88, *92*,
    120n, *133*, 142, 167, *170*
Gollob, H. F., 141, 168, *171*
Goodman, L. A., 273, *287, 288*
Gottfredson, M., 53, *63*
Gottman, J. M., 422, *423*
Gottschalk, A., 8, *26*
Graham, J., 8, 9, *26*, 31, 32, 110, *133*,
    183, *199*, 236, *237*, 274, 280, *288*,
    335, 336–338, 339, 344, 345, *352,
    353*, 359, 368, 369, *376*, 411, *412,
    416, 417*
Grandy, J., 388, *389*
Green, C., *392*
Greene, W., 101, *104*
Greffath, E., *392*
Griffiths, D., 167, *171*
Gu, C., 15, *26*
Gullion, C. M., 255, *258*
Guttman, L., 110, *133, 167, 171*

Haight, W., 59, *63*
Halverson, C. F., Jr., 266, *269*
Hamagami, F., 90, *92*, 141, 142, 148,
    149, 151, 153, 155, 156, 159, 166,
    167, *171–173*, 220, 229, 233, *238,
    239*, 339, *353*
Hammer, L., *199*
Hancock, G. R., 197, *199*
Hand, D. J., 300, *320*
Hannan, M., 148, *174*
Hansen, W., 183, *199*, 274, *288*, 339,
    344, *353*, 368, *377*, 411, *412*, 416,
    417
Hanushek, E. A., 101, *104*
Harford, T., 182, *199*
Harris, C. W., 139, *171*
Hartley, H. O., 363, *376*
Harville, D. A., 82, *92*
Hayduk, L. A., 67, *92*
Hayward, C., *199*
Hayward, P. A., 422, *423*
Healy, M., 120n, *133*
Heckman, J. J., 142, *171*
Hedeker, D., 51, *63*
Heise, D. R., 112, 113, *133*
Henderson, C. R., 75, *92*
Henry, N. W., 273, *288*
Hertzog, C., 256, *258*, 265, *269*
Hilton, T. L., 388, *389*
Hirschi, T., 53, *63*
Hofer, S. M., 110, *133*, 335, 338, *352*,
    359, *376*
Hoffmeister, H., 141, *170*
Hollis, M., 110, *134*, 335, *353*, 360, *377*
Holzinger, K. J., 216, *237*
Honzick, M. P., 205, *239*
Hopkins, B., 15, *26*
Hops, H., *237*
Horn, J. L., 139, 141, 142, 149, 155,
    167, 168, *170, 171, 173*, 203, 205,
    209, 212, *237, 238*, 422, *423*
Horney, J., 52, 53, 56, 61, *63*, 100, *104*
Horwood, L. J., 265, *269*
Hsia, J., 388, *389*
Hubbard, J. H., 8, *26*
Huizinga, D., 43, *63*, 412, *412*
Humphreys, L. G., 112, *133*, 247, 254,
    255, *258*
Hussong, A. M., 109, *133*, 167, *170*

Huttenlocher, J., 59, *63*
Hyatt, S. L., 274, 280, *288*

Inn, G., 183, *199*

Jackson, J. E., 101, *104*
Jackson, P. H., 367, *377*
Jagpal, H. S., 301, *320*
Jedidi, K., 301, *320*
Jennrich, R., 43, 44, 49, 61, *63*, 67, 76, *92*, 363, 375, *376*
Jo, B., 302, 304, *320*
Johnson, C. A., 339, *353*, 368, *377*
Johnson, R. A., *376*
Johnston, L. D., 296, *321*
Jones, L. W., 234, *240*
Jones, R. H., 82, *92*, 141, *171*
Jöreskog, K., 67, *92*, 112–114, *133*, 141, 154, 155, 167, *171*, 220, *238*, *258*, 260, 340, 345, *353*
Jozefowicz, D. M., 183, *199*

Kaplan, D., 8, *26*, 110, 125, *133*, *134*, 335, *353*, 360, *377*
Karim, M., 51, *63*
Kashy, D. A., 252, *258*, 268, *269*
Kasprzyk, D., 358, *375*
Keck, C. K., 140, *169*
Kennedy, B. P., 422, *423*
Kenny, D. A., 107, *134*, 244, 246, 248, 250–253, 255, 257, *257–259*, 262, 265, 268, *269*
Khoo, S., 302, 304, *320*
Kiecolt-Glaser, J., 116, *134*, 182, *199*, 220, *238*
Killen, J., 183, *199*
Kim, C., 116, *134*, 182, *199*, 220, *238*
Kim Boscardin, C., 304, *320*
Kistiakowsky, V., 388, *389*
Kowaleski-Jones, L., 191, *199*
Kraemer, H. C., 255, *258*
Kupersmidt, J. B., 418, *419*
Kupfer, D., 255, *258*
Kutner, M. H., 339, *353*

Laird, N., 37, *63*
Laird, N. M., 67, 68, *92*, 363, *376*, 409, *410*
Land, K. C., 302, *321*
Landis, P. K., 296, *321*
Lange, K., 156, *171*
Langeheine, R., 411, 412, *412*, *413*
Lapin, A., *392*
Lazarfeld, P. F., 273, *288*
Lee, S., 90, *92*
Lennon, M. C., *259*
Lerner, R. M., 169, *170*
Lesaffre, E., 301, *321*
Leyland, J., 422, *423*
Li, F., 167, *174*, 237, 335, *352*
Liang, K., 51, *63*
Liang, K-Y., 37, *64*, 141, *170*
Lidz, C. S., 422, *423*
Lillard, L. A., 51, 53, 62, *63*
Lind, J. M., 121, *135*
Lindsey, J. K., 141, *172*
Lindstrom, M. J., 375, *376*
Lippert, P., 141, *170*
Littell, R. C., 360, *376*
Little, K. B., 139, *171*
Little, R. J., 301, *320*
Little, R. J. A., 61, *63*, 110, *134*, 142, 166, *172*, 336, *353*, 357, 359, *376*, 379, *383*
Loehlin, J. C., 141, *172*
Lohmoeller, J.-B., 153, *172*
Long, J. S., 67, *92*
Longford, N. T., 67, 89, *92*, 142, 167, *172*
Lord, F. M., 206, 207, *238*, 273, 276, *288*
Lord, S. E., 183, *199*
Lord, S. R., 400, *401*
Lynch, K. G., 302, *321*

MacCallum, R. C., 116, *134*, 182, *199*, 209, 220, *238*
Mackey, M., 8, *26*
MacKinnon, D. P., 110, *133*, 335, 338, *352*, 374, *377*, *392*
Macready, G. B., 300, *320*
Madow, W. G., 357, *377*
Maes, H. H., 335, *353*
Majcen, A.-M., 244, *259*

Makov, U. E., 300, *321*
Makuch, R., 168, *174*
Malarkey, W., 116, *134*, 182, *199*, 220, 238
Manning, W. D., 273, *287, 326, 331*
Marbach, J. J., *259*
Marques, P. R., 396, *396*
Marsh, H. W., 107, *134*, 251, *258*
Marshall, I., 52, *63*, 100, *104*
Martin, J. M., 254, *257*
Mason, R., 205, *238*
Massioui, E. A. F., 8, 27
MathSoft, Inc., 361, *377*
Matier, M., 388, *389*
McArdle, J., 16, *26, 30, 32*, 90, *92*, 97, *104*, 114, 116, *134*, 141, 142, 144, 146–149, 151–156, 159, 163–168, *169, 171–174*, 180, 197, 198, *199*, 203, 205, 209, 212, 220, 223, 229, 233, *237–239, 339, 353*, 360, *377*, 381, *383*, 393, *394*
McCallagh, P., 53, *63*
McClearn, G. E., *401*
McCrae, R. R., 266, *269*
McDonald, R. P., 16, *26*, 141, 142, 144, 164, 167, *170, 173*
McLauchlan, G. J., 300, *320*
McLeod, J. D., 418, *419*
McNaughton, S., 422, *423*
Meehl, P. E., 324, 330, *332*
Menard, S., 43, *63*, 412, *412*
Meng, X. L., 364, *377*, 380, *383*
Meredith, W., 90, *92*, 114, *134*, 141, 154, 166, *173*, 181, 192, 197, 198, *199*, 203, 205, 212, 214, 220, 223, 226, 228, 229, 231, *239, 240*, 291, *320*, 360, *377*
Merrill, M. A., 222, 223, *240*
Miglioretti, D. L., 300, *319*
Miller, D., *392*
Miller, J. D., 388, *389*
Miller, P., 183, *200*
Milliken, G. A., 360, *376*
Millsap, R. E., 253, *258*
Moe, E., *392*
Moffitt, T., 296, *320, 321*

Molenaar, P. C. M., 77, 83, 89, *93*
Moll, L. C., 422, *423*
Morrell, C. H., 296, *321*
Mott, F. L., 140, 151, *169, 170*
Mulder, J., 164, *174*
Mussen, P., 205, *239*
Muthén, B., 90, *93*, 110, 114, 130, *133, 134*, 182, 192, 197, *198–200*, 212, 216n, *237, 239*, 292, 296, 299, 302–304, 314, *320, 321*, 335, 341, 345, *352, 353*, 360, *377*
Muthén, L., 110, *134*, 292, 296, 299, 314, *321*

Nachtsheim, J. C., 339, *353*
Nagin, D., 59, 62, *63*, 296, 301, 302, *321*
Nandrino, J., 8, 27
Neale, M. C., 16, *26*, 90, *93*, 154, 156, *173*, 335, *353*, 360, *377*
Nelder, J., 53, *63*
Nesselroade, J. R., 9, 13, 15, 19, 25, *26, 27*, 139, 146, 167, 168, *169, 173, 174*, 191, *200*, 223, *239*, 243, 246, 255, 256, *258*, 265, *269*, 339, *353, 401*
Neter, J., 339, *353*
Nisselson, H., 357, *377*
Novick, M. R., 206, 207, *238, 239*, 273, 276, *288*, 367, *377*
Nowack, A., 168, *174*
Nunnally, J. C., 207, *239*

O'Connell, E. J., 253, *257*
Olkin, I., 357, *377*
Olsen, M. K., 335, *353*, 371, *377*
O'Malley, P. M., 296, *321*
Ormel, J., 255, *259*, 265, *269*
Osgood, D., 52, *63*, 100, *104*

Pankratz, A., 142, 167, *174*

Patterson, C. J., 418, *419*
Patterson, G. R., 141, 164, *174*
Pearson, J. D., 296, *321*
Pedersen, N. L., 400, *401*
Peeke, L. G., 254, *257*
Pentz, M. A., 377
Perlmutter, M., 169, *170*
Peterson, J. L., 141, *174*
Pezard, L., 8, *27*
Phillips, D. A., 151, *170*
Phillips, S. J., 9, *26*
Piccinin, A. M., 338, *352, 359, 376*
Plomin, R., *401*
Ployhart, R. E., 273, *288*
Ponocny, I., 273, *288*
Poon, W., 90, *92*
Potthoff, R. F., 71, 81, 83, 85, *93*, 94, 96
Prescott, C. A., 155, *173*

Quinlan, S. V., 140, *169*

Rabash, J., 120n, *133*
Ramaswamy, V., 301, *320*
Ramsay, J. O., 325, *332*
Rao, J. N. K., 363, *376*
Raphael, K. G., *259*
Rathouz, P. J., 300, *319*
Raudenbush, S., 41, 45, 49, 51, 53, 59,
    61, 62, *62–64*, 67, 88, *92*, 98, 99,
    103, *104*, 122, *132*, 142, 149, 167,
    170, 185, *198*, 360, 363, *376*, 385,
    387, 410, *410*
Raykov, T., 167, *174*, 235, 236, *239*
Reichardt, C. S., 141, 168, *171*
Reitsma, P., 107, *132*
Renault, B., 8, *27*
Richardson, S., 365, *376*
Rietz, C., 243, *259*
Robbins, M. A., 229, *239*
Robinson, G. K., 75, 82, *93*
Robinson, T., *199*
Roeder, K., 302, *321*
Roehling, P., 183, *199*
Roeser, R., 183, *199*
Rogosa, D., 99, *104*, 107, *134*, 142, 163,
    167, *174*, 181, *200*, 220, 236, *239*,
    256, *259*

Rose, J. L., 9, *25*
Rosen, A., 330, *332*
Rosenberg, B., 67, *93*
Rosenthal, R., 330, *332*
Rousculp, S. S., 274, *288*, 411, *412*
Rovine, M., 71, 77, 84, 86, 89, 90, *92,
    93*, 152, *174*, 380, *383*
Roy, S. N., 71, 81, 83, 85, *93*, 94, 96
Rubin, D., 37, 61, *63*, 110, *134*, 142,
    166, *172, 174*, 330, *332*, 336, 337,
    353, 357–359, 364, 367, 372, *376*,
    379, 380, *383*
Rudinger, G., 243, 248, *259*
Rush, A. J., 255, *258*

Sacco, J. M., 273, *288*
Samejima, F., 411, *412*
Sampson, R., 53, 59, 62, *64*
Sandefur, J. T., 142, *174*
Sandland, R., 167, *171*
Saris, W., 164, *174*, 341, 345, 347n, *353*
SAS Institute, 341, *353*
Satorra, A., 90, *93*, 341, 345, 347n, *353*
Sayer, A., 30, *32*, 40, 45, *64*, 97, 99,
    104, 141, 149, 167, *175*, 182, 184,
    186, 197, *200*, 233, *240*, 265, *269*,
    340, *353*, 360, 377, 385, *387*, 394,
    418, *419*, 422, *423*
Schafer, J. L., 90, *93*, 154, *174*, 335, *352,
    353*, 357–359, 361, 364, 365, 367,
    368, 371, *377*, 380, 381, *383*, 405,
    406, 417, *417*
Schaie, K. W., 229, *240*
Schaufeli, W. B., 255, *259*
Schawitz, S. E., 168, *174*
Schluchter, M., 43, 44, 49, 61, *63*, 67,
    76, *92*, 363, 375, *376*
Schmitt, M. J., 244, *259*, 265, *269*
Schulenberg, J., 296, *321*
Schwartz, G., 299, *321*
Schwenkmezger, P., 244, *259*, 265, *269*
Scott, J., 388, *389*
Seltzer, M., 59, 60, 62, *63*, *64*
Seroczynski, A. D., 254, *257*

Shanahan, M. J., 381, *383*, 418, *419*
Shavelson, R. J., 192, *198*, 212, *237*
Shawitz, B. A., 168, *174*
Shedden, K., 296, 299, 314, *321*
Silverman, B. W., 325, *332*
Smagorinksy, P., 422, *423*
Smith, A. F. M., 300, *321*, 365, *376*
Smith, G., 100, *104*, 183, *199*, *200*
Smith, G. A., 400, *401*
Sobel, J. L., 339, *353*
Sörbom, D., 67, *92*, 114, *133*, 141, 154,
    155, 167, *171*, *174*, 220, *238*, *258*,
    260, 340, 345, *353*
Spearman, C., 234, *240*
Spence, M. A., 156, *171*
Spiegelhalter, D. J., 365, *376*
Spisic, D., 299, *321*
SPSS, Inc., 89, *93*
Stanley, J. C., 257, *257*
Stapleton, L., 197, *199*
StatCorp., 410, *410*
Statistics and Epidemiology Research
    Corporation, 389, *389*
Steiger, J. H., 121, *135*
Stein, P., 301, *319*
Stern, E., 411, *412*
Stern, H., 367, *376*
Stewart, H. B., 13, *27*
Steyer, R., 244, 245, 250, 255, *259*, 265,
    267, *269*
Stice, E., 116, *133*
Stoolmiller, M., 116, *135*, *237*
Strenta, C. A., 388, *389*
Stroup, W. W., 360, *376*
Stycker, L. A., *237*
Swineford, F., 216, *237*

Tabachnick, B. G., 67, *93*
Tanner, J. M., 139, 168, *174*
Tanner, M., 51, *64*
Terman, L. W., 222, *240*
Thelen, E., 9, 15, *27*
Thompson, G. H., 209, 213, *240*
Thompson, J. M. T., 13, *27*
Thompson, W. W., 418, *419*
Thum, Y., 44, 60–62, *64*
Thurstone, L. L., 205, 209, 213, 234,
    240
Tidball, M. E., 388, *389*

Tippetts, A. S., 396, *396*
Tisak, J., 90, *92*, 114, *134*, 141, 154,
    166, *173*, 197, 198, *199*, 220, 223,
    229, 231, *239*, *240*, 291, *320*, 360,
    377
Titterington, D. M., 300, *321*
Truglio, R., 254, *257*
Tucker, L. R., 209, *238*
Tuma, N., 148, *174*

Vallacher, R. R., 168, *174*
van de Pol, F., 411, *412*
van der Heijden, P. G. M., 300, *321*
Varady, A., *199*
Verbeke, G., 301, *321*
Vermunt, J. K., 411, 412, *413*
Vygotsky, L. S., 422, *423*

Wadsworth, K. N., 296, *321*
Walker, A. J., 167, *174*
Waller, N. G., 324, *332*
Wang, E. Y., 377
Ware, J. H., 67, 68, *92*, 363, *376*, 409,
    410
Warren, W., 5, *27*
Wasserman, W., 339, *353*
Wedel, M., 301, *320*
Wei, G., 51, *64*
West, B. H., 8, *26*
Westlake, J., 156, *171*
Whybrow, P. C., 8, *26*
Wichern, D. W., 368, *376*
Willett, J., 30, *32*, 40, 45, *64*, 97, 99,
    104, 107, *134*, 141, 142, 149, 163,
    167, *175*, 181, 182, 184, 186, 197,
    200, 220, 233, 236, *239*, *240*, 256,
    259, 273, 288, 340, *353*, 360, *377*,
    385, 387, 418, *419*, 422, *423*
Wilson, D., *199*
Windle, M., 244, 246, 249, 250, 254,
    255, *258*, 260, 265, 267, 268, *269*
Wittenberg, J., 301, *319*
Wohwill, J. F., 169, *175*
Wolf, S., 392
Wolfinger, R. D., 360, *376*
Woodcock, J. R., 142, 146, 147, 155,
    163, 166–168, *173*

Wothke, W., 335, *352*
Wugalter, S. E., 274, 280, *288,* 300, *320,*
  399, *399,* 405, *406,* 412, *412*

Xie, G., 335, *353*
Xie, H., 385, 386, *387*

Yang, C., 302, *320*
Yang, M., 51, *64*
Yau, L. H. Y., 301, *320*
Yosef, M., 51, *64*

Yucel, R., 365, *377*
Yung, Y. F., 301, *321*

Zautra, A., 244, 246, 248, 255, *258,*
  262, 265, *269*
Zautra, A. J., 248, *259*
Zeger, S., 37, 51, 54, 58, *63, 64,* 141,
  170, 300, *319*
Zill, N., 141, *174*
Zimowski, M., 99, *104*
Zonderman, A. B., 266, *269*
Zoref, L., *392*
Zucker, R. A., 296, *322*

Subject Index

AAPT. *See* Adolescent Alcohol Prevention Trial
Acceleration, 6, 13
Achieved stationarity, 366
Adolescent Alcohol Prevention Trial (AAPT), 183–184, 339, 344, 368–375, 416–417
Aggression in adolescents, and popularity, 385–386
Alcohol expectancies, 182, 393–394
Alcohol–tobacco comorbidity, 407–408
Alcohol use disorder (AUD), 407–408
AMOS program, 36, 335
Analysis of covariance (ANCOVA)
GLMM, SEM approach to, 68, 89, 97, 100
in SEM, 90–91
Analysis of variance (ANOVA), SEM approach to GLMM, 67–68, 76–77
LISREL model for repeated-measures ANOVA, 77–78
2 group × 4 time repeated-measures ANOVA, 71–75
ANCOVA. *See* Analysis of covariance
ANOVA. *See* Analysis of variance
Antisocial behavior, 152. *See also* Depressive symptomatology, antisocial behavior and
Attitude change, latent ordinal Markov models of, 411–412
Attractor(s), 13–15
definition of, 13
point. *See* Point attractors
AUD. *See* Alcohol use disorder
Augmented-moments matrix, 154–155
Autoregressive models, 107, 256–257
Autoregressive traits, 246–247

Basin of attraction, 13–15
BDCS. *See* Bivariate dual change score
Beck Depression Inventory, 395

Behavior Problems Inventory (BPI), 141, 152, 159
Bivariate dual change score (BDCS), 150, 161–163
Bivariate dynamic structural models, 149–151
Bivariate latent difference model, 159–163
Body mass index (BMI), 325–326
BPI. *See* Behavior Problems Inventory
Brief Symptom Checklist, 395
Bryk, Anthony, 35
Burst measurements, 25

Caldwell Home Observation and Measurement of the Environment (HOME) Scales, 395, 396
Caregiver stress, 420–421
CCS. *See* Constant change score model
Center for Epidemiological Studies— Depression Scale (CES–D), 244
Change
longitudinal factor models of, 227–228
model-based definition of reliability for measures of, 279–281
organism's use of information about, 5
as predictor or outcome variable, 5–6
rate of, 146
time-independent models of, 324
ways of measuring, 6
Chi-square test, 341
Classical reliability, 275–277
Classical test theory, 327
Classical true score theory, 146
Cluster analysis, 385–386
Cocaine use, 395–396
Cochran, William, 35
Cogeneric tests, 232
Cognitive growth, and environmental risk factors, 414–415
Cohort sequential designs, 229–233

Configurational invariance, 212
Constant change score model (CCS), 149, 157–160
Converged stationarity, 366
Correlated uniqueness, 251
Covariance components models, 35, 40
Covariances, 188–189
Covariates, time invariant, 293
Crosslagged latent curve model, 128–131
Cross-sectional factorial invariance, 209–212, 229
Curvature, 6, 13

DCS model. *See* Dual change score model
Depression, self-regulation of, 6, 8
Depressive symptomatology, antisocial behavior and, 108–131
    application of models, 121–128
        antisocial behavior and depressive symptomatology, 125–128
        antisocial behavior only, 121–123
        bivariate autoregressive crosslagged model, 125–126
        bivariate crosslagged latent curve model, 128, 129
        bivariate latent curve model, 126–127
        depressive symptomatology only, 124–125
        latent curve model (one factor), 122, 124
        latent curve model (two factor), 122–125
        simplex model with means, 121–122, 124
        tests of equality of means over time, 121, 124
    autoregressive model for, 110, 112–114
    combined autoregressive latent curve model for, 117–121
    crosslagged latent curve model, extensions of, 130–131
    empirical data, 109–111
    latent curve analysis, 114–117
    summary of substantive findings, 129, 130
Derivatives, 6, 15–16

Diagnostic and Statistical Manual of Mental Disorders, 407
Differential models, 30–31
Differential structural equation modeling (dSEM), 16
Drug use
    growth in, and modeling of prevention programs, 416–417
    home environment and infant behavior, effects of material cocaine use on, 395–396
    mediational effects of competence on propensity for childhood, 397–398
dSEM. *See* Differential structural equation modeling
Dual change score (DCS) model, 147, 158–164
Dynamical disease, 6, 8
Dynamical model(s), 29–30
    bivariate dynamic structural models, 149–151
    growth curve model vs., 8
Dynamical systems, 29

EM. *See* Expectation maximization
Empirical Bayes estimation, 295
EQS, 36
Error variance, 204, 207
Estimation theory, 41–42
Expectation maximization (EM), 37, 405

Factor analytic model, 206–209
Factorial invariance, 203–236
    aggregation and role of means in, 215–220
    cross-sectional, 209–212
    and longitudinal factor analysis, 223–227
    and selection theory, 212–214
    univariate development, methods for studying, 220–223
Factor score estimation using the regression method, 295
Fanspread, 181, 186
FIML. *See* Full information maximum likelihood
First derivative, 6

First difference, 146
First-order factors, 180
First-order parameterization, 186–187
Fisher scoring, 37
Fixed effects, 114
Fixed effects Markov simple model. *See* Autoregressive model
Full information maximum likelihood (FIML), 379–380

General growth mixture model (GGMM), 292–319
  conventional latent growth modeling vs., 292–296, 299–300
  and finite mixture modeling, 300–302
  and general latent variable modeling, 302–304
  heavy drinking, analysis of normative and non-normative development in, 312, 314–319
  math achievement development, analysis of, 304–313
  second-generation structural equation modeling vs., 296–299
General linear mixed model (GLMM), SEM approach to, 67–91
  and alternative approaches, 88–90
  and ANCOVA in SEM, 90–91
  covariance structure modeling, parameter estimation via, 76–83
    individual random effects, prediction of, 82–83
    random coefficients model, LISREL model for, 79–82, 94–95
    repeated-measures ANOVA, LISREL model for, 77–78
  examples demonstrating, 83–88
    Belsky–Rovine, 84–88
    Potthoff–Roy, 83–84, 96
  and general linear model, 67–71
  linear curve–random coefficients model, 75–76
  2 group × 4 time repeated-measures ANOVA, 71–75
General linear model, 67–71
GGMM. *See* General growth mixture model
Gibbs sampler, 365–368
GLMM. *See* General linear mixed model

Grip strength, stability and change in, 400–401
Growth curve model(s), 107–108
  autoregressive models vs., 256–257
  dynamical model vs., 8, 30
  limitations of simple conventional, 294–296
  and SEM, 291–292
Growth trajectory, 114

Heavy drinking, analysis of normative and non-normative development in, 312, 314–319
Hierarchical linear models (HLMs), 35–36, 39, 40, 360
  non-normal likelihoods (SEM vs. HLM), 49–60
    Level 1 models, expanding class of, 51–58
    Level 2 models, expanding class of, 57, 59–60
  normal likelihoods (SEM vs. HLM), 42–49
    complete data, balanced, 43–48
    complete data, unbalanced, 47, 49, 50
    observed data, balanced, 43
Hierarchical models, 35, 39, 142
HLMs. *See* Hierarchical linear models
HOME Scales. *See* Caldwell Home Observation and Measurement of the Environment Scales

Imputation, 357–358
  definition of, 357
  methods of, 358
  multiple, 358–361, 379–381
Incomplete data, handling, 156, 379–383. *See also* Missing-data designs
Individual change
  expanding model of, 99–101
  linear model for, 38–39
  and multilevel models, 102–103
Invariance
  configurational, 212
  factorial. *See* Factorial invariance pattern, 210
Invariance hypotheses, testing of, 191–194
Inverted Wishart distribution, 368

Item analysis, 326
Item nonresponse, 357–358

Latent class analysis (LCA), 292, 326–
330
Latent class models, 274–275, 300
Latent curve analysis, 36, 114–117
Latent curve model, 39
bivariate, 126–127
bivariate crosslagged, 128, 129
combined autoregressive, 117–121
extensions of crosslagged, 130–131
one factor, 122, 124
two factor, 122–125
Latent difference scores (LDSs), 142–169
bivariate results, 159–163
and classical true score theory, 146
definition of, 146
and key objectives of longitudinal
research, 139
models of, 147–148
overview of, as approach, 165–169
as rate of change, 146
trajectories over time, plotting, 163–
165
univariate results, 157–159
Latent growth models (LGMs), 36, 39,
141, 156
conventional, 292–294, 299
mediation analysis, as approach to,
390–392
second order. *See* Second-order latent
growth model(s)
Latent growth vector, 186
Latent ordinal Markov (LOM) models,
411–412
Latent profile analysis (LPA), 292
Latent rate score, 147
Latent score, 146
Latent state–trait (LST) model, 244–246
estimation of, 251–252
example using, 246
STARTS model vs., 248
Latent transition analysis (LTA), 279–
281, 292, 300, 399, 405
Latent transition models, 273–274
Latent variables, continuous vs.
categorical, 323–324
LCA. *See* Latent class analysis

LDSs. *See* Latent difference scores
LEM, 412
Level 1 equation, 294
Level 2 equation, 294
LGMs. *See* Latent growth models
Likelihood ratio test (LRT), 155
Likelihoods (SEM vs. HLM)
non-normal, 49–60
normal, 42–49
Linear oscillator
differential equation model of, 13–19
postural control, development of, 10–
13
LISCOMP, 36, 299
LISREL, 36, 67, 76–83, 98, 141, 154,
182, 186, 187, 345
MTMM model, 260–261
random coefficients model, LISREL
model for, 79–82, 94–95
repeated-measures ANOVA, LISREL
model for, 77–78
STARTS model, 260
LOM models. *See* Latent ordinal Markov
models
Longitudinal data, models for analysis of,
141
Longitudinal factor analysis, 223–229
Longitudinal research, 36
LPA. *See* Latent profile analysis
LRT. *See* Likelihood ratio test
LST model. *See* Latent state–trait model
LTA. *See* Latent transition analysis

MAR. *See* Missing at random
Markov chain Monte Carlo (MCMC),
365–368
Markov models, latent ordinal, 411–412
Markov simple model. *See* Autoregressive
model
Math achievement development, analysis
of, 304–313
conditional analysis, 309, 312
unconditional analysis, 305–311
Maximum-likelihood estimation (MLE),
37, 41–42, 154
MCAR. *See* Missing completely at
random
MCMC. *See* Markov chain Monte Carlo
Mean substitution procedure, 338

Measurement theory, 273
Measurement uniqueness, 188
Mediation analysis, 390–392
MI. *See* Multiple imputation
Missing at random (MAR), 359, 369, 373
Missing completely at random (MCAR), 336, 357, 369
Missing-data designs, 335–352
  in artificial-data study, 344–350
  planned, 339, 341–344
  three-form design, 339–340
  traditional procedures for handling, 337–338
  and types of missing data, 336–337
  for use with growth modeling, 340–344
Mixed linear models, 36, 294
Mixed models, 36, 39–40
MLE. *See* Maximum-likelihood estimation
MLWIN, 36
Model(s)
  estimating parameters of, 37
  hierarchical, 39, 142
  for individual change, 38–39
  mixed, 39–40
  multilevel, 39, 142
MPlus, 36, 299
MTMM. *See* Multitrait–multimethod matrix
Multilevel models, 36, 39, 67, 142
  linear models, multilevel, 36
  and within-individual change, 102–103
Multiple imputation (MI), 358–361, 379–381. *See also* PAN model
Multiplicative MTMM model, 253–254
Multistate model, 250
Multitrait–multimethod matrix (MTMM), 244, 250–254, 267, 268
  example using, 252–253
  model for, 250–252
  multiplicative MTMM model, 253–254
Multivariate development, methods for studying, 233
Multivariate survivorship analysis, 404
Mx program, 335

National Health Interview Survey, 141

National Longitudinal Study of Adolescent Health, 405–406
National Longitudinal Survey of Youth (NLSY), 109–111, 139–142, 151–154, 409–410
Noncentrality parameter, 341
Non-normal likelihoods (SEM vs. HLM), 49–60
  Level 1 models, expanding class of, 51–58
  Level 2 models, expanding class of, 57, 59–60
Normal likelihoods (SEM vs. HLM), 42–49
  complete data, balanced, 43–48
    compound symmetry, 45–46
    first-order autoregressive, 46
    heterogeneous Level 1 variance, random slopes and, 46
    homogeneous Level 1 variance, random slopes and, 46
  complete data, unbalanced, 47, 49, 50
  observed data, balanced, 43
NORM software, 335

Ordinary least squares (OLS) regression analysis, 185–186
Organism–environment coupling, 5

Pairwise deletion procedure, 338
PAN model, 361–375
  computational algorithms in, 365–368
  example using, 368–374
  features of, 362–365
Pattern invariance, 210
PCS. *See* Proportional change score model
Peabody Individual Achievement Test (PIAT), 409
Point attractors
  definition of, 8
  developmental change in, 8–9
Popularity, and aggression in adolescents, 385–386
Postural control, development of, 9–24
  differential structural equation models for, 16–19
  dynamical characteristics of postural control, 10–13

Postural control, development of
(*Continued*)
linear oscillator, differential equation
model of, 13–16
model misfit, age-based increase in, 22
participants, 9
procedure, 9–10
results, 19–24
Poverty history, and change in behavior
problems and self-concept, 418–419
Proc Mixed (SAS), 36, 360
Proportional change score model (PCS),
149, 157–160
p values, 195

Random coefficients model(s), 36, 39,
142
See also Growth curve models
linear curve, 75–76
LISREL model for, 79–82, 94–95
Random coefficients (random effects),
293
Random effects, 114
Random effects models, 36
Random shocks, 191
Rapid cycling bipolar disorder (RCBD), 8
Rate of change, 146
RCBD. *See* Rapid cycling bipolar disorder
Reliability
of categorical latent variables, 277–279
classical, 275–277
definition of, 273
in latent class analysis, 326–330
model-based definition of, for
measures of change, 279–281
properties of, for categorical data,
282–286
Repeat rate, 328
Residual state factors, 245
Rosenberg Self-Esteem Scale, 395

SAS, 36, 360
Science majors, change in field of study
among, 388–389
Second derivative, 6
Second-generation structural equation
modeling, 296–299

Second-order factors, 180–181
Second-order latent growth model(s),
179–198
adolescent alcohol expectancies,
application to, 182–186
average growth trajectory, estimation
of, 194–195
error covariance structures, alternative,
188–189
first-order latent growth model vs.,
393–394
first-order parameterization, 186–187
and first- vs. second-order factors,
180–181
multiple indicators, incorporation of,
195–197
rewriting measurement model as,
187–188
rewriting structural model as, 189–
191
and testing of invariance hypotheses,
191–194
Selection theory, and factorial invariance,
212–214
Self-concept, poverty history and change
in, 418–419
Self-regulation
definition of, 5
and developmental change in point
attractors, 8–9
and dynamical disease, 6, 8
SEMs. *See* Structural equation models
Sequential designs, cohort, 229–233
Simplex model, 113, 121–122, 124
Single trait, multistate model, 244
Slope, 6, 13
Software, 36, 37, 153–155, 179
S-PLUS, 361
Stability, 243
Stable traits, 246
STARTS model, 244, 246–250
components of score in, 246–247
example using, 249–250
LST model vs., 248
path diagram for, 247
sensitivity of, to small changes in
correlations, 248–249
specification and identification of,
262–263
STATA, 410

States, 241, 243, 247, 265, 330–331
Stationarity, converged, 366
Statistical vector field, 163, 165
Stress, caregiver, 420–421
Structural equation models (SEMs), 35, 36, 40, 141
  ANCOVA in, 90–91
  as approach to GLLM. See General linear mixed model, SEM approach to
  as approach to GLMM. See General linear mixed model, SEM approach to
  differential, 16
  and growth curve modeling, 291–292
  and latent curve analysis, 114
  non-normal likelihoods (SEM vs. HLM), 49–60
    Level 1 models, expanding class of, 51–58
    Level 2 models, expanding class of, 57, 59–60
  normal likelihoods (SEM vs. HLM), 42–49
    complete data, balanced, 43–48
    complete data, unbalanced, 47, 49, 50
    observed data, balanced, 43
  second generation, 296–299
Subpopulations, 208
Survivorship analysis, multivariate, 404

Tapestry Over Time, 402–403
Test theory, classical, 327
Three-form design, 339–340
Time-independent change models, 324
Time-invariant covariates, 293
TLI. See Tucker–Lewis Index
Tobacco–alcohol comorbidity, 407–408

Traitness, 243
Traits, 241, 243, 330
  autoregressive, 246–247
  dialectic balance between states and, 265–269
  stable, 246
Trajectory, 8, 114
Tucker–Lewis Index (TLI), 244

Uniqueness (unique variance), 204
Univariate development, factorial invariance and methods for studying, 220–223
Univariate latent curve model, 115, 116
Univariate latent difference model, 157–159
Univariate simplex model, 113

Vector field, statistical, 163, 165
Vector field plot, 13, 14
Velocity, 6, 13

WAIS–R. See Wechsler Adult Intelligence Scale—Revised
WAIS. See Wechsler Adult Intelligence Scale
Weak true score theory, 206
Wechsler Adult Intelligence Scale—Revised (WAIS–R), 233
Wechsler Adult Intelligence Scale (WAIS), 233
Wechsler–Bellevue Intelligence Test, 233
Wishart distribution, inverted, 368

Zone of proximal development (ZPD), 422–423

About the Editor

Linda M. Collins, PhD, is a professor of human development and the director of the Methodology Center in the College of Health and Human Development at Pennsylvania State University. Her undergraduate training took place at the University of Connecticut, where she received the Orbison Award as the outstanding senior majoring in psychology, and her graduate training took place at the J. P. Guilford Laboratory of Quantitative Psychology at the University of Southern California. Dr. Collins has focused her research on statistical methodology and measurement procedures for longitudinal data, particularly in the areas of human development and drug abuse prevention. She has worked extensively on an approach for fitting stage-sequential models in longitudinal data, called latent transition analysis, and on a related statistical software program called WinLTA. Her work on methodology and prevention has been funded by the National Institute on Drug Abuse (NIDA) for over 15 years. She currently directs a NIDA-funded center devoted to methodological innovation for prevention research. Dr. Collins is a Fellow of the American Psychological Association (APA) and the American Psychological Society, a recipient of the Cattell Award for outstanding early career contributions to multivariate behavioral research, a past president of the Society of Multivariate Experimental Psychology, and a recipient of Pennsylvania State University's Faculty Scholar Medal in the Social and Behavioral Sciences. She is also a core scientist in the Tobacco Etiology Research Network, funded by the Robert Wood Johnson Foundation. She is currently associate editor of *Prevention Science,* was an associate editor of *Multivariate Behavioral Research* and *Journal of Educational and Behavioral Statistics,* and served on the editorial board of *Psychological Methods.* Dr. Collins recently edited a special issue of *Multivariate Behavioral Research* on innovative methods for prevention research and is currently coediting a special issue of *Drug and Alcohol Dependence,* devoted to innovative methods for research on use of tobacco and other substances. She also coedited another volume in the APA's Science Directorate conference program series, *Best Methods for the Analysis of Change.*

Aline G. Sayer, EdD, is a senior scientist at the Murray Research Center at Harvard University. She received her undergraduate training from Temple University and her master's and doctoral degrees in human development and psychology from Harvard University. Her methodological research specialty is individual growth curve analysis, following the tradition of her thesis advisor, John B. Willett. Her substantive research focus is on the longitudinal development of children and adolescents at risk due to chronic illness conditions and substance abuse. She teaches courses in hierarchical linear models in the quantitative methods program at the University of Michigan and consults widely on the application of these models in developmental and educational research. She received the 1994 Human Development Dissertation Award from the American Educational Research Association and the Year 2000 Hugo G. Beigel Research Award from the Society for the Scientific Study of Sexuality.